Ancestors of
Jimmy and Rosalynn Carter

To my wife, Annette,
thank you for your help and support
and for enduring too many stories too many times.
And to my children, Joshua, Jeremy, and James,
may you have as many descendants as you have ancestors.

Ancestors of Jimmy and Rosalynn Carter

Jeff Carter

Foreword by President Jimmy Carter

McFarland & Company, Inc., Publishers
Jefferson, North Carolina

The present work is a reprint of the illustrated case bound edition of Ancestors of Jimmy and Rosalynn Carter, *first published in 2012 by McFarland.*

LIBRARY OF CONGRESS CATALOGUING-IN-PUBLICATION DATA

Carter, Jeff, 1952–
Ancestors of Jimmy and Rosalynn Carter / foreword by President Jimmy Carter.
p.   cm.
Includes bibliographical references and index.

ISBN 978-1-4766-7229-8
softcover : acid free paper ∞

1. Carter family.   2. Carter, Jimmy, 1924– — Family.
3. Carter, Rosalynn — Family   I. Title.
CS71.C323 2017   929'.20973 — dc23   2012018468

BRITISH LIBRARY CATALOGUING DATA ARE AVAILABLE

© 2012 Jeff Carter. All rights reserved

No part of this book may be reproduced or transmitted in any form or by any means, electronic or mechanical, including photocopying or recording, or by any information storage and retrieval system, without permission in writing from the publisher.

Front cover: John William Fulwood Murray's family. Left to right, possibly Alethea Lawhon (1814–1883), Nathan Murray, J.W.F. Murray (1833–1921) seated, Alma (1879) standing behind him, daughter Anna, Alethea Josephine (1842–1905) seated, John William (Papa) Murray (1871–1966) standing behind her; background © 2017 Shutterstock

Printed in the United States of America

McFarland & Company, Inc., Publishers
Box 611, Jefferson, North Carolina 28640
www.mcfarlandpub.com

TABLE OF CONTENTS

Foreword by President Jimmy Carter   1
Preface   3
Introduction   5

1. THE CARTERS	9
Jamestown	10
Bacon's Rebellion	20
The Thomas Carter Conundrum	24
Another Thomas Carter	32
Moore Carter and Jane Kindred	34
Kindred Carter and Mary "Molly" Odum	36
Isaac Carter and Sarah Browne	37
Kindred Carter and the Rozier Mystery	39
James Carter and Eleanor Duckworth	41
2. THE MORRIS, COX, AND ANSLEY ANCESTORS AND THEIR ANCESTORS	44
Monmouth County: A Haven for Baptists and Quakers Except for the Government	44
Thomas Cox and Elizabeth Blashford Puritanical Persecution	46
Lewis Morris of Passage Point: Uncle Lewis Morris of Tinton Falls; The Monmouth Riots	48
The Almys and the Cornells: They Thought Quakers Were Bad Until They Met the Antinomians	52
The Very Strange Case of Thomas Cornell	53
The Pottses Arrive from England	54
More Scots: All Is Forgiven Between the Ansley, Cox and Morris Families	55
More Taxes, the Regulators, and the Battle of Alamance	56
Duckworths and Ramseys and Carters and Ansleys	57
Wiley Carter and Ann Ansley	58
3. ANCESTORS OF MARY ANN DILIGENT SEALS	62
The Terrells: Polecat Swamp, Some Quakers Some Not, More Than One Affair	62
The Burnleys: Revolutionaries, Friends, and the Battle of Guilford Courthouse	64
The Barksdales: Early Virginians	65
The Muses and the Seales: An Illicit Relationship	66
A Tory Loyalist in the Family	67

The Seals: A Muse No More, the Yazoo Land Fraud	68
Littleberry Walker Carter and Mary Ann Diligent Seals	70
4. ANCESTORS OF CAPTAIN JAMES PRATT	**71**
The Kays	72
Captain James Pratt and Sophronia Cowan	72
5. ANCESTORS OF SOPHRONIA COWAN	**74**
Ireland and Charles II	74
Immigrations at Charlestown, Boonesborough, and the South Carolina Wilderness	76
The Clinkscales from Scotland, Probably Not That Ann Buchner	77
The Brownlees: More Irish Ancestors Who Marry Irish Ancestors	79
The Seawrights: The Battle at Pratt's Mill, Bloody Bill Cunningham, the Cloud's Creek Massacre	80
The Cowans: More Irish, More Revolutionaries	82
William Archibald Carter and Nina Pratt	84
6. ANCESTORS OF JAMES JACKSON GORDY	**86**
Perry Scott and Captain Allen McLane	87
Wilson Gordy and Mary Scott	89
The Helms Family, the Waxhaw Settlement and the Revolution	91
7. ANCESTORS OF MARY IDA NICHOLSON	**95**
The Nathaniel Nunn Nicholson Line	95
Patrick Jack	97
The Mecklenburg Declaration of Independence	97
Joseph Nicholson and Lillis McAdoo Jack	99
Were John Nicholson and John Candor Nicholson the Same Person?	99
Nathaniel Nunn Nicholson	102
The Very Interesting Dawson Ancestors	103
The Nicholsons from Ireland	105
The Gaines and Brown Families	106
Malekiah Dawson and Mary Marcus Brown and Back to Nathaniel Nunn Nicholson	109
8. ANCESTORS OF JOHN WILLIAM MURRAY	**112**
The Provable Murrays	113
The Albrittons	115
The Search for Susan Champion	116
The Bethunes in America	119
The Legend of Martin Bethune	121
The Short Ancestry of the Lawhons	122
The Short Ancestry of the Parkers and the Kellys	122
John William Fulwood Murray	123
9. ANCESTORS OF ROSA NETTIE WISE	**127**
If Not for Martin Luther, Half the Family Wouldn't Be Here	127
The Palatine Ancestors	130
The Trip from Wittenberg	132
Dutch Fork	133

The Coogles and the Kleckleys, Mt. Zion Evangelical Lutheran Church, More Civil War	134
The Wises	135
The Etheridges: In Theory, Five Names Are Enough	137

10. Ancestors of Wilburn Edgar Smith — 140

Colonial Maryland	140
The Prathers Arrived in 1622, the Odells, Ridgelys, and Biggers a Little Later	142
The Offutts and Captain Edward Brock Arrived Before 1672	145
The Isaac and Pottenger Families Arrived Around 1670	147
The Jacobs, Cheyneys, and Westalls Arrived in the Mid-1600s	148
The Halley, Haley, Hailey, Hawley, Holly Family	150
The Fulford and Bell Families	150
The Smiths	152
The Descendants of George Lynch Smith	160

Afterword: The Quest	163
Appendix A: What's a Cousin and How Do They Get Removed?	165
Appendix B: Pedigree Collapse	165
Appendix C: The Search for Kindred Carter's Wife	167
Appendix D: The Bethune Lineage in Scotland	168
Appendix E: Loyal "Regulators" Association	172
Appendix F: Land Grant to Ellis Marcus by the Earl of Granville	172
Appendix G: Wills	174
Last Will and Testament of Dr. Samuel Browne	174
Last Will and Testament of Francis Clinkscales, Sr.	175
Last Will and Testament of Charity Dysart	176
Last Will and Testament of William Nicholson	176
Last Will and Testament of Wilson Gordy	177
Last Will and Testament of Abel Ansley	177
Last Will and Testament of Joseph Pratt	178
Last Will and Testament of James Brownlee	179
Last Will and Testament of George W. Carter	179
Last Will and Testament of Peter Gordy	179

Chapter Notes 181
Bibliography 203
Index 211

Foreword by President Jimmy Carter

After I had been president for about two years, I had a call from Salt Lake City requesting a meeting in the Oval Office for the Elders of the Church of Jesus Christ of Latter Day Saints (LDS). Mormons had earlier been in trouble in several African nations because of false allegations that they denied membership to black people. I had interceded on their behalf and presumed that, once again, they had a request to make of me.

When the appointed time came, however, I was pleasantly surprised to receive a definitive analysis of the genealogy of my family, extending back twelve generations. In addition to a beautiful bound leather volume, there were a number of file folders containing census records, birth certificates, marriage licenses, land deeds, and other official documents.

In fact, I had little interest at that time in the history of my family, and all these data were filed away until I returned to my home in Plains in 1981. About the time I acquired my first word processor, I received a prepublication edition of the software for Family Tree Maker, and I slowly transferred my family records into the convenient spaces. As my relatives learned about this effort, I became the unofficial collector of information about other family members, and I learned that some of them were already concentrating on various branches of the family tree.

My grandfather's grandfather, Wiley Carter (1798–1864), had been the first ancestor of mine who moved to Southwest Georgia; he is buried about ten miles from my home. As his 200th birth year approached, I decided that we should have a family reunion, and we issued a brief news release about the planned event. I was inundated with mail, including letters from many people who were only distantly related to me, so we decided to limit attendance to Wiley's direct descendants.

More than 850 people attended, representing all twelve of Wiley's children. I distributed copies of the records I had, plus blank sheets on which additions and corrections could be entered. From this, we prepared a printed book encompassing the revised data, and then I kept my records current by adding information received by mail from interested families.

This outlines the limit of my involvement — just a record keeper. Then there was a complete turning point in 2008, when my youngest son, Jeffrey, decided to assume my duties as family historian. He has contacted other relatives who are studying their own family histories, examined birth, death, and marriage records in churches and courthouses, census data in all the involved states, family Bibles, land deeds, military service in all wars, immigration records, and LDS data available online. He has learned some of the finer techniques of research from Kenneth Thomas, the preeminent genealogist in Georgia, with whom he has formed a close friendship.

In addition to titillating anecdotes about many of our ancestors, there have been some intriguing revelations about the first members of the Carter family to settle in America. Jeff has devoted meticulous research to distinguishing among the four Thomas Carters who lived in colonial Virginia around 1650. There has been an intense debate about these interrelationships for several generations.

Of more interest to general readers will be Jeff's humorous but informative account of his experiences as a family researcher. The book also provides, quite often, a uniquely personal insight into important historical events, some of which were instrumental in shaping our character as a nation. An especially good aspect of this book is that conclusions are based on proven facts; if there are doubts about the authenticity of a statement, Jeff lets it be known.

It is a delightful book to read.

PREFACE

Much of the genealogy of President James Earl Carter and First Lady Eleanor Rosalynn Smith has been published — at least in the form of the names of the parents and the name of the child who was next in the lineage. Genealogy has always been of great interest to our family and we have an extensive collection of family documents, some more than two hundred years old. Several years ago, I became the custodian of these documents and while reading through them I became intrigued with the lives of our family's ancestors. I began conducting research to fill in the gaps and attempted to trace every ancestral line back to the original immigrant to America. After I had their names, I wanted their stories.

Many people have helped and I wish to thank all of my relatives who gave me copies of their family records and old photographs. Special thanks are due Allethea Wall, John Wise, and Sybil Carter for their interest and encouragement. I have also found relatives I did not know before starting my research, and finding Rubye Lewis has been a special treat. She not only shared her lifetime's collection of research on the Smith family, she was also available for hour-long telephone conversations even though she is in her 80s. Joe King, another newly found relative, kindly shared his collection of documents, including several Civil War era letters written by George Lynch Smith's sons. They are intriguing pieces of a still unsolved mystery.

I am especially indebted to Kenneth Thomas, who has done an enormous amount of work on the family's genealogy and is an expert on the Carter line in Georgia. Ken not only made his extensive collection of documents on both the Carter-Gordy and Smith-Murray lines available to me, he also provided insight and encouragement during the project.

Dr. Bascom Hayes has been of tremendous help deciphering the Carter records in Jamestown. Dr. Hayes is the preeminent researcher on the colonial Carters in Virginia and a direct descendent of our ancestor Thomas Carter. After twenty years of research, Dr. Hayes has concluded that our Captain Thomas Carter of Isle of Wight was probably the son of William Carter and that Thomas Carter of Barford was probably the son of Major Thomas Carter, finally making the pieces fit. His documentation, which he generously shared with me, is persuasive.

I especially want to thank Ken Thomas, Rubye Lewis, and Joe King for donating their collections of papers and documents to the Carter Presidential Library. Dr. Barry Hayes has also made arrangements to donate his collection to this library.

I was fortunate to find Darrin Carter of Newport News, one of the most astute researchers on colonial Virginia and Jamestown. Darrin's extensive knowledge of the era and willingness to travel across Virginia researching and gathering documents from several libraries was a great help.

As anyone who has attempted genealogical research covering four hundred years knows, the records are incomplete, dates are ambiguous or contradictory in some cases, and the spelling of names is inconsistent. Nevertheless, all errors are my own.

A Note on Dates

Throughout the book, the reader will note that some years are presented with a slash notation, as in 1639/40. Genealogists and researchers who deal with pre-1752 documents will be familiar with this presentation, but an explanation will benefit those who may not.

Great Britain adopted the Gregorian calendar in 1752. Prior to that, using the Julian calendar, New Year's Day was on March 25. March 24 of one year was followed by March 25 of the next year. Part of the Gregorian calendar reform changed New Year's Day from March 25 to January 1.

The calendar change affected the perception of dates in the Julian calendar, which Great Britain and its colonies had been using since 1582. After the reform, until March 25 of each year, old Julian dates are a year behind that same year in the new calendar. For example, George Washington was born February 22, 1732. However, if you had actually asked Washington (before he was 20 years old when the new calendar was adopted) what his birth date was, he would have told you February 11, 1731, because he was born when the Julian calendar was still in effect.

This ambiguity of which year is being referenced exists in all Julian dates occurring between January 1 and March 24 from 1582, when the Julian calendar was introduced, until 1752, when the Gregorian calendar was adopted. Great Britain and her colonies used the double date with the slash notation to signify that one of these Julian dates is being referred to in Gregorian notation and the year portion of the date is noted as Julian/Gregorian to remove the ambiguity of which year is being specified. From our point of view here in the Gregorian world, the year we would think of the date as being is always the larger numbered year listed on the right side of the slash.

INTRODUCTION

Except in rare cases in this book, I have included only our direct ancestors and members of their immediate families, our great aunts and uncles, and only after the families reached America. Even so, between Jimmy Carter's Gordy and Carter lineages and Rosalynn Carter's Murray and Smith lineages, there are a lot of ancestors. For the Carters, the provable line goes back to Thomas Carter, who was in Isle of Wight, Virginia, before 1650. The Carter and allied lines encompass a few more than a hundred direct ancestors. Adrian Bryan Gordy was born around 1660, most likely in Scotland but there's a case for France, and emigrated to Maryland. There are about ninety known ancestors in the Gordy and allied lines. David Murray was probably born in 1598 in Angarsk, Scotland, or he may be from Ireland; there is no solid proof for either. The first provable Murray ancestor was in Virginia in the mid 1700s. The Murray and allied lines have almost a hundred direct ancestors. The earliest member of our Smith line to reach America is in dispute; it could be before 1650 or it could be the late 1700s. There are almost a hundred more direct ancestors in the Smith and allied lines which are provable and several more that are probable.

Given the four hundred or so grandmothers and grandfathers who have been identified, the problem arose as to how to present them in a somewhat coherent manner. Typically, genealogical data is presented in ancestor or descendant charts that start with a person then get larger and larger through time as grandparents double in number with each generation. (more or less; see Appendix B: Pedigree Collapse). After a few generations the rows in the charts contain hordes of people, most of whose only connecting attribute is that they are members of the same generation. This system arbitrarily groups disparate people and blurs families.

Andrew Seawright, who arrived in South Carolina from Ireland around 1740, had very little in common with Joseph Duckworth, who was of the same generation but lived in New Jersey. What was happening in their lives was that the Seawrights were living close to the Cowans and intermarrying with them and the Duckworths were living close to the Ramseys. Rosalynn Carter's German Palatine refugee ancestors, fleeing the murderous rampage of the Catholic Church and Louis XIV, who were determined to exterminate them because they were Lutherans, banded together in such a tight group that from the time they arrived in South Carolina between 1732 and 1752 until her grandmother Rosa Nettie Wise was married around 1900 in Plains, there had been only one marriage in Rosa Wise's linage on either her father's or mother's side to a person who was not a Palatine or the direct descendant of a Palatine.

In colonial times most of our ancestors were pioneers establishing themselves in the wilderness on land they bought from the Indians or land they were granted by the colonial governments in land patents.* They lived in towns that they built themselves. Very, very few lived in established cities. They lived as pioneers together, their children married each other — which is of course how they became our ancestors — and then they moved to new areas together. Where that was the pattern, I have traced whole interconnected family groups together.

Our ancestors also lived and participated in historic times that influenced them in patterns they probably could not have discerned. We have a lot of Quaker and Baptist ancestors who were persecuted and who banded together. Those that lived in colonial New England were driven out by the theocratic governments there. The freedom of religion touted by the Puritan governments applied only to other Puritans. In Boston, the fanatical Cotton Mather, who claimed to have seen witches fly, persecuted everyone who was not a Puritan. He incited the population, preaching that the Quakers' rejection of Puritanism by itself was a possible manifestation of demonic thought and therefore might be an indication of witchcraft. However, witchcraft was extremely hard to prove. So led by Massachusetts, most of the New England governments outlawed Quakers just for being Quakers, something much easier to prove. Puritan officials confiscated the Quakers' land and jailed the ones who remained in their states. Most of our Quaker ancestors who lived in New England during that time fled to the havens of Rhode Island and New York, then to the Quaker and Baptist towns of Middletown and Shrewsbury in New Jersey and from there to North Carolina. Then, when the governor of Georgia gave them a large tract of land, the Quakers built Wrightsborough and moved there.

The Revolutionary War also led to a convergence. There are about twenty-five families in which we had a direct ancestor who fought in the Revolutionary War and survived. As a payment for service, those ancestors were given land or extra chances in land lotteries. There wasn't any land to be given away in places like Virginia or New York. The available land was in the Georgia frontier and so they converged there. These Revolutionary War ancestors are more or less traced both in family groups and are included as larger, more disparate, groups converging in Georgia.

As to the information about our ancestors, it varies vastly. For the Ansley, Cox, Duckworth, and Carter families at Wrightsborough, I probably have enough wills and deeds with land boundary descriptions and plats to reconstruct a good part of the settlement, not to mention that I have a map from 1758 of the original layout of the town. On the other hand, I don't know Robert Lindsay's wife's name. When I say "probably," I "kind of" know it from a lot of non-definitive sources but don't have genealogically acceptable proof. "Might be" means it's my current best-guess speculation that doesn't rise to the "probably" level. A family legend is just that, a legend handed down — being maybe so, maybe not, but usually with at least a grain of truth. By far, almost all of the lineages can be proven and the proofs and sources are cited for evaluation. New information is being discovered all the time and is welcome. If a great story is disproven by new facts, then so be it. I'll just change it to "We used to believe ... but it was later disproven" and keep the story anyway while discrediting it at the same time.

When I began researching, I initially thought that our ancestors moved a lot more than they actually did. In a lot of cases, they stayed where they were and counties formed and were renamed around them. For instance, in 1825 a portion of the territory ceded to

---

*A land patent is an original grant of land never before owned by anyone. At the time this definition was made as flexible as necessary so that the people in power could be accommodated.

the United States by the Treaty of Indian Springs was made into Lee County, Georgia. Three years later, in 1828, Randolph County was made from a part of Lee County. In 1830 Stewart County was formed from a portion of the Randolph territory. In 1831 on the day after Christmas, Sumter County, where our family has lived since before the county existed, was formed from a part of Lee County. In 1853 portions of Stewart County went to form parts of Webster County, which was originally named Kinchafoonee County after the creek which runs through it. Later, portions of Stewart County were divided to form Quitman County, Marion County, and Chattahoochee County. Our ancestors lived in all of these counties since the land was in the original Lee County. This makes tracing deeds and finding wills interesting, my not knowing in advance which county ended up with them. When relevant, I have made mention of the county divisions. However, if I refer to people as living in a county before that county was formed, take it to mean that they lived in the part of the former county that would later become the county I claim they lived in.

Special note should be given to the formation of counties in North Carolina since so many of our ancestors lived there. Many of our ancestors lived in the same area, although the county name changes make it appear they were more dispersed. The Albemarle region was the first area opened to colonization in North Carolina and this area is where our ancestors lived for over a hundred years through numerous land boundary changes. Albemarle County was formed in 1664. By 1689 it had been divided to form Chowan, Currituck, Pasquotank and Perquimas precincts. In 1722, the part of Chowan west of the Chowan River was formed into Bertie Precinct. In 1729, parts of Bertie, Chowan, Currituck, and Pasquotank were formed into Tyrrell Precinct. In 1739 Albemarle County was abolished and all the precincts became counties. All was quiet for two years, then in 1741, Bertie County was divided again to form Edgecombe County and Northampton County. In 1759, Hertford County was made from parts of Bertie County, Chowan County, and Northampton County. Our ancestors and relatives lived in all of these counties and in many cases had lived there since before the original Albemarle County was divided.

I have assumed that people might read parts of this and not remember what the Peace of Westphalia was, might have forgotten that Frederick V was a Calvinist, or they might have misplaced the knowledge that after Cromwell died, Charles II was restored to the throne and that his brother James was the Duke of York until Charles died and James ascended to the throne as King James II. If Martin Luther had not nailed his 95 theses to the door of the Castle Church in 1517, Eleanor Rosalynn Smith would not be in Plains, Georgia, to marry Jimmy Carter. If the Puritans in New England had not banned Quakers and Baptists, there would be no Jimmy Carter in Plains to ask her to marry him. Therefore, I have included short historical vignettes to provide some context to historical phenomena that were affecting and afflicting our ancestors or in which they were actively participating. Hundreds of thousands of pages have been written about the English capturing New Amsterdam from the Dutch, the Dutch subsequently retaking it, the peace treaty that gave the land back to the English Crown, and how all of that contributed to the history of New York and New Jersey. When I condense it to a page or two, a lot is left out. These vignettes are included only to provide context and are not meant to be exhaustive historical disquisitions.

As for the spelling of names, there are a number of variations, orthography apparently not being considered very important until the late 1800s. Some of our ancestors used different spelling variations in their names between the signing of one deed and the signing of the next. Some anglicized their names when they moved to the colonies; some in the same family did not or preferred another variation. I have a will in which the Murray name is spelled five different ways and the name James Murray uses initially declaring it as his will is spelled differently than his signature at the end. In some cases, I have also labeled some names with the designations I, II, III, and so on to try to help track and clarify who is whom. Our families have a remarkable propensity to reuse names and the labels are used to distinguish parents, children, and grandchildren and are not actually part of the person's name. There are a lot of names. In many cases, when listing the brothers and sisters or children of an ancestor, unless there is a story about them, I have placed them in footnotes. No disrespect is intended.

My original intent when I began researching our family was to trace every ancestral line back to the original immigrants to America, a goal I soon discovered to be impossible. The records don't exist anymore because a courthouse burned, orphans never knew who their parents were, or, in a few cases, the records are not there for reasons that are completely inexplicable mysteries. The search soon became a quest to find information about our family's ancestors, the result of which is this narrative, mostly about the people but partly about the quest itself. What I found has amazed me.

Our family includes weavers; cabinet makers; preachers; farmers; ancestors who had illegitimate children; ancestors who were illegitimate children; shoemakers; a Hessian soldier who fought against Napoleon; politicians; jail breakers; ancestors who saw Jamestown burn; Methodists; Quakers; Presbyterians; Baptists; Lutherans; revolutionaries in England who lost and were thrown out; revolutionaries in Ireland who lost and were thrown out; revolutionaries in Scotland who won and left; revolutionaries in the colonies who won and stayed; wheelwrights; orphans; ancestors who were trapped in their house and burned to death by Tories; ancestors whose brothers were Tories; dual ancestry ancestors; slave owners; indentured servants; the first woman to drive a car in Chattahoochee County; ancestors from England, Scotland, Wales, Ireland, Germany, and Switzerland; prisoners captured by the Union army during the Civil War; ancestors I can find nothing about; ancestors who fled Europe and were saved by Queen Anne after Louis XIV joined forces with the Catholic Church to kill them because they were Lutherans; mechanics; grist mill operators; ancestors who engaged in sword fights; ancestors who died of smallpox, measles, malaria, typhus, typhoid, rattlesnake bites, lightning, and one who was killed by a train; one who was fantastically wealthy; one I suspect was a double agent in the late 1600s; at least thirty-four who fought in the Revolutionary War; more than that who fought in the Civil War, one of whom traveled and fought with Stonewall Jackson and was kind enough to leave his diary for me; ancestors who probably saved other ancestors' lives during the Civil War and never met each other; veterans of the War of 1812; a mother whose babies froze to death while they were being pursued by the British during the Revolution; tanners; saddle makers; ancestors who set up a mysterious secret fund to undermine the colonial government of New Jersey; ancestors who can be traced back almost a thousand years; ancestors who did nothing noteworthy except have more ancestors; an ancestor who made a bargain with God to save himself from drowning and broke that bargain decades later and drowned that night; ancestors who fought with Lee and surrendered at Appomattox; an ancestor who was a spy for Washington at Valley Forge and fought with him there and at White Marsh; ancestors who fought with Lafayette during the Siege of Yorktown; and an ancestor who made a very special promise to his best friend before the Battle at Guilford Courthouse during the Revolutionary War on the morning of March 18, 1781, that he had to keep.

Chapter 1

THE CARTERS

In 1979, Noel Currer-Briggs published *The Carters of Virginia: Their English Ancestry*, in which he traced our Carter ancestry to John Carter, vintner of London. John was a wine merchant and a member of the Vintners' Company, one of the Great Livery Companies of London. The livery companies were trade guilds of London and virtually controlled commerce in England from the 15th century until the early 17th century. The Vintners' Company was the eleventh largest of the trade guilds and accounted for a large portion of England's imports, although by 1600 it was not quite as large as at its peak around 1450 when wine accounted for almost a third of all of England's imports.

The livery companies held royal charters from the king as monopolies until the livery companies were severely curtailed by Edward VI around 1552. Under Charles I, the Vintners' Company regained much of its influence, but its association with the House of Stuart led to political and financial attacks by Oliver Cromwell and the Puritan Parliament when they came to power.

During their heyday, the livery companies were expected to provide private financing for the king's projects and they provided explorers and adventurers for much of the expansion of the empire. In the early 1600s, the companies and their members invested in the Virginia Company and they were a huge and important part of the establishment of the Jamestown colony.

John Carter died in 1630 and in his will he named his children: George, William, John, Thomas, Robert, Anne, Elizabeth, Mary, Sylvester, and Isabel. William Carter first appears in the Jamestown records in 1622 and John and Thomas arrived in 1636. All of the brothers seem to have arrived in Virginia shortly after they reached their majority age. There is no proof that William, John, and Thomas Carter in Jamestown were John Carter's sons or that they were brothers, although the circumstantial evidence is overwhelming. They worked for the Vintners' Company and were business associates and friends with the same people and families that they and their father lived near and had business associations with in London and Hertfordshire. Unfortunately, most of the Vintners' Company records in England were destroyed in the Great Fire of London in 1666.

Col. John Carter* was the father of Robert "King" Carter, probably the wealthiest man in all of the colonies and the most famous of all the very early colonists in Virginia. The best genealogists and researchers have traced his descendants. By contrast, very little is known about Maj. Thomas Carter. In fact, neither his wife's name nor any of his children

---

*Because of the family's reuse of names, William Carter's brothers are referred to henceforth by their eventual ranks as Maj. Thomas Carter and Col. John Carter in an effort to simplify keeping track of the particular John Carter and Thomas Carter being referred to.

are positively known. There seem to be no documents at all pertaining to his family. Col. John Carter ran the Vintners' Company operation in colonial Virginia. His brother Maj. Thomas Carter and his probable brother William Carter worked with him. By 1640/41 Col. John Carter was appointed to the House of Burgesses for Nansemond County. By 1652 he was a justice of the Lancaster court and represented Lancaster County in that house.

Currer-Briggs believed, as do many genealogists, that our ancestor Captain Thomas Carter was the son of the Thomas Carter (Maj. Thomas Carter) who arrived in Jamestown in 1635, despite there being unresolved issues that arise by accepting this lineage. The most outstanding problem is that Maj. Thomas Carter was known to have been born in 1610 and his presumed grandson Thomas Carter (III) was born around 1648. Two generations of landed gentry in 38 years in an era of arranged or agreed marriages is very unlikely. Currer-Briggs was well aware of these issues, and after examining the evidence and describing the problems that arose, wrote that he could find no satisfactory solution. However, Currer-Briggs' book was mainly about the English ancestry of the Carters and he did not extensively research the colonial documents in the United States, relying on older published accounts of the Carter lineage in America.

After examining both the records from England and the colonial records in America, it now seems most probable that our Captain Thomas Carter was the son of the William Carter who had arrived in Jamestown by 1622; that William was the son of John Carter, vintner of London; and that he was the brother of Col. John Carter and Maj. Thomas Carter. Most modern American genealogists, relying on century-old genealogies that are demonstrably flawed, do not yet accept this interpretation. These conclusions are speculative but the evidence is persuasive.

Jamestown

Three hundred and two years before Jimmy Carter was born, William Carter, his probable great-great-great-great-great-great-great-great-great-grandfather, first appeared in the records of James City County, Virginia, in March of 1622 when he and some other young men were charged in court with killing and eating a calf.[1] At the time, William probably did not know that the calf belonged to former deputy governor Sir George Yeardley.

There are a few remaining records about William's early life in Jamestown. In February of 1623 he was living in Dr. John Pott's house in Jamestown, by January 24, 1624, when a muster was taken of Jamestown's inhabitants, William was living in the rural part of the island. A lawsuit over the ownership of a bed, in which William was called to testify on August 14, 1626, identifies him as one of George Menefie's apprentices employed at Menefie's forge in Jamestown.[2] Menefie was one of the most successful merchants in Jamestown and operated a thriving trade in tobacco with London. When William worked for him, Menefie owned the ship *Desire* and sometime later purchased the *William and George*. Our ancestor William Carter may have been indentured to George Menefie under an arrangement between Menefie and William's father, John Carter, in London.

Thirteen years after William was known to be in Jamestown, two of his probable brothers[3] arrived in the colony. Thomas Carter and his brother John sailed from "*Ye Port of London, imbarqued in the Safety, John Graunt, Master,*"[4] to Virginia in 1635 when Thomas was 25 years old and John was 22. Also on the *Safety* were Bartholomew Hoskins, a Vintners' Company operative and probably a business associate of the brother's father, John Carter, and Robert Pettaway,[5] who was either a business partner of the Carters or soon would be. Robert Pettaway's daughter Elizabeth would eventually marry William Carter's son William Jr.

In 1618, shortly before William Carter was known to be in Jamestown, the Virginia Company implemented the headright system to distribute land and encourage immigration and expansion of the colony. The headright system provided fifty acres of land for every person transported to the colony. Wealthy persons could pay the passage for others, usually being repaid through five to seven years of work as an indentured servant by the person transported. Immigrants who could pay for their own passage received the fifty acres for themselves and for each member of their family. First and second generation colonists were awarded two headrights, good for one hundred acres, when they reached majority age.

Headrights could be accumulated for years to form grants of large areas of land. They could also be transferred, bought and sold, and could even be inherited. There was no system in place for accounting for headright claims and fraud was rampant. Duplicate claims, the use of fictitious names, and the filing of the same headright claims in different counties were common practices and, for the most part, ignored. The colony wanted to expand. Although the cost of transportation was more than the cost of fifty acres of land, the system was a bonanza for the sea captains who sometimes claimed entire passenger lists as well as themselves and their crew as headrights, regardless of who actually paid for their passengers' transportation and in spite of the fact that the sailors would be leaving the colony when their ship sailed back to England. Our early Carter ancestors were sea captains.

William Carter and his brothers and business partners used the headright system to acquire land suitable for building ports and docks for themselves and for the Vintners' Company. William's first patents in 1636 brought the important Bay Tree Neck site into the business, a site which was owned by William the rest of his life and sold in 1660 by his widow Alice and his son George. Bay Tree Neck was probably an important shipping station for the Vintners' Company and in two years William had patented two thousand acres along the river there.

William Carter's first land patent is interesting because it named his three wives, for whom he claimed a fifty acre headright each for their "personal adventure." He also claimed Edward Bland, an important London businessman and partner in the Vintners' Company. A year later, William patented 200 more acres next to his original patents and then consolidated his hold on the Bay Tree Neck in 1638 with the patent of another thousand acres near or adjoining his previous patents, claiming headright grants for twenty persons. Apparently no one cared that fourteen of the headrights were the same people he had claimed in his original patent in 1636.[6]

William Carter himself was claimed as a headright at least five times, indicating some of his voyages to England and back. Edward Drew, who was a respected vestryman and was nominated for sheriff, claimed William as a headright on September 8, 1636,[7] and again on April 9, 1648.[8] Edward was probably the father of Richard Drew, William Carter's neighbor in Surry County. Richard Axom [Exum] and Thomas Godwin claimed William on a joint patent on May 22, 1650.[9] Richard Axom's descendants would still be neighbors of the Carters 150 years later in North Carolina. By July of 1676, Colonel Thomas Goodwin was speaker of the House of Burgesses. During his term, the House of Burgesses passed the "Bacon Laws" during Bacon's Rebellion.[10] Mr. Thomas Peck claimed William as a headright on April 6, 1655,[11] and Mr. William Underwood claimed him on September 10, 1658,[12] about three years after William died in 1655.

Major Carter was also listed as a headright upon returning from his voyages. The first headright claim for Maj. Thomas Carter was probably by Arthur Smith on September 10, 1637. Smith also claimed headrights for John Bancroft and Thomas Croxton.[13] John Bancroft was the brother of Charles Bancroft, whose granddaughter Jane Moore married William Carter's grandson Thomas Carter. Thomas Croxton was a relative of Alice Croxton, who married William Carter. On July 25, 1638, Maj. Thomas Carter was claimed as a headright by Edward Sparshott[14] and on March 24, 1639, he was claimed as a headright by John Walton.[15]

On February 15, 1642, Col. John Carter's business partner Epaphroditus Lawson established an important landing site for the Vintners' Company on the Nansemond River when he patented 1400 acres[16] next to land owned by Moore Fauntleroy. Part of the 1642 patent came from transporting 13 persons, among whom were Epaphroditus Lawson's son William Lawson and brother Roland. Col. John Carter was instrumental in helping his friend establish the patent for the landing site and on January 9, 1643, John Carter assigned another 450 adjoining acres to Lawson.[17] Evidence that this was Vintners' Company land is shown by the assignments and by Col. Carter reassigning parts of the land to Vintners' Company operatives as needed. When Epaphroditus Lawson died in 1652,[18] Col. Carter administered his estate and this land was not included in Lawson's will. Col. Carter arranged that it became the property of his cousin Edward Carter.

In 1639/40,[19] Lawne's Creek Parish was created by the House of Burgesses. The parish was formed from the part of James City Parish that was on the south side of the James River between the Lower Chippoke Creek and Lawne's Creek and from their sources to the James River and the creek separating Hog Island from the mainland. In 1642/43, Hog Island and the territory between the Lower Chippoke Creek and Sunken Marsh Creek were made into Chippokes Parish, which was soon absorbed by Lawne's Creek Parish. William Carter's land at Bay Tree Neck was about three miles down the Lower Chippokes Creek from the James River and included a bay at Sunken Marsh Creek. In 1652, the area became Surry County.

Lawne's Creek Parish is undoubtedly one of the most important places of convergence of Carter colonial ancestors in the history of the family. The families that lived in Lawne's Creek Parish with William Carter would intermarry and move and live together with the Carters for the next century and a half and more.

Maj. Thomas Carter and Col. John Carter operated from the Nansemond River and out of Isle of Wight, while their (probable) brother William Carter was located a few miles away in Lawne's Creek Parish. By 1642, Col. John Carter and his brother Maj. Thomas Carter had begun planning the expansion of the business to the north in anticipation of the lifting of the settlement restrictions. John Carter patented 1300 acres in Lancaster County on the Rappahannock River on August 15, 1642, part of what would become his famous plantation at Corotoman. Both men remained in the south for the time being because settlement restrictions north of the York River would not be fully lifted until 1650. In April of 1645, Maj. Thomas Carter and his brother John Carter witnessed a conveyance of land by Justinian Cooper to Col. John George. The land was part of Cooper's holdings on Pagan Creek in Isle of Wight.

By 1648, as the government settlement restrictions began to be lifted, many of John and William Carter's associates from Nansemond, including Moore Fauntleroy, Bartholomew Hoskins, and Epaphroditus Lawson, and their associates from Isle of Wight, including William Clapham, John Munger, and Nicholas George, also began patenting land about forty or fifty miles to the north in the Rappahannock River basin. Patents were filed on both sides of the Rappahannock River to protect the associates from the perfidy of Charles I, who had promised to give the entire Northern Neck to the Lords Proprietors to assure their loyalty. Other associates patenting land were William Newsome, Captain William Brocas, Thomas and Edward Dale, and Sir Henry Chicheley. One of William Newsome's many great-granddaughters married James Carter over 160 years later in 1816 in Warren, County, Georgia. Edward Dale was a neighbor of Col. John Carter, his plantation being next door to the Corotoman plantation. Edward Dale married Diana Skipwith, who, along with Sir Henry Chicheley, was a grandchild of Sir Thomas Kempe of County Kent, England. Edward Dale and Diana Skipwith's daughter[20] would eventually marry Thomas Carter of Barford, the probable son of Maj. Thomas Carter. Captain William Brocas owned land on the southern side of the Rappahannock River. After Captain Brocas died, Col. John Carter married his widow, Eleanor Eltonhead, whose sister Jane was married to Robert Moryson (Morrison), the brother of deputy governor Colonel Francis Moryson, who was a very close friend of Col. John Carter.

William Carter's associates speculated in the north, but their main attention was to the south in the Blackwater River basin in Surry and Isle of Wight. William's probable son, our ancestor Captain Thomas Carter, was born sometime between 1626 and 1628. He had probably finished his education in London and his training in the merchant marines by 1650 and had made several voyages between England and the Vintners' Company's landings in the colony. Sometime around 1650, Captain Thomas Carter married Elinor Cooke, the daughter of William Cooke, a Bristol-based mariner and an operative in the Vintners' Company. William Cooke, like Thomas Carter, spent much of his time at sea. Cooke moved to Virginia permanently in the early 1660s when he settled in Lawne's Creek Parish in Surry County.

Several other people important to the Carter family history also lived in Lawne's Creek Parish by the time Captain Thomas Carter's father-in-law William Cooke moved there. Among them were Charles Barcroft, a wealthy London merchant and vintner who had moved to Virginia in 1636, and John Moore, a merchant mariner from Bristol, England, who settled in Isle of Wight in 1640. Both Charles Barcroft and John Moore were ninth great-grandfathers (eleven generations) of Jimmy Carter. John Moore was the father of Thomas Moore, George Moore, and Katherine Moore, who also lived in Lawne's Creek Parish. George Moore married Charles Barcroft's daughter Jane Barcroft and their daughter Magdalen Moore married Captain Thomas Carter's son Thomas Carter, Jr., the grandson of William Carter. Katherine Moore married Robert Flake, Sr., one of the largest landowners in Isle of Wight and Surry County. Their daughter Joyce Flake married Captain Francis England, another neighbor in Lawne's Creek Parish and a business associate of the Carters.

James Sampson was a London shipwright who moved to Lawne's Creek Parish. He married Elizabeth Barcroft, the daughter of Charles Barcroft and his first wife, Dorothy Crosbie. Another neighbor in Lawne's Creek was Richard Piland, who married Elinor Moore, the sister of Magdalen Moore and the daughter of George Moore and Jane Barcroft.

John Munger lived in Lawne's Creek Parish before moving to Lancaster County. He was a close associate of the Carters and received one of the most interesting land patents of the Carter family history during that time. On July 29, 1650, Munger was granted land adjacent to Col. John Carter and his brother Maj. Thomas Carter on the Corotoman River. Among the headrights claimed by John Munger were Charles Barcroft, George Moore, and Edward Dale, whose daughter Katherine would marry Thomas Carter of Barford.

William Carter was responsible for the Carters' involvement in the Carolina Project[21]; the expansion of the family shipping and marine business south of the Blackwater River;

and preparing for the lifting of restrictions against settlements west of the Blackwater into the Carolinas. The Carolina Project was a plan to identify and claim bays and ports and suitable landing sites for the loading and shipping of tobacco.

Another neighbor in Lawne's Creek was Captain James Tooke, who owned land next to Epaphroditus Lawson's son William. Captain Tooke was one of the major operatives in the Vintners' Company working on the Carolina Project with William Carter. John Harvey, the nephew of Governor Sir John Harvey and the probable mastermind of the Carolina Project, married James Tooke's daughter Dorothy.

Many of these men were merchant mariners from London and Bristol who had relocated from England during the reign of Oliver Cromwell. They were also lifetime acquaintances and friends, and many of them were involved with the Vintners' Company or with another of the livery companies. As new territory opened in the Virginia and Carolina frontier, they gained control of land for ports and landing sites through the headright system and they and their families moved together into the new territory. Their children intermarried for generations.

Like the Carters, these men were Royalists. Most had fled England after Charles I was beheaded and Oliver Cromwell and the Puritan Parliament came to power. They were allies of Virginia governor Berkeley under whose influence the burgesses passed an act supporting Charles II as the heir and made it a treasonable offense to advocate support for the Puritan Parliament. After Governor Berkeley invited Charles II, then in exile, to come to Virginia, Cromwell and the Puritan Parliament responded by sending a naval fleet to Virginia and forcing the retirement of the governor.

The various partners in the Vintners' Company continued to patent land for themselves and the company at suitable docking and wharfage sites and to expand their holdings and the company's holdings as new land opened in the colony. In 1650, the restrictions imposed by the Virginia Company were lifted for settlements north of the York River and William's probable brothers Maj. Thomas Carter and Col. John Carter and their associates Epaphroditus Lawson,[22] Andrew Gilson, Moore Fauntleroy, and George Marsh from Nansemond County shifted their operations north into the Rappahannock region while William Carter concentrated on the south along the Blackwater River into the Chowan basin of North Carolina.

Records show that by 1653, both Col. John Carter and his brother Maj. Thomas Carter and a number of their associates had relocated to Lancaster County. In January of 1653, Col. John Carter administered the will of Epaphroditus Lawson in Lancaster County and in March of 1653 the Lancaster Court ruled in favor of Maj. Thomas Carter in a debt from John Seamor. On the first tithables lists in Lancaster County, issued October 24, 1653, Maj. Thomas Carter appeared on the roster of Epaphroditus Lawson's brother Rowland Lawson with five tithables.[23]

These records have been attributed to other "Thomas Carters," but they undoubtedly refer to Major Thomas Carter, as is proven by the Lancaster records. Major Thomas Carter was the only Thomas Carter on the Lancaster tithables list from 1653 until his death in 1658 and there are numerous official records of Lancaster County during that time identifying him by his title of "Major."[24]

On September 18, 1655, Col. John Carter sold his brother Maj. Thomas Carter part of the Brocas plantation on the south side of the Rappahannock River:

> Know all persons by these presents that I Tho. Carter of the county of Lancaster devise and am indebted in account to John Carter his heirs and assigns the gross sum of one hundred and fiftie pounds sterling of lawful money England to be paid in London, one hundred

pounds thereof to be paid the said John Carter of the County of Lancaster or his assigns at or before the tenth of June 1657 and for fifty pounds to be paid in like manner at or before the tenth of June next following the aforesaid.... I bind now my heirs, executors, administrators and assigns and also my plantation with ewes I bought of the said John Carter formerly belonging unto Capt. Wm. Brocas Esq. and also all my flock of cattle and do acknowledge this deed at the next court ... the tobacco to be paid at the dwelling of Thomas Carter formerly belonging to Capt. Wm. Brocs Esq.[25]

The indenture was signed by Thomas Carter and witnessed by his neighbor Diana Skipwith and by Anne Ebbason.

Maj. Thomas Carter, in his indenture acknowledging the purchase of the property, identifies the land as the land "I bought of the said John Carter formerly belonging unto Captain William Brocas" Col. John Carter had married Eleanor Eltonhead, the widow of Captain William Brocas, and sold part of the Brocas estate to his brother Maj. Thomas Carter. However, the land title was disputed by Captain Brocas' nephew John Jackson and the Jamestown court awarded the title to Jackson:

Order of the James City Court, August 1658: Whereas it appears to this court by ye confession of Capt. Will Brocus in his life time that Jo. Jackson was his sister's son, & therefore is now ye next heir in this Country to ye lands which he said Capt. Brocus died seized of. It is therefore ordered that ye sheriff of Lancaster forthwith put ye sd Jackson in possession of ye sd Capt. Brocus, decd.[26]

Maj. Thomas Carter never legally owned this land although he did apparently live there before the dispute over the title to the land was resolved; the indenture stated that the price in tobacco was "to be paid at the dwelling of Thomas Carter formerly belonging to Capt. Wm. Brocas." The transaction between Col. John Carter and Maj. Thomas Carter for the sale and purchase of the Brocas land was later voided by the Jamestown court.

Maj. Thomas Carter also attempted to buy 560 acres of land from George Marsh on January 14, 1656. The land adjoined Col. John Carter's Corotoman plantation and the terms of the deal called for half of the payment to be made on October 10, 1658, and the other half a year later:

This bill bindeth me Thomas Carter in the County of Lancaster planter my heirs executors and administrators to pay unto George Marsh merchant, his heirs executors, administrators or assigns the sum of eight thousand pounds of good well conditioned Virginia tobacco in leaf with cask to contain same being for the consideration of five hundred and sixty acres of land bought from him....[27]

However, by October 1658 Major Thomas Carter had died, and in 1660, during the estate proceedings in which his brother Col. John Carter was the administrator, the court caused the land to revert to George Marsh because of nonpayment. George Marsh subsequently sold the land to Col. John Carter:

This indenture made the 10 January 1660 witnessth that whereas there was sold by John Meridith, shipwright, a dividend of land containing 560 acres lying at the head of John's Creek and adjoining upon land of Col. John Carter as by patent dated 10 December 1652 more plainly appears unto George Marsh, merchant, And whereas the sd land was again sold by the sd George Marsh to Thomas Carter, deceased, which Thomas Carter in his lifetime misliking the title of George Marsh and refusing to pay 8,000 lbs of tobacco due consideration of the sd land.... This indenture testifyith that the sd George Marsh and his wife, for 7,000 lbs have sold the sd land to Col. John Carter.[28]

Although this transaction has been erroneously attributed to Thomas Carter of Barford by some researchers, the land was undoubtedly purchased by Maj. Thomas Carter, which is proven by the sale of the land in 1660 to Col. John Carter in which the land is clearly identified as having been sold to the deceased Thomas Carter—"whereas the sd land was again sold by the sd George Marsh to Thomas Carter, deceased" Thomas Carter of Barford was a child at the time and lived until 1700.

William Carter's son and our ancestor Captain Thomas Carter probably spent much of his time at sea and lived in England with or near his father-in-law William Cooke in the early 1650s. There are no records of him for several years. His older brother William Jr. died in 1654 and his father, William Sr., died by 1655 while Thomas was away. Then, in 1656, while preparing for an extended trip to London,[29] Col. John Carter received word that Captain Thomas Carter had arrived in London with a story of being captured by the Spanish fleet and being imprisoned by the Spaniards for two years until escaping on a Dutch ship.

Captain Thomas Carter had been captured by the Spanish "Plate Fleet," the fleet that went to Central and South America to collect treasure for the king of Spain. The English navy was extremely interested in the Plate Fleet because they wanted nothing more than to steal its treasure. When Captain Thomas Carter and his companions arrived in London with their story, they were picked up and interrogated by John Thurloe, chief spymaster for Oliver Cromwell. The *State Papers of John Thurloe* was published in 1742 and the intelligence gleaned from Thomas Carter and his companions was included in the entry of May 15, 1656. Thomas Carter, age 30, was "shipping in a small vessell to returne to the Burmudas, and touching at the island of salt Tartudas, were there taken the 25th of August 1654 by captain Domindo, comander of the ship called the *Pattach of Margaretta*, being one of the Spanish plate fleete." After months of sailing and after arriving in Cadis, they "made their escape to the Dutch admirall *Ruyter*, by whome, in a month's time, they were brought into the Tessell, and having stayed there about 15 dayes, came thence for England in the Norwich frigatt, captain Hutton commander, and arrived at Deale the 9th of May present."[30] If it can be proven that this was indeed our Captain Thomas Carter, then his year of birth can be firmly established as 1626, making it even more improbable that Maj. Thomas Carter, born in 1610, was his father, as has been claimed.[31]

Both Captain Thomas Carter and his uncle Col. John Carter, both royalists and staunch supporters of the House of Stuart, apparently operated from London for some time. There is unproven speculation that they and some of their associates were engaged in a scheme to divert tobacco to the Dutch in violation of the Navigation Acts and that they were secretly funneling money to Prince Charles. The Carters and other associates of the Vintners' Company were having considerable difficulties with the government of Oliver Cromwell, as were other Royalists. The war with Spain imperiled the Vintners' Company's sea traffic, opening shipping to attacks by the Spanish fleet, a distinct contrast to Charles I's alliance with Spain and the peaceful sea traffic that had ensued. Then in 1656, Oliver Cromwell's government implemented the "Decimation Tax," a 10 percent penalty levied on the Royalists to support government militias supposedly necessary because of the Royalists' conspiracies against the government. The Vintners' Company itself, having a longstanding relationship with the Stuarts, was the target of political attacks by the Puritan Parliament and was subject to special taxation.

Oliver Cromwell died in September of 1658 and his brother Richard was proclaimed as his successor, leading to new protest by the Royalists, who supported Charles II as the rightful heir. An indictment for treason was issued by the Lord Protector[32] in London against Col. John Carter. His nephew Thomas Carter was probably also wanted. Both men soon relocated to their holdings in Virginia. However, the treason indictment followed Col. John Carter to Jamestown and was proclaimed by Governor Matthews in April of 1659, leading to the arrest of Col. Carter. The indictment was entered into the official records of Jamestown:

> By the Governor & Capt General of Virginia Whereas the safety & peace of this Colony hath been much endangered by the exhorbatant and undue practices of some men in Contempt of the late Commission for the Government sent from his highness & the Lords of this Councill. There are therefore in the name of his highness the Lord Protector x x x to take into your safe custody the body of Colo John Carter & him safely to detain or take such sufficient security that he may answer on the third day of May next ensuing to such matters as may be objected agt him on the behalf of his Highness the Lord Protector before the Governor & Council at James City hereof fail not at your peril x x Dated 8 Apl. 1659. Signed Sam Mathews to the Sherif of Lancaster County or his Deputy. Record primo July 1659 per Edwd Dale Cl Curt.
>
> This is a true copy of the originall warrant by virtue of which original warrant Mr Travers now Sherif of this County did openly declare he did arrest the sd Colo John Carter according to the tenor of the sd warrant and is recorded in this Court 25th May 1659 per me Edwd Dale Cl Curt.[33]

Fortunately for the Carters in Virginia, Richard Cromwell's weak government collapsed and Richard was forced to resign in May of 1659. Virginia governor Samuel Matthews died in 1660, the same year Charles II was restored to power. The assembly in Virginia immediately reappointed Berkeley as governor and the treason indictment against his friend Col. Carter was never mentioned again in the official records.

Charles II did not reward the Virginians for their loyalty. Instead, he took steps to control the tobacco trade in an attempt to garner all of the profits from the commodity and to monopolize trade with the Dutch. In 1660, a stricter Navigation Act was passed by Parliament under which all goods sent to the colony were to be imported only from England and all tobacco could be exported only to England. The price of tobacco in Virginia fell below the costs of production.

Although the exact dates are unknown, both William Carter, Sr., and his son William Carter, Jr., had died by December 1655 when William Carter, Sr.'s widow, Alice Carter, deeded a parcel of land to Edward Pettaway. In court she stated that Pettaway had married Elizabeth, the widow of her son-in-law William Carter, Jr., and she agreed Pettaway should have 500 acres of land bequeathed by William Carter, Sr., to William Carter, Jr., by virtue of Edward Pettaway's marriage to William Carter Jr's. widow, Elizabeth.[34]

Alice Carter and her son George also leased 400 acres of William Carter Sr's. plantation to Augustine Hunnicutt for 99 years. These families were obviously friends and would be for generations. Augustine Hunnicutt's daughter Katherine married John Kindred and their daughter Jane Kindred married William Carter's great-grandson Moore Carter. John Kindred was Katherine Hunnicutt's second husband. Her first husband was Samuel Cornwell and their son Samuel Cornwell, Jr., married Sarah Tooke, the daughter of William Tooke, William Carter's neighbor in Isle of Wight, and the granddaughter of James Tooke.

Upon his return to Virginia around 1658, our ancestor Captain Thomas Carter was about 30 years old. He operated out of Lawne's Creek with his father-in-law, William Cooke. But, probably to insure the continuation of the Carolina Project while they consolidated their positions northward along the Rappahannock, his uncle John Carter and the

Vintners' Company operatives arranged for him to acquire a premium landing site in the south in anticipation of the expansion of the company along the Blackwater River and the Chowan River basins. In March of 1658 Captain Thomas Carter patented 220 acres in Nansemond County, claiming himself twice for headrights.[35]

This land had been originally patented for a Vintners' Company landing site in the 1640s and had been part of the holdings of Epaphroditus Lawson. After Epaphroditus died, the land became the property of Edward Carter. Captain Thomas Carter's land was either part of Edward's land or adjoined it. The re-patenting of this land was facilitated by Francis Moryson (Morrison), a friend, associate, and benefactor to Col. John Carter and an important official who helped the Carter family reestablish the titles to their land after the Restoration. Francis Moryson was a son of the influential Sir Richard Moryson[36] and was Governor Berkeley's deputy. A staunch Royalist, Francis had served under Charles I before Charles was beheaded and Cromwell took power in England. Francis was also the brother of Robert Moryson, who had married Jane Eltonhead, the sister of Col. John Carter's second wife, Eleanor Eltonhead.[37] Col. Carter's association with Francis Moryson apparently allowed him to have land re-patented whenever he deemed it necessary. Moryson would also be of help to the family later.

By 1659, Captain Thomas Carter was in Isle of Wight, the county adjacent to Nansemond, where he was a witness to the will of James Tooke, his deceased father's friend and business associate. In 1663, after his uncle Maj. Thomas Carter had died, Captain Thomas Carter moved to the Rappahannock region from Southside to help his uncle Col. John Carter with the expansion of the Vintners' Company's operations in the north and to serve as justice of the Lancaster court, an appointment almost certainly facilitated by his uncle. At the same time, Col. Carter assigned a parcel of Vintners' Company land in Lancaster County to William Cooke, Captain Thomas Carter's father-in-law.[38] This land bounded land of Thomas Chetwood and was therefore next door to, or very close to, Col. John Carter, Chetwood's neighbor. The land was most likely transferred to Captain Thomas Carter's father-in-law William Cooke for the use of Thomas while he helped his uncle with business in the north and served as justice of the Lancaster court. Thomas lived on the land until 1665, when he relocated back to Southside Virginia. William Cooke never lived on the land, and after Captain Thomas Carter moved back south to Isle of Wight, Col. Carter had the land transferred to Richard Lawrence, another key operative in the Carolina Project.

The Vintners' Company having established itself in the Rappahannock River basin after the restriction against settlements in the north were lifted, its operatives and others in the south prepared for the lifting of the restrictions west of the Blackwater River. Sir John Harvey, the former governor; Thomas Tooke, a prominent Quaker and the son of James Tooke; Henry Plimpton, a Carter relative; and Edward Bland had tried unsuccessfully to gain control of the entire area from the Chowan basin to the Roanoke River in the 1640s by negotiating agreements with the various Indian tribes. When the settlement restrictions were lifted twenty-three years later, it was Sir John Harvey's nephew, John Harvey the Younger, who masterminded the land grab. Edward Bland had surveyed the Chowan basin in 1650 and on September 25, 1663, with the lifting of the restrictions, Harvey implemented the plan he had engineered. The associates in the Carolina Project filed twenty-nine patents, virtually locking up the ports and landing sites in the Blackwater and Chowan basins deep into North Carolina. The patents are listed sequentially in Nugent's *Cavaliers and Pioneers: Abstracts of Virginia Land Patents and Grants*. All were filed on the same day. The grants and the people included were the following[39]:

"Thomas Hodgkin, 1000 acres in the bay of Carolina River beginning at a small creek called Cannaughsaugh."

"William Munday, 300 acres in Carratucks Creek falling into the Kecougtancke river which river falls into the Carralina." William Munday had served as an indentured servant of Col. John Carter.

"Thomas Sherwood, 880 acres on the North side of the Carolina River." Thomas Sherwood was a headright for Col. John Carter and was most probably the son of William Carter's neighbor William Sherwood. William Sherwood witnessed deeds in 1670 for John Kindred, the grandfather of Jane Kindred, who married William Carter's great-grandson Moore Carter.

"Thomas Keely (Keele), 800 acres in a bay of the Paspetanke River."

"John Battle, 640 acres on the westward side of the Paspetanke River." John Battle was the grandfather of John Battle, whose widow, Sarah Browne Battle, married our ancestor Isaac Carter, the great-great-grandson of William Carter.

"James Murdah, 420 acres on the west side of the Chowanoake River."

"Mr. John Lawrence, 625 acres on the west side of the Chowanoake River along Robert Lawrence's land recently surveyed for James Murdah." John Lawrence was the grandfather of William Lawrence, who married Penelope Browne, the sister of Sarah Browne Battle, who married Isaac Carter.

"Thomas Stampe and James Noakes, 300 acres on the north side of the Carolina River."

"Lt. Mount Wells, 600 acres on the west side of the Chowanoake River."

Mr. Robert Lawrence, the brother of John Lawrence, "625 acres on the west side of the Chowanoake River."

"Katharine Woodward and Philarete Woodward, 700 acres on the west side of the Paspetanke River beginning at the mouth of a large creek falling into the river."

"Robert Peele, 300 acres on the southwest side of the Paspetanke River between land of Doctor Relfe and John Battle."

"Mr. William West, 2500 acres on the east side of the Pequimmin River about 6 or 7 miles up the same river beginning at a point of land near the great Marsh nigh an Indian field, running N.E. etc. to the mount of a small creek called Curraticke and from thence up the said river of Pequemim."

"Samuell Davis, 950 acres on the north side of the Carolina River."

"Mr. Thomas Relfe, a physician, 750 acres on the south west side of the Paspetanke River beginning at the mouth of a swamp and running by land of Thomas Kelle."

"Mr. John Harvey, 600 acres on a small creek called Carrawtucks falling into the river of Kecoughtanke, which falls into Carolina River."

"Roger Williams, 350 acres of the north side of the Carolina River."

"William Jennings, 550 acres in New begin Creek."

"Mr. John Harvey, 250 acres of the River of Carolina." John Harvey, the mastermind of the expansion plan, claimed headrights for transporting five persons for this piece of property, one of whom was George Moore, father of Magdalen Moore, who married William Carter's grandson, Thomas Carter.

"Robert Lawry, 300 acres in a bay at the mouth of the New begin River."

"Thomas Woodward, Sr., and Thomas Woodward, Jr., his son, 2500 acres on the north side of the Paspetanke River beginning at the head of the easternmost branch of the Aranews Creek & towards the head of the North River." Thomas Woodward was the former assay master of the Mint under Charles I and had fled England for Virginia around 1649.[40] Thomas Woodward was the surveyor for Governor Berkeley for these grants.[41]

These grants were a coordinated claim of over 15,000 acres of the best landing sites and bays in a huge area of land encompassing hundreds of square miles of the Blackwater and Chowan basins. Later grants pushed the total land patented to over 29,000 acres. William Carter's descendants, as well as those of his business associates in the Vintners' Company, began to move south into southern Virginia and North Carolina to occupy and operate from the new landings.

The acquisition of landing sites and land in the north also continued. Francis Moryson was still in office in 1665 and he was instrumental in helping Col. John Carter re-patent a particularly interesting piece of land, 4000 acres owned by Samuel Mathews prior to Mathews' death.[42] Col. Carter must have been pleased to have the court declare the Mathews land deserted and to gain control of the land of his enemy, who as governor had him arrested for treason.

The last record for Captain Thomas Carter was on June 9, 1668, when William Tooke paid William Richardson 4300 pounds of tobacco for his share of a sloop, and court records noted that Thomas was to pay the remainder.[43] On May 3, 1669, Captain Thomas Carter's widow, Elinor Cooke, petitioned the Isle of Wight court for an appointment as administrator of his estate.

Bacon's Rebellion

By 1670, Virginia had become stratified, the outskirts of the colony still being a genuine frontier while the tidewater counties were relatively prosperous and no longer threatened by Indian attacks. The colonial aristocracy was entrenched. Governor Berkeley, through his power of appointment, controlled the offices in the province such as the sheriffs and justices. The assembly was also under his control through his patronage and by limitation of the eligibility qualifications of those people allowed to vote. After years of the governor and his friends using their positions to enrich themselves, widespread charges of corruption, public theft and unjust taxation were made. The Carters and almost all of their business partners were Royalists and strongly supported Governor Berkeley.

Adding to the colonists' discontent, Lord John Berkeley, the governor's cousin, sought a grant from the king to overturn the original patent and to grant the same region to himself and his friends. Charles II was indebted to Lord Berkeley for his support in the English civil war and issued this grant in 1669. The right to buy and sell land as well as to levy and collect taxes and rents was included in the patent. The colonists were outraged and alarmed and feared a takeover by the Proprietors. Then on February 25, 1673, in total disregard for any rights for the colonists, King Charles II took steps to regrant all of Virginia to Lord Arlington and Lord Culpepper, two of his most rapacious courtiers. There was no mention of the already existing government, and an additional tax of 50 pounds of tobacco was levied on all tithables. The breadth of the grant was stunning:

> First, the entire territory, tract and dominion, commonly called Virginia, with the territory of Accomack, with all rights, appurtenances and jurisdictions, together, with all rivers, waters and royalties whatsoever; are granted, as aforesaid, and bounded on the north, with

the dominion of Maryland; on the east, with the sea; on the south, with Carolina, with all islands within the said bounds, and within ten leagues of the shore.

2dly, the escheats of all lands, which shall become forfeit to his majesty, his heirs, or successors are granted as, above said, under uncertain compositions.

3dly, the quit rents, and other rents, payments, duties and reservations, upon any grants of the premises whatsoever, due to his majesty, are granted to the said lords, grantees, for the term above said; to be paid in specie, and not in commodity; together with the arrearages of rent to their own use, without account since the last day of May, 1669.[44]

By the nature of its coastline, the province was vulnerable to attack and difficult to defend. The James River was too wide to be defended and the material for building a fort was not available at the mouth of the river. Nevertheless, because of the threat of Dutch ships, it was decided by the governor and the assembly that a fort would be built at Point Comfort. Objections were raised that the fort should be built at Jamestown. But those objections were ignored and a fort, which proved useless, was built at Point Comfort, financed by a tax of 70,000 pounds of tobacco. When the Dutch Fleet did arrive in 1667, the fort proved completely ineffectual and the vessels anchored at Jamestown were easily seized. The merchants demanded again that a fort be built at Jamestown, even though they contributed nothing for defense except for port fees, which in all of 1667 amounted to £800. The construction of the fort was approved and was estimated to cost £15,000 at a time when the entire governmental revenue of Virginia was only £2000 a year, of which the governor received £1200. When the provincial government and Governor Berkeley decided to proceed with construction of the fort, a new tax was imposed. The Berkeley regime was assailed, and more charges of corruption, over-taxation and mismanagement were levied against him.

Even amid the rising discontent, Berkeley and his cronies could have probably maintained control had it not been for the Indian wars. Governor Berkeley controlled all trade with the Native Americans, which he regulated by licenses that were granted to his friends. Colonists could not trade with Indians, could not enter an Indian village without permission, and could not engage in land contracts with the Indians. The Indians' internal affairs were also regulated, and in 1662 the legislature went so far as to forbid the Indians from selecting their own chiefs and passed a law that they be appointed by the governor.

The peace between the Indians and the colonists of Virginia was broken with the murder of a settler in Stafford County. The Virginia militia was called out and the Indians were pursued and slaughtered. Minor retaliatory attacks by both sides followed until the Indians seized a fort a short way inside of Maryland. Captain Thomas Truman besieged the fort and when five Indian chiefs came out to negotiate a truce, Captain Truman's militia killed them all. A war of revenge ensued and the settlers appealed to Governor Berkeley for protection. However, the governor, fearing a war with the Indians would jeopardize his monopoly in the fur trade with them, refused to take action until the assembly sat. By the time the assembly convened, 800 more settlers had been killed. Nathaniel Bacon, citing the need for self defense of the settlers, organized several hundred settlers and began attacking the Indians.

Nathaniel Bacon came from an influential family and was a justice and member of the council but was not well liked by the government officials. A royal commissioner described him as a man of "an ominous, pensive, melancholy Aspect, of a pestilent and prevalent Logical discourse tending to atheisme, in most companyes not given to much talke, or to make suddain replyes, of a most imperious and dangerous hidden Pride of heart, dispising the wisest of his neighbors for their Ignorance, and very ambitious and arrogant."[45] Nevertheless, in the face of inaction by the government, his crusade against the Indians was extremely popular among the outlying settlers.

Berkeley demanded that Bacon cease his campaign against the Indians and charged him with treasonous activities by defying the authority of the king's representative. However, he offered Bacon a pardon if he would discontinue his fight and swear an oath of allegiance to the king and recognize his, Berkeley's, authority. Bacon did not respond to the offer. Governor Berkeley was outraged that the offer of a pardon was ignored and expelled Bacon from the council and suspended him from his office as justice of the peace. Bacon's suspension from the council freed him to run for the assembly, a seat he handily won because of his popularity with the people for his stance against the Indians. When his sloop approached Jamestown, it was fired upon and Bacon was captured. He then swore an oath of allegiance to the king and was pardoned. The rancor between Berkeley and Bacon continued and Bacon raised a force of 500 men and marched to the capital demanding a commission to make him commander of the provincial troops to fight against the Indians. The governor refused and, as soon as Bacon left Jamestown, he declared Bacon a rebel and ordered the militia to pursue him.

The insurrection lasted for months and during the height of the rebellion, one of the king's ships, the *Young Prince*, arrived, commanded by Captain Robert Morris. For four months, from September 19, 1676, until January 29, 1677, Robert Morris laid off the coast and monitored the situation and sent dispatches back to London. Morris met with government officials and received reports from the troops he had sent to help the governor's militia; he maintained a widespread network of spies. Several times at night, his ship was visited by a mysterious "Mr. Moore," who may have been our relative, either George or Thomas Moore. Mr. Moore also met with the governor and was obviously acting as an intermediary with Captain Morris and keeping him briefed on the situation on the ground. There were several instances where spying parties dispatched by Captain Morris would accidentally encounter Bacon's men, and after sometimes tense discussions, both parties would go their separate ways. There were also instances where the meeting of the two parties was not peaceful. All of this was recorded in a fascinating journal kept by Captain Morris which still survives today.

Bacon decided to capture Governor Berkeley and to send him into exile. To rally support he wrote and circulated a scathing manifesto charging the governor with levying unjust taxation, appointing unqualified friends to office for profit, and failing to keep the colony safe from corruption. He ended the document with this: "[N]ow let us compare these things togither and see what Spounges have suckt up the Publique Treasure and wither it hath not bin privately contrived away by unworthy Favourites and juggling Parasites whose tottering Fortunes have bin repaired and supported at the Publique charge, now if it be to Judg what greater giult can bee then to offer to pry into these and to unriddle the misterious wiles of a powerful Cabal."[46]

Bacon raised a force of three hundred men and approached Jamestown, causing Governor Berkeley to flee up the coast. Bacon sent a ship to capture the governor and when the ship arrived at Berkeley's camp, the governor invited the commander to his camp to discuss the matter; but during the negotiations Berkeley's men captured the ship and seized the commander. Governor Berkeley then returned to Jamestown while Bacon was away and, after promising pardons to all except the top leaders of Bacon's rebels, was welcomed into the city, whereupon Bacon and his men laid siege to Jamestown and burned it to the ground.

On October 18, 1676, Nathaniel Bacon suddenly became sick and died. Without his leadership, the rebellion faltered and his men dispersed. Berkeley's militia hunted down Bacon's top advisors and, avoiding the formalities of a trial, hung twenty-three of them. William Groves, who had married Elinor Cooke, the widow of Captain Thomas Carter, was a colonel in Bacon's Rebellion and was captured in 1676. On December 25, 1676, Colonel Groves escaped. Thirty or forty men under Captain Consent found him and three other rebels at Captain Francis England's house, which they had captured. Captain Consent shot and killed William Groves and captured the other three rebels.[47]

King Charles II sent a commission to investigate the uprising and after they arrived in January 1677, Governor Berkeley was recalled. He sailed back to England to explain his actions in person.

The commissioners investigating the rebellion announced that Charles II would protect all informers and petitioners who would come forward and state their cases, and a group of people from Isle of Wight presented to them a list of twenty-six "Grievances" against the unjust rule and corruption of Governor Berkeley and his allies. The grievances of "His Majesties 'Poor but Loyal Subjects'" were replied to by many citizens of the colony who had supported Governor Berkeley, among whom were the Carters and many of their relatives and business associates who had profited from Governor Berkeley's rule. Their reply to the Grievances was as follows:

> To the Right Hon. Herbert Jeffreys, Esqr., Sir John Berry, Knight, and Francis Morrison, Esqr., His Majesties Commissioners to enquire into the Grievances of His Majesties Subjects of Virginia.
>
> The humble Remonstrance of Divers of His Majesties Loyall Subjects in the Upper Parish of Isle of Wight County.
>
> Sheweth:
>
> That whereas His Most Sacred Majestie, hath most gratiously and compasionatly, vouchasefed to appointe and commissionate your Honors to enquire into the Grievances of His subjects of this Plantation notwithstanding the late desertion of the greater parte of this country, from their duty and allegance to His Majestie; and order thereunto, your Honors have been pleased to issue forth your declaration inviting the people to make known to you their Grievances, and especially such as they suppose, to occasion the late tumults, and in such manner to be made know unto you, as in your Honors said declaration is empressed; Whereupon certain persons of this county, have drawn up, to be presented to your Honors a certaine writing in the name of His Majesties "Poor but Loyall Subjects of the Isle of Wight County," there enumerating certain articles in the nature of Grievances of the People of the said county: But forasmuch as many of the honest, loyall and best affected people of the said county; besides your petitioners were never made privie to the said writing, nor the matter therein contained, before the publishing thereof, and conceiving, the same not to be framed and composed in that humble manner and nature as it ought to be, neither consisting of any matter, answerable to the directions, by your Honors given, in your said Declaration and least we allowe your petitioners as members of the said County, might be taken as concerned in the said writing.
>
> We humbly beg and lay hold of His Majesties most gratious Pardon, forasmuch, as we, or some of us, may have at some time or other since this Horrid Rebellion, either through fear, force, or otherwise, deviated from our duties and allegance to His Most Sacred Majestie.
>
> Next, We humbly beg of your Honors to admit of this our most Humble Remonstrance, as a protection against the said writing, or Pretended Grievances, and the composers thereof, most of them being active and solicitous instruments in the late Rebellion against His Majestie and his Governor within this country, who therein, as we humbly conceive, rather go about to justify themselves, in their late traitorous actions, then in humble manner, as they ought to do, beg his majesties pardon for their Offences. And we do further

the most humbly Remonstrate to your Honors that it is at present our greatest grievance that His Most Sacred Majestie, ever should have occassion to send his gracious Proclamation of Pardon, of Rebellion and Treason, into the country, and that his Majesties late Honorable Governor, Sir William Berkeley, who hath so long and so peaceably Governed this country for his Majestie and so much indulged the good and welfare thereof and the inhabitants (as is manifest he hath) should be not only so undutifully, but cruelly and barbarously dealt with:

And whereas your Honors do command, to make known what may be the chief Grievances, occationing the late tumults, we humbly conceive and believe it will so appear to your Honors, that Envy, Emulation, Malice, and Ignorance were the Cheife causes thereof.

Thus as in duty bound, Praying for His Majesties Temporal and Eternal Happiness and your Honors prosperity, we subscribe ourselves His Majesties Obedient and Loyall Subjects.[48]

Among those signing the remonstrance were Thomas Carter, the son of Captain Thomas Carter; his father-in-law George Moore and George's brother Thomas Moore; John Person, a son-in-law of William Cooke; Richard Piland, the brother-in-law of Thomas Carter's wife Magdalen Moore; James Lawson, who was most likely a son or brother of Epaphroditus Lawson, Col. John Carter's business partner; Captain Francis England, another business associate of the Carters who had married the niece of George and Thomas Moore; Richard Briggs, who died a year later and made Thomas Moore an overseer of his will and whose estate was appraised by George Moore[49]; Edmund Wickins, a fellow Captain in the merchant marines; George Cripps, who was appointed executor of the nuncupative will (an oral will) of John Godbehere, for which Captain Francis England and Thomas Moore posted security[50]; George Branch, Jr., the son-in-law of Captain Francis England[51]; John Newman, who with Thomas Moore posted security for the administration of the estate of Elias Fort; John Gutteridge, who lived next door to Captain Francis England on the Blackwater River[52] and whose estate was later appraised by Thomas Carter[53]; and John Carrell, who married the widow of Thomas Carter's uncle William Cooke and who, with Thomas Carter, was supervisor of the will of John Munger.[54]

A month later, on April 9, 1677, the signers of the "Grievances" recanted in the court of Isle of Wight, stating, "[W]e the subscribed having drawn up a paper in behalf of the inhabitants of Isle of Wight County as the Grievances of said county, seek pardon, and promise never to be guilty again of being false and scandalous [illegible] and ask mercy of Governor William Berkeley"[55]

Governor Berkeley died in London, never having met with the king.

The Thomas Carter Conundrum

There were three Thomas Carters in Lancaster County around 1650–1670 and they have been constantly confused with each other by modern genealogists and in historical publications.

Major Thomas Carter was born in London around 1610 and arrived in Virginia aboard the *Safety* with his younger brother Col. John Carter of Corotoman. Major Thomas Carter resided in Nansemond County before moving with his brother to the Rappahannock region to expand the family's merchant marine business to the north. Major Thomas Carter died in 1658.

Our ancestor Captain Thomas Carter was most probably the son of William Carter and the nephew of Major Thomas Carter and Col. John Carter, although there is no proof. Captain Thomas Carter was born around 1626, probably in Jamestown but maybe in England. He was a sea captain in the family's Vintners' Company business and spent much of his life at sea and in London. Captain Thomas Carter married Elinor Cooke and was a justice of the Lancaster court from 1663 until 1665, a post he almost certainly received with the influence of his uncle Col. John Carter.

The third Thomas was Thomas Carter of Barford, who was probably born around 1650 and who did not appear in the Lancaster records until 1670. Thomas Carter of Barford married Katherine Dale. Researchers of Thomas Carter of Barford have consistently confused him with both Maj. Thomas Carter and our ancestor Captain Thomas Carter. Charles Warner, a noted Carter researcher who theorized that there was no known association between the families, writes of *Debrett's Peerage* and others suggesting otherwise: "They appear to have taken over the characteristics of Thomas Carter of Barford, Lancaster County, and claimed them for President Carter's own line of Thomas Carters in Isle of Wight."[56] Actually, it appears that Barford researchers have claimed virtually every transaction by any Thomas Carter as that of Thomas Carter of Barford.

Most of the misidentifications can be traced back to two sources. Dr. Joseph Lyon Miller published an article in 1909, *Captain Thomas Carter and His Descendants*, in the *William and Mary Quarterly Historical Magazine*, and in 1912 published a book, *The Descendants of Capt. Thomas Carter of "Barford," Lancaster County, Virginia, 1652–1912*, about the descendants of Thomas Carter of Barford. Dr. Miller's book is a monumental work, but an additional century of research has uncovered more information. The other source of misinformation is a prayer book that supposedly belonged to Thomas Carter of Barford in which somebody wrote that he was "about 70" when he died in 1700. New evidence strongly supports the theory that Thomas Carter of Barford was born around 1650 and died when he was around fifty years old.

Dr. Miller opens his article thus: "Of the ancestry of Captain Thomas Carter of Christ Church parish, Lancaster County, Virginia, we know nothing, though it has been suggested that he may have been a brother or cousin of Col. John Carter of the same county and parish."[57] Of course, a century ago, Dr. Miller did not have the benefit of Noel Currer-Briggs' research and records on the English ancestry of the Carter family to know they were most probably uncle and nephew.

Dr. Miller also wrote that "Captain Thomas Carter [of Barford], appears first in the Lancaster records in 1653 when he paid tithes for himself and four servants. In 1663 he paid for twenty persons, and 1699 for nine; the number always varying according to the number of servants. It is important to note that there was only one Thomas Carter on the Lancaster tax rolls for each year. Captain Thomas Carter, Major Thomas Carter, and Thomas Carter of Barford were never on the tax list together. Nor was one or the other inadvertently left out. The tithables lists were posted on the church and courthouse doors to insure compliance. The penalties for concealing a tithable were severe — forfeiture of a servant or 1000 lbs. of tobacco to the informant.

The 1653 tithable records, which list a "Thomas Carter" and not "Captain Thomas Carter," as Dr. Miller wrote, refers to Maj. Thomas Carter, the brother of Col. John Carter, and not to Thomas Carter of Barford, the probable son of Maj. Thomas Carter. The 1653 tithables list on which Thomas Carter appeared was on the roster of Rowland Lawson, a neighbor of Col. John Carter and Maj. Thomas Carter and the brother of Col. Carter's business partner Epaphroditus Lawson. Roland had undoubtedly known Maj. Thomas

Carter personally for decades. Rowland Lawson was also a justice of Lancaster County charged with collecting the tax on the east side of the Corotoman River to the Rappahannock. There was only one Thomas Carter on the Lancaster tithables list from 1653 until 1658.[58] That Thomas Carter was undoubtedly Major Thomas Carter, who is known to have been living in Lancaster County during the time as proven by numerous official Lancaster records in which he is referred to, with his title, as "Major Thomas Carter."

Maj. Thomas Carter was on the Lancaster County tithables list in 1653 with 5 tithables, in 1654 with 4, in 1655 with 4, in 1656 with 9, in 1657 with 5 and in 1658 with 4. Maj. Thomas Carter died in 1658 and no Thomas Carter appears on the Lancaster tithables lists again until our Captain Thomas Carter moved there in 1663 to serve as a justice of the Lancaster court. Our Captain Thomas Carter then appears on the Lancaster County tithables list as "Captain Thomas Carter" in 1663 with 20 tithables, in 1664 with 18, and in 1665 with 15. After Captain Thomas Carter moved back to Isle of Wight in 1665, no Thomas Carter appears on any tax list in Lancaster County until Thomas Carter of Barford is listed in 1670 with 2 tithables.

Dr. Miller attributes the purchase of the Brocas plantation to Thomas Carter of Barford when he writes "Thomas Carter [of Barford] seems to have purchased his first land in Lancaster from Col. John Carter, as June 1, 1654, he acknowledged a debt due Col. John Carter for land, 12,352 pounds of tobacco to be delivered the following October at the dwelling house of the said 'Mr. Tho: Carter'; and 130 pounds sterling Sept. 18, 1655." As previously noted, this transaction was also a land deal made by Maj. Thomas Carter in a failed attempt to buy part of the Brocas plantation after Col. John Carter married Eleanor Eltonhead Brocas, the widow of Captain Brocas. The only Thomas Carter on the Lancaster County tithables list at the time was Maj. Thomas Carter, who is proven to have been living there during this time.

Dr. Miller also attributes the attempted purchase by Maj. Thomas Carter of George Marsh's land to Thomas Carter of Barford: "Jan. 14, 1656, George Marsh, Merchant, sold 560 acres to 'Tho: Carter in ye County of Lancaster.' Although many others have mistakenly identified the Thomas Carter involved in the purchase of George Marsh's land as Thomas Carter of Barford, it is abundantly clear that the transaction was with Major Thomas Carter. During the estate proceedings in 1660, after Maj. Carter's death in 1658, the land was sold to Col. John Carter and was clearly identified in the indenture as land sold to the deceased Thomas Carter: "And whereas the sd land was again sold by the sd George Marsh to *Thomas Carter, deceased*, which Thomas Carter in his lifetime misliking the title of George Marsh and refusing to pay 8,000 lbs of tobacco due consideration of the sd land" (italics added). Major Thomas Carter had refused to pay because he had died before the payment was due in 1658. Thomas Carter of Barford died in 1700.

Noel Currer-Briggs examined the records a hundred years later and shed a lot of new light on the situation but also was still at a loss explaining two particular records. On September 20, 1661, Thomas Carter re-patented the 220 acres of land that his uncle Col. John Carter had arranged for him to use as a base of operation upon their return from London. The following letter from Stephen Fox, who appears to have died at sea, to his brother John Fox was approved as a will in London in 1663:

> Stephen Fox Att Sea. Latitude 24 degrees. 7br ye 9th 1662. Aboard ye Restauracion. Loveinge Brother. These Certife you we sett sayle from New England the 5th August, encountered two storms, lost our mastes, thrown overboard fish and mickrell and pipestaves & 3 horses drowned, one of which was betwitx your selfe and my brother Thomas

soe that yow have lost all, as well as my Brother Thomas and myselfe and Peter. I knowe not whether I have saved any thing or noe till I come to some Port & I hope yow paid the £3 3c I charged to yow from Deale. I have sent 50 or 60 or 70 cwt of Tobacco in one Captain Thomas Carter's hands at Nuncemund in Jeames River.... Captain Jno. Whitty, who uses Virginia, knows the man, and will bring it home, which will be 70 or 80 apiece, and 70 or 80 amongst you all for mounringe. I am in hast the shipp being under saile. Your loveing Brother Stephen Fox. Administration 29 October, 1663, to Brother John Fox.

Currer-Briggs, noting that Major Thomas Carter had died by 1660, believed that the Thomas Carter referred to in Stephen Fox's will must have been Thomas Carter of Barford, in spite of the fact that Fox stated that Captain Thomas Carter was operating from Nansemond on the James River where our Captain Thomas Carter was known to live and Thomas Carter of Barford, who was probably about ten years old at the time, would eventually operate from Lancaster County on the Rappahannock River, almost 65 miles away by sea.

However, because Currer-Brigs believed that Major Thomas Carter had patented the 220 acres originally in 1659, he was at a complete loss as to how to explain the re-patenting of the same land to Thomas Carter in 1661 after Major Thomas Carter had died. He considered that the Thomas Carter who re-patented the land was our ancestor Thomas Carter, widely thought by modern genealogists to be the son of Maj. Thomas Carter. Here he ran into the problem of the ages of the Thomas Carters. Noting that a Thomas Carter who was the son of Maj. Thomas Carter would have been in his early teens, according to the American genealogists, and thus too young to have re-patented the land, Currer-Briggs could not make the ages work and confessed that he could find no satisfactory solution.[59] The ages did not work out because our Captain Thomas Carter (who did re-patent the land) was probably the son of William Carter and not Major Thomas Carter, who was born ten years after William.

Many patents were regranted during this time to protect the titles from Charles II's intentions to give Virginia to his allies. The 220 acres were declared deserted and regranted to Edward Carter on March 30, 1664, after our Captain Thomas Carter moved temporarily to Lancaster County to live on the land that Col. John Carter had arranged for Captain Carter's father-in-law, William Cooke, to patent for Captain Thomas Carter to use while he temporarily relocated to the Rappahannock and served as justice of the Lancaster court. This land was obviously the Vintners' Company's land controlled by Col. John Carter. After Edward Carter died, his wife relinquished the land and it was re-patented again by Thomas Tilly, another mariner, in November of 1685.

Besides claiming all of Maj. Thomas Carter's records as those of Thomas Carter of Barford, researchers further confuse Thomas Carter of Barford with our ancestor Captain Thomas Carter. Dr. Miller, remarking on the titles given gentlemen of the era, notes that "from his first appearance in the tax list of 1653 as "'Mr. Tho: Carter' until his death in 1700 he does not appear without the distinguishing 'Mr.' or 'Capt.'" In fact, in the subsequent records for Thomas Carter of Barford in Lancaster County for the thirty years after 1670 when he probably reached his majority age until his death in 1700, he is referred to as "Mr." Thomas Carter and never as "Captain" Thomas Carter. Expounding on titles given gentlemen, Dr. Miller even notes the Lancaster court records that state the following: "Oct ye 21st 1663 According to order the Oath of a Commissioner [justice] was this day Administered to Capt. Thomas Carter after which he sat in the Court," and citing the March 8, 1670, entry, "At ye request of Mr. Edward Dale, Mr: Tho: Carter is dep'td Clerke for said Dale for conformation of who in ye Clerke's place it is ordered by this Court."

Records from the same Court show that "Capt." Thomas Carter was administered the oath of justice and "Mr." Thomas Carter was appointed deputy clerk. Our ancestor Captain Thomas Carter was appointed by the governor as a justice of the Lancaster court and served from 1663 until 1665. He appears in the court records as "Captain Thomas Carter" seventeen times during this time. He is listed on the Lancaster tithables tax list as "Capt. Thomas Carter" during this time. After Thomas Carter of Barford appears in 1670, there are no more references to "Captain" Thomas Carter in the Lancaster records.

Another misidentification that has long persisted occurs when Dr. Miller wrote that on "March 8, 1670, Captain Carter married Katharine Dale, daughter of Maj. Edward and Diana Skipwith Dale, prior to 1670, as their son Henry was born in 1674 and he was at least the third and probably the fourth of their children."[60] Charles W.H. Warner, in his writing about the Carter family, states "Captain Thomas Carter of Corotoman married Katherine Dale, and Barford was the name of his home."[61]

Although Dr. Miller and Mr. Warner identify him as Captain Thomas Carter, the official records of the time refer to Mr. Thomas Carter. There are no official records whatsoever that refer to "Captain" Thomas Carter's marrying Katherine Dale. There seems to be no evidence that the Thomas Carter of Barford who married Katherine Dale was a captain of anything, nor is Thomas Carter of Barford ever referred to in any official records as "Captain" Thomas Carter after 1670 for the next thirty years until his death.

Between 1909, when Dr. Miller published *Captain Thomas Carter and His Descendants* in the *William and Mary Quarterly Historical Magazine*, and 1912, when he published *The Descendants of Capt. Thomas Carter of "Barford," Lancaster County, Virginia, 1652–1912*, a prayer book was discovered that belonged to Thomas Carter. The entry recording his marriage says "on Wedns^{day} ye 4^h Day of May 1670 — was Mar^d Mr Thomas Carter of Barford in ye County of Lancaster in Virg^a & Katharine Dale ye eldest Daugh^r of Mr Edw: Dale ye same County." Even in his own Prayer Book, Thomas Carter of Barford refers to himself as "Mr.," not "Capt." Other individuals known to be sea or militia captains are named in the prayer book and are referred to with the title of "Captain."

Dr. Miller speculated that "Captain Thomas Carter of Virginia [Thomas Carter of Barford] may possibly have been the youngest son of Ancell [Anscell] Carter, born Oct. 28, 1591, son of Wm. and Mary of Kimpson,[62] who settled in London. At the visitations of the Heralds from the Collage of Arms in 1634, Ansyll (Ancell) Carter of London, Grocer, had six sons living as follows: George, eldest son, John, Ansyle, William, James, and *Thomas, youngest son, who could not have been over three* or four years old in 1634. Capt. Thomas Carter of Virginia was born in 1630–31" (italics added).[63]

However, upon referring to the 1634 *Visitation of London*, Dollye McAlister Elliott, associate editor of the *Colonial Genealogist*, found that Ansyle (Anscell) Carter had no son named Thomas. His children were George, Anscell, John and Jane. Researching the Public Record Office in London, she found the will of Anscell Carter in which he named his sons, none of whom were named Thomas; and she found Anscell's son George's will in which he named his brothers, none of whom were named Thomas. Mrs. Elliot then examined the original 1634 *Visitation of London* in the Manuscript Department of the British Museum and confirmed that Anscell Carter had no son named Thomas.[64] Some Barford researchers have since claimed descent from other Bedfordshire Carters even though Mrs. Elliot, citing Thomas Fisher's *Collections Historical, Genealogical and Topographical for Bedfordshire* and F.A. Page-Turner's *Genealogia Bedfordiensis, 1538–1700*, proved that all of those Thomas Carters lived and died in Bedfordshire, England, and not Virginia.[65]

Mrs. Elliot correctly concluded that Thomas Carter of Barford was the son of Maj. Thomas Carter and that Maj. Thomas Carter was the brother of Col. John Carter (while also supposing that they could be nephew and uncle). She also speculated that Thomas Carter of Barford was the great-grandson of William and Mary (Anscell) Carter of Kempson and Barford, Bedfordshire, England, for which there is no proof whatsoever.[66]

Charles Warner speculated about the ancestry of Thomas Carter of Barford in *Northern Neck of Virginia Historical Magazine*:

> In 1635 Thomas Carter, age 25, and John Carter, age 23, arrived together on the ship, *Safety*, from England. Because of the close association between John and Thomas Carter in Lancaster County and the arrival of John and Thomas Carter on the same ship in 1635, it appears they were the same men. This identity is further strengthened by the associations surrounding Thomas Carter, referred to in 1626 as an "ancient planter" of Virginia. This title was given to the first property owners in the colony. That Thomas Carter ("ancient planter") and the Thomas Carter of the ship *Safety* was the same man is borne out by the identity of a fellow ship passenger, Bartholomew Hoskins. Both Hoskins and a John Carter owned Property in London near each other on Fleet Street and just off Fleet Street on Carter's Lane. Both Thomas Carter and Hoskins, listed as "ancient planters" of which there were very few, were in Virginia before and were in 1635 sharing passage for months at sea on a ship to Virginia. One John Carter, merchant, sued Bartholomew Hoskins, merchant, in 1641. All are identified as early Rappahannock landowners, Bartholomew Hoskins being the first Englishman to patent land in 1645 where Tappahannock and Essex County were later established after 1682. From 1651 to 1656 this was in that area then a part of Lancaster County. All known associations of these early Thomas Carters of 1626 and 1635 tie him to Lancaster County men. Therefore the evidence indicates that the early Thomas Carter ("ancient planter," of the ship, *Safety*, being probably the same as the Thomas Carter deceased by 1660) appears to be the father of Capt. Thomas Carter (c. 1630–Oct.22, 1700) of Barford.[67]

Although Mr. Warner's conclusion that Thomas Carter of Barford was the son of Thomas Carter of Archer's Hope, the "Ancient Planter," by virtue of sharing a voyage and a John Carter having sued Bartholomew Hoskins, seems odd, Bartholomew Hoskins was in fact on the *Safety* with (Col.) John Carter and (Maj.) Thomas Carter in 1635. Hoskins had also sailed to Virginia with Thomas Lee, another member of the Vintners' Company, in 1634. Lee had stayed in Hoskins' house in Elizabeth City, where he died ten days after his arrival in the colony. When Hoskins returned to London, Thomas Lee's widow, Joan (Jonne, Joane), hired him to return to Virginia and settle her husband's estate, giving Hoskins her power of attorney. Hoskins sailed back to Virginia on the *Safety* in 1635.

On December 21, 1635, John Carter of Sherley Hundred, having returned to London from Virginia, married Thomas Lee's widow, Joan, at St. Michael Bassishaw Church.[68] It was John Carter of Sherley Hundred who eventually sued Bartholomew Hoskins and not Col. John Carter of Corotoman, as Mr. Warner thought. Bartholomew Hoskins' wife Dorcas Foster Hoskins was in England in 1641 when she presented a petition to the House of Lords "on behalf of her said husband now in Virginia — that all proceedings in a suite commenced by John Carter and Joane his wife against the said Bartholomew Hoskins may be stayed."[69]

Thomas Carter the Ancient Planter was apparently much older than Mr. Warner thought and seems to have died around 1625, when Richard Kingsmill came into possession of his plantation near Jamestown, Kingsmill probably having married the daughter of Thomas Carter of Archers Hope[70] and inherited his land. Thomas Carter the Ancient Planter was much too old to be the father of Thomas Carter of Barford and had probably died about five years before even the earliest claimed dates of Thomas Carter of Barford's birth.

It is not known who made the entries in Thomas Carter of Barford's prayer book. There are three different authors identified as such by experts. The first author was assumed to be Thomas Carter of Barford himself until handwriting analysts proved that entries in the prayer book by the first author recorded marriages after Thomas of Barford had died. Serious genealogists and researchers now refer to the "first author," "second author," etc. The second author, recording the death of Thomas Carter of Barford in 1700, noted that Carter was "about 70 years old." Despite this entry made by someone who was somewhat unsure of his age, the most conclusive evidence of Thomas Carter of Barford's age are the tithables lists in Lancaster County, his age difference with his wife, and his appointment as deputy clerk of the Lancaster court.

An examination of the records shows that there was only one Thomas Carter on Lancaster county tithables lists at a time with significant gaps. Major Thomas Carter moved to Lancaster County in the early 1650s and appears on the tithables list, from 1653 until 1658. Major Thomas Carter died shortly after the tax list was issued in 1658. There is then a gap in the tithables list with no Thomas Carter listed until our ancestor Captain Thomas Carter moved to Lancaster County in 1663 and appears in the tithables list until 1665. There is again a gap with no Thomas Carter on the Lancaster list until 1670, when Thomas Carter of Barford appears on the list.

The tithables tax records for Lancaster County exists for the years between 1658 and 1663 and for the years between 1665 and 1670, but there is no Thomas Carter on them. Thomas Carter of Barford was not on the tithables list until 1670 because he had not yet reached his majority age. Thomas Carter of Barford's supposed age difference with his wife Katherine Dale is also unlikely. The currently accepted research holds that Thomas Carter of Barford was a peer of Katherine Dale's parents. A Thomas Carter witnessed deeds for Diana Skipwith and Edward Dale and many researchers claim that this Thomas Carter was Thomas Carter of Barford, who then married their daughter shortly before or after she turned eighteen.

Some researchers, noting the apparent age difference between Thomas Carter of Barford and Katherine Dale resulting from his alleged birth in 1630, have proposed that she was his second wife; some have even assigned children to this first marriage. Supposedly, Thomas Carter of Barford's first wife and all of his children died at some point somewhere.

There seems to be no evidence whatsoever supporting this supposition that Thomas Carter of Barford was ever married before his marriage to Katherine Dale or that he ever had children prior to his marriage to Katherine Dale. This legend undoubtedly can be attributed to John Carter of "The Nest," who wrote about his family in 1858 and attributed the story to his aunt, Miss Fanny Carter, who was born in 1738 and died in 1830. John Carter wrote that his aunt had told him this:

> Our ancestors came to Virginia about two hundred years ago & settled in Lancaster County. The first one of the Carters was my grandfather's grandfather Thomas Carter son of a London merchant of good family. I have heard said there was two brothers of them the other being a John Carter who settled south of the river in Essex but further I can't say.
>
> And I have heard said we are kin to old Robert Carter who is buried at old Christ Church in this County but have never found out how. He was very rich — some say the richest man in Virginia. Our old Ancestor Thomas Carter was about 21 years old when he came to Lancaster and he was a man of substance and position as a planter and tobacco trader. He was married twice. First to an English woman whose name I've never heard, they had 2 or 3 children who all died young. She died and he married a Miss Dale of good connections....

Miss Fanny Carter seems somewhat vague in her recollections, and in any case she was clearly mistaken, confusing Thomas of Barford with his probable father. The Thomas Carter who arrived with his brother Col. John Carter was Maj. Thomas Carter, who is shown on the ship records as having been born in 1610. He was certainly not Thomas Carter of Barford, who married Katherine Dale in 1670.

The most conclusive evidence of Thomas Carter of Barford's real age is that his father-in-law Edward Dale appointed Thomas of Barford as deputy clerk of the Lancaster court. Dr. Miller must have been troubled by the appointment as deputy clerk too, explaining it in his article: *"No office, provided it carried a salary, was too insignificant to be coveted by the most conspicuous and even the wealthiest citizens."*[71] In spite of this rather dubious assertion, it is ridiculous that Thomas Carter of Barford would have accepted an appointment as deputy clerk from his father-in-law five years after he had already served a term as a justice of the court, having been appointed by the governor. These are clearly two different people.

Thomas Carter of Barford's marriage to Katherine Dale was not a case of a forty-year-old mariner who was a captain in the militia, a plantation owner, and a former justice of the court being appointed deputy clerk shortly before marrying a 17- or 18-year-old girl. This was the clerk of the court Edward Dale giving his young son-in-law to be, Thomas Carter of Barford, a starting job as deputy clerk two months before Thomas married his daughter.

Thomas Carter of Barford being born around 1650 means that he was close in age to his wife Katherine Dale, who was born in 1652. They were married when she was eighteen and he was twenty instead of his being forty. His and Katherine's first child was born in 1671 when Thomas was in his early twenties and their last child was born in 1690 when Thomas was around forty, not when he was sixty years old.

Although unproven, Thomas Carter of Barford was probably Maj. Thomas Carter's son and he was probably born around 1650, fifteen or twenty years later than generally accepted by researchers who have confused him with his (probable) father. Thomas Carter of Barford being born around 1650 is much more plausible and clears up a number of unlikely occurrences. It was his father, Major Thomas Carter, who had witnessed the deeds of Diana Skipwith and Edward Dale. Major Thomas Carter had known the Dales for decades; they lived next door to his brother at Corotoman. Thomas Carter of Barford was a young boy when his father, Maj. Thomas Carter, died in 1658, and afterwards he probably lived with his uncle Col. John Carter on his uncle's plantation at Corotoman. The Dales were longtime friends and next-door neighbors. They were business partners of his father and uncle. Thomas Carter of Barford had grown up with and known Katherine Dale most of his life before marrying her in 1670, just two months after his future father-in-law gave him a job as deputy clerk of the court.

Official documents, land records and headright records for both Major Thomas Carter and Captain Thomas Carter have been attributed to Thomas Carter of Barford in the same publications with no explanation of how the major was demoted to captain. Land transactions in Lancaster County before 1658 have been attributed to Thomas Carter of Barford even though there was only one Thomas Carter on the Lancaster tithables list from 1653 to 1658, and that Thomas Carter is provably known to be Maj. Thomas Carter, identified as such in official Lancaster records. All of the Lancaster records before 1670 can be very credibly assigned to Major Thomas Carter and our Captain Thomas Carter; not surprising since those records are the records of Major Thomas Carter and our Captain Thomas Carter.

To confuse matters further, Thomas Carter of Barford named his son Thomas Carter. And, of course, so did our Captain Thomas Carter.

Another Thomas Carter

In May of 1669, after our Captain Thomas Carter's death, his widow, Elinor Cooke, administered his estate under the name Elinor Grove, "relict" of Thomas Carter. By then, Elinor had remarried, to William Grove,[72] who subsequently filed legal papers which identified Elinor as the wife of Thomas Carter, deceased, and which granted to Elinor personal property she and Captain Thomas Carter had owned for her to give to her heirs.

The only known child of Captain Thomas Carter and Elinor Cooke is our ancestor, the aptly named Thomas Carter, Jr., first identified in a deed made on the "9th day of Augt 1669 and in the One & twentieth year of the reigne of o^r Sov^{r}eign Lord Charles ye second of England Scotland ffrance* & Ireland King &c," in which his grandparents, William and Mary Cooke, sold Thomas Jr. 400 acres of land from the patent William Cooke and William Miles had been granted by Sir William Berkeley:

> Know all men by these p^{r}sents that wee William Cooke & Mary my now Wife late of the County of Isle of Wight in Virginia doe For diverse good causes & Consideracons us the s^d William Cook & Mary my Wife hereunto moveing and more especially For A valuable sume of Tobaccoe & Cask to us in hand secured before the signeing & sealing hereof Have given, granted, bargained alienated sould & sett over, unto Thomas Carter Junr sonne of Thomas Carter late of thes County deced and to his heires Executo^{rs} Adm^{rs} & Assignes For ever, Four hundred Acres of Land sictuate lying & being in the Isle of Wight County being bounded by marked Trees & included in A Pattent of Eleaven hundred Acres, of land granted by the Right hono^{ble} Sr William Berkley K^t, govern^r &c to Wm Miles & me the s^d William Cook It being the Land that I the said Cook & Mary my Wife lately lived upon before o^r removal into Surry County, To have & to hould all the said Four hundred Acres of land togerher wth all Edifices buildings, Orchards, ffences, Woods underwoods, and all other Appertences whatsoever thereunto belongeth ... signed: William Cook, Mary Cook.[73]

Thomas Carter, Jr., married Magdalen Moore, the daughter of George Moore and Jane Barcroft. George Moore had been granted a patent of 1400 acres of land "on the 2nd swamp of the Blackwater" in May of 1669. This land was just south of the Cooke plantation that William and Mary Cooke had sold to Thomas Carter, Jr., George Moore gave his daughter Magdalen and son-in-law Thomas part of that land, which adjoined the plantation Thomas had received from his grandparents the Cookes, as a wedding present on "ye 11th day of Augt A^o dom: 167<u>3</u> in ye 25th year of ye Reign of o^r Sov^{r}eign Ld Charles ye 2^d over England &c." The deed was filed in Isle of Wight:

> To all to whome these p^{r}sents shall come I George Moore of ye County of ye Isle of Wight in Virginia send greeting &c Know yee that I the s^d George Moore For & in consideracon of ye marriage between Thomas Carter of ye s^d / County & Magdalen ye daughter of me the s^d George, And in Pformance of the promise that I made to the s^d Thomas Carter Have given granted aliened enfeoffed & confirmed And by these p^{r}sent writing doe Fully

---

*The double F (Ff or ff) is thought to be a mistaken use in print of the medieval or Old English capital F as it appears written in antique English script. The old capital F looked very much like two small f's entwined and when handwritten English script was transliterated to typeset form, in many cases two lowercase f's were used in place of the capital F. All the double F's in this book are directly taken from the original sources.

Freely clearly & absolutely give grant aliene enfoeffe & confirme unto the said / Thomas Carter his heires & Assignes For ever, Four hundred Acres of Land out of my dividend or tract of Land conteining Fourteen hundred Acres scituate att or near the second Swamp of ye Blackwater in the said County granted to me by pattent dated the twelfth day of May 1669 wch s^d Four hundred Acres of Land hereby granted beginneth att A White Oak upon ye head of ye Beaver dam Branch & soe downe the s^d Branch to take in the Full quantity of 400 Acres, accordeing to the bounds menconed in the afores^d Pattent, granted to me the s^d George Moore....[74]

William Sherwood, the longtime business associate of Thomas Carter's grandfather, William Carter, witnessed the deed. William Sherwood was also William Carter's neighbor and evidently an associate and friend of John Kindred, for whom he witnessed other deeds. John Kindred's daughter Jane would marry Thomas Carter Jr's. son, our ancestor Moore Carter. Among other connections to the Carters, and especially William Carter and his descendants, William Sherwood also became the attorney for the estate of William Grove, who married Elinor, the widow of Captain Thomas Carter. He was probably the father of Thomas Sherwood, who patented land in the 1663 land acquisitions as part of the Carolina Project.

The deeds from his grandfather and his father-in-law conveying land to Thomas Carter, Jr., were dated August 9, 1669, and August 11, 1673. In that era, it would have been extremely rare for children to marry against the wishes of their parents and many marriages were arranged. Thomas Jr.'s grandparents, the Cookes, gave him a part of his plantation a few months after the death of his sea captain father, who owned no land. His in-laws, the Moores, gave him the adjoining piece of land four years later as a wedding present. It would not be surprising if the families had agreed to the marriage and planned the gift of Thomas Carter, Jr.'s plantation years in advance of the marriage. Thomas Carter, Jr., named his new plantation "Nanticoke."

Thomas Carter and Magdalen Moore probably had many children, as was the custom in the seventeenth century. Unfortunately there is no existing document listing them. Some of their children are easily proven; others, including our ancestor Moore Carter, are known only by circumstantial evidence.

Thomas and Magdalen owned eight hundred acres of land — four hundred that they bought for a cask of tobacco from William Cooke, and an adjoining four hundred acres on Beaver Dam Creek in Blackwater Swamp that they had received as a wedding present from George Moore. On January 9, 1679, Thomas sold to John Person (listed on the deed as "Parsons") fifty acres clearly identified as part of the land he had purchased from William Cooke:

Know all men by these p^{r}nts y^t I Thomas Carter of ye upper Parish of ye Isle of Wight County & Magdalen my Wife have For a valuable sume of Tob to me p^d before ye sealing & deliv'y of these p^{r}sents wth wch wee acknowledge or selves Fully sattisfied bargained sould & deliv'ed & doe by these p^{r}nts For us or [our] heires Ext^{rs} & Adm^{rs} For ever, bargaine sell & deliver enfeoff & confirme unto John Parsons of ye P̶ish [parish] & Country aforesd his heires & Afs For ever A certain piece or P̶cell [parcel] of Land contenig [sic] Fifty Six Acres Lyeing & being on ye East side of ye second Swamp of ye Maine Blackwater in ye P̶ish & County aforesd bounded ... ye s^d Fifty Six Acres of Land being P̶te [part] of Eleaven hundred acres of Land granted to Wm Miles & Wm Cooke ... sold and conveyed to ye s^d Carter ye 9th of Augt 1669....[75]

Thomas gave his son George, identified in the deed as such, two hundred acres of the land George Moore had given to him and Magdalen as a wedding present: "Thomas Carter of U.P. give George Carter, son of said Thomas and Magdalen — Whereas Geo. Moore of said Parish, father of Magdalen, by deed, 11 August., 1673, did in consideration of marriage, convey to said Thomas and Magdalen 400 acres, part of 1400 acres in Blackwater Swamp, pat. 5 May, 1669 — now they confirm to said Geo. Carter 200 of said 400 acres. 30 Dec, 1700."[76]

Sometime before he died in 1710, Thomas gave his son Thomas Jr. the other two hundred acres of the four hundred acres he and Magdalen had received from the Moores as a wedding present. Although there is no surviving document recording the conveyance, in 1733 or 1734 Thomas Carter, Jr., sold that two hundred acres to Samuel Person, the son of John Person, to whom his father, Thomas Carter, Sr., had previously sold the adjoining 50 acres.[77]

Thomas Sr. and Magdalen lived in Isle of Wight on their 350 remaining acres of the Blackwater River plantation. When Thomas died, in his will he left the remaining portion of his original 800-acre plantation to his "loving wife" and stipulated that after she died, the plantation should pass on to "our daughter Martha." After Martha's demise, the will stipulated that the land pass on to "my son Allecand [Alexander]." Martha married John Jones and when he died in 1736 or 1737 her mother Magdalen moved to Bertie County, North Carolina, to live with her. Magdalen and Martha then sold the plantation to Alexander for £3 Virginia money: "The land contains abt 350 A, and is prt. of a grtd. tract formerly taken up by William Miles by the sd. patent, which land Thomas Carter bought of Wm. Cook in 1669 by deed and in 1709 Thomas Carter, dec'd. left land in will to Magdalane, his wife, and Martha, his dtr., during their lives, and after their death to Alexander, his aforenamed son. Signed: Magdalane Carter, her mark, Martha Carter, her mark, Wit: Jno. Langston, Jr., James Carter, his mark, Sarah Floyd, her mark Rec'd. Feb 28, 1736."[78] In March 1737, Alexander sold the land to John Mangum for a nice profit at £12.

Moore Carter and Jane Kindred

The distribution and sale of the 800 acres of land known to have been owned by Thomas Carter and Magdalen Moore identifies their sons George, Alexander, Thomas, and their daughter, Martha. Their other children were our ancestor Moore Carter, John, probably Joseph, and Edward, none of whom received a part of the plantation. However, they did witness and participate in numerous transactions with other family members.

In 1710, when Moore Carter's grandparents, George Moore and Jane Barcroft, sold to Thomas Ward 100 acres of the 1400-acre plantation they had patented in 1669, Moore Carter and his brother George Carter witnessed the deed.[79]

On October 10, 1720, Moore Carter purchased 210 acres of land in North Carolina for £10 from John Dickinson, whose daughter Rebecca married a Carter cousin, Joel Newsome, the great-grandson of William Newsome, who had lived in Surry next to William Carter, the great-grandfather of Moore Carter. This deed was the first record of Moore Carter in North Carolina.

In 1723, Moore Carter patented 150 acres on the south side of the Potecasi Creek three miles north of his original land and near his cousin John Cooke. In 1724, the court recorded a conveyance of 200 acres from John Dickinson to Moore Carter on the north side of the Cutawhiskie "adjacent Browne." This land was adjacent to Dr. Samuel Browne, whose daughter Sarah married as her second husband Isaac Carter, Moore's son. Then on February

7, 1725, Moore patented land five miles north of his Cutawhiskie property on the south side of the Meherrin River adjoining more land owned by Dr. Samuel Browne. The next day, Moore witnessed a conveyance of 20 acres by John Dickinson to his brother Joseph Carter. The land adjoined Moore's land on the Potecasi Creek and in the deed, John Dickinson referred to Joseph, saying "for love, good will and affection which I bear to my beloved kinsman Joseph Carter."[80] Joseph had married Rachel, who was probably Rachel Dickinson, the sister of John Dickinson.

On August 11, 1725, Moore witnessed another deed for his brother when John Dickinson sold Joseph Carter 320 acres on the Potecasi Creek.[81] Moore Carter, James Bryn, and John Dickinson divided Joseph's estate in 1730 and Moore administered his brother John's estate in 1736.

Our ancestors Moore Carter and Jane Kindred had at least eight children, who are identified in the division of his estate on April 30, 1741,[82] with distributions to Jacob Carter, Kindred Carter, Isaac Carter, James Jones, Moor Carter, Bryant O'Quinn, father of Patience O'Quinn, granddaughter of the deceased, Katherine Carter, and Susannah Carter.[83]

Moor Carter lived next to his brothers in Northampton County, identified as such in a deed dated May 9, 1747, in which his brother Isaac Carter "of Society Parish"[84] sold a part of his land to Joseph Benthall — 200 acres of land for 25 pounds. The land was described as being adjacent to that of John Brown, "which was the line of Doctor Samuel Brown deceased," and adjacent to Moor Carter, "just over the N. Hampton County line" and adjacent to Jacob Carter and Isaac Carter.[85]

On April 13, 1742, after his father Moore Carter's estate was settled, Jacob Carter, then living in Northampton County, sold to his mother, Jane Carter, 150 acres on the south side of the Polepapa Creek for 6 pounds Virginia money.[86] That same day, Jane sold to Jacob "my whole right of thirds [her dower rights] of the plantation formerly belonging to my Husband Moore Carter decd" on Catawisky marsh for one shilling.[87]

Jacob Carter, describing himself as "heir at law to Moor Carter dec'd," made a deed of gift to Isaac of 200 acres of land for the "Love, good will and affection unto my well beloved brother Isaac Carter ... land on SS Meherin River ... an equal division of land granted to my father dec'd by patent Feb'y the first 1725...."[88] Jane later transferred the land she bought from Jacob to her son "Isaac Carter of Bertie County, 150 acres more or less that I bought from Jacob Carter on 15 Mar 1753 for the love, good will and affection I bear unto my son."[89] The land was adjacent to Dr. Samuel Brown, whose daughter, Sarah Brown Battle, would marry Isaac Carter.

On November 28, 1758, Martin Middleton sold Jacob Carter 200 acres on Fishing Creek, a transaction witnessed by his sister Sarah Carter Jones and his brother-in-law James Jones. Martin Middleton was Jacob's father-in-law, although the first name of the daughter Jacob married is not known.

Moore Carter and Jane Kindred's unknown daughter, who may have been Martha Carter, named for Moore's sister, married Bryan (Bryant) O'Quinn. When Martha died, Bryan O'Quinn, Joseph Jones and Frederick Jones posted a bond to Jane Carter, for 34 pounds, "obligation is such that we ... do save Harmless and Endemnify the s^d Jane Carter from all and every part of the estate of Patience O'Quin Granddaughter to Moor Carter Dec'd."[90]

Jane Kindred Carter died in February of 1764, shortly after having written a will dated January 27, 1764, in which she divided her estate between her "well beloved daughter Katherine Knight, my son Kindred Carter" and "son Isaac Carter." She named as executors her "well beloved son Isaac, well beloved son-in-law William Knight and my friend Joseph Benthall."[91]

Katherine Carter married William Knight. William was almost certainly a relative of Moses and James Knight, brothers who married two of Kindred Carter's daughters. Susannah Carter married William Skinner. Sarah Carter married James Jones, her first cousin, the son of her aunt Martha Carter and John Jones. Sarah died before her father, Moore Carter. James Jones was the beneficiary for their children of Sarah's portion of the inheritance in Moore's will.

Kindred Carter and Mary "Molly" Odum

Moore Carter and Jane Kindred's son Kindred Carter, the brother of our ancestor Isaac Carter, was born in 1710 in Bertie County, North Carolina, and died in 1777 in Edgecombe County. Although there is much speculation about the identity of Kindred's wife, she has been positively identified as Mary "Molly" Odum, the widow of Walter Browne, who died in 1735 (see Appendix C: The Search for Kindred Carter's Wife).

Kindred and Mary had four daughters. The oldest, Penelope, was born before 1740 and married Cary Whitaker. Charity Carter was born in 1740 and married Moses Knight. Charity and Moses had six children.[92] Priscilla Carter married James Knight, the brother of Moses Knight, who had married her sister Charity. Winifred Carter married Rueben Taylor and they had seven children.[93]

The first husband of Mary "Molly" Odum was Walter Brown, born a little before 1699 and the son of Dr. Samuel Browne. The name of Dr. Samuel Browne's first wife, the mother of Walter Browne, is unknown but his second wife was most probably Mary Jones and they had six children, including our ancestor Sarah Browne, who was born around 1710.

If it can be proven that Dr. Samuel Browne's second wife was indeed Mary Jones, it would be very interesting for our family. Mary Jones was born in 1675, the daughter of Matthew Jones and Elizabeth Albrighton. Elizabeth Albrighton was the daughter of Francis Albrighton, who was born in 1609 in England and immigrated to York, Virginia. Francis was also the father of George Albritton. George Albritton was the father of Ralph Albritton and Ralph was the father of Thomas Albritton. Thomas Albritton married a woman named Agnes and they were the parents of James Albritton. James Albritton married Elizabeth Lanier and they were the parents of Matthew Albritton. Matthew's daughter Martha Albritton was born in 1764 and married Nathan Murray. Nathan and Martha were the parents of Drury Murray, who married Susan Champion. Drury Murray and Susan Champion were the parents of John William Fulwood Murray and he married Alethea Josephine Parker. John William Fulwood Murray and Alethea Josephine had a son named John William Murray, who married Rosa Nettie Wise. They had a daughter named Frances Allethea Murray, who married Wilburn Edgar Smith. Frances Allethea Murray and Wilburn Edgar Smith had a daughter, Eleanor Rosalynn Smith, who, if Dr. Samuel Browne's second wife was indeed Mary Jones, married her ninth cousin once removed, James Earl Carter, Jr.

Sarah Browne married John Battle in 1726. John died April 30, 1740, when he was just 31 years old, and later that year Sarah Browne married our ancestor Isaac Carter.

Isaac Carter and Sarah Browne

Moore Carter and Jane Kindred's third child and our ancestor, Isaac Carter, was born about 1716 in Isle of Wight and lived until 1792, by which time he was living in Hertford County, North Carolina. Isaac married Sarah Browne, the daughter of Dr. Samuel Browne, and they had six provable children: James, Isaac, our ancestor Kindred, Parthenia, Jesse, and Lazarus. Matthew Carter is also probably their child.

Sarah Browne Battle was the widow of John Battle, and after John died Sarah married Isaac. Isaac became the administrator of John Battle's estate in care of John's minor children. John's brother William Battle petitioned the court to have Isaac either give up administration of the estate or post security for it. Isaac then turned John Battle's estate over to William to administer for the children. Isaac was in his 60s by the time of the Revolutionary War and was too old to fight. However, he was a Patriot and gave supplies and provisions worth over £10,000. Dr. William Price found the original vouchers for these contributions in the North Carolina Archives while he was the director of the archives.

Isaac's will was dated July 8, 1792, and was burned with the courthouse in 1830. Only the index of the will book survived, having been taken home the night of the fire by the county clerk. The fire was started by a citizen enraged by the slave rebellion led by Nat Turner. Ironically, the Nat Turner slave rebellion started on land once owned by the family of Isaac's mother, Jane Kindred. Benjamin Turner deeded to his son Samuel "the old Kindred plantation."

Isaac Carter and Sarah Browne's first child was James Carter, who was born around 1742 in Bertie County, North Carolina. His wife has never been proven but she was possibly Dolly Cotton, the daughter of Arthur Cotton.[94] Rev. E.S. Lucas of the *Southern Historical Press* discovered a surviving folder of Hertford County records which proved that James served in the Revolutionary War.[95] James is listed as Ensign James Carter and served in Major George Little's (Lytle) 3rd Company, part of the 10th Regiment, Continental Line, of Col. Abraham Sheppard. Col. Sheppard gave James his own command and put him in charge of his own company by April 1781.[96]

Further evidence that this is our family's James Carter is found in the Hertford 1784 tax digest, which shows that in the district of Captain James Carter's company there were several known neighbors of James Carter as well as his father, Isaac Carter. Governor Alexander Martin awarded James a state grant of 190 acres for his service on October 29, 1782. James subsequently sold this land to James Vinson in 1785. On January 2, 1787, James Carter received a land grant of 287 acres in Wilkes County, Georgia, and he and his brother Kindred moved to Georgia shortly thereafter. Most of his children moved with him.

Isaac Carter (II)

Isaac Carter and Sarah Browne's son Isaac Carter (II) was born around 1745 in Northampton County and died around 1805 or a little later in the same place but after that part of Northampton County became Hertford County. The number of Isaac Carters in the family has led to some confusion just as the number of Thomas Carters had previously.

In *The Colonial and State Political History of Hertford County*, Benjamin Winborne writes:

> In 1830 Maj. Isaac Carter was elected to the House with John H. Wheeler. Carter was said to be a wily politician, but Dr. G.C. Moore defeated him in 1831. He, however, recovered

and was re-elected in 1832, 1833 and 1834. He was the son of Maj. Isaac Carter, who died in Hertford County July 8, 1792, and who was a captain in the Revolutionary War of 1776. Isaac Carter, Sr., left a will in which he appointed his son, Lazarus Carter, his executor. His daughter Parthenia married Shadrack Rutland, November 12, 1775. Isaac Carter, Jr., was a major in the militia, and once Sheriff of the county.[97]

Benjamin Winborne collected personal documents and interviewed people for *The Colonial and State Political History of Hertford County* in an attempt to reconstruct the information lost in the 1830 courthouse fire. However, in this entry, he has confused Isaac with both his father and his son. The Major Isaac Carter who served in the house with John Wheeler and who was sheriff was actually the son of the Isaac Carter (II) discussed here and the grandson of our ancestor Isaac Carter who died in Hertford County in 1792. Our ancestor Isaac Carter was not a major in the Revolutionary War, having been born in 1717. It was his grandson who was a major in the Revolutionary War, although Isaac Carter, Sr., did provide provisions, as previously noted.

Isaac Carter (II) first appears in the North Carolina records on March 1, 1777, when he enlisted in Stephenson's Company of the 10th Regiment under the command of Colonel Abraham Sheppard, the company that his brother James also served in. Isaac reenlisted in Captain Bailey's Company of the 10th Regiment on May 25, 1781, and left service May 25, 1782. He then enlisted in Captain Evans' Company of the 10th Regiment on December 1, 1782. His service records show that he deserted on June 11, 1783, after the war was over.[98] He most likely just left and returned home.

Jesse Carter and Charity Vinson

Isaac Carter and Sarah Browne's son Jesse Carter was born between 1745 and 1750, probably in Northampton, North Carolina. Jesse married Charity Vinson, a neighbor who lived next to the Carters. Charity's family had a distinguished and interesting background stretching back to Jamestowne. Charity Vinson was the eighth child of Thomas Vinson, Jr., and Isobel (Isabel, Isabelle). Thomas, in his will dated January 15, 1762, and probated in 1764,[99] listed his wife and all of his children and bequeathed Charity Carter six acres of land on the south side of Bear Swamp.

Thomas Vinson, Jr., was the son of Thomas Vinson, Sr., and Sarah Jones. His mother is identified in a deed from May 11, 1713,[100] by which Thomas Vinson, Jr., sold land to Joshua Poythress. The deed identifies the land in Prince George County, Virginia, as belonging to Sarah, she having received it from Major Peter Jones, presumably her father.

The last known record of Major Peter Jones was his appointment on March 7, 1676, as commander of Fort Henry on the Appomattox River. Fort Henry had been built in reaction to the Indian Massacre of 1644, which led to the 1645 general assembly passing an act: "Be it enacted for the defense of the inhabitants on the southside of James River and the prevention of the great releife and subsistance to the Salvages by ffishing in Bristoll alias Appomattocke River, as also for the cutting down their corne or performeing any other service upon them. That there be a ffort forthwith erected, att the Falls of the said Appomattock River, nominated fforte Henry...."[101]

In 1636, the assembly enacted "that Capt. Abraham Wood whose service hath been employed att fforte Henery, be the undertaker for the said fforte, unto whome is granted six hundred acres of land for him and his heirs for ever; with all houses and edifices belonging to the said fforte, with all boats and amunition att present belonging to the said fforte,

Provided that he the said Capt. Wood do maintayne and keepe ten men constantly upon the said place for the terme of three yeares, duringe which time he the said Capt. Wood is exempted from all publique taxes for himselfe and the said tenn persons."

Fort Henry was also a trading post, handling furs as part of Governor Berkeley's network. When Abraham Wood died, the fort came under the proprietorship of Captain Peter Jones, who had married Abraham Wood's daughter. The fort was attacked by Nathaniel Bacon's forces during Bacon's Rebellion and Major Peter Jones was killed there while defending the fort. The location of the fort was of great strategic significance and Major Peter Jones' grandson founded the city of Petersburg on the site.

Charity Vinson's brother James was also identified in Thomas Vinson, Jr.'s will, having inherited his father's plantation on Bear Swamp, which was next to land that James Carter patented in 1782. James Vinson was the sheriff of Northampton County and his son, James Vinson, Jr., was captain in the militia and married Rhoda Benthall, the daughter of Joseph Benthall, whom Moore Carter's wife, Jane Kindred, had described as "my friend" and made an executor of her will. Rhoda and her father, Joseph Benthall, were also neighbors, Isaac Carter having sold them land adjoining his in 1747.[102]

Before James Carter and his brother, our ancestor Kindred, moved to Georgia, he sold his plantation to James Vinson in 1785. The plantation was then bought by John and Mary Vaughn, other neighbors of the Carters and Vinsons; and in 1798 Jesse and Charity Carter bought the plantation back from the Vaughns.

Parthenia Carter and Shadrack Rutland

Many of the family records, including Isaac's original wills and deeds, were burned in the Hertford Courthouse fire of 1830 or the Winton Courthouse fire set by Federal troops under Sherman in 1864. However, there was a controversy over Isaac's will which led to a court case between his heirs and provides proof of two other children of Isaac Carter and Sarah Browne.

Isaac Carter owned 58 slaves when he died in 1792. His son Lazarus, executor of his will, got into a legal dispute with Isaac's daughter Parthenia's husband, Shadrack Rutland, because on occasion and without any legal transfer, Isaac had given slaves to Parthenia during visits to Isaac's house. In his will, Isaac bequeathed the same slaves to Parthenia and Shadrack's children. Parthenia having already died, Shadrack contended that the slaves were his and therefore Isaac could not bequeath them to anyone in his will. The case eventually went to the N.C. Superior Court,[103] which ruled for Shadrack.

Kindred Carter and the Rozier Mystery

Isaac Carter and Sarah Browne's third child and our ancestor, Kindred Carter, was born in 1750 in Bertie County, North Carolina. Although there is no proof that he was a Quaker, he was certainly sympathetic to them and lived in or near Quaker communities almost his entire life. Sometime around 1780, Kindred and his brother James moved from North Carolina to Warren County, Georgia, on the Little Germany Creek. The land became part of Columbia County in 1790 and is now part of McDuffie County. In 1791, Kindred bought 100 acres of land in the Wrightsborough Township from Jonathan Sell, one of the men who had convinced Governor Wright to issue the grant of land to build Wrightsborough. Kindred then moved to Wrightsborough.

Kindred had four known children. Our ancestor James Carter was born in 1753 in Hertford County, North Carolina, and married Eleanor Duckworth. Henry Carter was born around 1775 in Bertie County, North Carolina. Martha and Jesse were born after 1785.

Nothing at all is known about Kindred Carter's wife and she has been the subject of much speculation. There is widespread misinformation that Kindred was married to Mourning Hickman, the daughter of Nathaniel Hickman and Sarah Strickland. He was not. Although I have seen the claim that Mourning Hickman was married to both of our Kindred Carters, both cases are easily disproven. The most common claim is that Mourning Hickman married our uncle Kindred Carter, who was born in 1710 and died in 1777 in Edgecombe County, North Carolina. Mourning Hickman was born between 1739 and 1745 and died after 1804. Kindred had four daughters and though Penelope's birth date is not known, Kindred's daughter Charity was born in 1740, Winifred was born in 1742, and Priscilla was born in 1760. Kindred's will was proved May 14, 1777, and in it he bequeathed his plantation to his wife, Mary (Odum), and named his daughters Priscilla Knight, Charity Knight, Winneford [sic] Taylor, and Penelope Whitaker. Besides having a different name than Kindred's wife, it is impossible that Mourning Hickman was the mother of children that were her age or older than she.

The claim that Mourning Hickman was married to Kindred Carter, our direct ancestor who was born in 1750 and died in 1801, is also easily disproved because Mourning Hickman was known to have been married to Jesse Pittman during this time. Jesse Pittman married Christian Hickman October 19, 1765, William Hickman bondsman, Thomas Cavenah, witness. According to the *Pittman Family Records*, 3rd ed., Jesse and Christian had two children: Patience, born about 1766, and Christian, born about 1768. Jesse then married Mourning Hickman sometime after 1777. Jesse and Mourning had four children: Hickman Pittman, born around 1780; Felix Pittman, born about 1781; Jesse Pittman, born around 1783; and Robert Pittman, born around 1785. Jesse Pittman's will was recorded in November 1793, Edgecombe County. The heirs named were his wife, Mourning, and his children: Hickman, Felix, Jesse, Robert, Patience, and Christian. His will was witnessed by Nathaniel Hickman, Jr., and William Hickman, two of Mourning Hickman's brothers.

During that same time, Kindred and his unknown wife had five children: an unknown daughter; James, born in 1773; Henry, born in 1782; Martha, born in 1784; and Jesse, born after 1785. When Kindred died in 1801, Martha and Jesse were orphan minors and they selected guardians. The original legal documents appointing their guardians are in the Georgia Archives. Since Mourning Hickman did not die until 1804, if she had been Kindred's wife neither of Kindred's children would have been declared an orphan and neither would have selected a guardian. Neither of the Kindred Carters in our family was ever married to Mourning Hickman. Kindred died in 1801 and did not leave a will; however, his estate distribution records positively identify four of his children.

After Kindred Carter died in 1801, in Columbia County, Georgia, James Carter, Anderson Rozier, Reuben Brownson, Robert Rozier and John Hayne posted a $7000 bond together to guarantee the administration of Kindred's estate, with James Carter and Anderson Rozier being appointed by the court to be coexecutors. When Kindred died, two of his children were minors, Jesse and Martha. Kindred's brother Jesse posted a $3000 bond to be Kindred's son Jesse's guardian and Robert Rozier posted a $3000 bond to be guardian of Kindred's daughter Martha Carter, who was about 16 or 17 years old at the time, having been born after 1781 and before 1784. Both children were minors over the age of fourteen and were able to choose their own guardians.

Martha Carter's choice of guardian seems unusual. There were several of her aunts and uncles living in the area who had children around her age and who would have been willing to be her guardian, just as Kindred's brother Jesse had become the guardian of his nephew. For Martha to choose the Rozier family, and for the extended Carter family to assent to her choice, implies a longstanding relationship between Kindred's family and the Rozier family. This speculation is reinforced by Anderson and Robert Rozier's willingness to help post a $7000 bond to guarantee the administration of Kindred's estate, Anderson Rozier's selection and willingness to become coexecutor of the estate with James Carter, and Robert Rozier's willingness to post a separate $3000 bond to become Martha's guardian.

Kindred's estate distributed his land to five heirs, although only four children were known: James, our ancestor who married Eleanor "Nellie" Duckworth; Henry, who married Rachel Davis; Jesse, who married Sarah Neal; and Martha Carter, who on September 24, 1805, married Alexander Rozier, the son of Anderson Rozier.

Three parts of the undivided tract were transferred through public auctions to satisfy debts. On January 7, 1810, William Wilkins, the sheriff of Columbia County, sold the portion of the land inherited by Martha Carter to satisfy a lawsuit brought by Mark P. Davis against Martha's husband Alexander Rozier. Mark P. Davis sold it to John Lamar on April 14, 1814. Then, on May 7, 1814, Henry Carter's one-fifth of the tract of land was sold at public auction by Sheriff William Wilkins to John Lamar to satisfy judgments in two lawsuits brought against Henry Carter by Charles W. Linn.

Jesse and James Carter sold their two-fifths of the land together to John Lamar on September 14, 1814. That sale accounted for the land distributed to the known children of Kindred. The other one-fifth of the land was a mystery until historian Kenneth Thomas found the deed that determined that the fifth heir was a daughter who married Anderson Rosar (Rozier). On March 7, 1810, Sheriff Reuben Sangstone sold the land to John Lamar at public auction to satisfy a fieri facias judgment from Justice Davis Ray's court in Columbia County in a suit brought by Henry Godwin against Anderson Rozier. The land was described as one-fifth of Kindred's undivided tract "by heirship and of right belonging to said Anderson."[104]

Kindred's unknown daughter must have died by March of 1810 for her presumed husband to have inherited her land. Unfortunately, she was not named in the transactions, and the documents conveying the land from the estate to her have still not surfaced. The discovery of the deed probably explains the biggest part of the Rozier mystery. Kindred's unknown daughter had married Anderson Rozier and after Kindred died, Martha Carter choose to live with her sister and the Roziers. Kindred's unknown daughter must have been Anderson Rozier's second wife, because her sister Martha married Alexander Rozier, Anderson Rozier's son, and Kindred could not have had a child old enough to be Alexander Rozier's mother nor would Martha have married her nephew. The names of Kindred's wife and daughter remain a mystery.

James Carter and Eleanor Duckworth

Thought to be Kindred's first child, although his unknown daughter may have been older, our ancestor James Carter, Jr., was born in 1773 in Hereford, North Carolina, and died on July 19, 1858, in Schley County, Georgia. Usually referred to as James Carter, Jr., to distinguish him from his uncle James Carter, Kindred's brother, James Jr. married Eleanor

"Nellie" Duckworth on January 31, 1798, in Columbia County, Georgia. Eleanor Duckworth, the daughter of Jeremiah Duckworth and Christiana Ramsey, was born in 1778 in Richmond, Georgia, and died in 1820 in Talbot County, Georgia. James Carter and Eleanor "Nellie" Duckworth had ten children: our ancestor Wiley, Felix, George W., James D., Epsey, Keziah, Littleberry, Marina, Martha, and Mary.

Felix Carter was born in 1800 in Warren, Georgia, and died in 1844. George W. Carter was born in 1801 in Warren, Georgia, and died in March of 1841. George married Winiford T. Miller on November 22, 1837, in Talbot County, Georgia.[105] A little more than three years later, George became ill and wrote a deathbed will a few days before he died. In his will, George noted that his wife was pregnant and divided his estate between his wife, his daughter, and his unborn child (see Appendix G: Wills).

The 1850 census of Talbot County shows Winiford Carter with two children: Georgia Ann, age 11 and probably the daughter that George called Sophronia in his will, and Martha, age 9. Georgia Ann Carter married Thomas J. Beach in Talbot County on June 1, 1853, when she was 14 years old. Martha Carter married Joseph E. Biggs on October 28, 1858. Joseph was the son of Joseph E. Biggs, Sr., an influential Methodist minister in Talbot County.

James D. Carter was born in 1803 in Warren, Georgia, the youngest son of James and Nellie Carter. James married Mary Harris, the daughter of Grey Harris, on June 8, 1847, in Talbot County.[106] James and Mary both died of tuberculosis within six months of each other. James knew he was sick and wrote in his will that he had "a disease that will sooner or later terminate my earthly existence" and left his household furniture and possessions and $300 to his wife, Mary. The rest of his estate he left to be equally divided between his wife and sons: "Mirabeaugh Carter, Jesse L. Carter and my youngest child yet unnamed."[107] After Mary died, her father, Gray Harris, was given custody of the two boys and in the 1860 U.S. Census, they were living with their grandfather and grandmother in Chattahoochee County, Georgia, both listed with the last name Harris. There was also an Elnora Harris living with them, age 7 years, having been born in 1854. Whether she was the "youngest child yet unnamed" of James D. Carter and Mary Harris is not known but seems probable. While Mirabeau was still a young boy, he ran away to Texas with a family named Williams. He eventually married Melinda Francis Harris in Sexton, Texas. Mirabeau died in Center, Texas, on January 8, 1928.

Epsey Carter was born in 1803 in Warren, Georgia, and died in 1867 in Houston, Alabama.

Keziah Carter was born in 1805 in Warren County, Georgia, and died between 1850 and 1860 in Talbot County. Keziah and Robert Hinton posted a marriage bond in Warren County on January 28, 1822, and were married January 30.[108] They had at least seven children.[109] Robert was a farmer, and a successful one, too. He and Keziah owned two plantations, one called Oakey Woods about four miles west of Talbotton, Georgia, and another named Piney Woods at Geneva, Georgia. Keziah died before 1860 and Robert died before June 28, 1868, when his son Robert Jr. began administering his estate. The returns of the sales of Robert's estate showed that he owned the "Homeplace" (Oakey Woods) of about 300 acres, and Piney Woods of about 700 acres, as well as 490 acres in Thomas County, 300 acres in Marion County, 490 acres in Worth County, and 161 acres in Walker County.[110]

Littleberry Carter was born in 1807 in Warren, Georgia, and died in 1847 in Talbot County, Georgia, having never married. He wrote a will March 29, 1847, in which he said that he was "labouring under bodily afflictions which I have reason to believe will speedily terminate my Earthly existence." Unfortunately, he was right. He died the next month when he was only 40 years old. Littleberry made his first cousin and "beloved friend" Jehu Carter executor of his will and gave him his buggy and harness. He bequeathed $200 to Georgian (Georgia Ann) and Martha Ellen Carter, the orphan daughters of his brother George W. Carter. He gave Madison Carter of Marion County three hundred dollars and gave five hundred dollars to his brother James D. Carter. He also owned land and he gave it to his brother Wiley — two lots in Stewart County, two lots in Lee County and another lot in Sumter County.[111]

James Carter and Nellie Duckworth's daughter Marina Carter was born in 1809 in Warren, Georgia, and married Edward Littleton on December 20, 1832.[112] They moved with Marina's father, James, to Talbot County and the 1850 Census shows Edward as a farmer with $380 worth of real estate. Not much is known about the family except that later records show an Edward Littleton in Terrell County, possibly a son.

Martha Carter was born in 1811 in Warren, Georgia. She married George H. Archer in Talbot County on February 20, 1837.[113] George and Martha had both died by March 1860 when Wiley, acting as administrator of the estate of his father, James Carter, filed a voucher in the Talbot County Court of the Ordinary identifying Mary Malonia Ellis as being Martha Carter and George Archer's daughter.[114] Wiley died in 1864 and the estate of his father, James Carter, had not been settled. Two more of Martha Carter and George Archer's children are identified in another voucher filed in Sumter County by Wiley's son Calvin Carter, who had taken over as administrator of James' estate.[115]

In 1978, Kenneth Thomas proved that Mary Carter was another daughter of James Carter and Nellie Duckworth. Mary was probably born around 1815 or a little thereafter and she married Eli Gray on June 15, 1841, in Talbot County, Georgia.[116] The marriage was not a happy one. Talbot County Superior Court records show that Mary Gray sued Eli for divorce in March and September 1844. Two juries voted for the divorce, which was not final until the September jury ruled and $1500 in alimony was paid. Eli, however, married Eliza Gray in Muscogee County in August. When the divorce settlement was shown to the Muscogee Court, a grand jury issued an indictment for bigamy against Eli. The state of Georgia paid Mary's brother $80 to go to Alabama to apprehend Eli but he never came to trial; his bondsman forfeited $600 after he fled. The drama may have been too much for Mary. Records from Talbot County show that Robert Hinton, husband of Mary's sister Keziah, administered Mary Carter's estate in 1848[117] when she would have been about 33 years old.

James Carter and Nellie Duckworth's firstborn child was our ancestor Wiley Carter, who was born in 1798 in Columbia, Georgia, and died on March 4, 1864, in Schley County, Georgia. Wiley married Ann Ansley on February 18, 1821. By then, Ann Ansley's ancestors had been in America almost two hundred years.

Chapter 2

THE MORRIS, COX, AND ANSLEY ANCESTORS AND THEIR ANCESTORS

Our earliest Carter ancestors were from Hertfordshire, England. For some of our allied lines, the original immigrants and where they emigrated from is also known. The Cox family was also from Hertfordshire, Thomas Cox having been born there in 1646. The Duckworth family came from nearby Lancashire. The Almys came from London and originally settled in Rhode Island. The Morris family came from England and were probably from London. The Clinkscales emigrated from Glasgow, Scotland. The Brownlees came from County Antrim, Ireland, and the Cowans came from County Down, Ireland. Andrew Seawright was born in Londonderry, Ireland, and his wife was from Donegal.

For other families, the immigrant ancestors have not yet been found but many of them had reached America very early. The Terrells were in New Kent, Virginia, by 1659. William Barksdale was born in Richmond County, Virginia, in 1675, and his wife was born in Virginia in 1677. James Kay was born in King County, Virginia, in 1662, and his family had probably been in the colony a generation earlier. Henry Randolph was born in Appomattox in 1689 and his wife Elizabeth was born in the same county in 1690.

Many left their home countries seeking freedom of religion and freedom from overly oppressive governments. Some found everything they were seeking. Some did not.

Monmouth County: A Haven for Baptists and Quakers Except for the Government

After the death of Oliver Cromwell and the collapse of Richard Cromwell's government, Charles II assumed the throne of England and, eager to reestablish the English crown claims to all of northern America, on March 12, 1663/64, made a royal grant and patent to his brother James, Duke of York.[1] The grant included the present-day state of New Jersey, part of New York, the islands of Massachusetts, most of Maine, part of Connecticut, and all of Staten Island and Long Island. To enforce the claim, which covered virtually all of the Dutch New Netherlands, King Charles II sent four ships under the command of Sir Robert Carre carrying a military force under the command of Col. Richard Nicolls, whom the Duke of York had commissioned to be governor of the territory included in the patent. The fleet arrived at New Amsterdam in August 1664 and demanded the surrender of all of the

New Netherlands. Dutch governor Stuyvesant eventually surrendered and the land passed to the control of the English crown.[2]

In a payoff for their support of Charles II during the English Civil War, the Duke of York granted New Jersey to "John, Lord Berkeley, Baron of Stratton, and one of His Majesty's most Honourable Privy Council, and Sir George Carteret, of Saltrum, in the County of Devon, Knight, and one of his Majesty's most Honourable Privy Council."[3] Berkeley and Sir Carteret were famously corrupt, Berkeley having to resign the Privy Council because of his blatantly corrupt financial transactions and Sir Carteret being faced with expulsion from the House of Commons for embezzlement and other corrupt practices until the king expressed his satisfaction with him, leading to his acquittal. Nevertheless, during the English Civil War, Berkeley had commanded the English forces against the Scots in 1638 and Sir Carteret had successfully defended the Isle of Jersey in the English Channel. Both were therefore favorites of the venal Charles II, who, after his ascension to the throne, had Cromwell's body dug up from the grave and hung.

The grant of New Jersey to Lord Berkeley and Sir George Carteret by the Duke of York conveyed to them the right to govern the province, which government was to be by delegates of the people to a general assembly, a governor, and a council. Phillip Carteret, Sir George Carteret's cousin, became Governor and abided by the terms of the prior grants to the people of Shrewsbury and Middletown in Monmouth County, New Jersey, that had been bestowed to them by Governor Nicolls upon the establishment of those settlements.

In March of 1672, Charles II and Louis XIV of France joined together to declare war on the States of Holland. During the war, the Dutch fleet recaptured New York and New Jersey. The peace treaty ending the war, signed February 9, 1673/74, restored to the English crown the towns and forts which had been taken during the war, so New York and New Jersey again passed back under English control. Then the question arose as to whether the grant to the Duke of York was still valid or, under the terms of the peace treaty with Holland, whether the land reverted to the Crown. Charles II settled the matter by regranting the same land to the duke again on June 26, 1674. However, the King had also, by proclamation on June 13, just a few days before the new grant, recognized Sir George Carteret as the sole proprietor of New Jersey, "he being seized of the province and jurisdiction thereof, and having sole power under us to settle and dispose of the country as he shall think fit."[4] These competing claims led to clashes between the two governors in the colonies, and the broad powers that Charles II had bestowed upon Carteret far exceeded the terms of the original grants and conditions under which Monmouth County had originally been chartered. Most important, Carteret wanted the people to now pay taxes in the form of quit rents.

While all this was swirling around the highest levels of government in England, Holland, and the colonies, the pioneers in Monmouth County were establishing their communities in the New Jersey wilderness. Suddenly, they were told not only that Carteret had sold vast tracts to William Penn, endangering their land titles, but also that Carteret now owned all of their property and they would now have to pay taxes and rent on the land they had cleared and the houses they had built. Furious and defiant, they pledged to abide only by the original terms of the grant by Governor Nicolls, which did not include rent taxes. Charles II issued three proclamations supporting Carteret and demanded that the people in Monmouth treat Carteret as their lord and pay the taxes he imposed. A campaign was then begun to subvert the government.

Thomas Cox and Elizabeth Blashford — Puritanical Persecution

In the middle of this controversy lived our ancestors Thomas Cox and Elizabeth Blashford and their family. Little is provably known about the early life and origins of Thomas and Elizabeth. Thomas Cox (1645–1681) probably emigrated from England and sometime before 1665 settled in Marshpath Kills on Long Island. Thomas was a Baptist and married Elizabeth Blashford (1645–1690) who was a Quaker and who may have moved from Massachusetts. They must have been of some stature in the colony because the colonial governor of New York, Richard Nicolls, signed their marriage license:

> Whereas I have received information of a mutual intent and agreement between Thomas Cox of Marshpath Kills in ye Lymmits of New Towne, and Elizabeth Blashford to enter into the state of matrimony, and that there lyeth no lawful obstacle or obligation on either part to hinder the performance thereof, I do hereby grant unto them Lycences so to do — and do also require one of ye Justices of ye peace of ye North Ryding of Yorkshire upon Long Island or ye Minister of some Parish therein to Joyne the said Thomas Cox and Elizabeth Blashford in Marryage, and to pronounce them man and wife and so to record them according to the law made in that behalf, for doing whereof this shall be sufficient warrant. Given under my hand and Seal at James Hart in New York this 22nd day of April, 1665. Rich. Nicolls.[5]

New York in the 1650s was becoming a haven of sorts for New England Quakers who moved there to escape religious persecution by the Puritans in Massachusetts or who had been banished from the Puritan colonies for their heretical religious views.[6] From the beginning of the Quaker movement in the 1640s in England, the sect embraced the Protestant "priesthood of all believers" philosophy and allowed and even encouraged women to proselytize and preach. To the Puritan leaders in Massachusetts, the practice was heretical, a public denial of Puritan religious beliefs, and therefore might be evidence of the influence of Satan, which in turn brought accusations of witchcraft.

In 1656, when Ann Austin and Mary Fisher, the first female Quaker preachers to reach Boston, arrived, deputy governor Richard Bellingham had them arrested while they were still on the ship *Swallow* in Boston Harbor. They were stripped naked and their bodies were examined for marks of the devil. The Quaker writings and papers found among their possessions were deemed evidence of "corrupt heretical and blasphemous Doctrines."[7] Their possessions were burned and the two women were thrown into jail in Boston, deemed so dangerous that the window to their cell was boarded over and a 5-shilling fine was imposed on anyone who tried to speak to them. They were incarcerated for five weeks and then exiled from the colony without trial.[8]

The next group of Quakers to arrive in Boston were jailed for eleven weeks and then sent back to England for being members of a "cursed sect of hereticks." During their imprisonment, the Puritan government passed a law allowing Quakers to be prosecuted just for being Quakers, a much simpler case to prove than witchcraft. Now they could be jailed for "tak[ing] upon them to be immediately send of God, and infallibly assisted by the spirit" and for holding "blasphemouth opinions, despising government and the order of God in church and commonwealth, speaking evil of dignities, reproaching and reviling magistrates andministers, seeking to turne people away from their faith, and gaine prosetyltes to theire pernicious wayes."[9]

During this period, the infamous Puritan preacher Cotton Mather was being called upon to examine the persons and evidence in Salem and Boston witchcraft trials, evidence that he almost invariably found and which led to the execution by hanging of several witches. He had the full backing of the Puritan government and later wrote *The Wonders of the Invisible World: Being an Account of the TRYALS of Several Witches Lately Executed in NEW-ENGLAND And of several remarkable Curiosities Therein Occurring*, published by a special command of the governor of the Province of Massachusetts Bay, in which he described his involvement in the prosecution of witches. Mather denounced the Quakers as heretics, cited their "quaking" as a sign of demonic possession and claimed Quakerism was the "grossest collection of blasphemies and confusions" that ever visited New England and that its practitioners were "madmen, a sort of lunaticks, daemoniacks, and energumens." His zeal in pursuing the Quakers was so vehement and well known that he fell victim to an apparent fraud, which many people easily believed, when a forged letter was circulated, allegedly written by Mather to the governor, imploring the governor to intercept William Penn's ship bringing Quaker settlers to Pennsylvania and to capture them all and to sell them, along with Penn, as slaves in Barbados.

Massachusetts Bay — which "CHARLES, BY THE, GRACE, OF GOD, Kinge of England, Scotland, Fraunce, and Ireland, Defendor of the Fayth, and co.," had declared in the charter of Massachusetts Bay in 1629 as a colony ("...whereby our said People, Inhabitants there, may be so religiously, peaceable, and civilly governed, as their good Life and orderly Conversation, maie wynn and incite the Natives of Country, to the Knowledge and Obedience of the onlie true God and Savior of Mankinde, and the Christian Fayth, which in our Royall Intencon, and the Adventurers free Profession, is the principal End of this Plantacion"[10]) — was decidedly hostile to the free profession of the Quaker faith.

New York was far more tolerant and, under the patent of Governor Nicolls, Monmouth County was formed and the towns of Middletown and Shrewsbury were established. Shrewsbury was predominantly a Quaker settlement and Middletown, where Thomas Cox and Elizabeth Blashford settled, was predominantly Baptist.

Thomas and Elizabeth moved to the land Governor Nicolls granted them and then paid the Indians who owned the land their full asking price, a condition of Governor Nicolls' patent and a practice that generated good will among the Indians. There is no other documentation for them for almost three years, until Thomas registers his cattle mark. Apparently, the cattle roamed freely in the area and ownership was signified by ear marks which were registered. In the book of the town clerk on January 4, 1668, it was recorded that "Tho Cocks his marke is the top of the right eare cutt off and a swallow taile and a hole in the left eare."[11]

In 1669 Thomas was made rate maker for the town. Later he became assistant deputy, then deputy, then in 1673 he was elected town overseer. In 1676 he was chosen to be a town deputy to meet with the governor about local affairs. Thomas died in August of 1681, by which time he and Elizabeth had six children. Thomas Ingram, the executor of the Thomas Cox estate and apparently a very good friend of the family, moved swiftly and married Elizabeth a month later as recorded in the town register: "Tho Ingham and ye wid. Elizabeth Cox were married by Cap. John, Bowne Justis of the peace in Middle Town, Sep. ye 9:1681." It was remarked that "the days of her mourning were not unduly protracted."

Of Thomas Cox and Elizabeth's six children, the oldest, not surprisingly, was named Thomas and he was our ancestor. Thomas Cox (II) was born February 11, 1668, and married a woman named Mary. She was probably Mary Wright but there is no proof of this identification. Thomas (II) apparently became moderately wealthy and very discontent. He signed a petition asking the Proprietors to appoint a competent governor. The second son,

John, was more outspoken and was heavily involved in the Monmouth County riots of 1701. The third son, James, was taxed on 300 acres of land and, very kindly for future generations seeking information, named all of his children in his will. The fourth son was Joseph, who married Catherine Shepherd, great-granddaughter of William Lawrence, who in turn was allegedly the son of Sir Henry Lawrence, president of Cromwell's council. James, Joseph and especially John Cox were politically active and were involved with a group to undermine the assembly and bring about elections. They were contributors to a mysterious fund called the "Blind Tack," which was used to further that goal.[12] Much of their political ire was directed at another of our ancestors, Lewis Morris, and his uncle.

Lewis Morris of Passage Point; Uncle Lewis Morris of Tinton Falls; The Monmouth Riots

Our ancestor Lewis Morris also lived in Monmouth County and was known as Lewis Morris of Passage Point to distinguish him from his uncle, who was also named Lewis Morris. Uncle Lewis Morris was in turn the nephew of Captain Lewis Morris, who had served under Cromwell during the English Civil War. After the restoration of Charles II, Captain Morris emigrated to Barbados and then to New York in 1673.[13] He acquired a large tract of land in Shrewsbury and started an iron foundry at Tinton Falls. Captain Morris died in 1691 and his manor passed down to his nephew Lewis Morris of Tinton Falls in a very contentious estate settlement. Lewis Morris of Tinton Manor, as he was known, was a vindictive politician of the highest sort, focusing his wrath on his political enemies and dispensing favors to his friends. He was arrested in September 1686 on a charge brought "on the oath of a negro woman named Franck."[14] The fact that the actual charge was not named probably indicates that it was scandalous indeed. Morris had the charge transferred to the court in Perth Amboy where the woman, who was most probably a slave, had no way to attend and therefore the charges were dropped.

Uncle Lewis Morris of Tinton Manor was made justice of the peace at the court in Middletown in 1687, and in 1692 he was appointed by Governor Hamilton as a member of the Council of New Jersey. Hamilton was a Scotsman and was despised by many of the residents of Middletown and Shrewsbury who claimed that his appointment was illegitimate by virtue of his being Scottish, which they thought precluded his ruling over free Englishmen. After his appointment, Lewis Morris of Tinton Manor ingratiated himself with Governor Hamilton and became one of his strongest supporters.

Lewis Morris of Tinton Manor also placed his nephew, our ancestor Lewis Morris of Passage Point, on the bench as judge. In 1694, Lewis Morris of Passage Point was indicted for stealing hay, a charge that disappeared in Lewis Morris of Tinton Manor's court. A grand jury then indicted Lewis Morris of Tinton Manor for fencing the highway. Even though he was sitting on the bench, the case was not called and he was ordered to appear at the next court to answer the charge. At the next court, Lewis Morris of Passage Point was arraigned for striking a man several blows. Lewis Morris of Passage Point explained to Lewis Morris of Tinton Manor "how matters stood"[15] and the case was dismissed with no evidence being presented and no trial.

In 1695, our ancestor Lewis Morris of Passage Point, possibly following his uncle's example in the treatment of women slaves, mistreated the wrong one and one of his slaves killed him by striking him in the head with a shovel.

At the next court, the indictment against Lewis Morris of Tinton Manor for fencing the road was again presented. Lewis was most likely fencing the public highway for his cattle, the highway providing an already cleared portion of (illegally) available land. During much of the five years that Lewis fenced the public road, our ancestor Thomas Cox was in charge of maintaining the road. Morris was again ordered to appear at the next court to answer the charge. The road fencing charge was presented again in 1698 and no action was taken, then again in 1699, and again no action was taken. The case never came before the court and so it is not known who was making the charges of fencing the road against Lewis Morris.

Governor Hamilton was replaced by Governor Basse in 1698 and Lewis Morris waged a vindictive battle to undermine him. Appearing in the court in Perth Amboy over which Governor Basse was presiding, Morris demanded by what right the court had been convened. Basse replied, "By the King's authority," which Morris vigorously denied. Morris was ordered to be arrested for open contempt. Swords were drawn but Morris was subdued and jailed and ordered to pay a hefty fine.[16] Upon his release from jail, Morris and some of his allies began traveling through the county bitterly denouncing Governor Basse. In May of 1699, another warrant was issued for his arrest:

> To the Sheriff of the county of Middlesex, his under sheriff or deputy, or either of them: Whereas we are informed that Lewis Morris of Tinton, in the county of Monmouth, and province aforesaid, Gent., did in April last in Perth Amboy in the said province, seditiously assemble with others and endeavor to subvert the laws of this province and did by malicious and reproachful words, asperge the governor of said province, contrary to the peace of our Sovereign Lord the King, and the laws in such cases made and provided. These are therefore to will and require, and in His Majesty's name, strictly to charge and command you to take into your custody said Lewis Morris, and to convey him to the jail of your county, and there safely to keep, until he shall give sufficient security in the sum of three hundred pounds for his appearance at the Court of Common Rights in Perth Amboy the second Tuesday of October next, then and there to answer the premise; and in meantime to be in good behavior to His Majesty and his liege people. Hereof fail not at your peril, and for so doing this shall be your warrant. Given under our hands and seals May 11, in the eleventh year of the reign of our Sovereign Lord William the Third of England, A.D. 1699, at Perth Amboy in province aforesaid."[17]

The next day, Uncle Lewis and his friend George Willocks were arrested and jailed in the Middlesex County jail. That night, between 2 and 4 o'clock in the morning, a group of "Malefactors and Disturbers of the King's Peace" assembled outside the jail with a wooden beam, battered down the door, and set Lewis and George free. Three days later, Morris sent the judges a letter:

> To Capt. Andrew Bowne, Mr. John Royce, Mr. Thomas Warne, and company, etc. Sirs. We are now able (God be thanked) to treat with you any way you see fit. If you had valued either your own or the welfare of the government, your procedure had been more calm. Your day is not yet out, and it is in your power to follow the things that make for peace, and if you do not at your door will lie the consequences. Our friends will not suffer us to be putt upon. Farewell. George Willocks, Lewis Morris.[18]

The judges convened the council, which requested a conference with the House of Representatives of the Provincial Legislature, then meeting in Perth Amboy, to request that an act be passed to suppress any insurrection. During the meeting of the legislature, Morris had a fabulously abusive letter delivered to Captain Andrew Bowne and other members of the council who were in attendance. Morris and Willocks then boarded a small sloop and began to sail up and down the river in plain view of the legislature building firing off their guns and shouting insults.

Governor Basse had had enough of this and other problems, and after appointing Captain Bowne deputy governor he sailed back to England. By this time the Proprietors themselves were split into factions and, looking for someone to calm the situation, they decided to appoint the one man with the experience to govern the province, the much hated former governor and Scotsman, Andrew Hamilton. Our Cox ancestors were appalled. Our Morris ancestors were overjoyed.

Soon it was discovered that Hamilton's commission was not signed by the required number of Proprietors and, much more serious, had not been signed by King William. Ignoring the flaws in the commission, Lewis Morris, his friend George Willocks, and others published the commission and welcomed Hamilton. Hamilton immediately appointed Morris as president of the council, ranking him second to the governor. Uncle Lewis Morris then fired all of his old enemies and appointed his political cronies in their place, almost all of them Scotsmen. Allegations of corruption soon followed. Members of the court and the sheriff's office were suspected and accused of accepting bribes and levying unlawful fees for which there was no accounting. The legislature passed an act making it easier for the courts and sheriff to seize property to be sold for taxes and the rents demanded by the Proprietors that the people were refusing to pay.

The people of Middletown and Shrewsbury were pleased with none of it. Thomas Cox and others signed a petition and sent it to the king requesting that a new governor be appointed and that the Proprietors be required to uphold the conditions of the original Nicolls patent.[19] Morris vowed to collect the taxes and rents, and three well respected Quakers from Shrewsbury stated in a written declaration that in their presence Lewis Morris had declared that he had no scruples of conscience like the Quakers and that he "would go through with his office though the streets run with blood."[20] The residents were inflamed; wild rumors circulated and in the midst of this several citizens of Middletown were called to sit on the grand jury.

The court convened March 26, 1700, and Eleazer Cottrell, the local blacksmith and the first man called to serve on the grand jury, refused on the grounds that the justices were illegally appointed by a Scotsman. He was jailed. Another citizen, Richard Salter, rose and objected to the arrest, repeating that the court convened by justices under the authority of a Scotsman who did not have King William's commission was illegal. He too was arrested. They then called up the former clerk and ordered him to turn over his records. He refused on the basis of the court's being illegal, but to avoid jail he offered instead to turn over his records if the justices would post a £10,000 bond to indemnify him against damages if it turned out that the court was later ruled to be a sham appointed by a usurper. The court adjourned for conference.

After the conference, it was decided to release the prisoners jailed for contempt and to instead impose fines on them and on several other Middletown citizens they also charged with contempt. Salter and Cottrell remained defiant and Cottrell was fined five pounds sterling, Salter fifteen. Uncle John Cox and nine other men were found in contempt of court and fined forty shillings.[21] Sherriff Johnson was ordered to seize enough of their property to sell to cover the fines and to present the money at the next court.

When the court reconvened in September, Sherriff Johnson reported the sad fact that not only did he not have the money but also that he and his deputies had been beaten by a mob in Middletown when he had attempted to seize their property to sell to cover the fines. More fines were levied against more citizens and the sheriff was again ordered to collect them. When Sheriff Johnson arrived in Middletown with 50 men he was met by over 100 citizens including the Cox brothers. The standoff was diffused with no violence when Sheriff Johnson decided that it was not an appropriate time to collect the fines.

Court convened again on March 25, 1701, in Middletown. Governor Hamilton was present as was Lewis Morris. A mob had gathered determined to prevent the court from sitting. Morris, however, had an unexpected surprise, a preplanned accusation and apparent false confession in a most unexpected case over which the court had no jurisdiction.

The court opened with the case of Moses Butterworth, who was accused of piracy, even though at the time only Admiralty courts had jurisdiction over piracy cases. Butterworth confessed that he had sailed with Captain William Kidd on Kidd's last pirate voyage to the East Indies and that he had then sailed with Captain Kidd to Boston. Uncle John Cox, Sam Willet and several others entered the courtroom and Willet declared that the governor and Justices had no authority to hold court. A drummer entered the court drumming loudly to drown out the proceedings and with him were 30 to 40 other men armed with clubs (the forthcoming indictments accused the men of being armed with clubs, the inductees would later claim that they had small sticks).

Butterworth was seized and grabbed onto a railing to keep from being rescued. A sword fight ensued and several people were injured. The prisoner was freed and the governor, Lewis Morris and the other justices, the sheriff, and the clerk of the court were taken prisoner and held for four days. The court records from three hundred years ago describe the incident vividly:

> Proceedings of Court of Sessions of Monmouth County at Middletown, relative to the putting Sundry Officials under guard.[22]
> At a court of Sessions held for y^e County of Monmouth at Middletown in y^e County afford^{ed} the province of East New Jersey, March 25 1701.
> Being present {Coll. Andrew Hamilton} Governor
>   {Lewis Morris} Esq^{res} of y^e
>   {Sam$^{L.L}$ Leonard} Gover^s Councill
>   {Jedidiah Allen}
>   {Sam^{Ll}- Dennes} Justices
>
> The Court being opened one Moses Butterworth who was accused of piracy (& had confessed y' he did sail with Capt William Kid in his last voyage when he came from y^e East Indies & went into Boston with him) & was bound to make his appearance at this Court y^t he might be Examined & disposed of according to his Maj^{ties} orders the s^d Butterworth was Called & made his appearance & when ye Court was Examining him one Sam^{ll} Willet In holder said y^t ye Gover^r & Justices had no authority to Hold Court & y^t he would break it up & accordingly went down staires to a Company of men then in armes & sent up a Drummer one Thomas Johnson into ye Court who beat upon his drum & severall of ye Company came up wth their armes & Clubs wch together wth ye Drum beating Continually made such a noise (notwithstanding open proclamations made to be silent & keep ye Kings peace) y^t ye Court Could not Examine ye prisoner at the Barr & when ther was as ye Court Judged betwixt 30 & 40 men Come up into ye Court some with their armes & some with Clubs two persons viz: Benjamin Borden & Richard Borden attempted to Rescue ye prisoner at ye Barr & did take hold on him by ye armes & about ye midle & forct him from ye Barr ye Constable & undersheriff by ye Command of ye Court apprehended ye s^d Borden upon wch severall of ye persons in ye Court assaulted ye Constable & undersheriff (the Drum still beating & ye people thronging up Staires wth their armes) & Rescued ye two Bordens upon wch ye Justices & Kings Attorney Generall of the province after Commanding ye Kings peace to be keept & no heed being given thereto drew their

swords & Endeavoured to Retake ye prisoner & apprehend some of ye persons Conserned in ye Rescons but was Resisted & assaulted themselves & ye Examination of ye prisoner torn in peices & in ye scufle both Richard Borden & Benj. Borden were wounded but ye Endeavours of ye Court were not Effectuall in retaking ye prisoner for he was Rescued & Carried off & made his Escape and the people viz: Capt Safetie Grover Richard Borden Benj: Borden Obadiah Holmes Obadiah Browne Nicholas Stephens George Cooke Benj: Cooke Richard Osborne Sam^ll Willett Joseph West Garret Bowler Garret Wall James Bollen Sam1' foreman Willm Winter Jonathan Stout James Stout Willm Hendricks John Bray Willm Smith Gersom Mott Abner Hewght George Allen John Cox John Vaughan Elisha Lawrance Zebulon Clayton James Grover Junr Richard Davis Jeremiah Evrington Joseph Ashton with others to ye number of about one hundred persons did traytorously seize ye Governour & ye Justices the Kings Attorney Generall & ye undersheriff & ye Clerke of ye Court & kept them close prisoners under a guard from tuesday ye 25th March till ye Saturday following being ye 29th of ye same same month & then Releast them.

    Vera Copia   P me Gav: Drummond Clark

At the next court, John Cox and several others were fined for contempt and misbehavior. Lewis Morris sailed to London and accusing the residents of Monmouth and Shrewsbury of being the rebels who were harboring pirates, one of the most inflammatory and serious charges of the time, tried to get the English government to send the navy and troops to New Jersey to support him. Several people disputed Morris' account of the residents of Shrewsbury and Monmouth, many of whom were known by the officials in London to be pious Quakers and Baptists. Governor Nicolls was in London at the time and disparaged Morris as a man lacking in character. The final blow to Morris' plan to rally the English military to his aid came when Queen Anne, who had just ascended to the throne, appointed her first cousin Edward Hyde to be governor of New York. Hyde agreed to abide by the original agreements of the Nicolls patent and scrupulously avoided any involvement in reviewing any of the previous court cases in Monmouth. The immediate controversy was diffused but the tax questions simmered for years.

Uncle Lewis Morris returned to New Jersey, and after New Jersey petitioned the Crown to be a state separate from New York, Lewis Morris became the first governor of New Jersey and served in that office until his death in 1746. His grandson, also named Lewis Morris, signed the Declaration of Independence as the representative for New York. In the *Dictionary of American Biographies* there is this entry included in Governor Morris' biography: "Morris' public career was never touched by the least suspicion of political jobbery."[23]

Before our ancestor Lewis Morris of Passage Point was killed by one of his slaves, he married Anne Almy. Her family was already in the colonies by 1631.

The Almys and the Cornells: They Thought Quakers Were Bad Until They Met the Antinomians

Anne Almy's father and our ancestor William Almy was born in 1601 in Belinden Parish, Kent County, England. He first came to New England with John Winthrop and made at least two trips back to England before moving to Rhode Island with his family.[24] William married Audrey Barlowe of Lutterworth in England in 1626.* William Almy and

---

*Audrey Barlow is a "gateway" ancestor to the descendents of Charlemagne. If you can trace back to a gateway ancestor, their line back through 39 or so generations to Charlemagne has been proven. There are an estimated 50 to 100 million descendants of Charlemagne after 39 generations, so it is not as exclusive as it may seem.

Audrey Barlowe's marriage certificate was found in 1910 and published by the British Record Society in *Leicestershire Marriage Licences, 1570–1729* that same year. By 1631 William was in Saugus, Massachusetts (now known as Lynn, Massachusetts), where the early records of the Massachusetts Bay Colony state that on June 14, 1631, he was "ffyned for takeing away Mr. Glouers cannoe without leave." There were other court actions, some that he won and some that he lost. In June of 1634, he was fined again for not appearing in court.[25] He was not in court because he had returned to England to collect his family and move to the colony.

William sailed with his wife, Audrey Barlow, and two children, Annis (Ann) and Christopher, from London to New England in 1635 on the *Abigail*, Robert Hackwell, master. The passenger list had, along with many other names, those of "Wm Almond, aged 34, Awdry Almond, aged 32, Annis Almy, aged 8, and Chris. Almie, aged 3."[26] They embarked in the ship on June 17, 1635.

William and his family were founders of the town of Sandwich near Plymouth Bay, where he was given a land grant in April of 1637. He and his family were all Quakers, members of the Society of Friends, and in 1641, in an increasingly hostile political environment and after the court confiscated a calf that belonged to him as remittance for an unpaid fine, he sold his house and land and moved with his family to Rhode Island, the only colony at the time that welcomed Quakers.

Ann Almy married the deputy governor of Rhode Island, John Greene, and stayed in Rhode Island. Christopher married Rebecca Cornell and established a shipping company serving Rhode Island and New Jersey.[27] Christopher and Rebecca are our ancestors. They moved to Monmouth and lived there for several years before returning to Rhode Island.

Descendants of the Cornell family eventually founded Cornell University. The family is interesting for other reasons too. Our ancestor Thomas Cornell Sr., father of Rebecca Cornell, was born in Essex County, England, around 1595. He married Rebecca Briggs, a brother of John Briggs. Thomas was an innkeeper and was fined several times for selling wine without a license. His friends and neighbors and his brother-in-law John Briggs were Antinomians, followers of Anne Hutchinson. The Antinomians believed that salvation was a matter of predestination and therefore they were under no obligation to obey the laws of ethics or morality. This dogma was the complete antithesis of everything the Puritans in Massachusetts stood for and Thomas' neighbors and brother-in-law were excommunicated along with Ann Hutchinson in 1637 and expelled from the colony. They fled and joined Roger Williams and John Trockmorton in Rhode Island.

Thomas arrived in Rhode Island about two years later, in 1640. In 1642 it was decided that Roger Williams should return to England and seek a royal charter for the colony they were essentially squatting on. Around this time Thomas Cornell moved to New Amsterdam, where the Dutch governor granted Thomas a land grant which came to be known as "Cornell's Neck." The grant to a non–Dutchman was exceedingly rare and the grant to Thomas was only the third one recorded. Thomas was driven from the land twice by Indians, the last time all of his property being burned. He returned to Portsmouth where he lived the rest of his life and where he is buried. Upon his death in 1655, he left all of his land to his wife, Rebecca. The estate was immediately challenged and was settled only when the land grant was produced and verified.[28]

The Very Strange Case of Thomas Cornell

Thomas Cornell Sr. and Rebecca Briggs had a son, Thomas Cornell (II), named after his father. In February of 1673, eighteen years after her husband had died, Rebecca was at home and apparently fell asleep while smoking a pipe. A fire started and the house burned with Rebecca in it. The coroner investigated and the fire was thought to be an accident until Rebecca's brother, John Briggs, went to the coroner and accused Rebecca's son Thomas (II) of starting the fire. A trial was held and the only evidence presented was the testimony of John Briggs, who clamed that his sister had appeared to him in a dream, "whereat he was much affrighted and cryed out, 'in the name of God, what art thou!' The apparition answered 'I am your sister Cornell' and twice said 'see how I was burnt with fire!'"[29] John Briggs testified that the apparition of his sister, Rebecca, had told him that her son Thomas had started the fire that had burned his sister to death. Based on the testimony of his uncle's dream, Thomas was convicted and hanged in May 1673. His wife, Sarah, was pregnant at the time and shortly after the hanging she gave birth to her third daughter. She named the child Innocent.[30]

Thomas Cornell Sr. and Rebecca Briggs had 10 children. Their ninth child was a daughter they named Elizabeth Cornell, a sister to Thomas (II), who had been hanged. Elizabeth Cornell married Christopher Almy in either Rhode Island or Monmouth, New Jersey. Christopher Almy and Rebecca Cornell had nine children. Their second child, and our ancestor, was Elizabeth Almy, born on September 29, 1663. Elizabeth Almy married Lewis Morris of Passage Point. Lewis Morris and Elizabeth's son and another of our ancestors, Richard Morris, was born in 1690. Richard Morris married Mary Porter on June 19, 1714.[31] Their son Job Morris was born in Monmouth in 1735.

The Pottses Arrive from England

Thomas Cox (II), the son of Thomas Cox and Elizabeth Blashford, and his wife Mary had a son, Thomas Cox (III), born June 23, 1700. Thomas (III) married Rebecca Potts, the granddaughter of Thomas Potts and his wife Joan of Derbyshire, England.

Thomas Potts was the sole surviving son of Richard and Anne Potts of Chesterfield, Derbyshire, England, where church records show that he was baptized on July 12, 1647.[32] When he was about 30 years old, he emigrated to Burlington, Pennsylvania, and the arrival of his ship was described in letters that were later published:

> In the 10th month O.S. 1678, arrived the *Shield*, from Hull, Daniel Towes commander, one of the ships mentioned in the above letter, and dropped anchor before Burlington, being the first ship that came so far up Delaware: Against Coaquanock [the Indian name for the site of present-day Philadelphia]—being a bold shore, she went so near in turning, that part of the tackling struck the trees; some on board then remarked it was a fine spot for a town: A fresh gale brought her to Burlington: She moor'd to a tree, and the next morning the people came ashore on the Ice, so hard had the river suddenly frozen. In her came ... [a list of passengers, including] Thomas Potts, his wife and children ... and several more.[33]

Thomas was a tanner and established a successful business in Philadelphia where he lived until his death on September 4, 1726, when he was 79 years old.[34] He was buried at the Pennypack Baptist Church, which had been founded in 1688 and still stands today in the historic Pennypack Park in Philadelphia.

When Thomas died, he left a will mentioning his only surviving son, also named Thomas. The younger Thomas Potts had been baptized in England on December 30, 1677, and had made the journey to America on the *Shield* when he was an infant. He married Mary Records, the daughter of Nathaniel Records, who lived in Mansfield Township,

Burlington County. Their marriage is listed in the old Burlington Book of Court Records.[35] Nathaniel obviously liked his son-in-law and on March 8, 1702, he executed a deed and gave Thomas a little over 200 acres in two plots in Burlington. The deed itself is wonderful genealogically, naming Nathaniel, his daughter Mary, his son-in-law Thomas, identifying his residence and confirming the marriage.[36]

Ancestors Thomas Potts and Mary Records were Baptist and the Pennypack Baptist Church records show that they were both baptized June 29, 1707. They were also among the original founders of the Baptist Church at Southampton in Bucks County, Pennsylvania, in 1746. Their son Joshua Potts was the first pastor there. Thomas died in 1754 and was buried in the Baptist cemetery at Bordentown, Pennsylvania. His tombstone is still there and the inscription can still be read:

> Here Lyeth the Body of
> Thomas Potts who
> Departed this Life February
> the 2nd 1754. Aged 76 Years
> and one Month.

Thomas Potts and Mary Records had eight children — five sons and three daughters — seven of which survived to adulthood, the eldest girl having died young. Their second daughter, Rebecca, married our ancestor Thomas Cox (III). Their third daughter, Mary, married his cousin John Cox, a son of James and Anne Cox.

In 1733 our ancestors Thomas Cox (III) and Rebecca Potts had a daughter they named Rebecca Cox. Rebecca Cox married Thomas Ansley, the son of William Ansley, who had arrived in Monmouth County before 1735. William Ansley's wife was also named Rebecca, which was apparently a very popular name in the early 1700s.

More Scots: All Is Forgiven Between the Ansley, Cox and Morris Families

Our seven-generations-ago ancestor William Ansley was born in 1710 and first appears in early records when he joined the Old Tennent Presbyterian Church in Monmouth County, New Jersey, on June 8, 1735. William Ansley married Rebecca, whose last name is unknown. Rebecca joined the church a year later, possibly giving an indication of their wedding date; having married Thomas she then joined his church. Their son Thomas was baptized at the Old Tennent Church in Monmouth on March 20, 1737.[37] The Old Tennent Church was established by Scottish Presbyterians fleeing the despotic persecution of Charles II, who especially disliked the foes of his Catholic Scottish allies. So William was probably an immigrant from Scotland and, being a Presbyterian, he would not have been allowed to live peacefully in the Puritan theocracy of Massachusetts. William and Rebecca Ansley had several children; among them were two of our ancestors, Thomas Ansley (1737–1809) and Mary Ansley (1745–1815).

Apparently the rancor between the Ansley, Cox and Morris family had been smoothed over by the middle 1700s. Job Morris married Mary Ansley on May 17, 1760, when she was only 15 years old. Thomas Ansley married Rebecca Cox, the daughter of Thomas Cox (III) and Rebecca Potts, on November 1, 1760.[38] Both couples are our ancestors.

A few years later, on February 13, 1765, Jacob Morris, Job Morris' brother, married Elizabeth Ansley,[39] the sister of Thomas and Mary Ansley. There are many references to Job

Morris marrying Elizabeth and to Job and Jacob supposedly being the same person, with "Job" being a nickname. However, the colonial records make it clear that Job and Jacob are two different people, brothers of one family who married sisters of another family.

Thomas Ansley and his wife Rebecca Cox had a son in 1761 that they named Able Ansley. Shortly thereafter, with the passing away of Uncle Lewis Morris making the political life less exciting, and because of the increasing hostility against Quakers and Baptists, they moved from Monmouth to Orange County, North Carolina, which at the time was a haven for Quakers. Their sons and daughters and their wives and husbands moved with them and by sometime shortly after November of 1760 almost the entire clan had moved from New Jersey to North Carolina.

More Taxes, the Regulators, and the Battle of Alamance

Seeking to enrich themselves, Governor William Tryon of North Carolina and his allies began to levy excessive taxes, most of which they allegedly kept for themselves. The poorest land and land in the western mountainous regions, the very area in the back country to which the Quakers and Baptists had moved, was taxed at the same rate as the most fertile farmland; and it was required that the taxes be paid in hard currency, which was scarce and hard to come by. The Quaker and Baptist communities began to see their land and stock being confiscated and transferred to the governor and his friends, some of whom became the wealthiest people in the colony through their corrupt practices. The Regulator movement was formed to protest the higher taxes and corruption, and many of the Quakers and Baptists were part of it. Organized by Herman Husband, the Regulators' protests ultimately turned to violence. Governor Tryon, who had arrived in 1765, was a veteran army colonel and formed a militia to deal with the protests.

In 1770, a mob entered the home of a particularly corrupt official of Orange County, beat him, and ransacked his house. Some officials, many appointed by the governor himself, became afraid to go to their offices and Governor Tryon, a governor appointed by the Crown and a trained military officer, could not tolerate the situation. He demanded that the Regulators disband and when they did not he called out the militia and confronted them in Hillsborough. The Regulators asked for negotiations and presented the governor with a petition protesting the taxes and corruption in his government. The next morning the governor responded with a proclamation demanding their surrender and accusing them of rebellion against the king:

> Alamance Camp, Thursday, May 16th, 1771. To Those Who Style Themselves "Regulators: In reply to your petition of yesterday, I am to acquaint you that I have ever been attentive to the interests of your County and to every individual residing therein. I lament the fatal necessity to which you have now reduced me by withdrawing yourselves from the mercy of the crown and from the laws of your country. To require you who are now assembled as Regulators, to quietly lay down your arms, to surrender up your leaders, to the laws of your country and rest on the leniency of the Government. By accepting these terms within one hour from the delivery of this dispatch, you will prevent an effusion of blood, as you are at this time in a state of REBELLION against your King, your country, and your laws. (Signed) William Tryon.[40]

At noon, Mr. Robert Thompson, one of the Regulator negotiators, attempted to leave and return to his camp but was detained on orders of the governor. Heated words were exchanged and Governor Tryon pulled his gun and shot and killed Mr. Thompson. Immediately realizing his mistake, the governor raised a white flag, which was fired upon by the Regulators. The governor ordered his men to open fire but they hesitated until a Regulator yelled, "Fire and be damned!" and the Battle of Alamance began.

It was the first time in history that the British military attacked the colonists in what many historians now rate as the first battle of the American Revolution. The Battle of Alamance was a decisive defeat for the Regulators. The poorly armed Regulators had no military experience and were no match for trained British militia with artillery, and they were quickly overwhelmed. Several were captured and were later tried in Hillsborough on charges of high treason and hanged.

As the political atmosphere in North Carolina became more hostile to the Quakers, this group began to look to the new colony of Georgia, which practiced religious tolerance of all sects except Catholics, who were not welcome in the colony. On September 1, 1767, a group of Quakers from North Carolina led by Joseph Maddock and Jonathan Sell presented a petition to Governor Wright saying they desired to move from North Carolina and become settlers in the province of Georgia. They requested a section of land in the area along the Savannah River that had recently been ceded by the Cherokee and Creek Indians. In February of 1769, Maddock and Sell presented Governor Wright with another petition saying that 70 families had already moved into the area on the land that had been reserved for only 40 families and they requested that they might have a larger extent of land and that roads might be run. They also requested the right to make land grants. Governor Wright agreed and granted them land amounting to more than 44,000 acres.[41] The Quaker leaders ordered that 1000 acres be surveyed and laid out for a town, which they named Wrightsborough in honor of the governor.

Thomas Ansley was one of the original recipients of a land grant in the new settlement and moved there shortly afterwards. In Wrightsborough, the Ansleys met the Duckworth family, who had also moved from North Carolina.

Duckworths and Ramseys and Carters and Ansleys

By the time the Duckworths moved to Wrightsborough the family had been in the colonies for almost a hundred years. John Duckworth arrived in New Jersey from Ireland on December 1, 1684, under a four-year indenture as a "yeoman" to William Dockwra.[42]

The name of John Duckworth's wife is not known but his son and our ancestor William was born in 1685 in Burlington County, New Jersey. William married a woman named Grace, whose last name is also unknown. In 1715 William served in the New Jersey militia under Captain George Carrick assigned to the 5th Company of Colonel Thomas Farmers New Jersey Militia Regiment.[43] William Duckworth died in 1727 in Hanover and his widow, Grace, was apparently very sick. In 1728, in what she termed as her last illness, Grace had the Burlington County court appoint guardians for her son Joseph and her daughters Anna and Mary Duckworth.[44]

Our ancestors Joseph Duckworth and Esther Ong were married June 1, 1737, in Burlington County, New Jersey.[45] Joseph and Esther had six children, among them Jacob and Joseph Jr., while they lived in New Jersey. By 1740, Joseph and Esther had moved to North Carolina where a daughter, Charity Jane Duckworth, and a son, our ancestor Jeremiah Duckworth, were born in Anson County, North Carolina. By 1760, Jeremiah had married Christiana

Ramsey, the daughter of John Ramsey Jr. and his wife Johannah Stewart. Christiana was born March 29, 1742, in Maryland,[46] the family having moved there from Pennsylvania where they had been members of the Donegal Presbyterian Church near Mt. Joy.

Jeremiah Duckworth was a member of the Regulator movement in North Carolina and signed public petitions against Governor Tryon, including the infamous Regulator Advertisement #9 with its long list of attached grievances[47] protesting the unfair taxation and corruption that characterized the Tryon administration. After the Battle of Alamance, the family decided it was time to move away from the increasingly hostile political atmosphere in North Carolina and in January of 1772 Jeremiah Duckworth and his wife Christiana Ramsey petitioned for and received three hundred acres of land on the little Kioka River near Wrightsborough, Georgia.[48] The land they were granted was next to the Ansleys'.

By mid-1772, the Carters, the Duckworths, the Ansleys, the Coxes and the Morrises had all moved to Wrightsborough or the immediate area. They all owned land adjoining the other families or very close by. They bought and sold land to each other and they witnessed each other's deed transactions and wills. And their children married each other.

Jeremiah Duckworth and Christiana Ramsey had eight children: Joseph Duckworth, born about 1770, Randal Duckworth, born in 1771, William Duckworth, born in 1774, Eleanor Duckworth, born 1778, Allen Duckworth, born in 1782, Phoebe Duckworth, born about 1784, Jacob Duckworth, born about 1786, and Christina Duckworth, born about 1788.

Thomas Ansley and Rebecca Cox had eight children: Abel Ansley, born about 1761, Samuel Marlin Ansley, born February 22, 1765, Thomas Ansley Jr., born July 27, 1767, William Ansley, born in October 1770, Joseph Ansley, born February 5, 1775, Rebecca Ansley, born in 1775, Nancy "Ann" Ansley, born in 1776, and James Ansley, born in 1777.

Eleanor "Nellie" Duckworth married James Carter, the son of Kindred Carter. James Carter and Eleanor "Nellie" Duckworth are great-great-great-grandparents of Jimmy Carter. Able Ansley married his first cousin Lydia Morris, the daughter of Job Morris and Mary Ansley. They are great-great-great-grandparents of Jimmy Carter. James Carter and Eleanor "Nellie" Duckworth's son Wiley Carter married Ann Ansley, the daughter of Able Ansley and Lydia Morris.

Our ancestors were not the only members in these families to marry each other. James Carter's first cousin Jesse Carter married Phoebe Duckworth. William Duckworth married Rebecca Ansley and Joseph Duckworth married Nancy Ansley. The Carter cousins married the Duckworth sisters. The Duckworth brothers married the Ansley sisters. In the next generation, Wiley Carter's sister Epsey Carter married Thomas Ansley Jr., the son of Thomas Ansley and Rebecca Cox.

Wiley Carter and Ann Ansley

Our ancestor Wiley Carter married Ann Ansley on February 18, 1821, and they moved from Wrightsboro to Warren County on the west side of Rocky Comfort Creek. Wiley also owned more than four hundred acres on the east side of the creek and he farmed both plantations, raising corn and oats. Wiley and Ann Carter had eleven children, all born in Warren County:

Amanda Carter was born in 1822 in Warren County, Georgia. She married Jordan

Lyon on November 4, 1838,[49] and after Jordan died Amanda married Wiley G. Sammons in 1858.[50]

Caroline Carter was born on September 13, 1823, in Warren County, Georgia. Caroline married Hansel Beckwith August 30, 1838, and they had seven children.[51]

Calvin G. Carter was born on February 1, 1825. Calvin married Mary "Polly" Davis on May 27, 1847. Calvin and Mary had seven children.[52]

Out ancestor Littleberry Walker Carter was born in 1832 and died November 27, 1873, in Warren County, Georgia.

Euphrasia Carter was born in 1829 in Warren County, Georgia. Euphrasia married James Stuart and they had a son, Homer Stuart. After James died, Euphrasia married Barnabas Hart December 9, 1847.[53] They had two daughters, Sarah Nancy Hart and Mary Virginia Hart. Mary Virginia Hart was probably born in 1848 shortly before Barnabas died. Euphrasia married again on November 23, 1849, to Cato Abbot,[54] who became Mary Virginia's guardian. Euphrasia and Cato Abbot moved to Sumter County, Georgia, sometime between 1850 and 1806 and then moved to Butler County, Alabama.[55] Euphrasia and Cato Abbot had seven children.[56]

Ann W. Carter was born in 1842 and married John J.W. Ford around 1859.[57] John was listed as a cotton broker in the 1870 census and as a druggist in the 1880 census.

Jane Carter was born February 26, 1834, and married Isaac Hart in Warren County, Georgia, on November 7, 1848.[58] At the time of the 1850 census, Isaac and Jane were living in Marion County, Georgia, and by 1870, they had moved to Ellaville, Georgia. Jane and Isaac had five children.[59]

Julia Ann Carter was born on June 26, 1836. Julia Ann married Francis M. Mize. They had seven children.[60]

Wiley Carter Jr. was born in 1840 and married Rachel McGarrah in 1864 in Warren County. Wiley and Rachel had fourteen children.[61]

Louisiana Virginia Carter married John H. Rumph in either 1854 or 1855. John was listed as a cotton broker in the 1870 census. Virginia and John had five children.[62]

Jesse Taliaferro Carter was born on August 26, 1846, in Warren County, Georgia. Jesse married Nancy Jane Spivey October 26, 1865. They had seven children.[63]

About four miles east of Wiley lived Carroll Usry, another prosperous farmer. There was bad blood between Wiley and Usry over Usry having publicly accused Wiley's wife of adultery. A confrontation over a slave resulted in Wiley's shooting and killing Carroll Usry. Our family's understanding of the story has long been that Usry stole one of Wiley's slaves and Wiley swore out a warrant and went with the sheriff to reclaim his slave. Wiley and Usry had words and the situation escalated until both men drew their guns and Wiley shot Carroll Usry. There are several holes in the 150-year-old story. Why was there a dispute over the slave if Wiley clearly owned him and why did the sheriff allow Wiley to confront Usry? The current owner of the Usry plantation wrote a small tract describing the night that Wiley and Carroll Usry had their fatal confrontation. The story was handed down from his great-grandfather, who owned the land next to Wiley, and was told to him many times by his father. His story is a much more plausible tale and is supported by the known facts of the case.

Besides farming, Usry was also a slave trader and he had one slave, said to be the "perfect specimen," with whom he made a deal. Usry would take him to a distant slave auction and sell him for $1000 or more. The slave would then run away and return to Usry's plantation. In return, Usry would show him a good time, allegedly letting him have his choice of the female slaves and not requiring him to work. After a few months, Usry would take him to another far-off slave sale and sell him again.[64] From trading slaves and farming Usry had become very wealthy and he kept his money in gold. Wiley was a deputy sheriff under Sheriff Augustus Beall[65] and when the slave selling scam was discovered, Wiley swore out a warrant and joined Sheriff Beale's posse to arrest Usry.

Wiley and Usry had been enemies for a long time, Usry allegedly having slandered Wiley's wife, publicly accusing her of infidelity. When the posse arrived at Usry's house, it was already nighttime and dark. Wiley shouted out to Usry that they had a warrant for his arrest and told him to come out peacefully or they would come in to get him, dead or alive. Usry loaded his gun and a huge and profane argument broke out between the two men, each cursing and threatening the other. As the night wore on, Usry slandered Sarah again and told Wiley that, come daylight, he was going to come out and kill him and "send him to Hell akicking."[66]

The argument raged through the night and when daylight came, Usry opened the front door and stepped out onto the porch. Wiley was a few yards away and as Usry raised his gun to shoot, Wiley raised his gun too and shot and killed Usry. A trial was held in Warrenton in April 1844 and Wiley was acquitted on the grounds of self defense.

Usry may have been warned that his slave trading fraud had been exposed. Two days before he was killed, Usry bought a large iron kettle and sent his family away to spend the day with neighbors. When they returned home, the iron kettle and all of Usry's gold was gone. Usry had not told anyone where he had buried the gold before Wiley shot him and although his family searched for it, they did not find it. Owners of the Usry plantation and others, including uninvited "guests," have been searching the land for the treasure for over 150 years, using metal detectors in modern times; but Usry's iron kettle and the gold have never been found.

Ann Ansley died in 1848 and Wiley married Sarah Chestnut Wilson on January 30, 1849.[67] Wiley and Sarah had a son, Sterling Carter, born November 15, 1851, in Warren County. Shortly afterward, Wiley sold his plantation in Talbot County jointly to his son Littleberry Walker Carter and his son's father-in-law, William Seals, and Wiley and his family moved to Schley County.

By 1849, Wiley had become wealthy acquiring land in several counties in Georgia and also speculating as a land developer in Florida. The 1849 Tax Digest shows that Wiley owned twenty-nine slaves and more than 5,642 acres of land in Warren, Lowndes, Appling, Baker, Muscogee, Stewart, Sumter, Marion, and Lee counties. When Wiley died on March 4, 1864, he left in his estate $22,000 for each of his twelve children, the equivalent of about $300,000 each in today's money. Unfortunately, it was Confederate money that would soon be worthless.

At the outbreak of the Civil War, Wiley Carter Jr., Jesse Taliaferro Carter, and Littleberry Walker Carter enlisted in the Confederate 11th Battalion's Artillery, the "Sumter Flying Artillery." Originally, the Sumter Flying Artillery was one battery of six cannon and 200 men organized by Captain Allen Cutts. All three brothers served in Cutts' Battalion. After arriving at the battlefield of First Bull Run the day after the battle in 1861, they were assigned to General J. E. B. Stuart. They fought at Dranesville on December 20, 1861, then wintered in Culpepper, Virginia. They moved to Warrenton in March of 1862, then to Richmond and to the defense of Yorkton in April. During the Seven Days campaign, the Sumter

Battalion served in the Artillery Reserve. The Battalion then fought at Antietam, Fredericksburg, Chancellorsville, the Bristoe Campaign, Mine Run, and the Battle of the Wilderness. The Sumter Artillery then moved to Petersburg for the defense of that town. The Battalion fought at Appomattox but only a few surrendered there.

Wiley Carter Jr. enlisted in the Sumter Flying Artillery Battalion on July 30, 1861, our ancestor Littleberry Walker Carter Jesse enlisted March 1, 1862, and Jesse enlisted December 15, 1862, after he turned 16 years old.[68] Walker Carter has an intriguing notation in his service records in that he was absent from the muster in November and December of 1862 because he was "on detail by order of Gen. Lee."[69]

Jesse served with the Sumter Artillery except for September through December 1864 during which time he was "detached duty as musketeer by order of Col. Walker but paid on company roll."[70] Wiley Carter, Jr. was seriously wounded on May 24, 1864, at Hanover Junction, Virginia, and was admitted into the General Hospital at Howards Grove, Richmond, Virginia, on May 26, 1864. Wiley retired from the battalion in October 1864 and joined the Invalid Corps, P.A.C.S., where he served until the end of the war.[71]

After the battle at Appomattox, the Sumter Flying Artillery Battalion broke into small groups and fled south. Many never surrendered but Wiley, Jesse, and Littleberry Walker Carter all were taken as prisoners of war, surrendered to Brig. Gen. M. McCook by Maj. Gen. Sam Jones, C. S. A., at Tallahassee, Florida., May 10, 1865. They were paroled in Albany, Georgia, May 23, 1865.[72]

In 1851, Littleberry Walker Carter married Mary Ann Diligence Seals. Mary Ann's ancestors were Virginians and some of them had arrived in the 1600s.

Chapter 3

ANCESTORS OF MARY ANN DILIGENT SEALS

Mary Ann Diligent Seals was the wife of Littleberry Walker Carter and a great-grandmother of Jimmy Carter.

Only a few of Mary Ann Diligent Seals' ancestors can be provably traced back to their countries of origin. However, they can be traced back several hundred years. Mary Ann Diligent Seals' ancestors came from Virginia and they arrived there quite a long time ago. William Terrell was born in Virginia in 1659, his wife Susanna Waters was born there in 1667. Elizabeth Oxford was born in Hanover in 1698. William Barksdale was born in Virginia in 1675, his wife in 1677, and his father before 1662. Henry Randolph was born there in 1689, his wife Elizabeth Epps in 1690. The first Burnleys were there by 1715. Judith Powell was in Virginia by 1756 and her parents may have arrived in 1731.

Many of the records of early Virginia have been destroyed. Jamestown, Virginia, was founded in 1607 and remained the capital until 1699, during which time the town burned three times. After William and Mary College was founded in 1693 in Williamsburg, that town became more important. After a fire in 1698 burned the Jamestown State House down for the third time the capital was moved to Williamsburg into a new building with no fireplaces. But it was cold in Williamsburg, and fireplaces were added in 1723. That statehouse burned to the foundations in 1747, destroying many valuable records. The capital was moved to Richmond, Virginia, and the statehouse there burned twice, the last time when Benedict Arnold captured Richmond in 1781. In 1865, during the Civil War, one-third of Richmond was burned again and many documents which had survived for 250 years were lost.

Relatives in our extended family have gone to extraordinary lengths searching courthouses and other archives to gather and copy the records which still exist.

The Terrells: Polecat Swamp, Some Quakers Some Not, More Than One Affair

William Terrell was born in 1659 in New Kent County, Virginia. New Kent was formed from York County in 1654 and has a long and distinguished history. Martha Dandridge was born there in 1731 and the church where she married George Washington is still active today. Patrick Henry was born there too, in St. Paul's Parish, the same part of the county that the Terrells lived in and which later became Hanover County. Unfortunately, many of the earliest records of the county were destroyed in the Revolutionary War and even more were burned in courthouses during the Civil War. Because of the destruction of the records, it is impossible to sort out every relevant land deed in the early colonial history, but it seems certain that William Terrell's father was also named William Terrell and that both patented land in Polecat Swamp along the Polecat Creek.[1] Distinguishing the patents between father and son with certainty cannot be done.

William Terrell married Susannah, whose first name is identified in a power of attorney she granted to her son David to relinquish her dower rights[2] for a land deed in Polecat Swamp.[3] A pamphlet published in 1909 by a Terrell descendant identified her as Susannah Waters but no proof was offered.[4]

The area where they lived in St. Paul's Parish had an active Quaker community and although there is no evidence that William and Susannah were members of the Society of Friends, several of their children were. David Terrell became overseer of the monthly Quaker Cedar Creek meetings and his brother Henry was also actively involved with the Quaker community and sometimes helped his brother oversee the meetings. Both brothers had property seized for refusing to pay the Church of England's tax levy that was used to pay the parish priest's salary, to which they objected, being Quakers whose ministers were not paid and also not wishing to support the Church of England. Both were also fined for not attending militia meetings. David married Agatha Chiles, the daughter of Henry Chiles. Henry married her sister, Ann Chiles.[5]

Other members of the family were not so religiously inclined. William Terrell Jr. was fined for not attending church and in 1732 he was brought into court on adultery charges along with Rachel Jordan. This was a very serious charge and Rachel would have been publicly whipped had William Jr. not come forward to claim and pledge to support the child which resulted from the affair.[6]

Another son, John Terrell, was in court on several different occasions because of his illicit relationship with Elizabeth Harrison, with whom he fathered three out-of-wedlock children even though he had a wife, Sarah. After each child John was heavily fined and placed under bond not to meet Elizabeth again, but he continued the relationship anyway. Eventually he and Elizabeth fled the colony. It would have taken an act of the general assembly to grant Sarah a divorce but the court did seize John's estate and transfer it to her.[7]

Another of William Terrell and Susannah's children, one of our many-generations-ago great-aunts, Anne Terrell, is the link providing the Carter family with a distant kinship to President Obama.[8]

William and Susannah's son Joel Terrell was born in 1692 and married a woman named Elizabeth. Terrell family tradition says she was Elizabeth Oxford. Joel and Elizabeth Terrell are great-great-great-great-great-great-grandparents of Jimmy Carter. They lived in St. Paul's Parish through the name changes of the county and died there in the same place, which was then called Hanover County. Joel bought and sold land in the area and acted as a processioner there in 1747. Land deeds of the time are interesting to read and difficult to follow. Boundaries are typically described as something like "starting at the northwest corner of John Brown's patent, thence southeast 60 chains to a dogwood tree, thence south 800 yards past the pond to a white oak stump, thence westwardly 400 yards to a light colored oak stake, thence northwest to an outcropping of rock, thence...." Since the markers were of an ephemeral nature, every year or so the parish church would appoint someone who, along with the landowner, would "procession" around the boundaries of their land verifying landmarks and restoring them as necessary.

In 1724 Joel Terrell and Elizabeth had a daughter they named Hannah. Hannah Terrell married Israel Burnley from Goochland,[9] Virginia. They are our seven-generation ancestors.

The Burnleys: Revolutionaries, Friends, and the Battle of Guilford Courthouse

The first Burnley to reach the colonies was probably John Burnley. The register of Saint Peter's Parish shows there was a John Burnley living there in New Kent County, Virginia, before 1700. There is a tantalizing tale that he came to Virginia from England on a ship manned by French sailors who mutinied on the voyage but, unfortunately, I haven't been able to track this story down. John's wife was probably Phoebe Davis.[10]

In 1704, Saint Peter's Parish was divided and in 1720 the part that John Burnley and Phoebe (probably) Davis lived in also became part of Hanover County. John and Phoebe had several children, one of whom was our ancestor Israel Burnley, who served in the Revolutionary War. Israel Burnley married Hannah Terrell, Joel Terrell and Sarah Oxford's daughter, who lived nearby.[11] Israel, along with Hannah's two brothers, Major Henry Terrell and Captain Peter Terrell, moved to Bedford County, Virginia, to the area that became Campbell County. In 1783 or 1784 Israel and his brother-in-law Captain Peter Terrell and their families moved to Wilkes County, Georgia. At that time Wilkes County was a huge area, one of eight counties into which Georgia was originally divided. Israel bought 600 acres and was granted a land patent of 900 acres in September 1780. The land was on both sides of the Little Falling River and Israel built and operated a grist mill there.[12] He died in Wilkes County in 1790 and his wife, Hannah, died there about 1792. Israel Burnley named all of his living children in his will, which was proved in January 1791.

Israel and Hannah had several children. Their fourth child, Joel Terrell Burnley, was killed in the Revolutionary War in the trenches during the siege of Yorktown.[13] His name is inscribed on a plaque at the Victory Monument in Yorktown, Virginia, as one of the 106 Americans who died there.

Another of Israel Burnley and Hannah Terrell's sons and our ancestor, Henry Burnley, also served as in the Revolutionary War. He enlisted in 1776 as a private in Capt. Henry Terrell's company in the Fifth Virginia Continental Line. Israel served two years in the Fifth Virginia Line, fought at Williamsburg, Suffolk, Norfolk, and Springfield, and then joined General Washington at White Marsh. He then volunteered under Colonel Morgan, Colonel Butler, and Major Morris at the battle of Burgoyne. He fought at the Battle of Chestnut Hill and Guilford Courthouse. He was discharged at Valley Forge by Colonel Russell and Colonel Davis, having been commissioned an ensign in 1780 in Captain Lawson's company of volunteers and in 1782 having been promoted to lieutenant.[14]

Henry applied for a Revolutionary War pension in 1834 and two of his original commissions were attached to the application. The first, dated October 28, 1780, designated him as ensign. The commission bears the signature of Thomas Jefferson, governor of Virginia. The other commission, dated March 7, 1782, appointed him as lieutenant and was signed by Benjamin Harrison, governor.

The Burnleys, the Barksdales, the Davenports, and the Terrells all lived near each other in Virginia and obviously knew each other well. Israel Burnley had married Hannah Terrell and their daughter, Susannah Burnley, married John Barksdale, the son of Collier and Sarah Barksdale and brother of our ancestor Lucy. John and Susannah moved to Wilkes County, Georgia, near her parents in that part of Wilkes County that became Warren County in 1793. Unfortunately, both John Barksdale and Susannah Burnley died there in 1803 after having contracted malaria.[15]

Our ancestor Henry Burnley was a good friend of John (Jack) Smith Davenport, who had married Lucy Barksdale, the families having lived close to each other for almost 100 years. Henry Burnley and Jack Davenport served together in the Revolutionary War at the Battle of Guilford Courthouse, which took place on March 15, 1781. Family legend has it that in the early morning fog before the battle, Henry and Jack were nervously talking and Jack Davenport told Henry that he was afraid he was going to get killed in the battle and asked Henry to take care of his wife, Lucy. Of course, Henry reassured him that nothing was going to happen to him in the battle but he promised Jack that he would take care of Lucy if anything did happen. During the Battle of Guilford Courthouse, Jack Davenport was shot in the chest and seriously wounded. He died a few weeks later. Henry Burnley kept his promise. He married Lucy Barksdale Davenport on the 13th of July 1782.[16]

By 1782 when Lucy Barksdale married Henry Burnley, her family had already been in the colonies for over a hundred years.

The Barksdales: Early Virginians

Our ancestor William Barksdale arrived in Virginia along with 115 other immigrants who were transported by William Mosley and John Hull. When they actually arrived or what ship they came on is not known but Mosley and Hull applied for a land patent on February 20, 1662, with a claim for 5800 acres, having transported 116 persons with a bounty of 50 acres each. It is probably safe to assume that William arrived shortly before then, as land patent requests were usually filed fairly quickly. When the land patent was granted, Mosley and Hull were deeded 5798 acres, 2 rods, and 13 perches instead of 5800 acres.* It seems they lost out on about an acre and a half.

The William Barksdale who arrived with Mosley and Hull seems too old to fit in with other records and it was probably his son, also named William Barksdale, who is our provable ancestor and who married a Miss Collier. This William Barksdale's will was probated in 1773 and three of his sons participated in the administration of his will, one of whom was Colliar Barksdale.[17]

---

*For those unfamiliar with archaic measures of length, a rod was once defined as 11 cubits, a cubit being six palms, a palm being the width of four fingers. One cubit was generally the length between the tip of a man's thumb and his elbow, which is about 18 inches. Noah's ark was 300 cubits long, 50 cubits wide and 30 cubits deep, making it about 450 feet long, 75 feet wide and 45 deep, in case you've ever wondered. Measuring lengths by the widths of four fingers was highly variable and, as more precise measurements became necessary, a rod was defined as the length between the end of the plow and the nose of the oxen. This measurement soon became unacceptable. So, in the 15th century a rod was defined as the length of the left foot of 13 men. This too eventually became unsatisfactory and in the early 1600s, Edmund Gunter, the English astronomer and mathematician who invented the slide rule, officially defined a rod as 5.5 yards or 16 ½ feet and a pole and a perch and a rod were all defined to be the same length. However, local customs variously defined a perch as between 18 and 24 feet as late as 1820. Four poles equal one chain and 10 chains equal one furlong. An acre was one chain by 10 chains or one chain by one furlong.

Colliar Barksdale, a great-great-great-great-great-grandfather of Jimmy Carter, bought and sold land in the Tidewater area of Virginia and was a tobacco farmer. There are very few records of Colliar Barksdale still existing, so the exact date and place of his birth are unknown. He married Sarah, whose last name is not known but who might have been Sarah Reynolds. Their son Joseph fought in the Revolutionary War as did another son, John, who served as a second lieutenant in Captain William Harvey's Company of the Virginia militia. Colliar and Sarah also had several daughters, one of whom was our ancestor Lucy Barksdale, who is mentioned in Colliar's will.[18]

In 1786, Henry Burnley and Lucy Barksdale's daughter and our ancestor, Elizabeth Burnley, was born in Virginia, but the family would soon move to Georgia. There they would meet the Seale and Muse families.

The Muses and the Seales: An Illicit Relationship

John Muse (Mewes) was born in England in 1633. The exact date of his arrival in the colonies is unknown but he was in Virginia by 1668. John Muse had several children, among whom was a son, Thomas Muse. Around 1710, Thomas Muse had a son, our ancestor James Muse Sr., who married Sophia Pope,[19] the daughter of Humphrey Pope and Amey Veale. When Humphrey Pope died around 1734 he left his estate to his daughter Sophia in his will. Our ancestors James and Sofia were living there by 1735.

James was repeatedly sued by his creditors over his debts and in 1753 he and his wife Sophia moved to Bladen County, North Carolina. The part of Bladen County that they lived in was known as the Deep River region, which in 1754 the state of North Carolina formed into Cumberland County. The Muse family and the Seale family lived next to each other and were obviously close friends. Both William Seale Sr. and James Muse were justices in Cumberland County, and James Muse's daughter Lydia married William Seale's son Charles. In September of 1753, James Muse Sr. appeared in court in Cumberland County and transferred all of his property to his son James Jr. in an attempt to protect his assets from his creditors. Charles Seale was a witness to the transaction.

James Muse Sr. and Sofia Pope had a daughter, our ancestor, whom they named Sophia Pope Muse after her mother. An apparent illicit relationship between Sofia Pope Muse and William Seale Sr., the father-in-law of her brother, resulted in the birth of William Seale Muse. At that time in North Carolina, there was a requirement for bastardly bonds, bonds posted by the father to support the child in case he did not assume financial responsibility. However, in this case both families were prominent and wealthy and apparently friendly with each other and no such bond has ever been found. Sofia Pope Muse, the daughter, married a man named Runnels whose first name is unknown. When her father died in 1758, he left part of his estate to her and his illegitimate grandson: "I give to my daughter Sophia Pope Runnels one horse to be valued at five pounds to her and her heirs forever. Further it is my will and desire all the remainder of my estate unto two parts — One part to my daughter Annabarbary Muse and the other part to be divided between my daughter Sophia Pope Runnels and her son William Ceal [sic] Muse to them and their heirs forever."[20]

After the death of her husband, James Muse Sr., Sophia, the mother, sold their land in Cumberland County and she and some of her children moved to Craven County, South Carolina, and lived next to her daughter Lydia and son-in-law Charles Seale. At least two of her sons fought in the Revolutionary War. Our ancestor William Seale Muse fought for the Patriots; his brother James fought for the Loyalists.

A Tory Loyalist in the Family

At the beginning of the American Revolution, the Highlander Scots in North Carolina were the best friends that King George III had in the colonies. The land grants and the strong affinity with King George's family stretching back to the English Civil War and the fight against Cromwell made the Scots natural allies with the British Tories. A large number of the immigrants from Scotland came to North Carolina in 1775 after the land bounties were reestablished and they were greeted by Governor Martin, who at the time was exiled on a ship at the mouth of the Cape Fear River, he having been driven from the colony.

In January of 1776, Thomas Rutherford issued a call for all supporters of the king to rendezvous at Cross Creek on the Cape Fear River on February 12, 1776, and to prepare to restore Governor Martin to office. When few responded, Brigadier General Donald McDonald asked that all loyal subjects join his army. He promised that their families and property would be protected and that each man that joined him would be granted a 200-acre bounty. Great-uncle James Muse Jr. was an ardent Loyalist and the captain of a company of light horse under McDonald's command. He joined with about fifteen hundred Loyalists to begin the march to Cross Creek for the rendezvous. Colonel James Moore, commander of the Patriot troops, reached Rockfish Creek first and blocked McDonald's path downstream on the western bank of the Cape Fear River, forcing him to cross to the east bank at Campbellton. The Loyalists now would have to cross the river again at Moore's Creek Bridge 18 miles above Wilmington. The Patriot commanders Colonel Richard Caswell and Colonel Alexander Lillington reached Moore's Creek Bridge first and fortified their position. The crossing at Moore's Creek Bridge was located in a natural choke point, surrounded by a nearly impassable swamp, and was a terrible place for a battle. Adding to the Loyalists' misfortune, General McDonald became ill and command fell to Colonel Donald McLeod, who approved an assault on the bridge on the morning of February 27, 1776.

The battle was disastrous for the Highlanders. The Patriots had removed most of the planks from the bridge and had zeroed in their artillery. The battle lasted only a few minutes but the victory was decisive. The Patriots lost only one man, Private John Grady of Duplin County, who became the first soldier from North Carolina to be killed in the Revolutionary War, while the Highlanders lost 70 men. Eight hundred and fifty Highlander soldiers were captured along with 350 guns, 1500 rifles, 13 wagons, and a box containing £15,000, about a million dollars in today's money.[21] Colonel McLeod, who had led the charge, was dead with 20 bullets in his body. General McDonald was captured lying in his sickbed.

The results of the relatively small skirmish were widespread. The attack and subsequent victory inflamed and bolstered the revolutionary spirit building in the colony and greatly dampened the willingness of the Loyalists in North Carolina to declare themselves. Lord Cornwallis, waiting with his fleet at the mouth of the Cape Fear River for troops who never arrived, abandoned his plan to attack North Carolina and withdrew to regroup and launch an ineffective attack on Charles Town instead. The newspapers in New England wrote glowing stories with huge headlines and the battle was credited with causing the North Carolina Provincial Congress to pass the Halifax Resolves on April 12, 1776, authorizing the provincial delegates at the Continental Congress in Philadelphia to vote for independence from Britain, making North Carolina the first colony to make such a declaration.[22]

Among the Tory officers captured at the Battle of Moore's Creek Bridge was Captain James Muse Jr. Captain Muse managed to escape while being taken as a prisoner to Philadelphia and returned to his home in North Carolina. Upon hearing of his return, the committee of safety in North Carolina sought to arrest him but he apparently fled to London where he lived for many years. The committee confiscated his plantation for his part in the Battle at Moore's Creek Bridge and it was not until after he died that his wife, Charity, was able to get part of the land returned.

The Seals: A Muse No More, the Yazoo Land Fraud

There is much less information available regarding the Revolutionary War history of Captain James Muse's brother and our ancestor William, who fought for the Patriots. He is listed in the records of Hancock County as one of their Revolutionary War veterans and he was awarded land, but little else is known.

In August of 1785, William Seale Muse and his wife Judith Muse were awarded a land patent of 250 acres in Wilkes County, Georgia, for his service in the Revolutionary War. In November of 1785, William Seale Muse bought an additional 250 acres on Long Creek in Wilkes County from Nathan Bostick. Sometime shortly thereafter he and his wife dropped the name Muse and in August of 1786 they sold the Long Creek land under the name of William Seals and Judith Seals.[23] In the 1827 Georgia land lottery, in which Revolutionary War veterans were allotted two draws, Williams Seals was awarded additional land in Muscogee County, Georgia, and Henry Burnley was awarded land in Carroll County.

The Seals and the Burnleys bought and sold land in Wilkes and Hancock counties, some in Columbia County and elsewhere in the general area. I was going to trace some deeds to see if I could determine where they probably met, which they did, because their children Spencer Seals and Elizabeth Burnley married each other. However, I soon discovered that Wilkes County became Elbert, Lincoln, Oglethorpe and parts of Madison, Taliaferro, Warren, Hart, McDuffie, and Green counties. Columbia was divided into parts of McDuffie and Warren County. Madison county was formed from portions of Clarke, Elbert, Franklin, Jackson, and Oglethorpe counties. Greene County was formed from Wilkes County and parts of Washington County. Taliaferro County was formed by taking portions of five other counties: Wilkes, Greene, Hancock, Oglethorpe, and Warren. Hart County was formed from territory that formerly was Elbert and Franklin counties. Franklin at one time included all of Barrow and Jackson counties, significant portions of Oconee, Clarke, Madison, Banks, Hart, Stephens counties and parts of Gwinnett, Hall, and Habersham counties. I didn't trace the land deeds. Spencer Seals met Elizabeth Burnley after their families had been awarded land grants and moved to Georgia shortly after the Revolutionary War. They were married November 25, 1805.[24]

Spencer Seals also drew land in the Georgia Land Lottery of 1805. To enter the lottery people paid a small fee, generating just enough money to cover the costs of the lottery itself. Land lots were surveyed and tickets were placed in a barrel with the lot number printed on them. Huge numbers of people entered the lotteries and all were oversubscribed, so blank tickets were added to compensate. Names were placed in another barrel and a ticket was drawn from each barrel. People either drew a land ticket and became a "Fortunate Draw" or they drew a blank ticket and did not receive land.

The lottery system itself came about as a reaction to one of the most famous scandals in the state's history, the Yazoo Land Fraud, which began when a secret society formed in 1785, called the "Combined Society," whose members' purpose was to use their influence to get the Georgia legislature to grant them huge parcels of land, specifically during the creation of Bourbon County, which is now the area around Natchez, Mississippi, but which then was part of Georgia.

The deal collapsed with the repeal of the Bourbon County Act but the Combined Society stayed together and in 1789 they formed three companies, the South Carolina Yazoo Company, Tennessee Company, and the Virginia Yazoo Company headed by Patrick Henry, governor of Virginia. They convinced the Georgia assembly to sell 20,000,000 acres of land to the Yazoo companies for $207,000. Governor Telfair signed the law selling the land in December of 1789, but that deal fell through when the Yazoo companies tried to swindle the state by paying in old and worthless currencies.

In 1794, four new Yazoo companies, the Georgia Company, the Georgia-Mississippi Company, the Upper Mississippi Company, and the Tennessee Company, were formed by some of the most powerful people in the country, including James Wilson of Pennsylvania, signer of the Declaration of Independence and at the time a justice of the U.S. Supreme Court; Congressman and Revolutionary War hero General Wade Hampton of South Carolina; Matthew McAllister, the first U.S. district attorney for Georgia; Governor George Matthews; and Georgia senator James Gunn. Senator Gunn was in charge of bribing officials and arranged the distribution of money and land to legislators, state officials, and newspaper editors.

The Georgia legislature sold them 35,000,000 acres for $500,000, a huge area encompassing most of present-day Alabama and Mississippi.[25] Governor Matthews signed the enacting legislation on January 7, 1795. Even before the bill authorizing the sale was passed, a mob protesting the corruption tried to lynch several members of the legislature. Afterwards, the protests mounted to a fevered pitch and U.S. senator James Jackson resigned his seat in Congress and returned home to Georgia vowing to have the legislation rescinded even if he had to shoot everybody involved with its passage.

In the following election, almost everyone involved in the scandal was swept from office. Legislation rescinding the sale was passed and the new governor, Jared Irwin, signed it into law in February of 1796. A ceremony was held and the original bill and all the copies, as well as all of the records of the land sales, were burned on the lawn of the state capitol. Money collected from the sale of the land was returned but a few people refused to accept the refunds and claimed the land. Lawsuits were filed that which went on for years. Georgia ceded all of its territory west of its present border to the United States in 1802 for $1,250,000, including all of the Yazoo land and the accompanying legal disputes. The dispute was eventually settled by the U.S. Supreme Court in the case of *Fletcher vs. Peck*, which upheld the contract and ruled for the remaining landowners. It was the very first case tried before the Supreme Court to be based on the Contract Clause[26] of the new United States Constitution, and the rescinding legislation was the first state law to be declared unconstitutional. The reformers, though, were much admired. Irwin County was named for Governor Irwin and Jackson County was named for Senator Jackson.

After the Yazoo land scandal, Georgia implemented the lottery system which was thought to be less susceptible to corruption. Almost three-quarters of the land in the state was distributed to male residents over 21 years old, orphans, and widows in seven different land lotteries held between 1805 and 1832, giving away the land taken from the Creek and Cherokee Indians. The lotteries limited political favoritism to land along the major rivers and lakes in the state, areas which were exempted from the lotteries.

Spencer Seals, a "Fortunate Draw" and the son of William and Judith Seals, married Elizabeth Burnley, the daughter of Henry Burnley and Lucy Davenport, on November 25, 1805. Our ancestor William Archibald Seals was born to them in 1814. William built and operated a large flour mill on Rock Comfort Creek in Warren County and lived there until he died in 1863. He married Eliza Harris February 9, 1834.[27] Eliza was the daughter of

Nathan Harris, who was probably born in Halifax County, North Carolina, around 1778. Nathan married Rhoda Champion June 1, 1805, in Warren County.[28] There are no other records for Rhoda Champion but she may have been the daughter of John Champion.

In 1838, William Archibald Seals and Eliza Harris' daughter, Mary Ann Diligent Seals, was born, the great-grandmother of Jimmy Carter.

Littleberry Walker Carter and Mary Ann Diligent Seals

Wiley Carter and Ann Ansley's fifth child was our ancestor Littleberry Walker Carter, born in 1829. Littleberry married Mary Ann Diligent Seals on January 3, 1851,[29] and they had four children. Jeremiah Calvin Carter was born April 4, 1855, in Warren County and died June 7, 1925, in Sumter County. Eliza Ann Carter was born on December 31, 1856, in Warren County and died September 25, 1891, in Americus, Georgia. William Archibald Carter was born November 12, 1858, in Sumter County, Georgia, and died September 4, 1903, in Cuthbert, Georgia. Nanny Isabel Carter was born in 1866 in Sumter County, Georgia.

In November of 1873, Littleberry Walker Carter and D.P. McCann got into an argument over the ownership of a "flying jenny," a small merry-go-round. The local newspaper, the *Weekly Sumter Republican*, reported on the altercation, which had turned to violence, in its November 21, 1873, edition:

> On Saturday afternoon last there was a difficulty in this place between two citizens, one living in the city and the other in the country. The country gentleman was severely cut in the head and in the side of his neck. We learned that he is doing as well as could be expected, and as the matter will undergo judicial investigation, will forebear making any comments.[30]

A week later in two articles, the newspaper reported about the death of Littleberry and a murder indictment against McCann:

> We have just learned (9 o'clock PM) of the death of Mr. Walker Carter, from injuries received some eight days ago at the hands of Mr. D.P. McCann.
> Sumter Superior Court.... True bills were found by the Grand Jury against ... State vs. D.P. McCann, murder.[31]

On December 5, 1873, the newspaper reported on the end of the family tragedy:

> In our issue of Thursday last, we published the death of Mr. Walker Carter caused from wounds inflicted on his person by D.P. McCann. This morning it is our sad duty to record the death of his very excellent wife which took place at her residence Thursday night, but a few hours after the remains of her beloved husband were confined to mother earth. Mrs. Carter was a most estimable Christian lady, and her sudden death was caused from grief. Her tender heart could not withstand the shock of the death of him she so tenderly loved. May he who doeth all tidings for his own glory, send comfort to the hearts of those who have so recently been deprived of their earthly parents.[32]

Littleberry Walker Carter and Mary Ann Diligent Seals' third child, and Jimmy Carter's grandfather, William Archibald Carter, was born November 12, 1858. On September 8, 1885, William Archibald Carter married Nina Pratt, the daughter of Civil War captain James Pratt. The Pratts lived in Abbeville, South Carolina, and their known ancestors were almost all from Scotland and Ireland.

Chapter 4

ANCESTORS OF CAPTAIN JAMES PRATT

Joseph Pratt and his brothers were some of the earliest settlers in Abbeville County, South Carolina, although records are sparse. Joseph is listed on the 1800 South Carolina census as living in Abbeville. In his will, proved in 1824, Joseph bequeathed property to his wife Elizabeth, his daughters Emma, Nancy, and Sarah, and to his sons — our ancestor William, Thomas, and Joseph (see Appendix G: Wills). Correspondence from a member of the Pratt family, with no supporting documentation, says Joseph Pratt of Abbeville was the son of a William Pratt of Orange County, Virginia, who in turn was the son of Griffin Pratt, who was born in 1635 and who emigrated from England in 1666.

William Pratt's daughter Sarah, who was 94 years old when the 1850 census took place, listed her place of birth as South Carolina so it is not unreasonable to assume that Joseph, William, and the Pratt families were in the state by the mid–1750s. In the 1750s there were other Pratts in Virginia but there is no known connection between those families and William Pratt of Abbeville. The first documentation of William Pratt is an award of a land grant for 100 acres in Craven County, South Carolina, in July of 1766.

Our ancestors William Pratt and his father, Joseph, built and operated a grist mill on a branch of the little Hogskin Creek a few miles north of the town of Abbeville. Pratt's Mill was burned by Colonel "Bloody" Bill Cunningham during the Revolutionary War.

In 1822, the South Carolina legislature commissioned Robert Mills to create an atlas to be used for the next census. The atlas was published in 1825 and the map of Abbeville County shows Pratt's grist mill and the places where several of William Pratt's neighbors lived, including the Clinkscales, the Lindseys, the Seawrights, and the Cowans. All of these families had members who were our ancestors. Since the original Pratt's Mill had been destroyed in the Revolutionary War, there is some question as to whether this is the exact location of the original mill, but it's probably pretty close.

William Pratt served as a private in the Revolutionary War in the South Carolina militia under the command of Captain John Norwood. Captain Norwood's log shows that William Pratt supplied his company with hogs and corn and that after the battle of Pratt's Mill on October 3, 1781, William Pratt put in a requisition for compensation for his horse lost in the battle. William, James, and John Pratt all put in claims for service rendered during the Revolutionary War.[1]

William married Mary Drennan and they had several children, one of whom is our ancestor James Pratt, who was born on March 11, 1788. James Pratt married Sarah Lindsay, a daughter of Robert Lindsay, who lived only a few miles from him. James bought and sold land in the area and in 1824 he bought 550 acres on the Big and Little Hogskin creeks and

Little River in Abbeville District. When James died in 1828, he left his plantation to his wife and his three sons, William, Robert, and our ancestor John.

John Pratt, a great-great-grandfather of Jimmy Carter, was born in 1810 in Abbeville County and married Mary Kay. The Kays had been in the colonies since at least the mid-1700s and had lived in Virginia and Maryland before moving to Abbeville.

The Kays

The first provable records of our ancestor Robert Kay in the colonies are when he purchased land between the Occoquan River and Bull Run in 1747 in Virginia. Robert and his son James bought and sold land in Virginia until 1794, when Robert bought a parcel of land on Broadmouth Creek and moved to the area that would become Pendleton County, South Carolina, north of Abbeville County.

Robert's wife, and therefore a possible maternal ancestor of the Carter line, is almost certainly, but not provably, Elizabeth Strother.[2] Elizabeth Strother was the daughter of Robert Strother, who in turn was the son of William Strother II, who was born in England in 1630 and emigrated to Virginia. William Strother II married Dorothy Savage about 1651 and they bought land and settled near Richmond, Virginia, on a plantation which adjoined that of Augustine Washington. Another of William and Dorothy's sons, William Strother III, inherited the land, and after he died in 1726 his plantation was bought by Augustine Washington and became the birthplace of George Washington.[3]

The Strothers' lineage has been well researched by the Strother family, written about in many well documented books and publications and the line has been traced back hundreds of years to ancestral England. If the Robert Kay and Elizabeth Strother marriage can be proven, it would also provide a link between the Carter family and President Zachary Taylor, who is the great-great-great-grandson of William and Dorothy Strother.

Robert Kay and his wife Elizabeth had several children, among whom was our ancestor James Kay who married Grace Elgin. On June 30, 1787, James and Grace Kay had a son, James Kay Jr., who would become a famous and influential preacher. The Rev. James Kay Jr. married Elizabeth Ann Clinkscales on August 27, 1806. Elizabeth Ann Clinkscales was the daughter of Francis Clinkscales and Mary Carpenter and the sister of Francis B. Clinkscales, who is also an ancestor.

In August of 1794, James Kay had surveyed a plot of 258 acres on a branch of the Hogskin and Corner creeks in Abbeville County, South Carolina.[4] The last record of James Kay and Grace Elgin is in the 1820 census where they are listed as being over 45 years old.

Our ancestors Rev. James Kay Jr. and Elizabeth Ann Clinkscales' daughter, Mary Kay, was born November 30, 1809.[5] Mary Kay married John Pratt, the son of James Pratt and Sarah Lindsay. Mary Kay and John Pratt's son, James Pratt, was born December 11, 1830. In 1854, James Pratt married Sophronia Cowan.

Captain James Pratt and Sophronia Cowan

After South Carolina seceded from the Union in December of 1860, the state authorized the formation of a regiment of infantry for six months. Col. Maxie Gregg, a lawyer from Columbia, was appointed commander of the regiment, the First South Carolina Volunteers.

Their first action was April 12, 1861, when parts of the regiment came under artillery fire during the attack on Fort Sumter. The following month, the regiment was transferred to the Confederate army and was sent to Virginia where it stayed until June when it was disbanded, its commission having expired. Col. Gregg and Col. Hamilton were asked to reorganize and form a new regiment under the same name. The new First South Carolina Volunteers was subsequently sent to Virginia as part of the brigade of Gen. Joseph R. Anderson under the command of Col. Hamilton.

In the early spring of 1861, James L. Orr was authorized by the Confederate government to raise a regiment of ten companies. Jimmy Carter's great-grandfather, Captain James Pratt, joined Orr's Rifles when it was formed, mustering in on July 20, 1861.[6] Colonel Orr resigned after he was elected to the Confederate senate in December 1861 and command of Orr's Rifles was given to Col. J. Foster Marshall. In April of 1862, the regiment was ordered to Virginia and was assigned to J.R. Anderson's Brigade.

The Twelfth, Thirteenth, and Fourteenth South Carolina Volunteer Infantry regiments were formed during the summer and were placed under the command of Col. Gregg after he had been appointed brigadier general in the Provisional Army of the Confederate States in December of 1861. Gregg's Brigade was assigned to Gen. Ambrose Powell Hill's division and was ordered to Richmond, Virginia, where they camped on the Chickahominy River about seven miles from Richmond. In June of 1862, the First South Carolina Volunteers and Orr's Rifles, also camped near the Chickahominy River, were assigned to Gregg's Brigade. These five regiments served together for the rest of the war and fought at the Seven Days' Battles, second Bull Run, Chantilly, Antietam, Shepherdstown Ford, Castleman's Ferry, Fredericksburg, Chancellorsville, Gettysburg, Falling Waters, the Bristoe Campaign, Mine Run, the Wilderness, Spotsylvania Court House, North Anna, Cold Harbor, the Siege of Petersburg, First Squirrel Level Road, Jones Farm, First Pegram's Farm, and Five Forks. Finally, they surrendered at Appomattox Court House.

Captain Pratt served with Orr's Rifles until he was seriously injured at the battle at Jones Farm on September 30, 1864, with a gunshot wound to his left arm.[7] He applied for wounded retirement and the application was approved by the Medical Examining Board.[8] Admitted into Jackson Hospital in Richmond, Virginia, for treatment on October 1, 1864, Captain Pratt was furloughed out of the army on October 21, 1864.[9]

In 1854, James Pratt had married Sophronia Cowan. By the time Sophronia was born in 1835, her ancestors had been in America for more than a century and a half.

Chapter 5

Ancestors of Sophronia Cowan

Jimmy Carter's paternal grandmother was Nina Pratt, the daughter of Captain James Pratt and Sophronia Cowan. A lot of Captain James Pratt's ancestry has been lost and it has been impossible to trace any of his ancestors beyond their arrival in the colonies, although one line, the Kays, can be probably traced back to Virginia in 1662, which is a respectable length of time ago. Sophronia Cowan's line is quite different and many of them can be traced to the immigrant ancestors. They were from Scotland and Ireland.

Sophronia Cowan's great-great-great-grandfather Andrew Seawright was from Londonderry, Ireland, and his wife Mary Eleanor Dickson was from Donegal. Their son James Seawright married Elizabeth McCullough, who was from Londonderry. Sophronia's great-grandparents, Andrew Cowan and his wife Ann, came from County Down. Her great-grandfather James Brownlee and his son George came from County Attrim and had sailed from Belfast. Her great-great-great-grandparents Andrew Clinkscales and Mary Preston were from Glasgow, Scotland. All of them were Presbyterians, driven from their homelands by King Charles II.

Ireland and Charles II

After the end of the English Civil War, Cromwell's soldiers confiscated much of the land in Ireland and settled there. Ireland at the time had two main industries; by far the largest was the export of cattle to England. After Cromwell's death and the restoration of Charles II, the English landowners renewed their strenuous objections to the competition from Ireland. Several laws were passed by the sympathetic English monarch, and in 1680 a law was passed implementing an absolute prohibition against the importation into England of Irish cattle, sheep, swine, bacon, beef, mutton, butter, and cheese.

Though a much smaller industry, trade with the new colonies boosted the Irish economy and helped support its fleet. Having an advantageous geographic position close to the colonies and very good ports, Ireland had profited from the English Navigation Acts, which prohibited trade with the colonies except on English ships. In the original Navigation Act of 1660, Irish vessels had been given all the privileges of English vessels. However, in 1696 the act was amended, banning the importation of any goods directly from the colonies to Ireland. Together, these two laws banning Irish farm exports and banning imports from the colonies had a devastating effect on the Irish economy.

With the ban on exporting sheep and mutton in place, Irish farmers turned to the production of wool and clothing. Soon thousands of Irish workers were engaged in the industry, prompting the English manufacturers to object and to petition for the destruction of the industry in Ireland. The House of Lords petitioned the King that "the growing manufacture of cloth in Ireland, both by the cheapness of all sorts of necessities of life, and the goodness of materials for making all manner of cloth, doth invite your subjects of England, with their families and servants, to leave their habitation to settle there, for the increase of the wool manufacturer in Ireland, which makes your loyal subjects in this Kingdome very apprehensive that the future growth of it may greatly prejudice the said manufacture here."[1] The House of Commons joined in urging King William to use "utmost diligence to hinder the exportation of wool from Ireland, except to be imported hither, and for the discouraging the wool manufactures."

A tax was imposed on the exportation of wool clothes and flannels and Ireland was prohibited from the exportation of any wool or any woolen manufactured products to any other country except England. Further, Ireland was also restricted to exporting to only six ports in England and from only six towns in Ireland. The English merchants were still not satisfied, and in 1699 the British Parliament passed an act prohibiting the export of wool or wool products from Ireland to any other country whatsoever. The ruin of the industry was absolute. Unemployment was rampant and those not the beneficiaries of the primogeniture laws (the right of the eldest son to inherit all the property of his father) had almost no prospect of accumulating wealth and property.

The final blow came with an amendment of the Test Act, which had been passed under Charles II and which required an oath of allegiance and supremacy as a condition of acquiring property in towns. Papist families were forbidden to settle in towns and it was ordered that all crosses, pictures, inscriptions, and objects of public devotion not of the Church of England should be destroyed by the magistrates. The Church of England, then in control of the government, amended the act so that no person who acted as a Protestant outside the rites of the "Established Church" could inherit land. If a Protestant landholder died and the heir was a Catholic then the Catholic heir would be skipped and the land would pass to the next of kin who was Protestant, except if the Protestant was a Presbyterian, in which case he too was to be passed over. The taking of Communion according to the rites of the Anglican Church was made a condition of holding any office. Presbyterians, Independents, Huguenots, and Quakers were not protected. The Bishops then launched an attack on the Presbyterian ministers, whom they considered unsanctified and with whom they had a bitter history, the Presbyterians refusing to acknowledge the authority of the Church of England or Catholic or Anglican bishops, declaring that the office had no foundation in the scriptures. In Belfast, it was announced that all children of Protestants not married in a proper Church should be treated as bastards, and prosecutions were brought against people accused of being fornicators for cohabiting with their wives.[2]

At the same time in the colonies, bounties were being offered for immigrants. Land was being offered for free along with a year's supply of food and provisions for any Protestant family willing to move there and cultivate the land. Representatives of the colonial governments and private ventures circulated throughout Ireland with advertisements and glowing descriptions of the New World. A huge migration began from Ireland to the colonies that reached such proportions some members of the Irish government expressed alarm that the countryside was being depopulated. By 1790, 26 percent of the white populations of Georgia and South Carolina were from Ireland.[3] The overwhelming majority of them were Presbyterians, as were all of Sophronia Cowan's Irish and Scottish ancestors.

Immigrations at Charlestown, Boonesborough, and the South Carolina Wilderness

An entry in the *South Carolina Council Journal* references the ship that our Seawright and Brownlee ancestors' families sailed on to the colony as having arrived in port in Charles Town:

> His Excellency the Governor acquainted the Board that a vessel was arrived in the Port of Charles Town with about 70 persons from Ireland who were come into this Province on encouragement of Bounty given by an Act of Assembly passed the 25th day of July 1761. That in order that no time might be lost in settling those persons in either of the two new townships lately laid out for Foreign Protestants he had ordered those people to attend with their petitions. His Honor the Lieutenant Governor thereupon observed that in order to distinguish those townships from the others in the Province names should be given them and proposed that the one at Long Cane should be called Boonesborough and the other Belfast. The Council agreed in opinion with his Honor and it was Ordered accordingly.

Our ancestors and relatives were given land in Boonesborough.

Upon arrival, the families were processed into the colony quickly. Each family wrote a petition declaring that they were immigrants and desired to move to the colony and listed their family members. Papers were required certifying that they were Protestants. The petitions were presented to the council, sometimes within a day of their arrival, and upon approval of petitions, which in most cases happened during the same council meeting, land was allocated and a small amount of money was given to the new colonists for them to buy supplies. Very soon they were on their way to their new homesteads. From the comforts of the 21st century it is hard to imagine what our ancestors endured and the hardships they overcame. The following is excerpted from a book written by Robert Witherspoon in the late 1700s describing his experience as a child sailing from Ireland to South Carolina and making the identical journey as our ancestors:

> We went on shipboard the 14th of September, and lay wind-bound in the Lough at Belfast 14 days. The second day of our sail my grandmother died, and was interred in the raging ocean, which was an afflictive sight to her offspring. We were sorely tossed at sea with storms, which caused our ship to spring a leak: our pumps were kept incessantly at work day and night; for many days our mariners seemed many times at their wits' end. But it pleased God to bring us all safe to land, which was about the first of December.
>
> We landed in Charleston three weeks before Christmas. We found the inhabitants very kind. We staid in town until after Christmas, and were put on board of an open boat, with tools and a year's provisions and one still-mill. They allowed each hand upwards of sixteen, one axe, one broad hoe, and one narrow hoe. Our provisions were Indian corn, rice, wheaten flour, beef, pork, rum, and salt. We were much distressed in this part of our passage. As it was the dead of winter, we were exposed to the inclemency of the weather day and night; and (which added to the grief of all pious persons on board) the atheistical and blasphemous mouths of our Patrons and the other hand ... our men came up in order to get dirt houses to take their families to. They brought some few horses with them. What help they could get from the few inhabitants in order to carry the children and other necessaries up they availed themselves of. As woods were full of water, and most severe frosts, it was very severe on women and children.... My father had brought on shipboard four children, viz.: David, Robert, John, and Sarah. Sarah died in Charleston, and was the first buried at the Scotch Meeting House graveyard. When we came to the Bluff, my mother and we children were still in expectation that we were coming to an agreeable place. But when we arrived and saw nothing but a wilderness, and instead of a fine timbered house, nothing but a mean dirt house, our spirits quite sank....

My father gave us all the comfort he could by telling us we would get all those trees cut down, and in a short time there would be plenty of inhabitants, so that we could see from house to house. While we were at this, our fire we brought from Bog Swamp went out. Father had heard, that up the river-swamp was [another settler] although there was no path, neither did he know the distance.... We watched him as far as the trees would let us see, and returned to our dolorous hut, expecting never to see him or any human person more. But after some time he returned and brought fire. We were soon comforted, but evening coming on, the wolves began to howl on all sides. We then feared being devoured by wild beasts, having neither gun nor dog nor any door to our house. Howbeit we set to and gathered fuel, and made on a good fire, and so passed the first night. The next day being a clear warm morning, we began to stir about, but about mid-day there rose a cloud southwest attended with a high wind, thunder and lightning. The rain quickly penetrated through between the poles and brought down the sand that covered them over, which seemed to threaten to bury us alive. The lightning and claps were very awful and lasted a good space of time. I do not remember to have seen a much severer gust than that was. I believe we all sincerely wished ourselves again at Belfast. But this fright was soon over and the evening cleared up, comfortable and warm....

People were much oppressed in bringing their things, as there was no house there. They were obliged to toil hard, and had no other way but to convey their beds, clothing, chests, provisions, tools, pots, etc., on their backs. And at that time there were few or no roads and every family had to travel the best way they could, which was here double distance to some, for they had to follow swamps and branches for their guides for some time.... Another source of alarm was the Indians. When they came to hunt in the spring, they were in great numbers in all places like the Egyptian locusts, but they were not hurtful. We had a great deal of trouble and hardships in our first settling, but the few inhabitants continued still in health and strength. Yet we were oppressed with fears, on divers accounts, especially of being massacred by the Indians, or bitten by snakes, or torn by wild beasts, or being lost and perishing in the woods. Of this last calamity there were three instances.[4]

The Boonesborough Historical Society Website lists several of our ancestors, including George Brownlee, Andrew Cowan, Andrew Seawright, James Seawright, and several family members, as Boonesborough Township Original Settlers.[5]

Not all of Sophronia Cowan's ancestors were Irish. The Clinkscales family emigrated from Scotland to Maryland and were living in Port Tobacco by 1791.

The Clinkscaleses from Scotland, Probably Not That Ann Buchner

Our ancestor Adam Clinkscales was born in Glasgow, Scotland, in 1700.[6] The exact date he arrived or how he got to the colony is unknown. The first record that appears of him in the colonies is his giving testimony in probate court during the hearing of the will of John Barron[7] on August 19, 1719, in Port Tobacco, Charles County, Maryland. Tobacco at the time was the basis for Maryland's economy and it was used as currency. Goods were bought with tobacco and fines, church tithes, and even taxes were assessed and paid in pounds of tobacco. At the beginning of the eighteenth century, Port Tobacco was a very important trade and naval town, included on the earliest colonial maps and growing to be the second largest city in Maryland before the river changed course and the port became unnavigable. Adam most likely emigrated there because of the lure of the booming economy and availability of jobs, a huge difference compared to Glasgow.

Adam Clinkscales' wife was Mary Preston or Prenton. Adam and Mary had a son, Adam Clinkscales Jr., who was born around 1720 or 1721. He married a woman named

Ann, whose last name is speculative but she is claimed to be Ann Bucher (Buchner), the daughter of Hans Martin Bucher. Hans emigrated from Bern, Switzerland, on the ship *Billender Oliver*, Samuel Merchant master, and landed in Philadelphia on August 26, 1735. The Buchers were probably Lutherans fleeing the religious persecution in the Palatine region. Beginning with the *William and Sarah*, forty-three vessels bringing immigrants from the area are recorded in the ten years before and including the year 1736. The immigrant passengers in these ships numbered about 8,000 over those 10 years. Forty-one of these ships were described as bringing "Palatines," one "Palatines and Switzers." One other, Samuel Merchant's *Billender Oliver*, brought forty-five "Switzers, late inhabitants of the Canton of Berne, in Switzerland, now from South Carolina." Nearly all the ships sailed first from Rotterdam, but as it was necessary to clear from an English port for the colonies, they were "last from" Dover, Falmouth, Deal, Plymouth. Bristol, or Cowes.[8] The peak immigration of Palatine refugees was in 1752, about which more is written later.

Other documents refer to an Ann Buchner of unknown parentage from Scotland, also without any primary source or documentation, but this seems much more likely. It is highly speculative in any event since Ann Buchner has not been proven to be the Ann who married Adam Clinkscales. But leading credence to the theory is that Adam and Ann Clinkscales' grandson was named Francis Bucher Clinkscales, a very close spelling in an era when names were spelled in a variety of ways.

Adam Clinkscales and Ann had several children. Their son William Clinkscales was born somewhere around 1752 and joined the Maryland Militia as a private in 1777, serving in the 26th Battalion in Captain Hezekiah Garner's Company. He is listed in the Maryland State Archives as having served in the Revolutionary War in the Continental Troops from Charles County, Maryland, in 1781.[9]

Another of Adam and Ann's sons and our ancestor, Francis Clinkscales Sr., was born around 1739 and married Mary Carpenter. Francis Clinkscales was also a Revolutionary War soldier, he served with his brother William in the 26th Battalion of the Maryland Militia under Captain Garner. His Revolutionary War service is commemorated by a memorial marker placed in an Anderson County cemetery upon which the following is inscribed:

> Revolutionary War Soldier and Patriot Francis Clinkscales SGT-26th Batt., Charles Co. Militia, MD under Captain Hezekiah Garner signed Oath Of Allegiance, Charles Co., MD. Born Circa 1739 in Charles Co., MD Died on January 12, 1838 in Anderson Co., SC Buried in this cemetery, actual burial site unknown Marker placed by Major John Bowie Chapter, DAR. May 14, 2005

Neither William nor Francis Clinkscales applied for a pension for their Revolutionary War service, which is unfortunate because in the pension applications the veterans describe where they served and the battles they were engaged in. However, Edward Miles did apply for a pension and in his application he described how the 26th Battalion, along with he and his companions William and Andrew Clinkscales, who could vouch for his service, were attached to the 4th Regiment under Major Roxbury and ordered to Yorktown where they were placed under the command of General Lafayette and took part in the Siege of Yorktown.[10] After the war in 1789, Francis Clinkscales Sr. moved to Abbeville, South Carolina, and resumed his trade as a tailor. In 1792 he moved to Anderson County[11] and died there in 1838. Francis named all of his children in his will, which was written a few years before his death.[12]

Francis Clinkscales Sr. and Mary Carpenter's children Francis Bucher Clinkscales and Elizabeth Ann Clinkscales were born in Maryland shortly before the family moved to Abbeville, South Carolina. Francis B. Clinkscales was born on October 13, 1786, and Elizabeth Ann Clinkscales was born June 4, 1788. Both Francis and Elizabeth Ann are our ancestors. After the move to Abbeville, South Carolina, Elizabeth Ann Clinkscales met and married Rev. James Kay and they were grandparents of Captain James Pratt. Also in Abbeville, Francis B. Clinkscales met and married Eleanor "Ally" Brownlee, the daughter of George Brownlee and Sarah Caldwell. The Brownlees emigrated from Belfast, Ireland, in 1768.

The Brownlees: More Irish Ancestors Who Marry Irish Ancestors

Our seven-generation ancestor James Brownlee and his children, along with his brother John Brownlee, John's wife, Alice, and their children, are all listed on the passenger roll of the *Brig Lord Dungannon*, Robert Montgomery master, which came to Charlestown, South Carolina, from Belfast, Ireland, in 1768, carrying 154 passengers.[13] James' wife was Jean Webb, who died in Ireland before they left. An ad published in a Belfast newspaper, alerting the passengers scheduled on the voyage that the Brownlees were on, announced that the sailing date was imminent:

> The Passengers who have engaged go to Charlestown by the Brig LORD DUNGANNON, are desired to take Notice, that she will be clear to sail against the Time appointed, or at [ ] as Monday the 11th latest. She wants about thirty of her Complement, but they will not detain her a Day after she be clear, and those who offer [first?] will be preferred. With respect to such as shall not appear to fill their Engagements by the 11th [ ] at [ ], the Owners will not look upon themselves as why longer [ ]. October 5, 1767.[14]

James Brownlee's son and our ancestor, George Brownlee, was born February 17, 1756, and was listed as being 11 years old on the *Brig Lord Dungannon's* manifest. The family was awarded land and lived in the Boonesborough Township in the area that would eventually become Dew West, South Carolina.[15] In fact, many of the Brownlee family still live in that area today.

George Brownlee served in the Revolutionary War as a private in the South Carolina militia and his grave marker at the Greenville Presbyterian Church cemetery commemorates his service as such. In 1786 or 1787, after his war service, George Brownlee married Sarah Caldwell in Abbeville[16] and he and his family lived in Abbeville and Newbury County until they died.

George and Sarah had eight children.[17] Their daughter and our ancestor, Eleanor "Ally" Brownlee, was born in 1791 and married Francis Bucher Clinkscales around 1809 in Abbeville. Francis B. Clinkscales was the son of Francis Clinkscales Sr. and Mary Carpenter, and Francis B. is a link in the double Clinkscales ancestry. His granddaughter, Sophronia Cowan, would eventually marry his sister's grandson, Colonel James Pratt, and they would become Nina Pratt's parents.

Francis B. Clinkscales and Eleanor Brownlee's daughter Sarah Brownlee Clinkscales was born November 9, 1811. Sarah married John Cowan the son of another family which had emigrated from Ireland. John's grandparents had moved to Abbeville in the early 1700s and the Cowan family had known and lived near the Seawrights for decades. The families had fought in the Revolutionary War together and several of their children had married each other.

The Seawrights: The Battle at Pratt's Mill, Bloody Bill Cunningham, the Cloud's Creek Massacre

The Seawrights also came to South Carolina from Ireland as a result of the act passed by the general assembly of the colony of South Carolina on July 25, 1761, extending the Bounty Act. The copy of the original act has been significantly damaged and what we know about it comes from the act that was passed repealing it. The Bounty Act was passed for the benefit of religious refugees fleeing from persecution and applicants were required to have certificates showing they were Protestants. The act also benefited the colony by attracting settlers who could be given land where the colonial government wanted them and thus provide a buffer between Charles Town and the sometimes hostile Indians.

Our ancestor Andrew Seawright and his wife and family, along with his brother Samuel Seawright and his family, left Ireland on November 23, 1762, on a 70-passenger ship and sailed for 85 days to Charleston, South Carolina.[18] Arriving in Charleston on February 19, 1763, Andrew Seawright and his wife Mary Eleanor Dickson were granted 400 acres of land in Boonesborough. Andrew's son James and his wife Elizabeth McCullough, who had met each other on the voyage from Belfast, were granted 200 acres of land, as were several other Seawrights who had immigrated on the same ship.[19]

As did many of the Irish Protestant immigrants who came to South Carolina as a result of the Bounty Act, both Andrew Seawright and his son James served South Carolina in the Revolutionary War. Andrew, who was born in 1712, was 65 years old when the war began and was too old to fight; he supplied the Patriots with food. James joined the South Carolina Militia and fought in several battles. In 1777, while James was away with the militia, Tories attacked the Seawright homesteads and set fire to Andrew Seawright's house and burned him to death inside. Next, they attacked James and Elizabeth's farm but Elizabeth had been alerted and gathered her children and hid in the cane fields while the Tories burned their farm. Her two infant children, William and Elizabeth, froze to death during the night.[20]

One of Andrew Seawright's daughters married into the Miller family and one of his nephews, John Miller, applied for a pension for his Revolutionary War service after pensions were authorized in 1832. In his application he mentions the battle around Pratt's Mill, which was near the Seawrights' home and farm:

> This declarant was born in Abbeville County South Carolina on the 21st of January A.D. 1766–7, where he continued to reside until the close of the Revolutionary War. This declarant states that sometime in the year 1780, or 1781, he joined a Company of Rangers in Abbeville County South Carolina commanded by Captain John Norwood to goe [sic] out against the Cherokee Indians who were then very hostile on the frontiers. He states that they were marched out towards Georgia and were absent about a month, after the expiration of which time he states they returned home. Sometime after this declarant states the Indians became very troublesome, and this declarant then enlisted under the same Captain, John Norwood, to serve for 9 months, in the protection of the State of Georgia and South Carolina. This declarant states that they were marched out of Abbeville County (SC) to the line, and were employed in ranging against the Cherokees. This declarant states they were out on this service 6 months, and during this time they were stationed at a place called Pratts Mills, where they were attacked by a party of Cherokees and a Tory by the name of William Cunningham, leading a body of Tories; they were attacked in the night, and were compelled to retreat, this declarant states that his Captain was grazed by a ball, and was knocked down, but, soon recovered. Declarant states that after this he was again engaged in the same service on the line, until the close of the war.[21]

In support of John Miller's pension application, his cousin George Miller, who was also Andrew Seawright's nephew, gave a sworn affidavit before the Tennessee Gibson County Court in which he gave a much more descriptive account of the battle:

> This day in open Court came George Miller Cousin of John Miller this said Applicant and saith that said John Miller was born in Abbeville District South Carolina in the year of our Lord 1766 or 7 of Religious parents and carefully brought up by them until the first day of July 1776 that the Cherokee Indians broke out along our frontier and killed all that they could amongst those that were killed was Captain Smith and his family and destroyed all that he had, then the said Captain's commission fell to my Uncle Andrew Miller this John's father. And he had to camp and be but little more at home but be in constant service until the 17th day of January 1781 at Tarleton's defeat there amongst the few that fell he was one, then the Captain's commission fell to John Norwood, this John Miller being a boy well grown and active did not get leave to stay at home in safety but had often to be in camp for man nor boy could get leave to stay at home if they ventured to stay if they were caught they were either killed or chopped with sword. I had a sword drawn over my own head before I was 9 years old but he staid about home until about the first of July 1781 there was a heavy draft made for men to go to General Green Nathanael Greene] before the Battle of the Eutaw [Eutaw Springs] then our frontier was to guard and this Captain John Norwood was ordered to stay along the line with his Company, gather all the men and boys that was able to bear arms that they could carry a gun, amongst the rest I remember well of seeing the said John Miller passed and repassed our house was a frontier House and they often passed us they rode the line from Saluda River on the east to Savannah River on the west the breadth of Abbeville District a distance of about 40 miles and sometimes over both rivers I remember to hear of them being over both, but the first thing that happened to them was that memorable night at Pratts Mill that he mentions in his writing that report said 500 Indians and Tories headed by William Cunningham broke them up and they lost all their horses and saddles and bridles. They have burned the Mill and went about one mile and burn the house but the people were out of it, then the next they came to was our old uncle John Johnston's there they caught 7 girls 4 of them young women and 3 that were not grown the Tories would not let the Indians kill them but they stripped them naked as they were born and turned them loose amongst them 5 of them came to my father's naked and 2 of them was driven out the other course, the Indians set fire to the house and burned it. My uncle [Andrew Seawright] in it they burnt every house & barn on the place and destroyed all his living. Then we were moved about one mile off my father's house was taken for a station then this John Miller was at the station with the rest of the company. I was there almost every day he being raised on the frontier and used to the woods and a James Lindsey was taken for spies and rode spies (I think in January the Tories attacked the station one night but could not take it.) In the spring this John Miller at the request of his Mother moved her off about 8 miles....[22]

At the time of the Battle at Pratt's Mill, General Pickens was in the area and part of his contingent of troops were chasing Bill Cunningham trying to put a stop to his reign of terror. Hearing that Cunningham and his Tories were in the nearby vicinity of Cloud's Creek, General Pickens dispatched Captain Turner and Captain Butler, along with 23 men, to find him. "Bloody" Bill Cunningham trapped them in a house where they held out for several hours against Cunningham and 250 men until Cunningham's men set a nearby shed on fire, forcing their surrender. When the Patriots came out of the house, they were disarmed and gathered into a group. Bloody Bill then ordered his men to hack them to death with their swords.[23]

Elizabeth McCullough lived until 1788 and died when she was only 36 years old. Her husband James Seawright lived until 1790 and died when he was 48. The family members are buried in the Greenville Presbyterian Church cemetery in Abbeville County in the

Donalds, Greenville, South Carolina, vicinity. Their tombstone inscriptions read as follows:

> Elizabeth McCullough 1752–1788 Born in Ireland and wife of James Seawright, Sr.
> James Seawright Pvt. SC Militia Revolutionary War 1742–1790 son of
> Mary E. Dickson and Andrew Seawright
> Andrew Seawright, Sr. Whig Patriot 1712–1777
> Wife Mary Eleanor Dickson 1716–1795 Pioneers from Ireland

George Brownlee is buried is this same cemetery.

James Seawright and Elizabeth McCullough had a daughter, our ancestor Jane Seawright, born January 31, 1771, in Abbeville. Jane Seawright survived the attack by Bill Cunningham on the family farm, which had happened when she was six years old. Jane married Isaac Cowan.

The Cowans: More Irish, More Revolutionaries

Our Cowan family history traces the line back to County Down in Ireland and describes three different groups of Cowan brothers emigrating to America from the same general area of Northern Ireland between 1720 to 1726 and settling in Lancaster and Chester counties, Pennsylvania. One of these brothers was our ancestor Andrew, for whom there are records of his being paid for his services in the French and Indian War.

At least two Cowan brothers, Andrew and James, moved into the Ninety-Six district of South Carolina.[24] In 1763, Andrew married Ann, whose last name is unknown now. Later that year, Andrew and Ann had a son, our ancestor, whom they named Isaac. Isaac Cowan enlisted in the Revolutionary War as a private and by the end of the war he had been promoted to major. He later became Colonel Isaac Cowan, having served with distinction.

Isaac Cowan married a young Irish girl from the Seawright family, Jane Seawright, the daughter of James Seawright and Elizabeth McCullough. Isaac Cowan and Jane Seawright had two known children, a daughter, Jane Cowan, who married William Richley, and a son, John S. Cowan, our ancestor, who was born in 1806. John Cowan married Sarah Brownlee Clinkscales, the daughter of Francis B. Clinkscales and Eleanor Brownlee.

John Cowan and Sarah Brownlee Clinkscales had eleven children. Isaac B. Cowan was born in 1830 and died in 1846 when he was sixteen years old. James M. Cowan was born in 1832. Jane Eleanor Cowan was born in 1834 and lived until 1895. Our ancestor Sophronia Cowan was born in 1835 and died when she was thirty. Malinda Cowan was born in 1837 and died in 1854 when she was seventeen. Mary L. Cowan was born in 1838. Martha Edna Cowan was born in 1839 and died the next year, in 1840. John Wesley Cowan was born in 1842. William Tully Cowan was born in 1845 and lived until 1906, having endured being wounded and taken prisoner during the Civil War while serving with Sophronia's husband, Captain James Pratt, in Orr's Rifles. Sarah Elizabeth Cowan was born in 1846 and lived until 1901. Louis (Lewis) Francis Cowan was born in 1848 and died in 1854 when he was six years old.

John Cowan died on December 27, 1874, in Due West, the town that had been formed from land that had originally been Boonesborough. His will contains something of a peculiarity in that he divides his estate among his wife and nine other heirs, all of whom he explicitly names except for his granddaughter and our ancestor, Nina Pratt, whom he refers to as "the legal family heir of my deceased daughter Sophronia who in her lifetime was the wife of the James Pratt."[25]

John Cowan is buried in Lindsay Cemetery, which is about 2 miles from Due West. His tombstone inscription reads, "Erected in memory of John Cowan born March 16, 1805. died December 27, 1874. He was a Deacon of Greenville Presbyterian Church and having lived a Christian life he died in the triumph of FAITH." John's wife, Sarah Brownlee Clinkscales, is also buried in Lindsay Cemetery. Her grave stone inscription reads, "Sacred to the Memory of Sarah B. Cowan, consort of John Cowan, who was born November 9, 1811 and departed this life March 6, 1852."

Several of our other relatives are also buried there, including an infant son and daughter of James and Sophronia Pratt, Captain Isaac Cowan and his wife Jane, Joseph Pratt and Thomas Pratt. On May 27, 2009, the Lindsay Cemetery was listed in the National Register for Historic Places. Altogether, there are over 100 graves in Lindsay Cemetery. There are, however, no Lindsays there.

John Cowan and Sarah Brownlee Clinkscales' daughter, Sophronia Cowan, married Captain James Pratt. They are great-grandparents of Jimmy Carter.

Left: William Archibald Carter (1858–1903). This photograph was taken around 1899 and is one of two known photographs, and the only known portrait photograph, of W.A. Carter. This photograph was found after years of searching and it was given to President Jimmy Carter by me on Father's Day when he was 80 years old, the first time he had ever seen a photograph of his grandfather. *Right:* Nina Pratt (1863–1939), the wife of William Archibald Carter, photograph taken around 1899.

Sophronia Cowan Pratt died when she was only thirty years old. She is buried in the Lindsay Cemetery too, and inscribed on her gravestone is, "My wife, Sophronia C. Pratt. Erected by her husband Captain James Pratt. Born October 5, 1835. Died November 11, 1865."

Captain James Pratt and Sophronia's daughter, Nina Pratt, was born on November 5, 1863. Nina married William Archibald Carter, the son of Littleberry Walker Carter and Mary Ann Diligent Seals.

William Archibald Carter and Nina Pratt

President Jimmy Carter's grandfather, William Archibald Carter but known as Billy Carter, married Nina Pratt September 8, 1885. Three years later, they moved to Rowena, a small crossroads community in south Georgia. They had five children: Ethel Carter, born in 1887; William Alton Carter, born in 1888; Lula Carter, born in 1891; James Earl Carter Sr., the father of President James Earl Carter, born in 1894; and Jeanette Carter, born in 1900.

Billy Carter was a sawmill operator. He eventually acquired four hundred acres of land, a cotton gin, three sawmills, and a roadside store. He also planted a ten-acre vineyard and made about three thousand gallons of wine each year.[26]

In 1903, a dispute over a desk in a store Billy had rented to the Taliaferro brothers resulted in a fight between Billy and Will Taliaferro and Will's brother. Billy was badly beaten with bottles and after he left the store, Will Taliaferro followed him outside and shot him in the back of the head. The Americus *Times-Recorder* newspaper reported the attack in its September 3, 1903 edition:

Fatal Affray At Arlington

Will Carter, Formerly of Americus Probably Killed.

Mr. William Carter, formerly of Americus, a brother of Mr. J.C. Carter residing here and cousin of Mr. Will Carter of this city, is probably dead at Arlington, the result of a difficulty with two citizens named Taliaferro the day previous.

Only meager details of the affair have been received here.

Mr. Carter was cut and shot at the same time, it is said, and while the difficulty occurred on Wednesday, he was still alive yesterday.

As stated, the details of the tragedy are not known here. The first information of the affair was received here yesterday, while later in the day a telegram was received announcing that Mr. Carter was rapidly sinking.

He is well known in Americus and has many relatives and friends here who deeply deplore the unfortunate affair.[27]

William Archibald Carter died the next morning. His brother, Jeremiah Calvin Carter, was with him when he died and gave additional details to the newspaper, which reported on the murder again the next day:

Death Results From Injuries

Will Carter Died Yesterday Morning

Son Witnessed the Assault

Had Trouble With Tolivers Over Rental of Store — Was Badly Beaten Then Shot — Was Much Esteemed by His Neighbors

---

> William Carter died at Arlington yesterday morning from wounds inflicted by the two Tolivers, it is alleged, in a difficulty that occurred between then at Arlington on Thursday, an account of which was given in yesterday's Times-Recorder.
>
> Only brief particulars of the tragedy were known here until yesterday.
>
> Mr. J.C. Carter, a brother of the deceased, returned to Americus yesterday noon and gave some additional particulars of the killing, though not a complete account.
>
> Mr. William Carter rented a store to the men who killed him, and the trouble grew out of this fact. It is said that Mr. Carter was badly beaten with bottles, and that as he attempted to leave the store one of the men shot him in the back of the head with a pistol.
>
> Mr. Carter's son, twelve years of age, was an unwilling witness to the fearful tragedy.
>
> He lingered until yesterday morning when death resulted. His brother, J.C. Carter of Americus, was at his side when he died. Mr. J.C. Carter will return to Arlington this morning to attend the funeral, as will other relatives in Americus.
>
> Mr. William Carter was 43 years old and leaves a wife and five children. He was well known in Americus and highly esteemed.[28]

Calvin Carter settled Billy's affairs in Arlington and moved the family back to Plains, Georgia, in 1904.

William Archibald Carter and Nina Pratt's son, James Earl Carter Sr., who was seven years old when his father was murdered, married Bessie Lillian Gordy. They are the parents of President Jimmy Carter.

About ninety direct ancestors of Bessie Lillian Gordy are known.

Chapter 6

ANCESTORS OF JAMES JACKSON GORDY

The first Gordy in the colonies was Adrian Gordy, who was transported by William Brereton to Maryland in 1675 and listed in Brereton's headright claim as Adrian Gardey. It is not known where Adrian was transported from, although speculation centers on England, Ireland, and Scotland. Adrian married Mary Disharoone and he is listed in the will of his father-in-law, Michael Disharoones, filed in Somerset County, Maryland, in 1690. Adrian is thought to be the father of our ancestor Peter Gordy Sr. Peter was a twin and both his and his brother Moses Gordy's wills were filed on the same day, July 15, 1775, in Worcester County, Maryland.

Peter Gordy Sr's. will, dated June 22, 1772, names his wife Catherine and their seven children, including our ancestor Peter Gordy Jr.[1] Peter Gordy Jr. was born around 1735 in Somerset County, Maryland, and his son Peter Gordy III was born around 1775 in Worcester County, Maryland, Worcester County having been formed from Somerset County in 1742.

The second of two known photographs of William Archibald Carter, taken around 1895–1896. Left to right: William Archibald Carter standing beside the bicycle, daughter Ethel, daughter Lula standing in front of Nina Pratt, Ben Talliaferro, son Alton, and Mariah, their cook.

Peter (II) married Ruth, probably Ruth Wilson, the daughter of Samuel Wilson. By 1803, Peter Gordy (II) and his wife Ruth had moved to Hancock County, Georgia, and they later moved to Muscogee County, Georgia, where Peter died about 1844. Peter Gordy and Ruth had eight known children, among whom was our ancestor Wilson Gordy.[2]

William Scott of the Thirlestane clan was born in Scotland before 1700. A strong supporter of the Church of Scotland and a bitter opponent of the Catholic Church, he joined with the Covenanters and eventually the religious persecution convinced him to leave Scotland and move with his family to Ballymacran in northern Ireland. Very little is known about him, but he must have been a man of some wealth because he had substantial land holdings and maintained a deer reserve for hunting. His only known son was Joseph Scott, born soon after 1700. After Joseph died around 1750, his daughter and five sons emigrated to the colony of Pennsylvania and settled near Lancaster. Our ancestor William Scott and his brother Zaccheus eventually left Lancaster and moved into the southern part of Pennsylvania that became Delaware. Here William met and married another Scotch/Irish immigrant. William Scott and his wife had three known children: our ancestor Perry Scott, and his brothers, John and James. In 1758, William enlisted for service in the French and Indian War serving under Captain McClughan in Delaware. He was killed in the last few months of the war.[3] All three of William Scott's sons fought in the Revolutionary War.

Perry Scott and Captain Allen McLane

Captain Allen McLane is an unknown hero of the Revolutionary War. Born in Philadelphia in 1764, McLane was the son of fairly prosperous parents. When his father died in 1775, he left McLane more than $15,000 worth of property. In 1769, Allen married Rebecca Wells, the daughter of the sheriff of Kent County, Delaware, and moved there, settling near his in-laws. When the Revolutionary War began, McLane was involved in one of the first skirmishes against Lord Dunmore and joined a Delaware regiment of volunteers. He fought at White Plains, Trenton, and the Battle of Princeton. His capabilities brought him to the attention of General George Washington, who promoted him to captain on January 13, 1777. Attached to Colonel John Patton's Company of Foot, he was sent to Delaware to raise a company. Paying the bounty out of his own money, he enlisted 91 men.[4] Among those that joined McLane was our ancestor Perry Scott, who enlisted in McLane's Company on April 10, 1777.[5]

The company's first major action was at Chestnut Hill during the nighttime attack of General Howe, the last battle at Whitemarsh before Howe withdrew for the winter to Philadelphia and General Washington to Valley Forge. Gen. Howe's attack was fierce and he drove back a regiment of Pennsylvania militia and a regiment of Continental troops. General Joseph Reed's horse was shot from under him and fell, pinning the general to the ground. The British rushed forward to bayonet him, but McLane and his company rode in and in a vicious saber fight rescued the general.[6]

McLane's Company soon became favorites of Washington's, and he broke them out as an independent unit and deployed them as spies and scouts. On November 7, 1777, Washington ordered McLane and his men to take "the post most advantageous for watching the enemy, sending out the necessary parties and patriots for that end. You are to prevent as far as possible all intercourse between Philadelphia and the country, suffering none to go to the city without papers given by the authority of the commander-in-chief."[7]

Perry Scott and McLane's scouts were also assigned to forage for the starving troops at Valley Forge, at one time becoming almost the sole source of food for Washington's troops by raiding British supplies and attacking British foraging parties. In one foray through Maryland and Delaware, McLane's Company, with Perry Scott, gathered 1500 fat hogs, 500 head of cattle and 200 horses for the army at Valley Forge.

Perry Scott and McLane's Company gathered intelligence and operated a spy network in Philadelphia and the surrounding countryside for Washington, and they were the first to enter the city after the British withdrew on June 18, 1778. They captured several British soldiers who had remained in the city.

Because of the incredible dangers in spying and raiding, by the summer of 1779 McLane's Company had lost almost three-fourths of its men. During the May session, the Continental Congress passed an act annexing McLane's Company to the State of Delaware. Washington had already issued an order to that effect and McLane petitioned the Congress to pass the act. The act passed in June of 1779 with the Congress noting that McLane's Company, through hard service, had been reduced to only twenty troops. The survivors, including our ancestor Perry Scott, are listed in Delaware's colonial council records.[8]

Allen McLane and his men were then assigned to Major Henry Lee, "Light Horse Harry," and Perry Scott's Revolutionary War records change his designation from Perry Scott in Captain Allen McLane's Company in the Regiment of Foot commanded by Lt. Col. John Parke to Perry Scott, 4th Troop, Lee's Legion.

Perry's war records end after July of 1779, shortly after his company, serving with Lee's Partisan Legion and General "Mad" Anthony Wayne, stormed and captured the British fortress at Stony Point on the Hudson River.

Alexander Garden, another member of Lee's Legion and aide-de-camp to Major General Nathanael Greene related a humorous story about Perry Scott in his *Anecdotes of the Revolutionary War in America,* which he published in 1822:

> While the Legion lay at Mr. Izard's Villa Plantation, near Bacon's Bridge, anxiously looking forward to the evacuation of the Capital, having long assiduously attended to the duties of camp, my superior officer, Captain Handy, advised me, as there was little appearance of an immediate call for active service, to visit a friend in the neighborhood, and enjoy the luxury of a comfortable meal. I was not unthankful for the favor, and with great satisfaction rode to Mrs. Barnard Elliott's, a few miles distant, from whose hospitality I was certain to meet a hearty welcome. Dinner was served up, and I was about to take my place at table, when a dragoon galloping up, presented a note from Captain Handy, requiring me, without delay, to join the regiment about to cross the Ashley, with orders to harass the rear of the retiring enemy, who were on the eve of departure. I had no alternative, and without a moment's hesitation, set out.
>
> Arriving at the Villa, I found that the regiment had already moved, and hastening forward, speedily joined it. Encamped for the night at Parker's, below Dor'chester, and expressing to Handy and Manning, my companions, the disappointment recently experienced, and the cravings of immediate appetite, a soldier, who had heard the conversation, with great civility, said, "While on our march, Perry Scott purchased of a negro, who was passing us, a turkey, which we have cooked. If you will partake of it, Lieutenant, I have a leg and a little rice, altogether at your service." It was not a moment to refuse. The leg and rice were produced, and my friends and self ate our scanty portion with great relish. We had halted at Parker's during the night, to give General Wayne an opportunity of crossing, with a large body of infantry, the Ashley Ferry; and at early dawn moved forward to join him, but not before a second soldier had presented to Manning, the other leg of the turkey purchased by Scott. Soon after our junction with the infantry, General Wayne, escorted by the whole of the cavalry, moved forward to reconnoiter the enemy's position at Shubrick's.

The usual hour of refreshment having passed, with little appearance of relief from our Commissary, a third soldier advancing, said, "I hope Captain Handy will not refuse from me, a leg of the turkey which Scott purchased the last night on the road, as it is a particularly fine one: and I wish, with a tempting mess of rice, to offer it to him." The third leg was eaten; and, to shorten my story, for three succeeding meals, still another, and another leg of Scott's purchased turkey were presented. The mystery was soon explained. A messenger, with dispatches from Head Quarters to General Wayne, brought an order also, that the knapsacks of the troops should be strictly examined, as Mr. John Waring's poultry-house [had] been robbed, and thirty turkeys carried off, about the time of our removal from Izard's. Search was accordingly made, but not a feather found that could justify suspicion of criminality in any Legionary Soldier. A detachment of Pennsylvanians were but a little removed from the spot, and as they enjoyed high reputation for their partiality to delicate fare, this unceremonious transfer of property, was generally attributed to them.[9]

Perry Scott's son, John R. Scott, married Rebecca Radney and moved from Delaware to Baldwin County, Georgia. Their only daughter, Mary Scott, married Wilson Gordy, the son of Peter and Ruth Gordy.

Wilson Gordy and Mary Scott

Wilson Gordy was born January 30, 1801, and married Mary Scott in Baldwin County, Georgia, on November 26, 1825.[10] Their first child, John W. Gordy, was born about 1826 and died when he was only sixteen years old. John and our ancestor James Thomas Gordy were born in Baldwin County, as were their brothers Green Berry Gordy and Gilbert Perry Gordy. Wilson and Mary Scott and their family then moved from Baldwin County to Muscogee County, Georgia, and the rest of their children were born there.[11] Sarah Rebecca Gordy was born about 1834 and married John Webb on May 22, 1852, then moved with him to Tennessee. William Scott Gordy, Henry Mitchell Gordy, Mary A. Gordy, David Crockett Gordy, and George Gaines Gordy were all born in Chattahoochee County.[12] David died when he was fourteen years old. All of Wilson Gordy and Mary Scott's surviving sons fought in the Civil War.

Green Berry Gordy was born about 1830, moved to Louisiana and remained a bachelor.[13] When the war started, he enlisted for one year on April 6, 1862, in Captain Fuller's Louisiana Cavalry. The Company eventually became Company G, Balch's Battalion, 18th Tennessee Cavalry, then Captain Harrison's 2nd Regiment, Kentucky Cavalry, and finally the 6th Regiment Louisiana Cavalry. Green Gordy served when the unit was Company G, Balch's Battalion, 18th Tennessee Cavalry. Green supplied his own horse and arms, for which he was paid forty cents a day.[14] Green Gordy survived the war and became a wealthy businessman and farmer in Louisiana. To his misfortune, he was killed while being robbed in Red River County, Louisiana, in April 1885.[15]

Gilbert Perry Gordy, Wilson Gordy and Mary Scott's sixth child, was born about 1831[16] and married Martha George on September 30, 1859. On May 6, 1862, Gilbert enlisted in the Chattahoochee Rangers in Columbus, Georgia; Captain Beverley A. Thornton's Company, Crawford Regiment, Georgia Cavalry. The company subsequently became Company B, 3rd Regiment of the Georgia Cavalry[17] and fought at New Haven. Gilbert was promoted to lieutenant on April 17, 1863, before the regiment fought in the Battle of Murfreesboro, then at Chickamauga, Chattanooga, Knoxville, the Battle of Atlanta, and then in skirmishes in northern Alabama and the Carolinas. In one of the later battles in Alabama or South Carolina, Gilbert Gordy was shot and he died of his wounds on October 4, 1864.

Gilbert's daughter, who was only about three years old when he was killed in the war and who with her mother had moved to Oklahoma, died in 1930. In her will, she left Gilbert's uniform to Chattahoochee County on the condition that it would remain in the county.[18] The uniform was sent to the Cusseta Chapter of the United Daughters of the Confederacy and when the chapter disbanded in 1940, the uniform became the property of the probate office. A note entitled "The History of This Suit" was left with the uniform which said in part, "On the old Gordy homestead ... about three miles west of Cusseta, wool was sheared from sheep, thread was spun from this wool and cloth was woven from this thread on a hand loom and this suit cut and sewed by hand by Mrs. Mary Scott Gordy for her son Gilbert Perry Gordy. He left Columbus, Georgia, with the Chattahoochee Rangers on Oct. 29, 1861 and after engaging in many battles died from wounds on Oct. 4, 1864."

The uniform includes a black leather hat, butternut officer's jacket with brass buttons, black wool pants, a pair of socks, a belt with a buckle and a hanger for his saber, and a red bandana. Below the left knee is a patched bullet hole, believed to have been made by the bullet that killed Gilbert. Wrapped in the bandana was a .53 caliber minié ball, identified in the note as the bullet that caused his death. The fragile suit is considered extremely rare and is valued at well over $100,000. It is being restored and preserved.

William Scott Gordy was born about 1836 in Chattahoochee County, Georgia.[19] During the Civil War, he enlisted in Company I, 64th Regiment, Georgia Infantry, on March 24, 1863. The 64th Regiment was one of the last units formed in Georgia and spent most of the war in Georgia and Florida. Shortly after William joined the regiment, the 64th was assigned to Wright's Brigade, Anderson/Mahone's Division, Hill's Corps, and sent with the Army of Northern Virginia to Richmond. William was either wounded or fell ill with a major ulcer in his left leg. He was admitted to the Jackson Hospital in Richmond, Virginia, August 27, 1864, where, in December, he was judged unfit for field service and detailed as a sentinel at the hospital. On April 3, 1865, six days before Lee's surrender, William was captured at the Jackson Hospital by Union troops and was transported to the prisoner of war camp at Point Lookout, Maryland. He became seriously ill at the prisoner of war camp and was admitted into the U.S. Army General Hospital at Point Lookout on May 28, 1865, where he was diagnosed with idiopathic erysipelas, a highly contagious acute streptococcus bacterial infection of the skin. Erysipelas, also known as "Ignis sacer," "Holy fire," and "St Anthony's fire," is known to enter the body through open wounds, and William undoubtedly contracted the disease through exposure of the ulcer in his leg. William Gordy, prisoner number 1148, died at Point Lookout on June 2, 1865, and was buried there in the prisoners burial ground.[20]

Henry Mitchell Gordy was born September 7, 1837.[21] During the Civil War, he enlisted on August 1, 1861, in Semmes Brigade, Company C, 10th Georgia Volunteer Infantry, known as the Chattahoochee Beauregards, and was sent to Williamsburg, Virginia. At the start of the war, John Paul Semmes, a banker and plantation owner from Columbus, Georgia, was appointed colonel of the 2nd Georgia Infantry. Gordy served with Semmes' Brigade in Virginia during the Peninsula Campaign and in the defense of Richmond after John Semmes had been promoted to general.

At the start of the Maryland Campaign, the Semmes Brigade joined the Army of Northern Virginia under Major General Lafayette McLaws' Division and fought at Crampton's

Gap. The Battle of Crampton's Gap was a tactical defeat for the Confederacy but a key strategic victory. The Union Army's VI Corps suffered 115 dead and 416 wounded. The Confederates suffered 113 dead and 759 wounded and the Union Army was successful in driving the Confederates from Crampton's Gap. However, even though outnumbered six to one, the Confederates managed to delay the Union Army for three critical hours, long enough for McLaws to reach safety on Maryland Heights and night to fall. General Franklin decided not to launch a second attack on McLaws during the night and allowed Stonewall Jackson's forces to reunite with the main body of the Confederate army at Sharpsburg.

The brigade was a key part of the Battle of Antietam,[22] then fought at Chancellorsville and Salem Church.

Gen. Semmes was killed at Gettysburg and the 10th Georgia Volunteer Infantry was reassigned and fought at the Battle of the Wilderness, Spotsylvania Court House, North Anna, Cold Harbor, and the Siege of Petersburg. Henry Gordy was seriously wounded on May 6, 1864, during the Battle of the Wilderness.[23] His unit lost track of him and he was listed as AWOL until he was accounted for in the regimental return in March of 1865.[24] Henry Gordy lived in Cusseta, Georgia, until 1922, although for the rest of his life he walked with a severe limp as a result of his wounds. He was believed to be the last surviving member of Semmes' Brigade.[25]

George Gaines Gordy enlisted in 1864 and served during the last year of the Civil War. His war records are missing. After the war, George represented Chattahoochee County in the legislature for two terms. His son, T.A. Gordy, was the first person to buy an automobile in Chattahoochee and the first rural mail carrier to use an automobile. His daughter, Mrs. Lucy Gordy Speight, was the first woman in the county to drive an automobile.[26]

After Mary Scott died, Wilson Gordy married Martha J. Sheffield on April 23, 1882, in Chattahoochee County.[27] Wilson died on January 21, 1890, and his will gives an interesting insight into the life of a successful south Georgia farmer of the time, listing his children and virtually everything he owned from his patent-lever double-screw silver watch to his corn sheller and oat cutter (See Appendix G: Wills).

Our ancestor James Thomas Gordy was born in 1828[28] and enlisted in Company B, Georgia State Guards, in 1864 during Sherman's campaign in Atlanta.[29] He was a wagon master for the Confederacy. After the war, James was a farmer and served as a tax collector and was a member of the Baptist church in Cusseta, Georgia, where he is buried. James married Harriett Emily Helms on October 26, 1854.[30]

The Helms Family, the Waxhaw Settlement and the Revolution

The territory between the Rocky River and the Catawba River, now Union County, North Carolina,[31] was inhabited by the Waxhaw Indians, a kindred tribe of the Catawbas. Around 1740, after contact with white explorers, a smallpox epidemic swept the area and decimated the tribe. The few remaining survivors abandoned their land and joined the Catawbas. Land agents advertised the land as being vacant and began recruiting immigrants. A large contingent of Scotch-Irish settlers had moved to Pennsylvania after the Siege of Londonderry and had settled in the frontier of the colony, where they immediately came into conflict with the local Indians. The settlement in North Carolina promised peaceable neighbors and a better climate and they were persuaded to move. The settlers established the Waxhaw Settlement in 1751. Among the immigrants were Andrew Pickens, the father of General Andrew Pickens of Revolutionary War fame; Andrew Jackson Sr., father of President Andrew Jackson; and Patrick Calhoun, father of John C. Calhoun.[32] The settlers built a Presbyterian church and recruited ministers. The church also served as a school building and, before the Revolutionary War, it was the only church and school in the area.

Also among the first settlers from Pennsylvania were our ancestor George Helms and his brothers Tilman and Jonathan.[33] In 1750, Thomas Helms, George Helms, Tillman Helms, John Helms, and Jonathan Helms were neighbors who lived on the Little River northeast of the Pee Dee River.[34] It is believed from land records that John Helms was the father of Tilman, George, and Jonathan Helms, and that Thomas was his brother.

Tilman Helms and his wife, who was probably Rachel Craig, had several children; among them were William, Jacob, Mary, Phoebe, and Tilman Helms Jr. Jacob Helms married Anna Pressley and Mary Helms married Anna's brother Richard Pressley.[35]

Our ancestor George Helms married Mary Margaret Faulkenborough (Faulkenberry, Faulkenbury, Fortenberry), the daughter of Jacob Faulkenborough. The Faulkenboroughs lived in Orange County, Virginia, and moved to Anson County, North Carolina. Orange County borders the Shenandoah Valley and was one of the major routes from Pennsylvania to North Carolina. George may have met and married Mary Margaret during the family's move from Pennsylvania or he may have met her after they arrived in North Carolina. George Helms and Mary Margaret Faulkenborough had six children. John was born in 1756 and married Susannah Presley. Our ancestor George Helms Jr. was born about 1758 and married Sarah Presley, Susannah's sister. Jacob Helms was born about 1760 and married his first cousin Sarah Helms, the daughter of Tilman Helms. Phoebe Helms was born about 1764 and married Charles Polk. Isaac Helms was born about 1767 and married Nancy Laney. Abraham Helms was born about 1771 and married his first cousin Phoebe Helms, another daughter of Tilman Helms.

Anna Pressley and Richard Pressley, who married Tilman Helms' children Jacob and Mary; and Susannah Presley and Sarah Presley, who married George Helms' children John and our ancestor George Jr., were all the children of Thomas Presley and all are listed in Thomas Presley's will of March 6, 1808.[36] It is through Thomas Presley's line, his father and brother, that the widely reported kinship between President Jimmy Carter and Elvis Presley was established.[37]

At the beginning of the Revolutionary War, most people in the region around the Waxhaw settlement were indifferent to the struggle until the Battle of Camden. After the capture of Charlestown, the Continental Army had been completely driven out of South Carolina. After it was re-formed at Charlotte, North Carolina, under Horatio Gates, and against the advice of his advisors, Gates led his ill prepared and untested Continentals to Camden, South Carolina, a strategically important crossroads. General Cornwallis and his Tory army met them there on August 13, 1780. The battle was a rout, with the experienced Tory army decimating the Continentals, who fled in panic at the first attack, Horatio Gates with them. The Continental Army suffered over 2000 casualties, including over a thousand men being captured, along with all of the Continental troop's artillery. General George Washington subsequently replaced Gates because of his cowardice and gave command of the southern army to Nathanael Greene.

The massacre in South Carolina, just fifteen miles southeast of the Waxhaw Settlement church, enraged the people. The British then provoked the population again by attacking the minister's house and burning it down along with all of his books. The Tories then declared war against all Bibles that contained the Scottish version of the Psalms. The formerly

James Jackson "Jim Jack" Gordy (1863–1948) with friends. Gordy is the man dressed in black with the black hat, second from left. The photograph was taken around 1895.

peaceful settlement became fully engaged in the war and furnished many of the Patriot troops at Hanging Rock, King's Mountain, Cowpens, and the Battles of the Waxhaws, Eutaw Springs, and Blackstocks. Almost every man in the territory belonged to some militia and fought on the Patriot side, although there are very few records. In most cases, rosters were not kept and the men are not listed on payrolls because very few of the Scotch-Irish settlers applied for pay. George Helms Jr. was one of the recruits from the Waxhaw settlement who fought in the Revolutionary War. He is the Patriot that Jimmy Carter's aunt Emily Gordy traced in order to join the Daughters of the American Revolution.

Our ancestors George Helms Jr. and Sarah Presley had seven children. Their firstborn child was a son whose name is unknown. Their daughter Clorinda was born in 1785 and tragically she drowned when she was a teenager. Elizabeth Helms was born in 1783 and married into the Yarbrough family. Isaac Hanley Helms was a captain in the Revolutionary War. Pamly Uriah Helms, the great-great-grandfather of President Jimmy Carter, was born in 1785 and married Elizabeth Fisher.[38] Charles Helms was born in 1793 and eventually moved to Talbot County, Georgia. Israel Helms was born in 1800 and married Francis Sikes.[39]

Pamly Uriah Helms and Elizabeth Fisher's daughter and our ancestor, Harriet Emily Helms, was born in 1836. She married James Thomas Gordy in 1854 and they are great-grandparents of Jimmy Carter. James and Harriett had nine children. John Thomas Gordy was born in 1855 and died in 1900. Francis Marion Gordy, who served as a state legislator, was born in 1857 and died in 1930. Mary Gordy was born in 1860. Our ancestor James Jackson Gordy was born in 1863 and died in 1948. James Jackson Gordy married Mary Ida Nicholson, a daughter of Nathaniel Nunn Nicholson. David Crockett Gordy was born in 1869 and married Sallie Nicholson, also a daughter of Nathaniel Nunn Nicholson. Charles Lee Gordy was born in 1871. William Mack Gordy was born in 1873. Arthur Gordy was born in 1875 and became a state senator representing Columbus. Frederick Gordy was born in 1878.

James Thomas Gordy also had another son, Berry Gordy, the child of a relationship he had with one of his slaves. Berry Gordy and his wife Lucy had a child born in 1888 they also named Berry Gordy. Berry Gordy (II) moved from Georgia to Detroit, lured there by the promise of jobs in the automobile industry. In Detroit, Berry Gordy (II) met and married Bertha Fuller and the couple had eight children. Their seventh child was Berry Gordy Jr. who served in the army in Korea. After returning from Korea, Berry Gordy Jr., married Thelma Coleman and became a songwriter. In 1957, Jackie Wilson recorded *Reet Petite*, a song that Berry had cowritten and that became an international hit. Jackie Wilson recorded four more of Berry Gordy's songs. Berry reinvested his money and began producing and promoting artists. His first big group was the Miracles with Smokey Robinson. Berry Gordy founded Motown Records and became one of the most successful music producers in America.

James Jackson Gordy married Mary Ida Nicholson, a daughter of Nathaniel Nunn Nicholson. A part of the Nicholson ancestry is speculative.

Chapter 7

ANCESTORS OF MARY IDA NICHOLSON

Mary Ida Nicholson was the daughter of Nathaniel Nunn Nicholson and Mary Elizabeth Dawson. Nathaniel's father married Francis Nunn and both the Nicholson line and the Nunn line can be traced back to the colonial era. With a few notable exceptions, almost nothing is known with certainty about the wives of the ancestors of the Nicholson or Nunn lines.

More is known of the ancestry of Mary Ida Nicholson's mother, Mary Elizabeth Dawson, and several ancestors can be traced back to the colonial era or to the original immigrant ancestors. The Dawson family itself can be traced to Jonathan Dawson, who was born in England around 1720. Jonathan Dawson's son married Repsema Nicholson, whose family can also be traced back to the immigrant ancestor. Repsema Nicholson's family is apparently unrelated to the Nicholsons of Nathaniel Nunn Nicholson, unless they share a common ancestor in Ireland.

Another major line in Mary Ida's ancestry is five generations of the Brown family, whose original immigrant ancestor was William Brown, born in 1706 in Ireland. The Gaines family contributed three generations of ancestors as did the Marcus family, which received a royal grant of land.

The Nathaniel Nunn Nicholson Line

Nathaniel Nunn Nicholson was the grandfather of Bessie Lillian Gordy and the great-grandfather of James Earl Carter Jr. Professional genealogists stop the lineage with Nathaniel's father, John Nicholson, disputing whether or not John Nicholson and John Candor Nicholson were the same person. There is very strong circumstantial evidence that the two were the same person. But since every occurrence in the records of John Nicholson could be attributed to John Candor Nicholson, who was not using his middle name or initial when he signed documents, there is no absolute proof and thus the lineage from Cuthbert Nicholson and the two generations that follow him to John Candor Nicholson has to be considered speculative. From Nathaniel Nunn Nicholson's father, John Nicholson, born in 1790 in North Carolina, there is adequate documentation to establish the line. If John Candor Nicholson and our John Nicholson are the same person, then the line is extended back to 1712 with some interesting ancestors. The whole conundrum is explained later, but there is no absolute proof either way.

Our possible ancestors Cuthbert Nicholson and Jennet Candor were both probably born in Philadelphia in 1712. They received a marriage license June 30, 1736, and were married in the First Presbyterian Church on the first of July.[1] Jennet Candor was the daughter of Josias and Mary Candour, who also had a son, Joseph. An oral history of the Candour family says that the Candour family immigrated from Enniskillen, Ireland, before 1735 and lived in Chester and then in Derry, Lancaster County, Pennsylvania.

Enniskillen (Ennis Killen) is a stunningly beautiful town on the Erne River in Northern Ireland with buildings still standing that were built in the early 1400s. The centuries-old Enniskillen Castle still stands in the center of town and is a popular tourist attraction now, but there were few tourists in Enniskillen when Josias and Rose lived there in the late 1600s. In 1689, Enniskillen and Derry were the focus of Williamite resistance in Ireland during the conflict which resulted from the ousting of King James II by his Protestant rival, William III. The Protestant civilians of Enniskillen organized a militia and began attacking and harassing the Jacobite forces in and around Ulster. The Jacobite army, 3000 poorly trained troops led by Justin McCarthy, marched on Enniskillen and were met by about 2,000 "Inniskilliniers" commanded by Colonel Berry. Fifteen hundred Jacobites were killed. Of 500 who tried to flee by swimming the Erne River, only one survived. Over 400 Jacobite prisoners were taken, including Justin McCarthy. The Orange Order, named after the victor, William of Orange, still celebrates the victory today and the battle is commemorated in the Irish ballad "The Sash."

The battle did not end the war, which raged for years. The aftermath of the conflict led to the destruction of the Irish clan system and was responsible for the largest Irish migration in history, in which Josias and Rose took part.

Josias and his wife Rose are buried in the Donegal Presbyterian Church Cemetery in East Donegal Township, Lancaster County, Pennsylvania, along with their son Joseph and his wife Mary. Their graves are marked by a horizontal sandstone slab which is engraved with the following:[2]

> Here lieth the body of
> Rose Candour
> who departed ye life
> Aug. the 23d day, 1739, aged 57 years
>
> Here lyeth the body of
> Josias Candour
> who departed this life Oct: the 11th, 1748
> aged 82 years
>
> In memory of
> Joseph Candour
> who departed this life April 20th, 1784
> aged 71 years
>
> In memory of
> Mary Candour
> who departed this life July the 22d, 1797, aged 55 years

Cuthbert and Jennet had three sons born in Philadelphia: George Nicholson, born about 1737; John, born about 1738; and our possible ancestor Joseph, born about 1739. Sometime between 1750 and 1767, Cuthbert Nicholson and Jennet moved to Mecklenburg County, North Carolina, with their three sons. Cuthbert is on the tax rolls in Philadelphia in 1750. Deeds recorded in Mecklenburg County show that on January 9, 1767, Cuthbert Nicholson bought 131 acres on Sugar Creek from George Augustus Selwyn.[3] In 1770, Cuthbert bought another 72 acres on Sugar Creek from John and Elizabeth Mitchell.[4]

Patrick Jack

Also living in Mecklenburg County, in the little town of Charlotte, was another Irish immigrant, Patrick Jack. Patrick and three of his brothers emigrated from Ireland to Pennsylvania around 1730.[5] Patrick was descended from William Jack, one of thirteen ministers of the Presbytery of Lagan in northern Ireland who were expelled from the country by Charles II for nonconformity to the Church of England. Around 1760, Patrick Jack moved to Charlotte, following the migration of many others moving south as the colonies were established and land grants were issued. He first bought land in Rowan County between the Grant and Second creeks, where he lived for almost two years before selling his land and moving to Mecklenburg County.[6] His business ventures proved to be successful and by 1775 he and his son Captain James Jack owned several city blocks in Charlotte. His home was on the corner of the block next to the courthouse and he opened it as a public house of entertainment.

In 1771, eastern and central North Carolina were overflowing with political intrigue. Royal governor Tryon and his officer's were openly charged with corruption and extortion by the Regulators. People were outraged by the palatial home Gov. Tryon built with funds skimmed from taxes he had imposed. In Charlotte, Queen's College had been built for the education of young men. The college was only two blocks from the courthouse and three blocks from Patrick Jack's home. King George II repeatedly denied the college's request for a charter, enraging the people in Charlotte who considered the refusal a deliberate snub. The college operated without a charter in defiance of the king and the governor. Regular militia musters were held and people gathered to discuss politics and news. One of the most popular meeting places was Patrick Jack's house.

Patrick Jack and his wife, Lillis McAdoo, had four sons and five daughters: James, John, Samuel, Robert, Charity, Jane, Mary, Margaret, and our ancestor Lillis McAdoo Jack. Their son Captain James Jack attended the Convention of Delegates in Charlotte when it convened on March 19th and 20th of 1775.

The Mecklenburg Declaration of Independence

At the Convention of Delegates in Charlotte in 1775, Captain James Jack was selected to deliver to Congress a copy of the patriotic resolutions they had passed. Congress was then in session in Philadelphia. Accordingly, as soon as the necessary preparations for traveling could be made, Jack set out from Charlotte on horseback. C.L. Hunter wrote of his trip in 1887 in the wonderfully entitled book *Sketches of Western North Carolina Historical and Biographical, Illustrating Principally the Revolutionary Period of Mecklenburg, Rowan, Lincoln and Adjoining Counties Accompanied With Miscellaneous Information, Much of It Never Before Published*:

> On the evening of the first day he [Captain James Jack] reached Salisbury, forty miles from Charlotte, before the General Court, then in session, had adjourned. Upon his arrival, Colonel Kennon, an influential member of the Court, who knew the object of Captain Jack's mission, procured from him the copy of the Mecklenburg Resolutions of Independence he had in charge, and read them aloud in open court. All was silence, and all apparent approval *(intentique ora tenchant)* as these earliest key-notes of freedom resounded through the hall of the old court house in Salisbury. There sat around, in sympathizing composure, those sterling patriots, Moses Winslow, Waightstill Avery, John Brevard,

William Sharpe, Griffith Rutherford, Matthew Locke, Samuel Young, Adlai Osborne, James Brandon, and many others, either members of the court, or of the county's Committee of Safety. The only marked opposition proceeded from two lawyers, *John Dunn* and *Benjamin Booth Boote,* who pronounced the resolutions *treasonable,* and said Captain Jack ought to be detained. These individuals had previously expressed sentiments "inimical to the American cause." As soon as knowledge of their avowed sentiments and proposed detention of Captain Jack reached Charlotte, the patriotic vigilance of the friends of liberty was actively aroused, and a party of ten or twelve armed horsemen promptly volunteered to proceed to Salisbury, arrest said Dunn and Boote, and bring them before the Committee of Safety of Mecklenburg for trial. This was accordingly done (George Graham, living near Charlotte, being one of the number), and both being found guilty of conduct inimical to the cause of American freedom, were transported, first to Camden, and afterward, to Charleston, S.C. They never returned to North Carolina, but after the war, it is reported, settled in Florida, and died there, it is hoped not only repentant of their sins, as all should be, but with chastened notions of the reality and benefits of American independence.

On the next morning, Captain Jack resumed his journey from Salisbury, occasionally passing through neighborhoods, hi [sic] and beyond the limits of North Carolina, infested with enraged Tories, but, intent on his appointed mission, he faced all dangers, and finally reached Philadelphia in safety.

Upon his arrival he immediately obtained an interview with the North Carolina delegates (Caswell, Hooper and Hewes), and, after a little conversation on the state of the country, then agitating all minds, Captain Jack drew from his pocket the Mecklenburg resolutions of the 20th of May, 1775, with the remark: "Here, gentlemen, is a paper that I have been instructed to deliver to you, with the request that you should lay the same before Congress."

After the North Carolina delegates had carefully read the Mecklenburg resolutions, and approved of their patriotic sentiments so forcibly expressed, they informed Captain Jack they would keep the paper, and show it to several of their friends, remarking, at the same time, they did not think Congress was then prepared to act upon so important a measure as *absolute independence.*

On the next day, Captain Jack had another interview with the North Carolina delegates. They informed him that they had consulted with several members of Congress, (including Hancock, Jay and Jefferson) and that all agreed, while they approved of the patriotic spirit of the Mecklenburg resolutions, it would be premature to lay them officially before the House, as they still entertained some hopes of reconciliation with England. It was clearly perceived by the North Carolina delegates and other members whom they consulted, that the citizens of Mecklenburg county were *in advance* of the general sentiment of Congress on the subject of independence; the fantasy of "reconciliation" still held forth its seductive allurements in 1775, and even during a portion of 1776; and hence, no record was made, or vote taken on the patriotic resolutions of Mecklenburg, and they became concealed from view in the blaze of the National Declaration bursting forth on the 4th of July, 1776, which only re-echoed and reaffirmed the truth and potency of sentiments proclaimed in Charlotte on the 20th of May, 1775.

Captain Jack finding the darling object of his long and toilsome journey could not be then accomplished, and that Congress was not prepared to vote on so bold a measure as *absolute independence,* just before leaving Philadelphia for home, somewhat excited, addressed the North Carolina delegates, and several other members of Congress, in the following patriotic words: *"Gentlemen, you may debate here about 'reconciliation,' and memorialize your king, but, bear it in mind, Mecklenburg owes no allegiance to, and is separated from the crown of Great Britain forever."*[7]

Patrick Jack was a lieutenant in the Third Lancaster Battalion,[8] but at the outbreak of the Revolutionary War he was well advanced in age. His views were so patriotic toward America and so widely known that when the British entered Charlotte on September 26,

1780, the commander of the British troop declared that "all of old Jack's sons are in the rebel army, and he himself is a promoter of treason."[9] Patrick Jack was dragged out of his sickbed into the street and his house was burned to the ground. His health turned worse and Patrick Jack died before independence was won.

During the Revolutionary War, Captain James Jack commanded a company under Colonels Polk and Alexander. After the war, he sold his property in Charlotte and moved to Wilkes County, Georgia, with his brother John Jack, who also had served in the Revolutionary War. Samuel Jack, Patrick Jack's third son, had commanded an artillery company during the Revolutionary War and afterwards stayed in Mecklenburg County and lived on Sugar Creek. Patrick Jack's eldest daughter, Charity, married Dr. Cornelius Dysart, a surgeon during the Revolutionary War. Mary Jack, Patrick Jack's third daughter, married Captain Robert Alexander, who had commanded a company during the Revolution under General Rutherford. Margaret Jack married Samuel Wilson and stayed in Mecklenburg. Patrick Jack's youngest daughter, and our possible ancestor, Lillis McAdoo Jack, married Joseph Nicholson.[10]

Joseph Nicholson and Lillis McAdoo Jack

Our ancestor Joseph Nicholson also fought in the Revolutionary War,[11] probably serving with members of the Jack family.

In April of 1778, Joseph Nicholson bought 34 acres of land on Sugar Creek close to his father.[12] The deed was witnessed by Joseph's brother John. In March of 1780, Joseph bought another 150 acres from William Elliot. Joseph apparently tired of farming and decided to start a business with his brother-in-law James Jack. The Mecklenburg County Court of Common Pleas issued Joseph Nicholson and James Jack an ordinary license in October of 1781. (An ordinary was a restaurant and tavern, without overnight accommodations, serving drinks whose prices were set by the court.) Apparently the court of common pleas liked the establishment run by Joseph and Jack, because they began to meet there and in January 1782 the minutes of the court record shows that the court paid $675 for a room and firewood to be used during the sitting of the court. In July 1782, the court also issued a license to Joseph to open a tavern in his house in Charlotte.

In late 1785 or early 1786, our ancestors Joseph Nicholson and his wife Lillis, along with two of his brothers-in-laws, John and James Jack, and their families, moved together to Wilkes County, Georgia. On January 31, 1786, Joseph bought 300 acres of land in Wilkes County on Upton's Creek for $280 from Thomas Carson and his wife. John Jack witnessed the deed.[13]

Joseph's father, Cuthbert Nicholson, died January 2, 1789, in Mecklenburg County and his mother, Jennet, died there about a year later on March 13, 1790. Both are buried in the Steele Creek Presbyterian Church Cemetery. The minutes of Mecklenburg County, North Carolina, Court of Common Pleas and Quarter Sessions, show that George Nicholson was appointed executor to his father's estate along with James Tagert.[14]

Were John Nicholson and John Candor Nicholson the Same Person?

I had never seen a reference to the parents of John Nicholson indicating that they were anybody other than Joseph Nicholson and Lillis McAdoo Jack, so I was surprised to find that professional genealogists do not consider the relation proven. I was even more surprised to find that I did not have ironclad proof either. Nevertheless, I do have strong circumstantial evidence.

There is no question that the Jack family and the Nicholson family were close friends and knew each other quite well. They lived in Mecklenburg together, their children intermarried, they witnessed each other's legal documents and some members of both families moved to Wilkes County, Georgia, together. In the last will and testament of Patrick Jack, made on the 19th of May, 1780, he devised the whole of his personal estate and the "undivided benefit of his house and lots to his beloved wife during her lifetime." After her death they were directed to be sold, and the proceeds divided among his five married daughters: Charity Dysart, Jane Barnett, Mary Alexander, Margaret Wilson and Lillie Nicholson. James Jack and Joseph Nicholson were appointed executors.[15]

The Lillie Nicholson mentioned in Patrick Jack's will was his daughter Lillis McAdoo Jack, who had married Joseph Nicholson, the executor of Patrick Jack's will. Joseph Nicholson and Lillis McAdoo Jack were the parents of John Candor, Joseph, James, George P., Charity, and Samuel Nicholson.

Sterling Grimes, William Garland Grimes, and Thomas Wingfield Grimes were the sons of John Grimes and Elizabeth Wingfield. John Grimes was a Revolutionary soldier and moved to Wilkes County, Georgia, after receiving a land bounty for his services.[16] The Grimes families were friends of the Nicholson and Jack families from way back. Charity Nicholson, the sister of our presumed ancestor John C. Nicholson, married Thomas Wingfield Grimes. Charity Dysart, Patrick Jack's daughter who had married Dr. John Dysart, mentions several of the relationships in her undated will, of which Thomas W. Grimes is an executor. Among others, Charity mentions "Charity Grimes, my niece," "nephews James H. Nichelson, John Candor Nickelson, William H. Jack, Patrick Barnett, and William Dysart Jack," "my cousin Joseph William Grimes" and friends "James Jack of Wilkes County and Thomas W. Grimes" (see Appendix G: Wills).

The Nicholson family also had other business arrangements with the Grimes and Jack families in Georgia and they witnessed each other's legal documents. John C. Nicholson witnessed a deed wherein Sterling Grimes sold a lot in Greensborough to his brother William Grimes.[17] John C. Nicholson and his brother also opened a tavern in one of William Grimes' houses.[18]

There are other records as well. When John's father, Joseph Nicholson, died in 1826, John and Thomas Grimes were appointed administrators of his estate, and Thomas and his brothers posted the administrative bond.[19] John C. Nicholson was not always successful in business. Some of his and his brother's land was seized in Greene County and sold at a sheriff's auction.[20] The same thing would happen to John Grimes later, in Muscogee County.

There are also records of John Nicholson without a middle initial. John Nicholson and Joseph Nicholson were eligible for two draws in the 1807 Georgia Land Lottery. John Nicholson witnessed the deed when Joseph Nicholson sold land to Samuel McCombs. However, none of this is proof that this John Nicholson or John C. Nicholson is the same John Nicholson who was the father of Nathaniel Nunn Nicholson, especially since all references to John Nicholson could be interpreted as referring to John C. Nicholson when he was not using his middle name or initial.

Proving that Nathaniel's father, John Nicholson, was John Candor Nicholson seems very difficult without somehow tying Nathaniel to other members of John Candor Nicholson's family and those records are not readily apparent, to say the least. There are no records of John Candor Nicholson's wife at all and there are no deeds whereby John C. Nicholson gave Nathaniel Nunn Nicholson land "for the natural affection I have for my son." The Wilkinson County courthouse burned down twice. There are no deeds before 1870, no tax digest before 1890, and no wills before 1820. There are a few marriage records from 1823 to 1828 and then no more before 1865.

Unsubstantiated sources say that our ancestors John Nicholson and Francis Nunn had several children besides the two proven: Nathaniel Nunn Nicholson and Nancy Nicholson. Their firstborn son was supposedly John Candor Nicholson Jr., born about 1789 in Wilkes County, which, if it could be verified, would be proof that Nathaniel's father was John Candor Nicholson.

In the 1840 Muskogee County census, there is a John Nicholson who is between 40 and 50 years old. He lived next door to Nathaniel Nunn Nicholson. It is reasonable to assume that the two brothers lived next to each other; the age of this John Nicholson is perfect for him to be Nathaniel's brother John Candor Nicholson Jr. and too young to be his father.

John Nicholson's father-in-law, John Nunn, registered for the 1827 Georgia Land lottery as a Revolutionary soldier and qualified for two draws. He won Lot 113, District 12, of Muscogee County on his first draw and Lot 193, District 23, of Muscogee County on his second draw. There are no records of John Nunn transferring the land to his son-in-law but the Nicholsons are soon afterwards living on the land in Muscogee County. In 1847, Muskogee County sheriff Jonathan Bethune seized John Nicholson's land in Muscogee County to satisfy a fieri facias judgment against him brought by Bedford S. Worrel, an attorney from Stewart County. The land was sold at a sheriff's auction and was described as being the "land where Hamilton Matthews now lives." Hamilton Matthews was the husband of Nathaniel Nunn Nicholson's sister Nancy. The land also adjoined Nathaniel Nunn Nicholson's land and Nathaniel bought it at the auction. The witness to the transfer of the deed was Sterling Grimes, the brother[21] of Thomas Wingfield Grimes, who was the husband of John Candor Nicholson's sister Charity. John Candor Nicholson was almost certainly John Nicholson, the father of Nathaniel Nunn Nicholson, but there is still no certain proof. Something will either turn up or not.

John Nunn was born in 1755 in North Carolina and was an avid supporter of Governor Tryon, serving as his deputy sheriff during the Regulator movement. When the Regulator movement became violent, John joined as a sergeant in Captain David Hart's Company of the Orange Regiment of Militia[22] and was actively involved in the Battle of Alamance, which broke the Regulators and caused our ancestor Jeremiah Duckworth and other Quakers to leave North Carolina for the more hospitable settlement of Wrightsborough in Georgia. There is no indication that John Nunn and Jeremiah Duckworth ever fought against each other and neither could have possibly known that, generations later, John Nunn's great-great-granddaughter Bessie Lillian Gordy would marry Jeremiah Duckworth's great-great-great-grandson James Earl Carter Sr. By the time of the Revolutionary War, John Nunn had changed sides and fought for the Patriots.[23]

John Nunn was a Fortunate Draw in the 1805 Georgia Land Lottery and was awarded land Lot 208 in Warren County. He took possession of the land June 12, 1806.[24] Our ancestor Frances Nunn would have been 21 years old at the time and undoubtedly moved to Georgia with her father at the same time. John Nicholson married Frances Nunn, the daughter of John Nunn and Eliza Pratt, in Warren County, Georgia, sometime before 1815 when their son Nathaniel Nunn Nicholson was born.

Nathaniel Nunn Nicholson

Before Nathaniel Nunn Nicholson married our ancestor Mary Elizabeth Dawson, he first married Martha Johns in 1833 and they had twelve children: James John, born in 1838, Martin Luther, born in 1840; William Jefferson, born June 2, 1843; Rebecca Lucinda, born December 8, 1845; Daniel Melson, born March 20, 1848; Nathaniel Nunn Jr., born in 1851; Samuel Pratt, born January 14, 1853; Martha E. "Mattie" Nicholson, born in 1856; twins Romulos and Calvin, born March 1, 1858; Mary Leah Mildred, born February 26, 1862; and an infant child.[25]

James John Nicholson enlisted as a private on June 4, 1861, in Co. C, 10th Regiment, Georgia Vol. Infantry of Norhtern Virginia, from Chattahoochee County — the "Chattahoochee Beauregards."[26] The 10th Regiment was assigned to Robert E. Lee's Army of Northern Virginia and fought in most of the big battles in the Civil War, including Back River, Yorktown, Lee's Mill, Williamsburg, Mechanicsville, the Seven Days Battle, Savage's Station, Allen's Farm, Malvern Hill, South Mountain, Antietam, Fredericksburg, Chancellorsville, Gettysburg, the Siege of Chattanooga, the Siege of Knoxville, the Battle of the Wilderness, Spotsylvania Court House, North Anna, Cold Harbor, the Siege of Petersburg, Cedar Creek, Sayler's Creek and Appomattox Court House. James surrendered at Tallahassee May 10, 1865, and was paroled in Albany, Georgia.

Martin Luther Nicholson enlisted on November 10, 1861, in Co. G, 31st Regiment of Ga. Vol., Evan's Brigade, Gordon's Division, Army of Northern Virginia.[27] He died in service in Savannah on January 30, 1862. Nathaniel filed a claim for his back pay but the payment was delayed while the army tried to determine the cause of death. The Confederate records show repeated inquiries, but if the cause of death was ever determined it is not in the existing records. Nathaniel had an attorney file another claim but there are no records of Nathaniel's being paid.

William Jefferson Nicholson enlisted as a private in Co. C, 10th Regiment, Georgia Vol. Infantry of Northern Virginia from Chattahoochee County. He enlisted almost a year later, May 6, 1862, in the same unit as his brother James John Nicholson. His Regiment fought at Mechanicsville in May, the Seven Days' Battles and Savage's Station in June, and Allen's Farm and Malvern Hill in July. William Jefferson contracted typhoid fever after the battle at Richmond and died September 5, 1862.[28] His unit was

The only known photograph of Nathaniel Nunn Nicholson (1822–1891), the father of Mary Ida Nicholson and great-grandfather of Jimmy Carter.

with the Army of Northern Virginia. William Jefferson was sick and was left in Richmond. He died the day after his brother James and the rest of the army, commanded by Robert E. Lee, crossed the Potomac and invaded Maryland on September 4 headed to Harpers Ferry on the 15th. William had never been paid during his four months of service and Nathaniel N. Nicholson was issued $44 cash for William's service, pay for four months at $11 per month. Nathaniel was also given William's clothing valued at twenty-five dollars.[29]

Daniel Melson Nicholson married a Spann and lived next to the Parkers in Richland. They moved to Florida. Daniel and Sophia Elizabeth "Bettie" Spann had a daughter, Mamie I. Vera Nicholson, who was born March 25, 1883, and lived in Webster County for more than 100 years. She married Samuel Brightwell in 1900.

The twin Romulus died the day he was born. Calvin seems to have died around 1870 when he was 12. Rebecca Lucinda Nicholson died when she was fourteen. My suspicion is that they died of typhoid fever, which swept through that part of Georgia during that time.

Nathaniel's wife Martha died in 1869 and Nathaniel remarried to our ancestor Elizabeth Dawson. Nathaniel and Elizabeth had three more children: Jimmy Carter's grandmother Mary Ida Nicholson, born February 10, 1871; Ira Brady Nicholson, born in 1872; and Sallie Estelle Nicholson, born in 1874.[30]

Elizabeth Dawson was the daughter of Malachi Dawson and Mary Marcus Brown. The Dawsons had emigrated from England in the early 1700s and they intermarried with another line of Nicholsons who had fled Ireland in the mid–1600s.

The Very Interesting Dawson Ancestors

Our immigrant Dawson ancestor, Jonathan Dawson, is believed to have been born around 1720 in England. Jonathan emigrated to North Carolina about 1743 and married Frances Rouse, who was from Edgefield County, South Carolina. Jonathan Sr. and Francis lived in the Cape Fear River area near Wilmington and their three known sons, Joseph, William, and our ancestor Jonathan Jr., were born there between 1745 and 1750. According to a Dawson family history,[31] Jonathan Dawson Sr. died at sea just before his son Jonathan Jr. was born; Frances married Gen. Williams of South Carolina and they moved back to that state.

There are deeds documenting that the family lived or owned land in Edgefield County until at least 1801 and Jonathan witnessed a will there in 1809. More definitive are the Revolutionary War records of our ancestor Jonathan Jr., who was by then living in the Ninety-Six District, and the records of his brother William, who was living in Edgefield County, South Carolina. Jonathan Jr. was a private in the South Carolina Militia and served under General Pickens. He also furnished supplies to the militia. His service under Gen. Pickens and his patriotic service of furnishing supplies are documented in the South Carolina Archives.[32]

Jonathan did not file for a Revolutionary War pension but his brother William did. William was a colonel in the Revolutionary War and also fought under Gen. Pickens. It is not unreasonable to speculate that the two brothers may have served together. William's pension application describes his service during the war and is quite interesting, although in the intervening 170 years since he filed the claim the document has deteriorated somewhat. Blanks indicate illegible words:

South Carolina
Edgefield District

On this first day of November the year of our Lord one thousand eight hundred and thirty two personally appeared before me in open court Richard Gantt one of the _____of said state now sitting in and for the District aforesaid. William Dawson a resident of the District and State aforesaid, aged seventy four years, _____ days who being first duly sworn according to the law, doth on his oath make the following declaration in order to obtain the benefit of the Act of Congress passed June the 7th 1832.

That he entered the service of the United States in July 1776, his first tour of military service being against the Cherokee Indians within the chartered bounds of the state's _____ in a militia company under the command of one Capt. Jefferson Williams of said District. The expedition was commanded by _____ Andrew Williamson who commanded _____ of So. Carolina militia. Encountered _____ in considerable forces at the Tupelo River, and again _____ days on subsequently at a place called Tama__ or _____ Town near the last mentioned place where several of the enemy were slain.

In the early part of 1779 the applicant repaired to his native place Cumberland County in No. Carolina _____ then and there drafted for three months and served in a company commanded by Capt. Nathaniel King, attached to Col. Johnsons Regiment and _____ Bates Brigade of North Carolina militia. _____ at crop _____ and from there was ordered to the South and effected a junction with the Army under the command of Gen. Andrew Williamson near Augusta. The applicant was at the defeat of the Army of Gen. Ash which was a detachment from Gen. Williams army, at Briar Creek in Georgia in 1779. In April following or May following the Army which was defeated at Briar Creek now under the command of _____ Lincoln commenced its march to the defense of [document torn] section of this state and engaged the enemy at the Battle of _ton_ which was fought in June 1779.

After this the applicant having a discharge from the _____ Capt. King to whose company he was yet attached _____ discharged _____ he returned to his home in Edgefield.

In ____ 1780 the _____ having all _____ of all the _____ County of South Carolina. Gen. Williamson _____ surrendered all the men (who he could) under his command near Cambridge.

_____ applicant having [?] been paroled remained in this situation till the fall of the same year when he volunteered in the service and _____ Expedition under the command of Gen. Elijah Clarke and _____ McCoy of Georgia which eventuated in an Engagement with a detachment of the enemy from the fort of Cambridge at Cedar Creek which was commanded by William Cunningham, then a Tory Colonel. Several were killed and wounded, amongst the latter of whom was Gen. Clarke. In May succeeding, the applicant _____ the army under the command of Col. Clarke and Gen. Pickens which united with a detachment of Gen. Greens Army Cavalry under Col. Lee at Augusta and was actively engaged at Fort Brown at the said _____ when Col. Brown surrendered the garrison [document torn] commands. From thence we repaired to _____ [document torn] in the vicinity of Cambridge and formed a junction with Gen. Green army which was then _____ before the fort at Cambridge attempting its reduction. This garrison was commanded by Col. Cruger. The sudden appearance of Lord Rawden in the vicinity of that place forced us to retreat from our function and make a movement towards to the low country in this state. At Eutaw our army encountered a considerable body of the enemy, in September 1781, who after a _____ several engagements retreated. In this last Expedition the applicant was attached to a company under the command of Col. Maxwell (then a resident of the District). The officers in the battle were Gens Green and Pickens, Col Martin, Col. Moore. _____ were those he had _____ so _____.

After this the applicant returned home to Edgefield where he now resides and attached to a militia company commanded by Capt. Henry King of Col. _____

From the fall of 1780 till the termination of hostilities in So. Carolina the applicant was frequently actively engaged in scout and reconnantering [sic] sorties against disaffected provincials severally called Tories. The applicant never received a discharge except the one from Capt. King. In the above declaration the applicant has _____ some of the principle events of his military campaigns and has omitted the details of his minor services which would easily fill up this [document torn] of time between the more prominent Events above [document torn] when he was not actually Engaged [document torn] were comparatively short and _____ a small _____ of time to those periods when _____ was engaged in the military service and added together would greatly exceed two years.

This deponent has no documentary evidence to add__ for the verification of this declaration but would refer to the accompanying certificate of _____ who was an active and efficient officer in the Revolutionary a corroboration in part of this said declaration.

The applicant hereby relinquishes every claim whatsoever to a [document torn] except the present and declares that his name [document torn] of the pension roll of any state. Except [document torn] pension which he hereby _____ on the sworn to and subscribed to day and year aforesaid.

(signed) William Dawson[33]

William's pension application file is quite long because he immediately became embroiled in bureaucratic redtape. There are numerous letters back and forth between William and people that he had served with and the bureau of pensions. William had to fill out new standardized forms and he spent years gathering affidavits from various people attesting to each part of his service. In his original pension application, William said that he had "omitted the details of his minor services," which of course the Bureau of Pensions decided they needed, but not until the end of 1840. William filed an amended statement of his service filling in the minor details in January of 1841, almost nine years after his original application, by which time he was 83 years old. The last correspondence between William and the Bureau of Pensions was February 20, 1841. There is also a letter in his file from someone in the Bureau of Pensions finally saying that they had no doubt that "the old man" had provided service even beyond what he had claimed and apparently that ended the case. William was awarded a pension of $80 a year for his service during the Revolutionary War. He died in 1848.

The Nicholsons from Ireland

Jonathan Dawson and Francis Rouse's son and our ancestor, Jonathan Dawson Jr., married Repsema "Repsy" Nicholson, who was born May 22, 1773. This Nicholson line seems to be completely separate from Nathaniel Nicholson's line, unless the two families were related long ago in Ireland. Repsy was the fourth generation of this Nicholson line to live in the colonies, her great-great-grandfather William Nicholson Sr. having been born in Ireland in 1669. The first record of William in the colonies is on April 23, 1698, when he witnessed the will of Joseph Matthew Commander in Pasquotank County, North Carolina. William Sr. died in 1728. His will, filed in Norfolk County, Virginia, was dated February 24, 1728, and proven May 17, 1728.[34] In his will, he left his plantation and houses to his oldest son, William Nicholson (II). He did give some land to his younger sons, including our ancestor George Nicholson, and his brother Lemuel with the provisions that they not sell their portion to anyone "out of the name Nicholson" and also "that my son William, Thomas and John Nicholson Shall have privilege to drive on and off the said land their hoggs" (see Appendix G: Wills).

By 1750, George and Lemuel Nicholson had moved to North Carolina. George witnessed a will in Edgecombe County and sold his brother 160 acres of land there in 1766.[35] Halifax County was formed from parts of Edgecombe County in 1758 and Nash County was formed from Edgecombe in 1777. George died in Nash County in 1780, possibly staying where he first moved to in Edgecombe County before Nash County was formed. In his will dated February 1773, George Nicholson mentioned his children: his firstborn son and our ancestor Wright, David, George, Edward, Malachi, Josiah, Teressa, Cloe, Elizabeth, and a granddaughter, Lydia. Wright Nicholson received only 5 shillings from his father's estate. Being the oldest, he had probably already received his inheritance.

The Nicholsons probably knew the Carters in Edgecombe County. The Carters lived close to the Hart, Pace, and Knight families and Moses Knight married Kindred Carter's daughter, Charity. In January of 1760, Thomas Hart sold 192 acres of land on Beaver Dam Swamp to John Pace in a deed witnessed by Kindred and Jesse Carter. In December of 1772, John Pace sold that same land on Beaver Dam Swamp to Wright Nicholson — George Nicholson's son and our ancestor. John Pace made a nice profit on the land, too; having bought it for a little over 31 pounds, he sold it to Wright 12 years later for 130 pounds. Moses Knight died in 1781 and the executors of his will were his wife Charity, Kindred's daughter; James Pace, John's son; and John Nicholson, George and Lemuel's brother.

Our ancestor Wright Nicholson sold the land on Beaver Dam Swamp to James McNeil in October of 1776 for 140 pounds and moved to Edgefield District, South Carolina. Wright served from the Edgefield District during the Revolutionary War. He enlisted as a private and was promoted to lieutenant before the end of the war.[36] He is also recognized for his "Patriotic Service" of providing beef for the military and was awarded a land grant of 830 acres in the Ninety-Six District for his services.

Jonathan Dawson married Wright Nicholson's daughter Repsema Nicholson and in his will, dated "One thousand eight hundred and seven and in the thirty first year of Independence of the United States of America," Wright divided his estate and left his daughter and our ancestor Repsy Dawson $250.[37]

In 1801, Jonathan and Repsy Dawson sold, for $250, 169 acres on "Mountain Creek of Big Turkey Creek of Stephens Creek of Savannah River" to Eli Stringer. Justice James Harrison certified the relinquishment of her dower rights by "Repsema Dawson wife of Jonathan Dawson."[38] Jonathan had been granted 196 acres in Edgefield County on Mountain Creek in 1797, and although it is not known when Jonathan and Repsema moved to Georgia, it was probably soon after. Our ancestor Malekiah (Malachi) Dawson was born in Georgia in 1808[39] and married Mary Marcus Brown on November 24, 1830, in Jones County.[40]

Mary Marcus Brown was the daughter of Hollinger Brown, whose family had come from Virginia, and Sarah Cassandra Marcus, whose family had moved to Georgia from Indiana.

The Gaines and Brown Families

Hollinger Brown was the son of John Brown and Mildred Gaines and the ancestry of the Gaines family is far from clear. In the *History of the Gaines Family*, L.P. Gaines reports that two brothers, Richard and Roger Gaines, emigrated from Wales to Virginia about 1620. The book also notes a statement by descendants of Captain Daniel Gaines that five brothers emigrated from Wales. A family history written by a granddaughter of Francis Gaines says four brothers emigrated. George Strother Gaines wrote a letter to a relative in 1864 which says seven brothers emigrated. In fact, four branches of the Gaines family say two brothers emigrated, five branches of the family say three brothers emigrated, four branches say five brothers emigrated, and two branches say it was seven brothers.[41] What is agreed upon is that a Richard Gaines was born around 1670 or 1680 in Culpepper, Virginia, and lived there until he died in 1755. There are surviving records of the inventory and settlement of his estate between 1755 and 1759. It is thought that this Richard had seven sons, including our ancestor Richard Gaines (II), and four daughters.

Richard Gaines (II) was born in 1726 and married Mildred Hollinger in 1747. He fought in the Revolutionary War, serving as a private and sergeant in the 5th Virginia Regiment under Lieut, Col. Holt Richerson.[42] Two of his brothers also served and were killed in the war at Braddock's Defeat. Richard and Mildred had at least six sons, and three of them, Captain Richard Gaines Jr., Robert Gaines, and Thomas Gaines, were also soldiers in the Revolutionary War.

Richard Gaines (II) and Mildred Hollinger's daughter and our ancestor, Mildred Gaines, was born January 1, 1761, and was baptized in Goochland Parish on March 15 of that year. She married John Brown, the son of William and Mary Brown, in Charlotte County, Virginia, February 1, 1779.[43]

Not a lot is known about John Brown's parents, William and Mary Brown, except that they were living in Virginia when he was born. Mary Brown's maiden name is not known nor is John Brown's birthday. What is known is that their son John Brown married Millie Gaines and that our ancestor Hollinger Brown was John and Millie's fourth son. Hollinger was born in Virginia on December 31, 1785, and the whole family moved to Georgia sometime after 1788. John and Millie Brown both died in Baldwin County, Georgia, in 1814.[44]

Hollinger met Sarah Cassandra Marcus after the move to Georgia and married her on December 29, 1808, in Baldwin County, Georgia.[45] Sarah was the daughter of Daniel Marcus, whose wife may have been named Mary. Daniel Marcus was another of our ancestors who served in the Revolutionary War.[46] Daniel was the son of Ellis and Mary Marcus, who lived in Edgefield County, South Carolina. Ellis Marcus was probably our immigrant ancestor of the Marcus line and he obtained a royal land grant in 1744 from the Earl of Granville from land given to Granville by King George the Second (see Appendix F: Land Grant to Ellis Marcus by the Earl of Granville).

Ellis Marcus died in 1789 and left a will,[47] written a few months before his death. In his will, Ellis left everything to his wife Mary except for the feather beds of his daughters who still lived with him, which he gave to them, and a few cows that he also gave his daughters. The will reflects the British primogeniture custom of the time and, after his wife's decease, he gave all of his land and the plantation house where he had lived to his eldest son, Joshua. His wife and son Daniel Marcus were made executrix and executor of the will, which split his personal belongings between his seven children after Mary died. Daniel Marcus was 26 years old and had no land of his own, his oldest brother having inherited his father's land and plantation, Daniel and his family, and Hollinger Brown and his wife Sarah Marcus and their family, moved to Jones County, Georgia, about the turn of the century. According to the 1840 agricultural census, Hollinger was living in Jones County where he owned 20 slaves, 9 of whom were working as farm laborers. Hollinger and Sarah moved to Stewart County shortly after that and lived there for the rest of their lives. The 1850 Slave Schedule showed Hollinger living in Stewart County and owning 29 slaves.[48]

Hollinger Brown and Sarah Marcus had seven children: Amelia Gaines, born May 4, 1810; our ancestor Mary Marcus Brown, born October 15, 1812; Brady Mitchell Brown, born April 13, 1816; Hollinger Daniel Brown, born June 6, 1819; Sarah Ann Elizabeth Brown, born October 22, 1822; Louisa Jane Brown, born February 15, 1825; and William Thomas Brown, born August 5, 1828.[49]

Hollinger Daniel Brown married Lydia Wadsworth Cole and his brother Brady married Lydia's sister, Nancy Cole. Brady Mitchell Brown was a hard man. His job was to round up runaway slaves or those away from home after dark. One man he found and whipped was a trusted slave of the Sneads. The Sneads were enraged over the incident and they and some friends approached Brady at his home. In the resulting confrontation, Brady Brown was killed. The Sneads and their friends immediately left town and although the Browns and Brady's wife's family, the Coles, sought them, they were never found. Thinking that the fugitives had fled west, the Coles posted a reward in several newspapers in Mississippi and Alabama:

The MISSISSIPIAN

The State Government is a Beautiful Structure — It Stands, However, on *the Naked Beach—The Union is the Dyke to Fence Out the Flood.*

| Pub. by G.R. | Fall Volume 1— No. 4 |
| JACKSON MI. | FRIDAY, MAY 14, 1841 |

[Front Page]

$1000 Reward

The subscribers will give ONE THOUSAND DOLIARS reward, for the apprehension and safe confinement of GARLAND SNEAD, GEORGE J. HUNT, PETER SNEAD & OWEN GRIMSLEY within the State of Mississippi; or we will give a proportional part for either of them.—Said men committed murder upon one Bradley M. Brown of Kemper county, Miss., on the 14th February 1841.

REUBEN COLE
JAMES M. COLE

Description:— Garland Snead is about 34 years of age weighs about 160 lbs, about 5 feet 7 or 8 inches high, fair complexion, prominent blue eyes, dark hair, heavy beard, with a few grey hairs, full face square built, under teeth project beyond the upper teeth, has a shrill sharp voice, his appearance genteel and prepossessing; on his left little finger, at the middle Joint, out-side there is a limp [lump?] about one-fourth of an inch high.

Peter Snead is about 38 years of age weighs about 140 lbs, about 5 feet 10 or 11 inches high, fair complexion, dark hair, little grey blue eyes sharp features, the upper teeth back of the eye-teeth out, awkward built, and quite awkward appearance and address, stoops some when moving.

George J. Hunt is about 40 years of age five feet 7 or 8 inches high, weighs about 150 or 60 Lbs, dark swarthy complexion, black hair, thin beard, heavy gloomy coarse features, with large light blue eyes, right eye blinks, and on close examination will be found blind in that eye, square built, slow spoken, a shoemaker by trade. Owen Grimsley is about 22 years of age five feet 9 or 10 inches high, weighs about 170 lbs., square stout built, dark complexion, dark hair, dark eyes, light beard, a shoemaker by trade. February. 20, 1941.

The New Orleans Bulletin, Louisville Journal, Free Trader, Natchez, Houston Telegraph, Texas, will give the above twelve insertions and forward their accounts to this office.

A Hollinger family legend says that years later in Palmer, Texas, by a quirk of fate, Brady's nephew, Hollinger Daniel Brown Jr., overheard a man from McKinsey, Tennessee, tell the story of Snead confessing to the murder on his death bed.[50]

Malekiah Dawson and Mary Marcus Brown and Back to Nathaniel Nunn Nicholson

Malachi (Malekiah) Dawson, the son of Jonathan Dawson and Repsema Nicholson, and Mary Marcus Brown, the daughter of Hollinger Brown and Sarah Cassandra Marcus, were married in 1830 in Jones County, Georgia, where Mary's parents lived. Malachi and Mary then moved and settled in Upson County close to Malachi's family. While living in Upson County, Malachi and Mary had seven children: Hollinger Dawson, born in 1832 and named after his grandfather; Ann, born in 1834; our ancestor Mary Elizabeth Dawson, born in 1836; Davis, born in 1840; Brady, born in 1842; Sarah, born in 1843; and John, born in 1848.[51]

Malachi was a prosperous farmer and owned nine slaves in 1850.[52] By 1860, Malachi and his family had moved to Marion County and his slaves had children. The 1860 U.S. Census Slave Schedules shows that Malachi owned twenty slaves, ten of whom were ten years old or younger. The Civil War was coming and Hollinger, Davis, and Brady joined the Confederacy.

Left: James Jackson Gordy (1863–1948), the husband of Mary Ida Nicholson and grandfather of Jimmy Carter. The photograph was taken around 1910. *Right:* Mary Ida Nicholson (1871–1951), the wife of James Jackson Gordy and grandmother of Jimmy Carter. The photograph was taken around 1910.

Lillian Carter, President Jimmy Carter's mother, and his brother, William Alton Carter, at the Carters' pond outside of Plains. The photograph was taken around 1945.

Davis Dawson joined Company B, Cutt's Battalion, the 11th Battalion Georgia Artillery known as the Sumter Flying Artillery. Several of our other Carter ancestors and their brothers also served with the Sumter Flying Artillery. Davis became violently ill at the end of August 1862 and was admitted into General Hospital No. 17 in Richmond, Virginia, on September 25, 1862. Davis was sick for several months and when he returned to duty in July 1863, he was assigned to guard duty in Georgia after the port surgeon in Macon declared him unfit for field service until he further recovered. Davis returned to his unit and was wounded in Gordonsville, Virginia, in November 1863. He was transferred to the Floyd House and Ocmulgee Hospital in Macon, Georgia, November 20, 1863, and deserted four days later.[53]

Brady Dawson joined Company G, 31st Regiment of the Georgia Infantry, Evans' Brigade, Gordon's Division, Army of Northern Virginia; enlisting November 10, 1861, the day the unit was formed. Martin Luther Nicholson, Brady's nephew[54] who would be killed in the Battle of Savannah, joined the unit the same day.

Hollinger B. Dawson enlisted as a 2nd lieutenant in Company I, 17th Infantry Regiment, Georgia, August 15, 1861, and helped form the unit, which was officially organized August 19. Hollinger was part of Benning's Brigade, Field's Division, Longstreet's Corps, Army of Northern Virginia. They were sent by train through Tennessee and saw their first combat in May 1862 during the Peninsula Campaign serving under Gen. John B. Magruder as he opposed the advance of Maj. Gen. George B. McClellan. After this battle, the brigade came under the command of Robert E. Lee and engaged the Union Army at the Battle of Garnett's Farm on June 27, 1862.

On July 1, 1862, the 17th fought in the Seven Days' Campaign, losing almost 300 men, including two regimental commanders. Hollinger and the 17th Infantry Regiment then crossed the Potomac with Lee and were engaged in the Maryland Campaign. They fought at Antietam, preventing Ambrose Burnside from crossing Antietam Creek. After Antietam, Colonel Benning assumed command of the 17th and they fought at the Battle of Fredericksburg. The final battle for Hollinger was at Gettysburg, where the regiment attacked and captured the Union Army defending Devil's Den at the foot of Little Round Top. Hollinger was captured at Gettysburg July 3, 1863, and was sent to the Union POW camp at Johnson's Island, Fort Delaware.[55] On December 22, 1863, Hollinger became one of the 2,927 Confederate military prisoners to die at the Fort Delaware prison camp. He is buried in Grave #111.[56]

Hollinger's sister, Mary Elizabeth Dawson, married Nathaniel Nunn Nicholson. Their daughter and Jimmy Carter's grandmother, Mary Ida Nicholson, was born February 10, 1871.

Mary Ida Nicholson married James Jackson Gordy on September 6, 1888, in Chattahoochee County, Georgia. President Jimmy Carter's mother, Bessie Lillian Gordy, was born August 15, 1898, in Stewart County, Georgia.

Chapter 8

ANCESTORS OF JOHN WILLIAM MURRAY

John William Murray was the grandfather of Eleanor Rosalynn Smith and the father of her mother, Frances Allethea Murray, or "Mother Allie," as we all knew her. John William Murray, who was always referred to as Captain Murray by his friends and Papa by his family, was the husband of Rosa Nettie Wise. Papa was born in Plains, Georgia, in 1871, and lived there all of his life until 1966.

The Murray line itself can be traced back to James Murray, who was born in Virginia in 1724. Before then, there are strong indications of the line but no positive proof. It may go back to David Murray, who was probably born in Angarsk, Perthshire, Scotland, in 1598,

Drury Murray (1787–1862), the great-great-grandfather of Eleanor Rosalynn Smith, and Susan Champion (1795–1878), the great-great-grandmother of Eleanor Rosalynn Smith. These are the Carter family's rarest photographs. The originals are full plate (8½" × 6½") daguerreotypes. They were taken around 1850.

but it is also possible that he was from Northern Ireland. Our Murray ancestors lived in Virginia for a generation or more; then they migrated south to Duplin County, North Carolina, and then to Onslow County, where they lived for three generations. Nathan Murray met and married Martha Albritton in Onslow County. The Albrittons had immigrated to Virginia from England in the mid–1600s and had lived in Virginia for four generations before moving to North Carolina. Nathan and Martha's son, Drury Murray, married Catherine Russell in Onslow County and when Catherine died, Drury became the first of our Murray ancestors to move to Georgia.

Drury's son by his second wife, Susan Champion, was John William Fulwood Murray, who was born in Georgia in 1833 and who married Alethea Josephine Parker. Alethea Josephine Parker's ancestry is almost totally unknown. Her parents were William John Parker and Alethea Lawhon. There is very little information about either of William John Parker's parents. Alethea Lawhon's parents were Noel Lawhon and Sarah Bethune and there is virtually no information about the Lawhons.

Rosa Nettie Wise and John William Murray, Rosalynn Smith's grandparents. This photograph is actually a composite of two photographs and was printed in their wedding announcement in 1904.

It is ironic that for three of Alethea Josephine Parker's grandparents there are almost no records, because the fourth, her mother's mother, was Sarah Bethune. The Bethunes immigrated from Scotland to South Carolina in the mid–1700s and their lineage is extraordinary and can be reliably traced for almost a thousand years.

The Provable Murrays

In the early 1700s, Virginia was awarding bounties in the form of fifty-acre headrights to persons who transported new immigrants to the colony. Most of the names of these immigrants, and the ships they arrived on, have been preserved in the records filed by the ship captains and others in their headright applications for land. Many of the immigrants from Scotland and Ireland were fleeing persecution or being exiled for their support of James Francis Stuart, the "Old Pretender" and son of deposed King James II. In the records of Virginia in the early 1700s, there are at least forty-five Murrays, most of who were named James or had a James in their family in honor of the Old Pretender. Our first provable Murray ancestor is James Murray of Nansemond County, Virginia. James' wife was probably Elizabeth Edwards and they had at least three sons: James Jr., David, and Jonathan Murray.

In May of 1725, James Murray bought 250 acres of land in Albemarle County, North Carolina, and moved there from Nansemond County, Virginia. Over the next four years,

James bought another 440 acres of land and sold 500 acres. James paid £32 for his 690 acres and received £51 for the 500 acres that he sold, making a handsome profit and still retaining 190 acres.[1]

It was an interesting time for James and his family to move to North Carolina. Lord Granville had instructed Sir Nathaniel Moore to establish the Church of England in North Carolina by legal authority and in 1702 the general assembly had passed a new tax of 30 pounds per precinct for the purpose of supporting a minister of that church. This was met with widespread discontent among the numerous Quakers, Lutherans, Presbyterians, and Independents. Sir Moore then appointed Thomas Cary as deputy governor. This was met with widespread discontent among the Proprietors, who disliked Cary and instead appointed their own man, William Glover, to the position. Cary responded by seizing the provincial records and declaring himself governor, which sent the colony into anarchy. In 1711, Edward Hyde arrived with an armed brig and a commission from the Proprietors appointing him deputy governor but Cary refused to yield. Hyde appealed for help to Alexander Spotswood, governor of Virginia, and Governor Spotswood sent his marines to North Carolina, where they arrested Cary and sent him back to London and his fate.

Charles Eden became governor in 1713 and it was during his administration that Edward Teach, "Blackbeard" the pirate, was plaguing the colony. Teach had accepted a pardon but after squandering his fortune in a licentious manner, he had returned to piracy. He was killed during a hand-to-hand fight in 1718 after being tracked down by Lt. Maynard, who sailed back to Bath with Teach's head mounted on a pole on his ship. Governor Eden had been darkly rumored to be a friend of Edward Teach and a major scandal swept the colony when a letter from Eden's secretary, intimating friendship and mutual respect with the governor, was found on Teach's corpse. Governor Eden died in March of 1722 and Governor George Burrington was appointed in January 1724. Governor Burrington was the son of a supporter of Charles I, seemingly his only qualification. So many complaints were lodged against him that he was replaced by Sir Richard Everhard in 1725.

James Murray would surely have known all of this before he decided to leave Virginia and move to North Carolina in 1725. He must have had good reason to leave Virginia and move to a much less stable colony; or perhaps he thought that the politics was at such a high level that ordinary people would be unaffected. What he probably did not know was the level of concern being expressed over the colony in London. South Carolina had already revolted against the Proprietors. Governor Johnston had been forced to leave and the colony had reverted to the Crown. The Proprietors of North Carolina were well aware of the instability of their colony and the example of South Carolina. When King Charles II proposed a buyout of their interest, all accepted except Lord Granville. Lord Granville became Lord Granville upon the death of his mother, the Countess of Granville. Before that, he was Lord John Carteret, the grandson of Sir George Carteret. James Murray, being from Virginia, would have been well aware of Lord Carteret. James had ended up in the Granville District after the other Proprietors sold their shares back to King Charles II and when the king offered land grants in the newly formed Onslow County in April 1741, James did the only reasonable thing. He applied for a land grant the next month, in May 1741,[2] and he and Elizabeth moved to Onslow County shortly thereafter. James Jr. and James Sr. eventually accumulated 940 acres in land grants.[3]

In 1754, James and Elizabeth's son and our ancestor, Jonathan Murray of Duplin County, bought 200 acres in Onslow County. In 1755, Jonathan was awarded a fifty-acre land grant in Duplin County but by then he had married Charity Jenkins and they had settled in Onslow County, so he and Charity sold that land to Abraham Herring for 30 pounds.

Charity Jenkins was the oldest child of Thomas and Margaret Jenkins of Onslow county. Thomas Jenkins bought and sold land in and around Onslow County and witnessed numerous deeds but did not leave any clues as to the identity of his parents. One day, for some reason, while Thomas was at the Onslow deed office, he wrote the names and birthdates of his seven children in the Onslow deed book. His entry was witnessed by Lewis Jenkins, possibly a relative. In the deed book, Thomas listed his children as "Charity Jenkins, July 23, 1735; Agnes Jenkins, October 20, 1737; Rebecca Jenkins, August 6, 1739; Jonathan Jenkins, March 6, 1741; son Rees Jenkins, March 19, 1743; Margaret Jenkins, March 2, 1745; Rey Jenkins, August 22, 1745. Signed: Lewis Jenkins, Registrar."[4]

In 1764, Jonathan Murray sold 50 acres in Duplin County to his brother James Murray Jr. The land adjoined land that James already owned and there is no record of Jonathan ever having bought it. Probably, James Sr. had given the land to his sons, and Jonathan, having established himself in Onslow, sold his part to his brother.[5]

Jonathan Murray's will is dated December 8, 1808, and in it he mentions five grandchildren, sons and daughters of our ancestor Nathan Murray, deceased: Hosea, Druery [sic], Mary, Serena, and Jonathan Murray. Jonathan's will also mentions his daughter Mary Hicks, son James Murray, son-in-law James Ballard, and his granddaughter Elizabeth Murray. Executors were his son James Murray and son-in-law James Ballard.[6]

Jonathan Murray and Charity Jenkins' son Nathan married Martha Albritton. Nathan Murray and Martha Albritton are great-great-great-grandparents of Eleanor Rosalynn Smith.

The Albrittons

The first of our Albritton ancestors to reach the colonies was probably Joseph Albrighton. Joseph was born in Staffordshire County, England, sometime around 1630, and immigrated to York County, Virginia, before 1650. Joseph is believed to be the father of Ralph Albritton, who was born in 1656 in York County and died there January 21, 1700/01. There is only circumstantial evidence that Joseph was the father of Ralph Albritton and, although his father is not provably identified, the descendants of Ralph Albritton are well documented. Ralph married Mary Wooten, the daughter of Thomas Wooten and Sara Wood from Isle of Wight[7] and they had eight children. Their oldest child was our ancestor Thomas Albritton, who was born August 1, 1682, in York County and died March 3, 1730/31, in Princess Anne County, Virginia.

Thomas Albritton moved from York County to Currituck County, North Carolina, and then back to Virginia to Princess Anne County, just across the border north of Currituck. Thomas was a saddle maker and farmer and he bought and sold land in all three counties. Thomas Albritton married twice. His first wife was Agnes, by whom he had two children: our ancestor James Albritton, born September 17, 1705, and a daughter, Agnes, born in March of 1706/07. Thomas' second wife was named Ann. In his will, he split his estate between his wife, Ann, and son, James, and left James his saddle making tools. James apparently did not get along with his stepmother and refused to act as executor of the will.[8]

James Albritton married Elizabeth. She may have been Elizabeth Lanier, the daughter of John Lanier and Elizabeth Bird but there is no proof of it. After his father, Thomas Albritton died, James and Elizabeth bought land in Beaufort County, North Carolina, in

1744. They then sold the Beaufort County land and moved to Onslow County in 1750. Then they sold the Onslow County land and moved back to Beaufort County. They then sold the Beaufort County land and moved to Pitt County. At some point, Elizabeth died and James married a woman named Ann from Onslow County.

In 1858, a man named Croom set fire to the Pitt County Courthouse while trying to destroy a will. The courthouse burned to the ground. It was rebuilt in 1877. In 1910, that courthouse burned in what was described in the newspapers as, "one of the worst fires in Greenville history," the Pitt County courthouse being in Greenville, North Carolina. Many of the Pitt County records are missing. However, James' sons are positively identified in a complex deed whereby land conveyed, "...to James Albritton Senr and by James Albritton Senr conveyed by his last Will and testament to us his four sons to Wit Thomas, James, Peter and Mathew Albritton,"[9] was sold to George Albritton.

James Albritton's son and our ancestor, Matthew Albritton, was born around 1734 and died in 1782 when he was 48 years old. He is believed to have married Susannah Oliver in 1757. Matthew and Susannah had five children. Their fourth child and our ancestor, Martha Albritton, was born in 1764. Martha Albritton married Nathan Murray in 1780 when she was about sixteen years old and they had seven children: Hosea, Mary, our ancestor Drury, Cyrene, Matthew, Jonathan, and James, who died at birth.

Nathan Murray served in the North Carolina Regiment during the Revolutionary War and several of his descendents have joined the DAR as a result of his service.

The Search for Susan Champion

Drury Murray was born January 8, 1781, in Onslow, North Carolina, and married Catherine Russell, also of Onslow, in 1813. They had three daughters: Martha, who was born in 1815; Dorothy, who was born in 1819 and only lived four months; and Elinor, who was born June 27, 1827. Catherine may not have recovered from the childbirth, as she died a few months later, on September 7, 1827, when she was about 28 years old. Two years later, Drury married Susan Champion of Onslow on September 10, 1829, and sometime thereafter they moved to Georgia. At least, that is the story you will encounter over and over when researching the family. It did not agree with our family history, and for good reason. The identity and origin of Susan Champion, whose name was actually Susannah, is one of the mysteries of the Murray family and there is almost no information about her except that she was born on September 10, 1795.

The first step in the latest search was to check the 1790 census of Onslow County, which was actually completed in 1792, but was still before Susannah was born. I had hoped that there would not be too many Champion families reporting female children under 10 years of age. Comparing it to the 1800 census to see who had new female children under 10, if there were few enough of them, Susan's likely parents might be identified in this way. In fact, there were not too many Champions listed in the 1790 census of Onslow County. There were none.

Drury bought and sold quite a few pieces of land, and three of his deeds in our collection of family documents are very interesting. On November 5, 1819, Drury bought 202½ acres from Lark Boyette. The land was listed as being "Lot 26 in Old Wilkinson County now Laurens County in the State of Georgia."[10] The next interesting deed was for "Lot 81, 1st District of the County originally Wilkinson, now Laurens County." Drury bought the lot from Jesse Young for $225 on December 10, 1825. Both men are described as being "of Laurens County."[11] The third interesting deed is dated January 19, 1828, and it records that "Drury Murray of the County of Laurens," bought from James H Kidd "Lot 55, 2nd District County originally Wilkinson, now Laurens County."[12]

Research of the abstract of the deeds of Onslow County at that time revealed two more interesting deeds. One abstract says, "February 13, 1818. Drury Murray sold to Greer Bishop for 25 dollars, 12½ acres of land which fell to my wife, Catherine at the death of her father. Test: David Gornto, John Russell."[13] The other one says, "February 13, 1818. Drury Murray sold to Jonothan Murray for 275 dollars land of south side of SW branch of New River in 3 different parcels."[14]

Drury sold his wife's land in Onslow County to Greer Bishop and sold his land to his brother who lived next to him. On the same day in February of 1818, Drury sold four parcels of land and in November bought 202½ acres in Laurens County, Georgia. What is most interesting is the dates of these deeds. They prove that Drury wasn't in Onslow County in 1829 to marry Susan Champion. Drury and Catherine had moved for good by mid to late 1818. Drury was in Laurens County, Georgia, and had been for years by 1829. In fact, there seems to be no evidence that Susan was ever in Onslow County. But there is evidence that she was born in North Carolina.

The 1850 United States Census of the 17th Division, Sumter County, Georgia, shows Drewry (Drury) Murray, 62 years old, and Susannah Murray, 55, living in Sumter County. Susannah is listed as having been born in North Carolina, as she is in the 1860 census. So, if Susan was from North Carolina but not Onslow County, then where was she from?

There were only about twenty Champion heads of households in North Carolina in the 1800 Census. In 1800, this probably represented three or so extended families of fathers, brothers and sons living close to each other. The Champions were named John, Jesse, William, Joab, Benjamin, Elias, James, Henry, and Isaac, among others.

The census shows that of the Champion households in North Carolina in 1800, only a few had daughters matching Susan Champion's age. James and Elias Champion of Cumberland County had one and two females under 10, respectively. Jesse, in Edgecombe County, had three, William, in Halifax County, had one daughter under 10. Joab Champion had a daughter under 10, but Joab didn't post his marriage bond until December 24, 1796, so he was married too late to be Susan Champion's father. Theoretically, that left only four possible fathers for Susan Champion: James, Elias, Jesse, and William. However, after I checked these Champions others turned up. Also, almost all of them moved, making them difficult to definitively trace more than 200 years later.

But if Drury had lived in Laurens County for over a decade before marrying Susan Champion in 1829, he most likely met her there. In the 1830 U.S. Census, there are nineteen heads of households in Georgia named Champion. The only one living in Laurens County was Elias Fort Champion. These Champion names were familiar, but from 150 years earlier and from the Carter line.

In Isle of Wight, Virginia, on September 28, 1696, Thomas Moore sold to Edward Champion Jr. the land that he had bought from Edward Cobb. The land adjoined Orlando Champion's land on the west side of the Blackwater Swamp. The deed identifies Edward Champion as the father of Orlando, names Benjamin and Alice Champion, and identifies George Moore as Thomas Moore's brother. Thomas sold the land for an amount of tobacco that he put in a trust for "my niece Magdalen Carter, the same amount for Priscilla Champion."[15]

Magdalen Moore was George Moore's daughter and Priscilla Moore was the daughter of his brother Thomas Moore. Magdalen Moore married Thomas Carter and Priscilla Moore married Edward Champion.[16] As Thomas set up a trust for the funds, the Priscilla Champion he mentions was probably a minor, the daughter of Edward Champion and Priscilla Moore — Thomas' granddaughter, and not his daughter, Edward Champion's wife.

Edward Champion and Priscilla Moore's son, Benjamin Champion, was born in 1680 in Isle of Wight and died in Surry County, Virginia, in 1735, Surry County being the county to the northwest of Isle of Wight. He married Elizabeth Williams and they had several children including four sons: John, Benjamin, Charles and William Champion. John Champion was born in Surry County, Virginia, in 1705 and married Lucy Hart. They apparently lived in Surry all of their lives and John died there in 1755. He and Elizabeth had four sons: John, Benjamin, William, and Hart Champion.

William Champion is most interesting. William married Mary Fort and they lived in Virginia and North Carolina before moving to Worth County, Georgia. Two of William and Mary's sons also moved to Georgia. Elias Fort Champion was born in 1773, in Cumberland, North Carolina, and died in 1865, in Laurens County, Georgia; Micajah Fort Champion was born February 15, 1790, in Halifax County and died in 1871 in Worth County, Georgia.[17] Elias Fort Champion and Micajah Fort Champion seem to be the only Champions in North Carolina who had daughters under ten years of age, as shown in the 1800 census, and who moved to Georgia.

On November 24, 1820, Elias Fort Champion sold to his uncle John Champion, both of Laurens County, Lot 108 in the 2nd District of "old Wilkinson County now Laurens County, Georgia."[18] The lot was 70 acres bordering on the Oconee River, for which John Champion paid Elias $50.00. The deed was witnessed by Samuel Faust and Susannah Champion.

Drury had been in Laurens County since 1818 and Susannah was there by at least 1820. Susannah was part of the Champion family that had lived with the Carter family in Isle of Wight, Virginia, in the late 1600's. The Carters and Champions had moved to Edgecombe and Halifax counties, North Carolina, together and then to Wilkes, Warren, and Laurens counties, Georgia, together. The Carters and Champions had then moved to Sumter, Marion, and Dougherty County, Georgia, together and still live near each other today, more than three hundred years after the families first met.

Susan Champion was born September 10, 1795, in North Carolina and married Drury Murray in Laurens County, Georgia, in 1829. Elias Fort Champion was born in 1773 in North Carolina and had a daughter under ten years old in the 1800 census. Elias was one of two known Champions in North Carolina who had daughters of the right age and who moved to Georgia and he was the only Champion who moved to Laurens County. In 1820, Susannah witnessed a deed for Elias in Laurens County. Susannah Champion was almost certainly a close relative of Elias Fort Champion although her exact relationship remains unknown.

Drury Murray and Susan Champion had four children: Mary Murray, born September 30, 1831; our ancestor John William Fulwood Murray, born August 9, 1833; Charity A. Murray, born March 16, 1837; and Queen Ann Elizabeth Murray, born April 12, 1839.[19]

On March 21, 1833, Drury bought 202½ acres of land in Lee County, Georgia, from Samuel Dasher for "one hundred dollars good and lawful money" and moved his family there from Laurens County. That part of Lee County became Sumter County later that year. On January 21, 1834, Drury bought an adjoining lot of 202½ acres, "originally in the county of Lee now Sumter," from William A. Morris for $225. On January 17, 1835, Drury bought another 202½ acres for $475 from Merril Williams. Also in 1835, Drury bought 202½ acres from Boling Whitlow for $100 and another 202½ acres from Edward Boyaw for $100. All of these lots were won by the owners in the 1827 Georgia Land Lottery, the fifth land lottery in the state, which divided Lee County into lots. Almost 200 years later, most of this land is still owned by our family.

Drury and Susan's son and our ancestor John William Fulwood Murray married Alethea Josephine Parker, the daughter of William John Parker and Alethea Lawhon. Alethea Lawhon's mother was Sarah Bethune and her extraordinary lineage can be traced back almost a thousand years in Scotland before they arrived in South Carolina in 1774 (see Appendix D: The Bethune Lineage in Scotland).

The Bethunes in America

The Jacobite uprising of 1745 ended with the Battle of Culloden Moor in April 1746. For all practical purposes, that was the final clash between the Jacobites and the Hanoverians and it ended the French-supported Jacobites' attempt to restore the House of Stuart to the throne of Great Britain. The majority of Highland Scots supported Charles Stuart, "Bonnie Prince Charlie," the "Young Pretender," who was the grandson of the deposed James II.

After Charles Stuart and the Scottish Highlanders defeated George II's Hanoverian army in Scotland, King George withdrew his forces from Flanders and, thus reinforced, began to reclaim the territory. The Jacobites supporting Charles Stuart were untrained, poorly armed, and divided along religious lines; the Catholic and Episcopalian Scots generally supported Stuart, while the Presbyterian Scots supported the British House of Hanover. Desertions by the Presbyterian Scots plagued the Jacobite army throughout the rebellion.

The two sides' final big clash occurred on April 16, 1746, at Culloden Moor. In a very unwise decision, Charles Stuart took personal command of the Jacobite army and held them in place waiting for the British to charge. But instead of mounting a charge, the British opened with a devastating artillery barrage against the Young Pretender's stationary army. Many of the clan chiefs who were leading their men were killed, and as the battle wore on it turned into a rout of the Jacobites. Between 1500 and 2000 of the Jacobite army were killed or wounded compared to about 300 of the British army. Charles Stuart fled and escaped, chased constantly by the British forces across the Hebrides Islands until he made it to Isle of Skye, where he escaped, with the help of Flora MacDonald, who in a famous ploy dressed Stuart in women's clothing and smuggled him aboard a ship. Stuart sailed from Skye to France and never returned to Scotland.

Thousands of Scottish prisoners were taken by King George's army and many were transported to the colonies and sold as indentured servants. The leaders were executed. The land of the rebellious clans was confiscated and sold. Over the following two decades, the clan system in Scotland was destroyed and many of the Highlanders were forcibly evicted during the "Highland Clearances." Our family had ancestors on both sides of the conflict, but whichever side they were on they, too, were affected by the huge transformation of Scottish society that resulted from the English rule and they joined many of their Scottish kinsmen and emigrated.

Colin Bethune and his wife Janet Frazer came to Wilmington, North Carolina, from

Isle of Skye,[20] Scotland, arriving in about 1772 aboard the ship *Baliol*.[21] The ship would gain some amount of historical fame two years later. After Flora MacDonald helped Bonnie Prince Charlie escape to France by dressing him up in women's clothes and smuggling him out of the country, she was arrested and imprisoned in the Tower of London. After she was released, she and her husband and family decided to emigrate to America. They left from Campbeltown, Kintyre, and landed in Wilmington, North Carolina, in the fall of 1774. They sailed on the *Baliol*[22] just two years after Colin and his wife Janet.

Colin Bethune and his family evidently were very successful in North Carolina. A history book of North Carolina biographies says this about him:

> In old Robeson and new Hoke County the name Bethune has been one of distinction for practical achievement and value of citizenship for many generations. A finer class of people exists nowhere than the North Carolina Scotch, and the Bethunes have their proper share of honors among this worthy race.
>
> A short time before the Revolutionary war Colin Bethune came from Scotland, and making settlement acquired land which was for many years the Bethune homestead in North Carolina. The old place is easily distinguished now, because it is the site of the state tuberculosis sanitarium, about ten miles west of Raeford in Hoke, but formerly Robeson County. A more beautiful bit of topography can hardly lie found in the entire state. Its selection for the tuberculosis sanitarium was based upon considerations of altitude, favorable climatic conditions, pure water, and the general charm and beauty of the landscape constituting an almost ideal environment.
>
> A son of Colin Bethune was Hon. Lauchlin [Laughlin] Bethune,[23] who represented this district of North Carolina in Congress in the days when Andrew Jackson was President. He was a man of learning and versatile ability, and his leadership meant much to the people of old Cumberland County.[24]

Colin Bethune arrived in America shortly before the Revolution and, like many of the Presbyterian Highland Scots, he probably supported the Tories. Immediately after the war supporters of the British were not in good standing in the former colonies and many were arrested and otherwise harassed and driven from the country. Quite a few of Colin's neighbors either moved back to England or moved to Nova Scotia. Colin did not fight in the Revolution and after the war he and his family stayed and apparently weathered the anti–Tory storm; but it seems that he did not get off without some recriminations.

In 1856, Rev. E.W. Carruthers wrote *Interesting Revolutionary Incidents and Sketches of Character, Chiefly in the "Old North State,"* in which he described the treatment of the post revolutionary Tory soldiers and sympathizers. He also described how many were driven from the States and remarked about how many good people were thus lost to their communities and how well those who remained had been integrated back into their societies and had prospered. Carruthers mentions Colin Bethune in a tantalizing sentence: "Col. Ray, Capt. McLean, Capt. McKay and others, also left very respectable families and connections. The same may be said in regard to many who were then only private individuals, and but little known. The Hon. Laughlin Bethune, for example, formerly a member of Congress, was the son of the Colin Bethune, who has been already mentioned as having been so maltreated when a prisoner." But Colin had not "been already mentioned." This is the only sentence about Colin Bethune in three editions of the book. There are no other references to Colin's being a prisoner or being mistreated — another story lost in time.

Colin Bethune died in 1781 and is believed to be buried in the cemetery at the Old Bethesda Presbyterian Church in Moore County, North Carolina.

The Legend of Martin Bethune

Besides Laughlin, Colin Bethune and Janet had another son, Martin Bethune, who was the great-great-great-great-grandfather of Eleanor Rosalynn Smith. Martin was born in 1740 in Isle of Skye, Scotland. Before they emigrated to South Carolina, Martin married Barbara Urquhart, who was also born in Skye. Martin Bethune and Barbara Urquhart's journey to America is a mystery as they don't appear to be listed on the passenger rolls of any ship. Martin would have been in his early 30s when his father Colin sailed, so it would be expected that his name would appear on the passenger list if they had traveled together. A document in our family records written by Martin Bethune's granddaughter Alethea Lawhon says he sailed in 1771 but she did not name the ship.

Martin and Barbara had six children. Nancy was born in 1768, Laughlin in 1769, and John in 1770. All of their births are listed as having been in Isle of Skye, Scotland. Their other children—our ancestor Sarah, born January 20, 1774, Margaret, born in 1775, and Daniel, born in 1780—were born in Cumberland County, North Carolina.

Martin received several land grants in the part of Cumberland County that in 1855 was formed into Harnett County, North Carolina. In 1792 he was issued two grants totaling 100 acres on the head of the Buck Yard Branch that he had applied for in 1785 and another 100 acres lying on both sides of Thornton's Creek that he had applied for in 1787. In 1794 he was issued two more land grants totaling another 150 acres on Thornton's Creek that he had applied for in 1791 and 1794. In 1794, he also applied for another grant and was awarded 92 more acres on Thornton's Creek in 1798. He is listed in the 1790 census of Cumberland County, North Carolina, as "Martin Beaton" living with three males over 16, two males under 16, and four females. Most likely, he applied for land grants as his children got older. In all, he was granted 442 acres in what is now a very nice area about 25 miles north of Fayetteville, North Carolina.

There is a legend about Martin Bethune, as told by Lady Barbara Urquhart to her children and grandchildren:

> In 1770, when Martin Bethune and his wife were newly married and living on the Isle of Skye, the young man kissed his lovely bride a pleasant goodbye and went to spend the day fishing from the rocks off the coast.
>
> Unobserved, the tide rose rapidly and Martin found himself unable to reach land. It was a large high rock upon which he stood, and as the water rose higher and higher, he began climbing toward the summit, but he soon saw that the fast rising tide would sweep him off the rock into the seething waters below. Death was staring him in the face. Then it was that he made a vow unto his Lord. He begged to be spared to walk on the land again, and to look upon the face of his wife once more. He vowed unto the Lord if He would grant the petition, he would forever observe that day, annually, by fasting and prayer. When he had reached the very top of the rock and while the waters were lapping his feet, a silent boat, rowed by a silent oarsman approached him and stopped for him to step in. He took a seat in the boat and was carried to shore. Not a word was spoken. Martin watched the silent oarsman disappear and then went home to tell his young wife all about his vow.
>
> In 1771, the family sailed for the Colonies in America. They settled on Cape Fear River in Cumberland County, North Carolina, passed through the hardships of the Revolutionary war, and reared a family of 6 children. Down to old age, Martin Bethune remembered and kept the vow he made to the Lord on the lonely rock off the Isle of Skye, Scotland.
>
> But one anniversary day, Martin met an old friend who came from Scotland and he forgot or ignored his vow, drinking with his friend from his homeland. That evening as he

went home, when his horse stopped to drink by the river, he fell from his horse, rolled into the river and was drowned.

His good wife always declared his life was cut short because of the broken vow.

Martin Bethune died in 1814. He drowned in the Cape Fear River.

The Short Ancestry of the Lawhons

Martin and Barbara Bethune's daughter Sarah Bethune married Noel Lawhon[25] February 16, 1796. Sarah and Noel Lawhon are great-great-great-grandparents of Eleanor Rosalynn Smith. Their children were John Lawhon, born March 25, 1834; Nancy, born December 29, 1798; Cynthia, born August 2, 1801; Daniel, born September 14, 1803; Angerone, born April 18, 1806; our ancestor Alethea Lawhon, born August 4, 1814; Sarah Barbara, born June 18, 1817; Martin, who burned to death at age 4; and Noel and Joel, born January 3, 1812.[26]

Noel Lawhon was born October 10, 1766, in Cumberland County, North Carolina,[27] and was still living there in 1783. By 1809, Noel Lawhon and Sarah Bethune were in Georgia and Noel was a justice of the peace in Washington County where he received two land grants in 1818. The parents of Noel Lawhon are thought to be John Lawhorn and Elizabeth of North Carolina and before that, Virginia. The Lawhons changed the spelling of their name so many times that it would probably be possible to trace them only by tracking their landownership and noting the names they used when the land was bought and sold. At a minimum, the family in Virginia used Lawhon, Lawhorn, Laughon, Lawhun, Langhorn and Laugharne for different spellings of their name.

Noel Lawhon's ancestry is only speculative. A John and Elizabeth Lawhon who may have been his parents did live in Johnson County and Edgecombe County, very near Cumberland County where Noel and Sarah lived. Deeds of the family show the spelling of their names Lawhon and Lawhorn more or less interchangeably. John Lawhon may have been the son of John Lawhon Sr. of Isle of Wight, Virginia, and who owned land on Tarraroe Creek. John Lawhon Sr. may have been the son of Charles Laugharne, a merchant mariner probably shipping tobacco from the colony to England and trade goods and passengers back to the colony.

It is ironic that the Lawhon line ends so quickly, considering that Noel Lawhon married Sarah Bethune, whose ancestry can be traced back for over a thousand years.

Noel Lawhon and Sarah Bethune's daughter, Alethea Lawhon, married William John Parker on April 25, 1833, in Lee County, Georgia.[28] They are great-great-grandparents of Eleanor Rosalynn Smith.

The Short Ancestry of the Parkers and the Kellys

William John Parker was born in Warren County, Georgia, May 23, 1812. Very little is known about his family except that he was the son of John Prescott Parker and Rachel Kelly of North Carolina.[29] William John Prescott was an active Master Mason serving in the Weston Lodge, No. 80, Free and Accepted Masons of Georgia; the Furlow Lodge No. 124 in Botsford, Georgia, which he helped form; the L. Dwelle Chapter, No. 17, in Lumpkin, Georgia; the Palmer Council, No. 9, in Lumpkin, Georgia; the Lawrence Chapter, No. 49, in Dawson, Georgia, of which he was a charter member; and the Fort Dade Lodge, No. 48, in Dade City, Florida, which he joined in 1887. He served as Worshipful Master for eleven years.

William John Parker's mother, Rachel Kelly, was the daughter of William Kelly, who served in the Revolutionary War under Col. Elijah Clarke. Under Col. Clarke, William Kelly fought in various skirmishes and small battles at Alligator Creek, Kettle Creek, Green Spring, Cedar Springs, and Musgrove's Mill. On March 26, 1784, William Kelly petitioned for and was awarded 287½ acres in Washington County, Georgia, as a bounty for his service during the Revolutionary War.[30]

Alethea Josephine Parker, the daughter of William John Parker and Alethea Lawhon, married John William Fulwood Murray, the son of Drury Murray and Susan Champion.

William John Parker (1812–1887), the great-great-grandfather of Eleanor Rosalynn Smith. The original photograph is an undated tintype likely taken around 1868.

John William Fulwood Murray

John William Fulwood Murray married Alethea Josephine Parker on November 15, 1860, shortly before he left for the Civil War. His father, Drury, built a cabin for them as a wedding present. Before J.W.F. Murray left for the war, Drury took him to a spot on the farm that he had selected as the site for the family's cemetery and had told him that he would be buried there when John returned from the war. Drury Murray died June 27, 1862, and was the first person buried in the Murray family cemetery.

John William Fulwood Murray enlisted in the Confederate army on May 8, 1862, at Savannah, joining Company H of the 13th Regiment, Georgia Volunteer Infantry, Evan's Brigade, Gordon's Division of the Army of Northern Virginia,[31] known as the Lawton-Gordon-Evans Georgia Brigade after its three principal commanders. The Brigade served under General Robert E. Lee from the Seven Days' battles at Richmond, Virginia, until Appomattox. It was organized in May 1862 and originally mustered almost 7000 men.

In August 1862, the brigade fought in the battles at Gaines Mill, Seven Days', Cedar Run, Groveton, Bristoe Station, and Second Manassas. J.W.F. Murray kept a diary during part of his service and about two months of it, covering the battles at Cedar Run, Bristoe Station, and Second Manassas, still survives, although some parts are torn and missing and some are now unreadable. Here are some excerpts:

> August 1, 1862 joined General Stonewall Jackson's troops and stood guard around General Jackson's camp.
>
> detailed to attend wounded [after the battle of Cedar Run, 9 August 1862].
>
> August 22. left camp about day light — waded 1 branch of the Rappahannock River marched on apiece & our Regt. was thrown out as skirmishers cracked another branch of the Rappahannock River at Whit Sulphur Springs. stood picket all night. it rained very hard both in the evening & at night. we were several times called to attention on account of the firing of the pickets. one of our Co. takes one prisoner & horse. two was also killed

The golden wedding anniversary of Rosalynn Smith's great-grandparents (seated) John William Fulwood Murray (b. 1845) and Alethea Josephine Parker (b. 1842), photograph taken in 1910. Rosalynn's grandparents are standing behind J.W. Murray to the left. Her grandfather, John W. Murray, is wearing a bow tie and her grandmother, Rosa Nettie Wise Murray, is standing to the left, partially hidden. Rosalynn's mother, Frances Allethea Murray, is the little girl in the front row, third from left.

(one ____) Cavalry captured 282 prisoners & taken & destroyed a considerable amount of stores. also tore up the RR beyond Warrenton.

August 24 left our position about daybreak & recrossed the river. went through Jefferson. marched some four or five miles & _____ stopped. remained all night.

August 25 left a little after sunrise and marched of force march all day _____ day _____ through Waterloo & Orleans. marched some 20 of _____ miles. _____ the Rappahannock River. struck camps between sunset & dark near Salem.

August 26 left camps a little after sunrise passed through Salem, _____ market, Wainesville & Stephensville. camped near Stephensville. captured 3 trains of cars at Stephensville or Bristol also taken Manassas & stores.

August 27 fell back a little. left my knapsack. cannonaded. fell back to Manassas. two of our men wounded & left. B _____ & ____. camped at & about Manassas.

August 28 marched out towards Col. Pepper Co. H passed through portion of Manassas's battle ground. sever fighting in the evening. drove the yanks from their position but at considerable lose of men. camped on the battle ground.

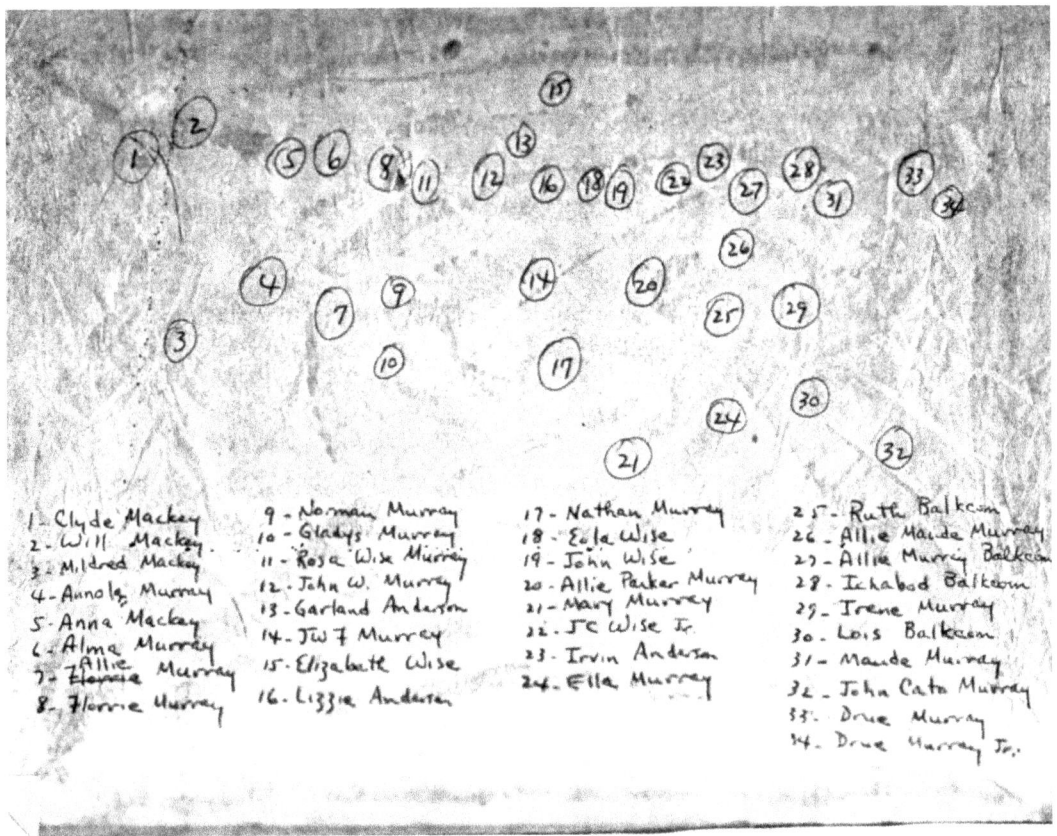

The golden wedding anniversary key identifies the known people in the golden wedding anniversary photograph; 34 relatives are identified.

> August 29 heavy cannonading and small arms off & on all day. one of Co. H killed _____ saw David and Daniel Champion _____ W.M. McLin though not while in action. the 13th made one charge in the evening.
>
> August 30 remained on & near the same ground. there was fighting going on all day. 2 of Co. H wounded _____ J.L. Etheridge & W.H. Lowell the former in the shoulder the latter in the side. camped on battle ground.

After the battle of Second Manassas, Company H fought at Antietam, Shepherdstown, Hatcher's Run, Fredericksburg, Chancellorsville, Winchester, and Gettysburg.

J.W.F. Murray was admitted into the General Hospital in Staunton, Virginia, on October 24, 1863, and probably missed the regiment's next battle at Mine Run on November 30, 1863. His next big engagements were at the Battle of the Wilderness in May of 1864 and then at Spotsylvania Court House. In June 1864, the regiment fought at Cold Harbor. In July, they fought at Harpers Ferry, Monocacy, and Winchester. In August, they fought at Deep Bottom and on August 17, 1864, J. W. F. Murray was wounded at the Third Battle of Winchester and furloughed home to Sumter County for 60 days. He was back with his regiment by December and fought at Hatcher's Run in February 1865, Petersburg and Fort Stedman in March, and Farmville in April. His last battle was at Appomattox Court House.

On April 9, 1865, he was present when General Lee surrendered at Appomattox and was taken prisoner by General U.S. Grant's troops. He was paroled about two weeks later.

John William Fulwood Murray and Alethea Josephine Parker had eight children.[32] Their fourth child was John William Murray. He was born June 12, 1871, and married Rosa Nettie Wise. John William Murray and Rosa Nettie Wise are Eleanor Rosalynn Smith's grandparents.

Chapter 9

ANCESTORS OF ROSA NETTIE WISE

Rosa Nettie Wise's parents were Francis Elizabeth Coogle and George Calhoun Wise. They married in Macon County, Georgia, in 1877. Both of their ancestral lines are from the Palatinate region in what is now Germany and Switzerland. They were all Lutherans from the province of Württemberg fleeing the religious persecution of the Catholic Church and Louis XIV. Most arrived in the colonies in the two major waves of Palatine emigration from Europe in 1732 and 1752, and they settled in the Dutch Fork region between the Broad and Saluda rivers in South Carolina, where they built towns, founded Lutheran churches, and lived together in tight-knit communities. When Francis Coogle was born in 1858, every one of her ancestors back to her immigrant great-great-great-great-grandparents were either Palatine refugees or descendants of Palatine refugees.

George Calhoun Wise's ancestors were also Palatine refugees from Württemberg who immigrated to South Carolina and settled in the Dutch Fork region. All of his ancestors in America back to his great-great-great-great-grandparents were either Palatine refugees or descendants of Palatine refugees except for one line, his father having married Rosannah Etheridge in South Carolina shortly before they moved to Georgia. Except for Rosannah Etheridge, both lines of ancestors were composed entirely of German and Swiss immigrants who came to South Carolina together, lived together in Dutch Fork, and then moved to Georgia together. The Palatine migration from Europe was historically unusual, but they had good reasons for leaving.

If Not for Martin Luther, Half the Family Wouldn't Be Here

The Holy Roman Empire, consolidated by the Emperor Charlemagne, lasted from the ninth century through the eighteenth and covered Eastern and Western Europe. In late 1516, Pope Leo X sent a Dominican friar named Johan Tetzel into the area of Europe that would become Germany to raise money for the construction of Saint Peter's Basilica. Friar Tetzel was the church's commissioner for "indulgences," indulgences being a means to acquire the forgiveness of punishments meted out by the church for sins which had been confessed to and had been spiritually absolved. Essentially, indulgences allowed the wealthy to buy their way out of penances, imprisonment, and even penalties of death imposed by the church for crimes against the faith. Martin Luther, a priest and religious scholar, protested the Catholic Church's sale of indulgences and on October 31, 1517, he sent a letter to the Archbishop of Mainz outlining his objections. He also nailed a copy of his letter, which became known as the 95 Theses, to the door of the Schlosskirche (Castle Church) in Wittenberg. Today this is viewed as a grand act of defiance, but in 1517 in Wittenberg it was a common practice at the university to post scholarly articles on the church doors alerting the academic community that a matter of faith was being challenged and was open to debate.

Reading the 95 Theses, it's clear that Martin Luther had launched an attack on the authority of the Pope and Article 86 was widely perceived to be a personal attack on the Pope's conduct. Translated, it reads, "Why does not the Pope, whose wealth is today greater than the richest of the rich, build just this one church of St. Peter with his own money, rather than with the money of poor believers?" The Archbishop of Mainz, who had incurred considerable debt purchasing his office and had negotiated with Friar Tetzel for a cut on the sales of indulgences, reacted poorly to the theses and, after examining them for heresy, the archbishop escalated the disagreement to Rome.

A case of heresy was brought against Luther and during the hearings in 1517 Luther informed the papal prosecutor, Cardinal Cajetan, that he did not consider the papacy to be consistent with the Bible. Cajetan tried to arrest him, but with the protection of a highly placed local official, Luther fled Wittenberg in the night and escaped. There were attempts to diffuse the situation until Johann Maier von Eck, determined to expose Luther, challenged him to a public debate. Luther accepted and during a heated exchange Luther proclaimed that the Bible did not give the Pope the exclusive right to interpret scripture and therefore neither the Pope nor the church councils were infallible. On June 15, 1520, Pope Leo X issued a papal encyclical entitled *Exsurge Domine*, which was a carefully worded rebuttal of Luther's 95 Theses, and Luther was threatened with excommunication unless he recanted. Von Eck proclaimed the encyclical in several towns and in December of 1520 Luther responded by publicly burning a copy of *Exsurge Domine* in Wittenberg. He was excommunicated by Leo X on the 3rd of January 1521, thus beginning the Protestant Reformation.

The influence of Luther's writings grew and soon thereafter the Castle Church banned private masses. By the end of 1522, people in Wittenberg were holding Lutheran services instead of Catholic masses. Lutheranism, an illegal religion, spread like wildfire. The conflict was partially assuaged by the Peace of Augsburg in 1555 in which the Catholic Church officially recognized Lutheranism as an acceptable religion.

However, by then several of the Germanic rulers had become Calvinist, a religion outside of the purview of the Peace of Augsburg. Lutheranism and Calvinism continued to spread, resulting in Protestants leaving the Catholic Church and worse, proclaiming that their lands no longer belonged to that church. By 1618 the stage was set for the Thirty Years' War between the Holy Roman emperors Ferdinand II, Ferdinand III, and Phillip IV of Spain against France, the Dutch, the Swedes, and the Danes and their militant Calvinist ally, Frederick V of the German Palatinate. The Thirty Years' War was the most destructive war fought in Europe up until that time and Frederick V was crushed in a series of battles with complex political ramifications. The war ended in 1648 with the signing of the Peace of Westphalia in which Calvinism was recognized as an officially accepted religion.

The peace treaty did not bring peace. The Franco-Dutch War, the War of the Reunions, the Nine Years' War, and others all ravaged Europe; and especially the Palatinate region, as control of the Rhine River was a highly sought after prize. Over 35 years, the Palatinate was invaded 32 times. Louis XIV, a fanatical Catholic ruler, revoked the Edict of Nantes in 1685 and made Protestantism illegal. The ensuing persecution led many French Huguenots to flee the country.[1]

In 1689, Louis XIV claimed the entire region on the eastern border of France encompassing the Rhine River and began the War of the Palatinate. Queen Anne, married to a Palatinate ruler, offered asylum to 3000 families for people willing to declare themselves Protestants and emigrate to America to act as a bulwark against the influence of the Catholic Church in the colonies. Tens of thousands of families fled down the Rhine, and Rotterdam was soon flooded with refugees, as was London. Overwhelmed by the influx, Anne dispersed the refugees everywhere, sending them to the Caribbean islands, into Ireland, and to William Penn's new colony where they became the Pennsylvania Dutch. The exodus of refugees continued for decades.

South Carolina, originally part of the territory of the Lords Proprietors, petitioned the king and became a Crown colony in 1721. By 1730 or thereabouts, Charles Town was an established and busy port. To encourage settlement in the wilderness surrounding Charles Town and to provide the city with a buffer against sometimes hostile Indians, King George II offered 50 acres of land to each family member willing to settle there. The bounty grants included tools and a year's supply of food, with the stipulation that the land be cleared and farmed.

Palatine Lutherans came to the area seeking land and religious freedom and many settled in the Newberry and Lexington districts between the fork of the Broad and Saluda rivers, an area which became known as Dutch[2] Fork. About 12,000 immigrants eventually arrived, and Dutch Fork was the most densely settled, becoming home to 483 settler families by 1760, almost all of whom were of German origin.[3]

John William Fulwood Murray's family in a photograph. Left to right: possibly Alethea Lawhon (1814–1883), Nathan Murray, J.W.F. Murray (1833–1921) seated, Alma (1879) standing behind him, daughter Anna, Alethea Josephine (1842–1905) seated, John William (Papa) Murray (1871–1966) standing behind her.

The Palatine Ancestors

Thirty-six people in Rosalynn Carter's grandmother's lineage were Palatine immigrants or their descendents. The first of our Palatine ancestors to arrive in the colonies were a shoemaker, Hans George Picklie (Bickley), and his wife Agnes along with their sons John, Thomas, and Jacob. The Bickleys sailed on the *Two Brothers* and arrived in Georgia on October 7, 1738.[4] They appear in the records of Lexington County, South Carolina, in 1748 when they receive land grants on High Hill Creek on the Saluda River. Their son John also received a bounty land grant of 100 acres on High Hill Creek, indicating that John was probably already married by the time they arrived in South Carolina, since bounty land grants were allocated at 50 acres per person. Thomas was still single and received 50 acres, also on High Hill Creek. Shortly after the Bickleys arrived in Dutch Fork, John and his wife, who may have been Rachel Nichols, had a daughter, our ancestor Anna Barbara Bickley, who was born in March of 1749.

The next ancestors to arrive seem to have been Johannes Kleckley, a former Hessian soldier who had fought against Napoleon, and his wife Elizabeth Rhodes. The Kleckleys walked to Charles Town after they arrived in North Carolina aboard the ship *Friends Goodwill* in 1750. They filed a petition for bounty land in January 1751. There is a family legend that Johannes Kleckley was sent by the Crown to help subdue the revolting colonists but when he got here he found a group of German-speaking people peacefully settled and worshiping as Lutherans, so he discarded his uniform, joined them, and became a farmer. The same story is related by Mrs. Mary Belle Powers in the *History of Mt. Zion Lutheran Church*, thus promoting the story from an unsubstantiated family legend to a documented family legend.

The height of the Palatine exodus from Europe was 1752, and in September of that year the *Snow Rowan* sailing from Rotterdam arrived in Charles Town carrying about 350 passengers. All of the passengers were Palatine immigrants from the Duchy of Württemberg in what is now Germany. It was quite common at the time for agents from the colonies to travel to a particular area and recruit an entire shipload of immigrants. Among the passengers were Matthew Kugler (later Coogle) and his wife Catherine whose last name is unknown. The Kuglers petitioned for and received 400 acres along a road to Dreher's Ferry. John Dreher was a prosperous businessman and owned the ferry and a grist mill, and later built Dreher's Canal and locks. His son, Gottfried Dreher III, named after his grandfather, was also known later as Rev. Godfrey Dreher, a famous Lutheran minister of Dutch Fork and the first president of the Lutheran Synod of South Carolina, which was formed at St. Michael's Lutheran Church. John Dreher donated the land where the church was built and is buried in the church cemetery. The church is still there on Highway 6 at Yacht Cove. John Dreher's house is there also, and is listed on the National Register of Historic Places. The grist mill is now under water, covered by Lake Murray.

Thomas Hamiter, his wife Catherine, and their children also arrived on the *Snow Rowan* in September of 1752, having sailed from Rotterdam with the Kuglers and the Weiss family. The Hamiters were also from Württemberg and may have known the Kuglers and the Weiss family in Württemberg since it was common then for families and friends to emigrate together. Thomas Hamiter petitioned for 300 acres between the Broad and Saluda rivers and received land along Cannon's Creek in Newberry County, South Carolina. The Hamiters' son, Johann Sebastian Hamiter, may have traveled separately from his parents. It was common for older children or fathers to remain behind finishing up family business before sailing on a later ship to rejoin the family. Johann may have sailed to Philadelphia before rejoining his family in Dutch Fork.

Also aboard the *Snow Rowan* was Ernst Frederick Weiss, who was born in Obermutschelbach, in the Duchy of Württemberg, in 1710, and married Anna Barbara Ruff in December of 1732 in the Evangelical Church of Nottingen in Baden, Germany. Ernst was a former Catholic and had to agree to raise his children in the Evangelical church in order to gain the blessing of Maria's parents for marriage. Ernst Weiss petitioned for and received 300 acres along the north side of the Saluda River near what is now the Lake Murray Dam.[5]

From the records of the Evangelical Church in Obermutachelbach, Baden, Germany, researched by our Wise relatives when they were writing *The Wise and Wyse Families of South Carolina*, we know that Ernst Friedrich Weiss and Anna Barbara Ruff had a son, Johann Georg Weiss, who was born in Obermutachelbach on November 23, 1742.[6] Johann was ten years old when the family sailed on the *Snow Rowan* to Charles Town along with about 300 other German passengers.

In December 1752, Johann Heinrich Leibbrand arrived in Charles Town with his wife Catherina Weiss and children aboard the *Elizabeth*, captained by John McCall.[7] Johann petitioned for and received 250 acres on the Twenty Mile Creek branch of the Saluda River under the name Heinrich Lybrand.[8]

The petitions and grants for bounty land were recorded in the *South Carolina Council Journal*, page after page of them, and almost all were worded similarly. Heinrich Lybrand's looked like all the rest:

> The Petition of Hendrick Lybrand humbly setting forth that the petitioner came into this province from Germany on the Encouragement given here to foreign Protestants and shipped himself and his Family on board the Ship Elizabeth bound from Rotterdam to this Port and has paid his passage money as appears by the Enclosed Discharge of Mr. John McCall, he is now Desirous to be a subject of his Majesty King George and to Live in this Province he has a wife and three children viz Christian aged 23 years Simon 18 and Maria Magarata 16 years for whom nor yet for himself has any Land been granted, prays to run out 250 acres of Land free of Charges and that he may have his most Gracious Majestys Bounty. Cha's Town, the 18th day of March 1853, Hen: Lybrand. The prayer thereof was granted.[9]

It was all the legalese of the time. He was a "petitioner," which he had to declare to get the bounty grant. He sailed with Captain John McCall, whose ship records would have been appended to the Council Journals showing that the Lybrands were immigrants. They declared themselves Protestants, another requirement as Catholics were not allowed. He was on the ship *Elizabeth*, tying his family to the ship's records. He "shipt himself," meaning he had paid his own way and therefore was not arriving as an indentured servant. He was "Desirous" of settling in the province, thus agreeing to stay, clear the land, and farm — a condition of the petition he was filing to get land. He declared his wife and three children. Along with Hendrick himself, that made five petitioners at 50 acres each, so they qualified for 250 acres. A closing nice word about the graciousness of the king, and the deal was done.

Also in December of 1752, Johann Jacob Kölle, a wheelwright from Baden-Württemberg, and his wife Anna Catharina Sigler and their children arrived in Charles Town aboard the brigantine *John and Mary*.[10] Johann petitioned for and received a 400-acre bounty grant, under the name Kelly, on Buffalo Creek near the Saluda River.

Besides all of these people being our ancestors, they share another common link. They all made the trip from Württemberg province, most from Wittenberg, and it was not a pleasant journey.

The Trip from Wittenberg

The voyage from Wittenberg to Rotterdam and from there to England and then to the colonies was incredibly difficult. In 1750, a Palatine schoolteacher named Gottlieb Mittelberger made the same journey from Wittenberg as our ancestors, except he sailed to Pennsylvania instead of South Carolina. Gottlieb kept a diary of his voyage entitled *Gottlieb Mittelberger's Journey to Pennsylvania in the Year 1750 and Return to Germany in the Year 1754*. Unfortunately his subtitle was *Containing Not Only a Description of the Country According to Its Present Condition but Also a Detailed Account of the Sad and Unfortunate Circumstances of Most of the Germans That Have Emigrated, or Are Emigrating to That Country*, indicating that his experience was not a pleasant one. Gottlieb returned to Germany in 1754 and printed a detailed account of his voyage in a pamphlet that was widely distributed in Germany. These excerpts describe the same voyage our ancestors undertook on sailing to America:

> This journey lasts from the beginning of May to the end of October, fully half a year, amid such hardships as no one is able to describe adequately with their misery.
>
> The cause is because the Rhine-boats from Heilbronn to Holland have to pass by 36 custom-houses, at all of which the ships are examined, which is done when it suits the convenience of the custom-house officials. In the meantime the ships with the people are detained long, so that the passengers have to spend much money. The trip down the Rhine alone lasts therefore 4, 5 and even 6 weeks....
>
> Both in Rotterdam and in Amsterdam the people are packed densely, like herrings so to say, in the large sea-vessels. One person receives a place of scarcely 2 feet width and 6 feet length in the bedstead, while many a ship carries four to six hundred souls; not to mention the innumerable implements, tools, provisions, water-barrels and other things which likewise occupy much space.
>
> On account of contrary winds it takes the ships sometimes 2, 3 and 4 weeks to make the trip from Holland to Kaupp [Cowes] in England. But when the wind is good, they get there in 8 days or even sooner. Everything is examined there and the custom-duties paid, whence it comes that the ships ride there 8, 10 to 14 days and even longer at anchor, till they have taken in their full cargoes. During that time every one is compelled to spend his last remaining money and to consume his little stock of provisions which had been reserved for the sea; so that most passengers, finding themselves on the ocean where they would be in greater need of them, must greatly suffer from hunger and want. Many suffer want already on the water between Holland and Old England....
>
> When the ships have for the last time weighed their anchors near the city of Kaupp in Old England, the real misery begins with the long voyage. For from there the ships, unless they have good wind, must often sail 8, 9, or up to 12 weeks before they reach Philadelphia. But even with the best wind the voyage lasts 7 weeks.
>
> But during the voyage there is on board these ships terrible misery, stench, fumes, horror, vomiting, many kinds of sea-sickness, fever, dysentery, headache, heat, constipation, boils, scurvy, cancer, mouth-rot, and the like, all of which come from old and sharply salted food and meat, also from very bad and foul water, so that many die miserably.
>
> Add to this want of provisions, hunger, thirst, frost, heat, dampness, anxiety, want, afflictions and lamentations, together with other trouble, as c.v. the lice abound so frightfully, especially on sick people, that they can be scraped off the body. The misery reaches the climax when a gale rages for 2 or 3 nights and days, so that every one believes that the ship will go to the bottom with all human beings on board. In such a visitation the people cry and pray most piteously.
>
> When in such a gale the sea rages and surges, so that the waves rise often like high mountains one above the other, and often tumble over the ship, so that one fears to go

down with the ship; when the ship is constantly tossed from side to side by the storm and waves, so that no one can either walk, or sit, or lie, and the closely packed people in the berths are thereby tumbled over each other, both the sick and the well — it will be readily understood that many of these people, none of whom had been prepared for hardships, suffer so terribly from them that they do not survive it.

I myself had to pass through a severe illness at sea, and I best know how I felt at the time. These poor people often long for consolation, and I often entertained and comforted them with singing, praying and exhorting; and whenever it was possible and the winds and waves permitted it, I kept daily prayer-meetings with them on deck. Besides, I baptized five children in distress, because we had no ordained minister on board. I also held divine service every Sunday by reading sermons to the people; and when the dead were sunk in the water, I commended them and our souls to the mercy of God....

That most of the people get sick is not surprising, because, in addition to all other trials and hardships, warm food is served only three times a week, the rations being very poor and very little. Such meals can hardly be eaten, on account of being so unclean. The water which is served out on the ships is often very black, thick and full of worms, so that one cannot drink it without loathing, even with the greatest thirst. O surely, one would often give much money at sea for a piece of good bread, or a drink of good water, not to say a drink of good wine, if it were only to be had. I myself experienced that sufficiently, I am sorry to say. Toward the end we were compelled to eat the ship's biscuit which had been spoiled long ago; though in a whole biscuit there was scarcely a piece the size of a dollar that had not been full of red worms and spiders' nests. Great hunger and thirst force us to eat and drink everything; but many a one does so at the risk of his life. The sea-water cannot be drunk, because it is salt and bitter as gall. If this were not so, such a voyage could be made with less expense and without so many hardships.

At length, when, after a long and tedious voyage, the ships come in sight of land, so that the promontories can be seen, which the people were so eager and anxious to see, all creep from below on deck to see the land from afar, and they weep for joy, and pray and sing, thanking and praising God. The sight of the land makes the people on board the ship, especially the sick and the half dead, alive again, so that their hearts leap within them; they shout and rejoice, and are content to bear their misery in patience, in the hope that they may soon reach the land in safety.[11]

Gottlieb landed in Philadelphia and continues his narrative to describe the terrible conditions that awaited indentured servants who had traded years of their life's work to pay for the voyage to the colonies.[12] Fortunately, our ancestors emigrated to South Carolina and were not indentured.

John Bickley, the son of a shoemaker, and his wife Rachel Nichols; Johannes Kleckley, the retired Hessian soldier and his wife Elizabeth Rhodes; Matthew Kugler and his wife Catherine; Ernst Frederick Weiss and his wife Anna Barbara Ruff; Johann Jacob Kölle, the wheelwright, and his wife Anna Catharina Sigler; and Johann Sebastian Hamiter, who made the voyage when he was seventeen, were all great-great-great-great-great-grandparents of Eleanor Rosalynn Smith.

Dutch Fork

Johann Christian Lybrand was born October 8, 1728, in Kleiningersheim, Bietigham, Germany, and arrived in Charlestown, South Carolina, aboard the *Elizabeth* in December 1752. He sailed with his parents, Johann Heinrich Leibbrand and Catherina Weiss, and his father named him as his 23-year-old son in his petition for a land grant upon arrival.

Christian Lybrand married sometime before 1756 when his son Christopher Lybrand was born in Lexington, South Carolina. Christopher's wife is unknown. His son, Christopher Lybrand (II), was born in 1773 in Lexington and married Barbara, whose last name is also unknown.[13] Christopher Lybrand (II) and Barbara had seven children.[14] Their first child was our ancestor Elizabeth Lybrand, who was born about 1797.

There is some confusion surrounding the names in the Lybrand family. Most records list Barbara and the children as the wife and sons and daughters of Christopher Lybrand. However, estate records list the same children as beneficiaries of Barnet Lybrand. Barbara either outlived Christopher and later married Barnet Lybrand or Barnet and Christopher were the same person. In 1878, Barnet Lybrand filed a claim against the government for supplies that the Union Army had appropriated from his farm during the Civil War. Unfortunately, his claim was denied when the Archive Office of the War Department checked[15] and found that he was listed on the muster roll of Captain Leaphart, Company C, 20th Regiment of South Carolina. In these documents, Barnet is referred to as Barnet C. Lybrand, the only instances where his middle initial is used. If his name was Barnet Christopher Lybrand, then the confusion would be cleared up.

When Barnett Lybrand died, he left the land owned by Barbara to her children, who sold it for $391.[16] The estate records refer to John Coogle as the husband of Barnett Christopher Lybrand's daughter, our ancestor Elizabeth Lybrand. John was the son of Peter Coogle and the grandchild of Matthew and Catherine Kugler, who had arrived on the *Snow Rowan* in 1752 and who had received a land grant of 400 acres near Dreher's Ferry. Peter Coogle is listed as the head of household in the 1790 census with a wife and one child. At that time, Peter and his family were living in Lexington and the child was probably John's older brother Daniel, John having been born in 1792 after the census was taken. Peter Coogle had several other children, including a daughter, Christina. Daniel and his brother John would later move to Georgia between 1830 and 1840 and become the founders of the Coogle family in Macon County.

The Coogles and the Kleckleys, Mt. Zion Evangelical Lutheran Church, More Civil War

Elizabeth Lybrand married John Coogle sometime around 1815 and they are great-great-great-grandparents of Eleanor Rosalynn Smith. John and Elizabeth had four children. Their firstborn child and our ancestor, John Thomas Coogle, was born May 24, 1817.[17] John Thomas Coogle married Harriet Rebekah Kleckley, the daughter of Rev. Jacob Kleckley and Francis Hamiter. John T. Coogle and Harriet Kleckley were great-great-grandparents of Eleanor Rosalynn Smith.

The Coogles and the Kleckleys owned land next to each other and the families had probably known each other since immigrating to South Carolina. Jacob Kleckley was born November 1, 1791, in Saxe Gotha, South Carolina, and was the son of Johannes Kleckley, the Hessian soldier who had been sent by England to fight against the revolting colonists but had instead decided to stay and join the Lutheran community. Jacob married Christina Coogle, the daughter of Peter Coogle, in April 1813, and they had two children[18] before Christina died in October of 1821. In January of 1822, Jacob married Francis "Fannie" Hamiter,[19] the daughter of Jacob Hamiter and Harriett Bickley. Jacob Kleckley and Francis Hamiter were great-great-great-grandparents of Eleanor Rosalynn Smith.

By the 1830s, there was also a thriving community of German Lutherans in the eastern part of Marion County, Georgia, which would become Macon County in 1837. Many of them had moved from the Dutch Fork area and had family ties there. David Coogle, the brother of our ancestor John Coogle, moved to the area sometime after the 1830 census was taken. In 1836 he wrote to the South Carolina Synod describing the Lutheran community and requesting that the Synod consider sending a Lutheran minister to settle in the area. The Evangelical Lutheran synod of South Carolina and Adjacent States held jurisdiction over all of the Lutheran churches at the time and the synod was the only means of obtaining a licensed Lutheran minister. The synod approved the request and in 1838 Rev. Jacob Kleckley received a license to "exhort" and "bury the dead." Jacob and Fannie, along with their children — our ancestor Harriett Rebekah Kleckley, John Jacob, Catherine, Joel Thomas, Rhoda Ann, David Hemiter, and Nancy Ann — together with five slaves, made the 250-mile trip from Dutch Fork in horse drawn wagons and were in Macon County, Georgia, by 1840. The first place of worship was a cabin near a spring, which retains the name Meeting House Spring today. The 1840 census shows many settlers in Macon County from the Dutch Fork area, and the church founded by Reverend Kleckley is still active today.[20]

Jacob Kleckley and Francis Hamiter had eleven children in all, including our ancestor Harriett Rebekah Kleckley. At least four of their sons fought in the Civil War. John Jacob Kleckley was born in 1826, David Hemiter in 1832, Joel Thomas in 1836. Jacob's son Daniel, his only son with his previous wife, also had two sons, Jacob A. Kleckley and John L. Kleckley, who fought in the Civil War. Jacob A. Kleckley joined Company C, 12th Regiment, Georgia Infantry, on June 15, 1861. Jacob was killed at Cedar Run on April 30, 1862, shortly after he turned 18 years old.[21] John L. Kleckley joined Company C, 12th Regiment, Georgia Infantry, on April 1, 1864. John Kleckley was wounded during the Battle of the Wilderness May 5, 1864. He had recovered and rejoined his unit in time to fight at Winchester, Virginia, on September 19, 1864, and at the Siege of Petersburg on April 2, 1865.[22] John Jacob Kleckley served as a private in the Georgia Militia.

David Hemiter Kleckley joined Company A, 10th Battalion, Georgia Infantry, on September 18, 1861. He was promoted to sergeant on April 28, 1863. David was wounded in the siege of Petersburg, Virginia, sometime between June 22 and June 27, 1864. After staying a week in the General Hospital in Petersburg, he was transferred to the hospital in Richmond, Virginia, on July 1 and remained there until December 14 when he was transferred to the Floyd House and Ocmulgee Hospitals facility in Macon, Georgia. A week later, he was furloughed, having lost the use of his hand.[23]

Joel Thomas Kleckley joined Company A, 10th Battalion, Georgia Infantry, on April 23, 1862, about seven months after his brother David had joined the unit. He was admitted into the Jackson Hospital in Richmond, Virginia, on August 17, 1864, with serious wounds. Joel was furloughed home to Oglethorpe, Georgia, October 23, 1864, after recovering from having his right leg amputated.[24]

Jacob Kleckley and Francis Hamiter's daughter, Harriett Rebekah Kleckley, married John Thomas Coogle, the son of Elizabeth Lybrand and John Coogle. John and Rebekah's daughter, our ancestor Francis "Fanny" Elizabeth Coogle, married George Calhoun Wise. Calhoun was descended from five generations of Palatines.

The Wises

Johann Georg Weiss was ten years old when he arrived at Charles Town with his parents aboard the *Snow Rowan* in 1752. Although there is no surviving documentation, Johann fought in the Revolutionary War at the Battle of King's Mountain, which was a major victory for the Patriots and resulted in Cornwallis' being pushed out of North Carolina. Teddy Roosevelt later wrote that the Battle of King's Mountain was the turning point of the American Revolution. Johann lost his horse but was unharmed in the battle. His musket was later passed down to his descendants until it was lost in a house fire. Unfortunately, Johann's military service records were lost in another fire but he received two land grants for his service.

Sometime around 1768, before he served in the Revolutionary War, Johann Georg Weiss married Anna Barbara Bickley, the daughter of Rev. John Jacob Bickley and Rachel Nichole, both of whom had sailed to South Carolina in 1738 aboard the *Two Brothers*. Georg Weiss and Anna Barbara Bickley had thirteen children and Anna lived to be 88 years old. When she died in 1837, her obituary said that of her thirteen children seven were still alive, along with sixty-four grandchildren and one hundred great-grandchildren. Of the Wises' thirteen children, three were sons: George Wise, born November 25, 1776; our ancestor John Wise, born September 25, 1779; and Frederick Wyse, born sometime in 1787.

The Weiss family lived very close to the Kölles. They had been awarded a land grant on High Hill Creek on the Saluda River and Johann Jacob Kölle (Kelly), the wheelwright who had arrived in Charles Town aboard the *John and Mary* in 1752 with his wife Anna Catherine Sigler, had been awarded land on Buffalo Creek, also on the Saluda River. The land grant to the Weiss family must have been very close to the Kölle land because these families obviously knew and liked each other very well.

Johann Kölle and Anna Catharina Sigler had a son, John George Kelly, who was 12 years old when he made the voyage with them to South Carolina; he had been born in 1741. John George Kelly married Mary Margaret and they had at least nine children. Among them were Mary Margaret Kelly, who was born October 25, 1775, and married George Wise; Anna Mary Kelly, who was born in 1779 and married John Wise; and Julia Kelly, who was born in the mid–1780s and married Frederick Wyse.[25] Three brothers married three sisters.

Our ancestors John Wise and Anna Mary Kelly had twelve children, six daughters and six sons.[26] Their firstborn son, George Wise, was married twice and he and his wives had five sons: John A. Wise, Michael Wise, Patrick Wise, Lemuel Wise and James Wise. Three of their sons fought in the Civil War. George's firstborn son was John A. Wise, who was born in 1827. John enlisted to fight in the Civil War on January 7, 1862. He joined the Holcombe Legion, South Carolina Volunteers, which consisted of an infantry regiment and a cavalry battalion. The cavalry battalion was later separated from the legion and increased in size to a regiment which was designated the 7th Regiment, South Carolina Cavalry. However, before the separation took place, John Wise was killed near Warrenton, Virginia, during the Battle of Second Manassas on September 19, 1862.[27] Patrick Wise was born in 1830 and he may have fought in the Civil War. He is referred to as Major Patrick Wise in the few references that exist for him.

George had two other sons who fought in the Civil War. Lemuel Wise was born in 1845 and joined Company G, 13th Regiment, South Carolina Volunteers, on August 28, 1861. His brother James, born in 1839, joined Company G with him on the same day. Both brothers almost immediately contracted measles. Lemuel died on September 18, 1861, about two weeks after joining the regiment. James died on September 30.[28] James was 22 years old, Lemuel was 16. George Wise received the back pay and a $50 bounty each for his two sons in July of 1863 — $69.80 for James and $83.60 for Lemuel.

The youngest son of John Wise and Anna Mary Kelly was Joel Wise. Joel married

Melissa Schumpert and their only son, John C. Wise, joined Company E of the Holcombe Legion, South Carolina Volunteers, on June 4, 1861. His surviving service records go only through December of 1861. John was killed during the Siege of Petersburg at the Crater.[29]

John Wise and Anna Mary Kelly's third son was our ancestor David Wise. David married Rosannah Elizabeth Etheridge, and it was the only marriage in Rosalynn Carter's grandmother's lineage since the families had arrived in South Carolina that was not a Palatine immigrant or one of their descendents.

David Wise's wife, Rosannah Etheridge, had two brothers, Guilford and Tyre Etheridge, who fought in the Civil War. Tyre enlisted in Company M, 7th Regiment of the South Carolina Infantry, on August 9, 1862. He contracted smallpox in November and was admitted into the Howard's Grove Smallpox Hospital where he stayed until February of 1863. He relapsed in May and spent another month in the General Hospital at Camp Winder in Richmond, Virginia. After returning to duty, Tyre was captured at North Anna on May 23, 1864, and remained a POW at the Point Lookout prison camp until he was exchanged in a prisoner swap in May of 1865.[30] Guilford Etheridge enlisted in the 14th Infantry, South Carolina, on August 12, 1861, and was killed at Gettysburg.[31]

In addition to Rosannah's brothers, three sons of David Wise and Rosannah Etheridge served in the Civil War: William J. Wise, Tyre Wise, and Rosalynn Carter's great-grandfather George Calhoun Wise. Calhoun Wise was 17 years old when he enlisted with his brother William J. Wise in Company B, 14th Infantry, South Carolina Volunteers, on August 12, 1861, at Camp Butler. Most of William's records have been lost. William died of disease shortly after the Siege of Petersburg, Virginia, when he was 23 years old.[32]

Shortly after our ancestor Calhoun Wise enlisted, he was wounded in the battle at Frayser's Farm on June 30, 1862, and his service records list him as being in the hospital for several months afterwards. He rejoined his unit in time to fight at Fredericksburg in December of 1862 and Chancellorsville in May of 1863. George Calhoun was hospitalized with wounds again in September of 1863 immediately after the battle Sharpsburg/Antietam where his brigade fought. Calhoun had rejoined his unit by the end of October. His unit then fought at Falling Water, the Bristoe Campaign, and Mine Run. On May 6, 1864, his brigade fought in the Battle of the Wilderness. Calhoun was seriously injured and his left leg had to be amputated.[33]

On February 27, 1864, William and Calhoun's brother Tyre Wise enlisted in the same unit as they had: Company B, 14th Infantry, South Carolina Volunteers. Tyre's war experience was intense and short. He fought at Spotsylvania, North Anna, Jericho Ford, Cold Harbor, Deep Bottom, and Petersburg. Shortly after the battle of Petersburg, Tyre contracted an undiagnosed disease and died at the Jackson Hospital in Virginia on August 24, 1864.[34] Tyre was 17 years old.

It is clear that the Wise family and the Etheridge family were quite fond of each other and at least eight of their children married each other. The Etheridge family was probably from England and probably moved to Virginia around 1630. Unlike our Palatine ancestors, their records were not written in German. However, they turned out to be almost as indecipherable.

The Etheridges: In Theory, Five Names Are Enough

David Wise married Rosannah Elizabeth Etheridge and both are buried together in the Lebanon Cemetery in Plains. Rosannah was born in 1821 and lived until 1900, the daughter of William Etheridge and Letha Lucy Jennings. There seems to be agreement but no proof that Lucy was the daughter of William Jennings, who was born in 1787 and lived until 1846, and Nancy Dove, who was born in 1784 and lived until 1840, both from Edgefield County, South Carolina. The William Jennings who married Nancy Dove is the son of John Jennings, but he may or may not have been Lucy's father. That seems to be the extent of what is provable about the family.

The Etheridge family genealogy is very difficult to decipher because this branch of the family has five names: Aaron, Caleb, Thomas, William, and Lott, which were used over and over with every male descendant in every generation, each seemingly naming their sons after their father and brothers. There are numerous documents about the family — wills, deeds and tax lists — in which all of these names are used repeatedly. An article about the Etheridge family genealogy was written for *Historical Southern Families*, and almost every entry is qualified by "probably" or "maybe." The article says that Aaron Etheridge and his brothers, Lott and Caleb, moved from Norfolk County, Virginia, to Edgecombe County, North Carolina, in the early 1740s and that two of the three brothers "seem" to have married daughters of Robert and Jean Clark. It seems "probable" that Rachel and Agnes Clark were the wives of Aaron's younger brothers, Lott and Caleb, for there is "some probability" from his will that Aaron's wife was named Emily. That is not very definite.

Discussing the 1790 census of Halifax County, the article says that William Etheridge is shown with one grown son, probably William Jr., because the census shows only two other Etheridges in Halifax County, both named Caleb. The tax list of 1782 shows a George Etheridge in District 11 of Halifax County who was possibly a son of a Lott Etheridge because the only other Etheridge there was a third Caleb Etheridge. "Probably" and "possibly" don't provide a lot to be sure about.

Frances Allethea Murray (1905–1997), Rosalynn Smith's mother. The photograph was taken about 1930.

Several land transactions were discussed. Caleb, Aaron, William and Thomas Etheridge bought and sold land to each other and to their children and they deeded land and property to their children in their wills, and every entry is qualified by its perhaps being this Caleb or perhaps being that Thomas.

The tax list of 1782 for Halifax County shows Aaron Etheridge Sr., William Etheridge Sr., Robert Etheridge, Caleb Etheridge Sr., Aaron Etheridge Jr., and Caleb Etheridge Jr., all owning stock, presumably cattle. The explanation accompanying this is that all the younger Etheridges in the list were sons of Caleb, because Aaron Etheridge, in his will, mentions only one son, William, but the William mentioned above was probably a son of Aaron's son William — again, not very precise.

The *State Records of North Carolina* show that three Etheridges — Robert, Aaron, and Caleb — were all soldiers in the Revolutionary War in Captain William Brinkley's Company of the First Regiment of North Carolina Troops, commanded by Col. Samuel Jarvis. They all fought in the Battle of Brandywine, which took place on September 11, 1777, a decisive victory for the British that left Philadelphia undefended so that the British captured the city the next day without firing a shot. Major General Nathanael Greene estimated that Washington had lost between 1200 and 1300 men at Brandywine. The next big battle that the Etheridge brothers all fought in was the Battle of Germantown, where they were defeated again, although when the news of their audacious attack reached Europe it was later credited as being a major influence on the French court's deciding to throw its support behind the Americans. The next battle the Etheridges fought in was the Battle of Monmouth, the largest one-day engagement in the war measured by the number of troops involved. These Etheridges were probably the sons of one of the Calebs.

David Wise married Rosannah Elizabeth Etheridge. Their son George Calhoun Wise, the great-grandfather of Rosalynn Carter, was born April 17, 1842. George Calhoun Wise and Francis "Fanny" Elizabeth Coogle were the parents of Rosa Nettie Wise, who was born on October 12, 1880, in Plains, Georgia. Rosa married John William (Papa) Murray, who was born on June 12, 1871, also in Plains, Georgia. Their daughter Frances Allethea Murray was born on Christmas Eve in 1905.

Frances Allethea Murray, known to our family as Mother Allie, married Wilburn Edgar Smith on June 21, 1905, and they were the parents of four children. William Jerrold Smith was born May 5, 1929. Murray Lee Smith was born January 19, 1932. Lillian Allethea Smith was born November 10, 1936. Their first child was born August 18, 1927. She was Eleanor Rosalynn Smith.

Chapter 10

ANCESTORS OF WILBURN EDGAR SMITH

Wilburn Edgar Smith, the father of Eleanor Rosalynn Smith, was born on November 20, 1896. Edgar was the son of William Juriston Smith and Sarah Eleanor "Aunt Sally" Bell. The provable Smith ancestry ends with the Rev. George Lynch Smith, born in 1779, but the information does not stop there.

Eleanor Rosalynn Smith's ancestry through her grandmother Sarah Eleanor Bell can be traced back for ten generations to several pioneer families who settled in Maryland starting with the establishment of the colony. Jonathan Prather and Jane McKay, Colonel Henry Ridgely and Elizabeth Howard, John Bigger and Ann, Richard Isacke and Elizabeth Sharpe, Richard and Charity Cheyney, Richard Wade and George Westall Sr. were all Rosalynn's great-great-great-great-great-great-great-great-grandparents. At least forty-two of her grandmothers and grandfathers had emigrated to, or were born in, Maryland before 1700.

Colonial Maryland

King Charles I gave Lord Baltimore the Charter for Maryland in 1632 and many of the first settlers came there from Virginia. Edward Bennett, a wealthy Englishman, invested in the Virginia Company in 1620 to send 200 settlers to Virginia. Bennett was the commissioner of Virginia at the court of England and owned a fleet of ships which traded with the colony, bringing settlers and supplies to the colony and returning with tobacco. In February of 1622, the first 120 settlers that he sponsored arrived in the ship *Sea Flower* and settled at Warroscoyack, now known as Isle of Wight. Less than a month later, on Good Friday, March 22, 1622, the great Indian Massacre occurred and most of the settlers were killed. Undeterred, in July 1622 Bennett sent more settlers on the ship *James* and more in October on the *Gift of God*. In 1623, he sent more settlers on the *Hopewell*. In all, he and his family transported over 800 settlers to Virginia.

Sarah Eleanor Bell (1875–1951), Rosalynn Smith's grandmother and the wife of Wilburn Juriston Smith. The photograph is thought to have been taken around 1900.

In 1642, Edward Bennett's nephew Richard Bennett arrived and settled on the Elizabeth River next to his uncle's plantation. Richard sent a delegation to Boston to secure a Puritan minister for an Independent Church of England which had been built at Sewell's Point near Bennett's 2000-acre plantation. When the ministers arrived in Virginia, they were opposed by Governor Berkeley and his chaplain; through the governor's influence, the Virginia legislature passed a law prohibiting ministers who did not use the *Book of Common Prayer* from holding services. The Puritan ministers returned to Boston, but in 1644 Governor Berkeley's own chaplain, Reverend Thomas Harrison, became a Puritan. Soon, the vestry of the church presented a complaint against him before the governor and council "for not reading the booke of Common Prayer and for not adminstring [sic] the sacrament of Baptisme according to the Cannons and for not catechising on Sunnedayes in the afternoon according to the act of Assembly."[1] Harrison moved to Nansemond County where there was a strong Puritan community and later fled the colony, moving to Maryland.

Mr. William Durand, another Puritan, took over the ministerial position and on Sunday, May 28, 1648, Richard Conquest, the high sheriff of Lower Norfolk, went to the church and observed Durand taking the pulpit to preach. Conquest

Wilburn Edgar Smith (1896–1940), on the left, and Frances Allethea Murray (1905–1997) and an unknown friend. This photograph was taken around 1924 before the couple were married and it is the only known photograph with both of Rosalynn Smith's parents in it.

ordered everyone to disperse and return to their homes, which they refused to do. Durand was arrested but several parishioners forced the sheriff to release him. In November, Durand was arrested again and an attachment was placed on his property. Thomas Marsh posted 5600 pounds of tobacco as security for Durand's release.

In Maryland, William Stone, an influential Englishman and pioneer, met with the exiles, and with the agreement of Lord Baltimore, he assured them of religious liberty. Lord Baltimore, a Catholic, was in a perplexing position; opposition in Parliament had arisen after Charles I had granted him a charter for the colony because it was deemed contrary to the interest of the established church. Officials in Virginia had no inclination to help the Maryland colony and complained about losing two-thirds of Virginia's territory. Lord Baltimore had spent an immense amount of money founding the colony, which was yielding no returns.

The execution of Charles I inflamed the Royalists in Virginia and the assembly passed an act denouncing the execution and proclaiming Charles II as the rightful king. The act made it treason to speak against the House of Stuart or in favor of a Puritan Parliament. In this increasingly poisonous political atmosphere, at the county court of 1649, an indictment was read: "Whereas, Mr. Edward Lloyd and Mr. Thomas Meeres, commissioners, with Edward Selby, Richard Day, Richard Owens, Thomas Marsh, George Kemp and John Norwood were presented to the board by the sheriff, for seditious sectuaries for not repairing to their church, and for refusing to hear common prayers—liberty is granted till October next, to inform their judgments, and to conform themselves to common law."[2] Thomas Marsh and his family, along with Durand and his family, left the colony and fled to Maryland. Their land and their tobacco security were seized.

By this time, William Stone, a Protestant, had been appointed governor of Maryland. Governor Stone had promised Lord Baltimore that he could and would bring a large number of settlers to his colony. An Act was passed declaring that "...all who professed Jesus Christ as their savior should have equal justice."

Before the October deadline to appear in court in Virginia to face sedition charges arrived, all of the indictees were in Maryland. Edward Lloyd had been a burgess and justice in Lower Norfolk. Governor Stone considered him such a desirable immigrant that he appointed him commander of Providence and gave him the authority to make land grants. John Norwood had been the first sheriff of Lower Norfolk. Richard Bennett moved to Maryland the same year, taking the role of Elder of the Puritan Church, and began to transport immigrants. With Maryland's guarantee of religious freedom, persecution in Virginia, and land being distributed through headright grants, along with the recruitment of immigrants by highly influential people in the colony, immigration into Maryland began to boom at the new settlement in Anne Arundel County.

Governor Berkeley continued his campaign to undermine the colony in Maryland and informed his ally, Charles II, then in exile, of the refuge given by Maryland to "all kinds of sectaries and schematics and ill-affected persons, adherents to the rebels in England who for this cause had been driven from Virginia,"[3] causing Charles to revoke Lord Baltimore's rights. The Parliament in England eventually seized control of both colonies and Maryland came under Puritan control.

The Prathers Arrived in 1622, the Odells, Ridgelys, and Biggers a Little Later

Of all of the ancestors of Eleanor Rosalynn Smith to immigrate to Maryland, Thomas Prather's (Prater) family probably arrived first. Thomas was the son of Thomas Prather and Margaret Quintyne. He was born in 1604 in Wiltshire, England, and was baptized December 26, 1606, at St. Mary's Church in Marlborough, Wiltshire, England. Thomas was from a wealthy family of landed gentry; his family owned the estate and manor at Latton on Eton Water in Wiltshire. However, Thomas was the second or possibly third son, and under the primogeniture laws his eldest brother stood to inherit his father's entire estate.

Thomas Prather was educated and would have been well aware of the events occurring in England and the colonies. He was certainly aware of the offer of the headright land grants in the colonies and probably followed the news from Virginia closely. England was awash with tales of riches to be had in the New World, and with no realistic prospects of obtaining any substantial part of his father's inheritance, Thomas decided to leave England for the new Virginia colony. To do so, he indentured himself to Captain Richard Shepard and sailed to Virginia on the ship *Marie Providence* in 1622, at the age of eighteen.[4] Captain Shepard sold Thomas' indenture warrant to John Powell in Elizabeth Cittie, Virginia,[5] and Thomas worked for John Powell for five years to fulfill the obligations of the indenture. The Powell and Prather families had a long history of associations and intermarriages in England and John Powell was most probably a cousin to Thomas.

John Powell had come to Virginia on the *Swallow* in 1609 and was an "ancient planter." In 1622, deputy governor Argall gave him land on the east side of the Hampton River in Elizabeth Cittie. The land was later confiscated by Governor Yeardley on behalf of the Virginia Company and the company compensated Powell for the clearing and buildings. On September 20, 1624, Powell patented 150 acres of land in Elizabeth Cittie and was described in these documents as a yeoman.

After serving his indenture, Thomas Prather received his headright grant of 50 acres. He married Mary in 1627. Some historians think that she was Mary Mackay; others think that she was Mary Powell, the daughter of John Powell. Thomas and Mary Prather had six known children. Jonathan Prather Sr., our ancestor, was born between 1630 and 1635 in Virginia and moved to Maryland in 1658. He died in Calvert County, Maryland, in 1680. Jonathan married a woman named Jane, who lived until 1713 at Brookfield Plantation in Prince George's County, Maryland. After Jonathan died, she remarried before May 17, 1684, to John Smith, a wealthy Scotsman from Calvert County, Maryland.[6]

Jonathan and Jane Prather had six children. Their oldest child, our ancestor Jonathan Prather (II), was born in Maryland in 1666. Jonathan (II) married Elizabeth Bigger, whose parents had immigrated to Maryland from Ireland. John Bigger, the son of James Bigger and Rebecca Parker of Carnmoney, Antrim, Ireland, was transported to Calvert County, Maryland, in 1652, by Captain John Boage of Patuxent Manor,[7] when John Bigger was 18 years old. John Bigger completed his indenture service in 1654, a relatively short time. He was reportedly a horse trader of some ability and at least once was called as an expert witness by the provincial court of Maryland to give testimony about the age of a horse that was at the center of a dispute.[8]

John Bigger married a woman named Ann, who was probably Ann Truelock. When he died, he left a will dated November 12, 1675, in which his wife, Ann, was named as executrix, she was left 200 acres on Freason's Creek and was left in charge of the entire estate while their children were minors. John and Ann Bigger were probably, but not provably, the parents of our ancestor Elizabeth Bigger born in 1670 in Prince George's County, Maryland.

Jonathan and Jane Prather's son Jonathan Prather (II) married Elizabeth Bigger. Their daughter Ann Prather was born in 1702. Ann married Henry Odell, the son of Thomas Odell. They were great-great-great-great-great-great-grandparents of Eleanor Rosalynn Smith.

Although no one knows for sure, Thomas Odell was thought to have been born in Derbyshire, England.* Walter George Odell in his *Origin of the Odells of Maryland* relates an old tradition with the Odells that the emigrant was shipwrecked off the coast of Virginia

---

*Another member of the Odell family from Derbyshire, thought to be a relative of Thomas Odell, emigrated to New York. Family members later moved to New Hampshire and eventually to Minnesota, where Clinton Odell invented a brushless shaving cream. As automobiles become popular, Clinton Odell's son Allan came up with a marketing idea and convinced his father to invest $200 in the plan. In 1926, Allan placed the first four Burma Shave signs on Route 35 near Minneapolis. Eventually, over 7000 sets of Burma Shave signs were placed in 45 states as the advertising campaign became a phenomenon.

in about 1650 and landed in that colony. Thomas allegedly arrived on the ship *Virginia Merchant* and, if so, he arrived in a spectacular manner.

The 1649 voyage of the *Virginia Merchant* is well known, but not because Thomas Odell may have been aboard. King Charles I, after having been held prisoner for years, was beheaded in front of Whitehall Palace on January 30, 1648. The leaders of Virginia were avid supporters of the despotic ruler and by October had passed an act declaring that anyone voicing support for the beheading of the king could be tried as an accessory after the fact. The act made to be treason the denial of the right of succession by Charles II or the denial of the Royalists' right to govern Virginia. Colonel John Norwood, a loyalist in exile in Holland; Major Francis Morrison; Major Richard Fox; and Thomas Woodward, the former assay master of the mint to Charles I, met in London and bought passage on the *Virginia Merchant* to sail to the hospitable colony of Virginia. The *Merchant* was a large ship for the time, a three-hundred ton brigantine mounting thirty guns and carrying 330 passengers. The ship struck a reef off Cape Hatteras in a violent storm and during the tempest lost her forecastle and mainmast. Passengers were swept from the deck and after the storm passed, the *Virginia Merchant* had been reduced to a drifting hulk.

Colonel Norwood kept a diary and wrote about the shipwreck. In his writings, he claims that the ship drifted near an island and the ship abandoned him and his companions there. A more likely version of the story is that upon seeing the island, Norwood and his companions commandeered some remaining small boat and abandoned the others on the ship to their fate. The ship eventually drifted into the Yorke River and the remaining passengers were saved. Governor Berkeley in Virginia was notified and dispatched a rescue party to the island, where Norwood and his companions were found and brought safely to Virginia. If Thomas Odell was on the *Virginia Merchant*, his arrival in the colonies was one of the most exciting of all of our ancestors.*

From 1694 until 1698, Thomas was a county coroner for Anne Arundel County. He also served as a militia officer and as one of Her Majesty justices for Anne Arundel County.[9] In April 1691, Thomas married Sarah Ridgely (Brewer), the daughter of Colonel Henry Ridgely and (probably) Elizabeth Howard. Their son Thomas (II) was born January 7, 1692, and Henry was born April 15, 1698.[10]

Colonel Henry Ridgely emigrated to Maryland with his brother, William Ridgely. His grandson, Judge Nicholas Ridgely, published a manuscript of Colonel Ridgely's collection of family papers and Bible records before his death in 1777. Judge Ridgely's manuscript traces the Ridgely family in Annapolis and Delaware to their ancestor the "Hon. Henry Ridgely, of Devonshire, England, who settled in Maryland, in 1659, upon a royal grant of 6,000 acres. He became a Colonel of Militia, member of the Assembly of the Governmental Council, Justice of the Peace, and Vestryman of the Parish Church of St. Ann's."[11]

Colonel Ridgely's first wife is identified in his request for land: "Henry Ridley demands lands for transporting himself, which is entered in Buries book, and Elizabeth Howard, his wife, and John Hall, Stephen Gill, Richard Ravens and Jane his servants, in the year 1659." In 1661, "James Wardner (Warner), who had left Virginia with the other Puritans, and Henry Ridgely were granted a certificate for 600 acres, called 'Wardridge,' on the north side of South River, joining a tract, 'Broome,' formally Richard Beard's, adjoining Neale Clarke's."[12] James Warner's children married into the Ridgely family and James assigned his rights to

---

*The *Virginia Merchant* was lost for good on March 26, 1661, when she struck rocks and sank off the coast of Bermuda. She was eventually found by treasure hunter Teddy Tucker and is now a diving attraction.

the land to Colonel Ridgely in 1665 in a transaction that was one of the burnt records of 1704.[13]

Colonel Ridgely had three wives. Judge Nicholas Ridgely's Bible entry about himself identifies his father, Henry Ridgely, as the son of Colonel Ridgely's wife Sarah Warner.[14] Before August 9, 1695, Colonel Ridgely married the widow of Maureen Duvall, a wealthy and influential member of the provincial commission.*

Although there seems to be no proof of which one of Colonel Ridgely's wives was her mother, there is no doubt that Colonel Ridgely was the father of Sarah Ridgely, the wife of Thomas Odell. Thomas and Sarah Odell's children, Thomas (II) and Henry, are mentioned in Colonel Ridgely's will, written in 1705, with codicils, which was probated in 1710.[15]

On April 6, 1700, Thomas Odell bought two tracts of land in Baltimore County from James Murray.[16] The tracts were called "Athel" and "Murray's Addition" and both were located on the Patapsco River on Hunting Ridge. A year later, on March 25, 1701, Thomas purchased an 800-acre tract of land called "Darnell's Grove" on the west side of the Pawtuxet River and moved to Queen Anne's Parish in Prince George's County. In 1705, he and his father-in-law, Henry Ridgeley, were elected vestrymen of the St. Barnabas Episcopal Church in Queen Anne's Parish. Thomas Odell died in 1722 and in his will, which was probated in the Prince George's County Court April 11, 1722, he left land to his sons, Thomas (II), Henry, and Rignall, and personal property to his daughters, Ann and Sarah.

Our ancestor Henry Odell, the son of Thomas Odell and Sarah Ridgely and Colonel Henry Ridgely's grandson, was born in Anne Arundel County, Maryland, in 1698. Henry was left 500 acres of land in his father's will and lived on the plantation with his wife, Ann Prather, the daughter of Jonathan Prather and Elizabeth Bigger. Their son, Thomas Odell (III), was born July 28, 1726, in Queen Anne's Parish; a great-great-great-great-great-grandfather of Eleanor Rosalynn Smith. Colonel Henry Ridgely died in 1738 and in his will he divided his plantation between his two sons, Thomas (III) and Rignall (II).

Henry and Ann's son, Thomas Odell (III), married Keziah Offutt, whose ancestors had already been in the colony for three generations.

The Offutts and Captain Edward Brock Arrived Before 1672

Keziah Offutt was the granddaughter of William Offutt and Mary Brock. Mary's father was our ancestor Captain Edward Brock, an Irishman who had immigrated to Calvert County, Maryland. The exact date when Captain Edward Brock arrived in the colony is not known, but he was well established by 1681, as proven by an entry in the St. Mary's council records in which is a description of his farm having been attacked by Indians:

> At a Council held in the City of St Maries the 26th Day of September Anno Domini 1681:
>
> Memdû [memorandum], this following information being delivered into his L^{spps} [Lordship's] hands by Capt Ninion Beale was by his L^{spp} ordered entred in the Councill booke viz.
>
> Upon the 31st Day of August last divers Indians came to the house of Edward Brock, the which Indians came to damage unto the s^d Brock in taking away at least four barrels of his Corne out of the field and broke open six hogsheads of Tobacco taking what they thought good, and the remainder heaving it about the Plantation and in the Swamps and killed three of his hoggs.

---

*Maureen Duvall was an ancestor of associate justice of the Supreme Court Gabriel Duvall, President Harry Truman, and actor Robert Duvall, among others.

> Upon the 10th Day of September now present there came a great party of Indians about 150 of them to the house of Edward Brock the which Indians did him much damage in breaking open his two hides of tobacco more taking what they thought good and to the value of two hides of tobacco uncured, and three great hogs they killed then, and have taken away about Six barrels of Corne out of his Loft and about 3 barrels of Corne out of the field, and made several attempts to have broke into his house to have robb'd him, and lay sore upon him from 12 a Clock on the tenth Day until 9 Clock on the 11th Day.[17]

Captain Edward Brock died in 1714 and in his will he named his son-in-law William Offutt as executor. William declined the executorship and the back of Captain Brock's will was so endorsed.[18]

William Offutt emigrated from Scotland and settled in Prince George's County sometime before 1694. King William III and Queen Mary were Presbyterians and had ascended to the throne of England in 1689. William Offutt was also a staunch Presbyterian and he began to accumulate a vast amount of land from grants from the king for his service to the Crown and support of the Presbyterian Church.

William received an initial land grant of 101 acres in 1694 next to land owned by Ninian Beall, Samuel MacGruder, and Captain Edward Brock. These men received grants for and purchased immense tracts of land in the area which is now Washington, D.C., and they are credited with establishing the first Presbyterian churches in Maryland and Virginia. William Offutt was closely associated with Colonel Ninian Beall. In 1704, Ninian Beall gave land to Nathaniel Taylor, a prominent Scott Presbyterian minister who arrived with a congregation from Fifeshire in 1690, for "ye erecting and building a house for ye service of Almighty God, that parcel of land being a part of a tract called ye Meadows, lying on ye western branch of the Patuxent River in Prince George's County" Beall made "a number of his kinsmen trustees,"[19] including William Offutt.

After receiving a grant for "Offutts' Delight," William married Mary Brock, the daughter of his neighbor Captain Edward Brock. William lived in the reign of six Protestant monarchs and received land grants from William III, Queen Anne, King George I and King George II.

"Calverton Edge" and "Addition to Calverton Edge," 948 acres total, were surveyed by and granted to Ninian Beall in 1688 and 1695. Ninian deeded the land to William Offutt in 1701 and 1702.[20] William patented a 100-acre tract called "Offutt's Adventure" in April 1715. "Covert," a 406-acre tract, was surveyed for him in May 1715 and "Clewerwell" was surveyed for him in July 1715. The 500-acre "Outlett" was surveyed in September 1715 and the 600-acre "Younger Brother," in August 1717. "Offutt Pasture," containing 613 acres, was surveyed for him in November 1722 and "William and James" in 1723. "Clewerwald Enlarged," containing 2000 acres, was surveyed for Offutt July 17, 1728, and "Bear Den," containing 200 acres, was surveyed in April 1729.

When he died in 1732, William Offutt owned over 4100 acres of land. He and his sons owned Great Falls near the present-day Washington, D.C.; "Offutt's Crossroads," which is now Potomac, Maryland; Offutt's Island, near Cabin John's Bridge near today's Interstate 495; part of the present-day Georgetown; and the land where the Capitol and the White House were later built.

William and Mary Offutt had eleven children. William Offutt Jr. was born around 1700 and married Jane Joyce about 1720. They were great-great-great-great-great-great-grandparents of Eleanor Rosalynn Smith. On November 25, 1725, William Offutt Sr. gave "Clewerwell" and the "Enlargement" to his son William Offutt Jr. and his wife Jane Joyce. The deed of gift was acknowledged by William's wife, Mary.[21]

Keziah Offutt was born February 2, 1735,[22] and married Thomas Odell, the son of Henry Odell and Ann Prather. On April 21, 1771, their daughter Eleanor Odell married Benjamin Jacob of Queen Anne's Parish, Prince George's County,[23] the son of Mordecai Jacob and Jemima Isaac.

The Isaac and Pottenger Families Arrived Around 1670

The first of the Isaac (Isacke) line in Maryland were two brothers, Edward and Joseph Isaac, who arrived in the colony around 1670. Edward was a captain in the English army and reportedly came to the colony in charge of Scottish political prisoners exiled by Cromwell at the end of the civil war in England.[24] Joseph Isaac's name first appears in the Maryland records in his will dated December 26, 1688, and probated February 23, 1689, in which he mentioned his wife, (Jane) Margaret, his sons, Richard and Joseph; his daughters, Elizabeth and Rebecca; and his stepsons Joseph Brown and James Clifford.[25] All of the children were minors.

Our ancestor Richard Isaac was born in 1679 in the part of Calvert County that would become Queen Anne's Parish, Prince George's County, Maryland, in 1705, and lived there as a gentleman planter his entire life, until he died in June of 1759. Richard was a vestryman of the parish, and in 1753 he was a justice of the peace.

Richard Isaac married Sarah Pottenger, the daughter of John Pottenger and Mary Beall. Mary Beall's parentage is not proven and is the subject of some controversy. Mary Beall was thought to have been born in Collington, Prince George's County,[26] in 1658, the daughter of Ninian Beall, one of the largest landowners in Maryland. However, later research cast doubt that the Mary Beall who married John Pottenger was Ninian Beall's daughter.

In 1637, King Charles I mandated that the *Book of Common Prayer* be used in religious services in Scotland. Opposition to the new liturgy was declared to be treason and citizens who did not attend services at their local church under the control of the Episcopalian curates were subject to fines, jail and torture. The king believed in the divine right of the monarch: that God had appointed him to rule and that he was the spiritual head of the Church.

Ninian Beall and his relatives lived in the seaside village of Largo in the County of Fife, near Edinburgh, Scotland. Like many lowland Scots, they were Presbyterians and utterly rejected the idea that anyone but Jesus Christ could be the spiritual head of the Church. In 1638, a group of Scots including Ninian and his relatives signed the National Covenant, confirming their opposition to interference by the Stuart kings in the affairs of the Presbyterian Church. "Covenanter" ministers continued to hold secret services, an offense that became punishable by death. Covenanters were arrested and forced to take oaths of loyalty to the king and to acknowledge his role as the head of the Church. Failure to do so could result in immediate execution. As the repression of the Presbyterians continued and escalated in Scotland, and in an effort to counteract the religious repression, an Episcopalian bishop named Montgomery was killed. One story holds that Ninian was somehow implicated in the plot and in 1655 he fled Scotland and emigrated to Maryland.

Ninian married Ruth Moore in 1668. Ruth was the daughter of Richard Moore, barrister of St. Mary's County, and his wife Jane Moore. This couple had several children, including a daughter named Mary. A Mary Beall married our ancestor John Pottenger, and several references state that the Mary Beall who married John Pottenger was the daughter of Ninian Beall and Ruth Moore. However, that may not be the case. Research shows through property transfers that Ninian's daughter, Mary, married Andrew Hamilton; these transfers and suggest that the Mary Beall who married John Pottenger was Ninian's niece, who was born in

Largo, Scotland, in 1658, and who later emigrated with a Scottish Presbyterian minister and joined the Beall family. Land transfers between the parties refer to each other as "father-in-law," "son-in-law," "cousin" and "brother," terms with less precise meaning in 1650 than are assigned to them today. Weighing the evidence, Ninian Beall was probably not the father of the Mary Beall who married John Pottenger. It seems much more likely that Ninian Beall was her uncle and that her father remains unknown. At best, Mary's lineage is unproven in spite of the numerous references stating knowledge of her parents as being fact.

Fortunately, there is no controversy about the children of John Pottenger and Mary Beall because they are listed in the vestry book of the All Hallows Parish Church. Sarah was born July 20, 1688; Mary was born October 22, 1689; John was born August 20, 1691; Samuel was born April 11; 1693; Robert was born February 25, 1694 or 1695; Rachel was born June 20; 1700, Jemima was born October 2, 1702; William was born May 3, 1704; and Verlinda was born October 18, 1706.

Richard Isaac, the son of Joseph and Jane Isaac, married Sarah Pottenger, the firstborn child of John Pottenger and Mary Beall, and they are great-great-great-great-great-great-grandparents of Eleanor Rosalynn Smith. Their children are also listed in the All Hallows Parish Church Vestry book. Mary was born May 4, 1712; Rachel was born July 2, 1716; Kezia was born February 5, 1719; Richard was born January 21, 1720 or 1721, Drusilla was born April 5, 1723; and our ancestor Jemima was born May 21, 1727.

Jemima Isaac married Mordecai Jacob. The Jacob family had immigrated from England in the mid–1600s.

The Jacobs, Cheyneys, and Westalls Arrived in the Mid–1600s

John Jacob was born in Dover, Kent, England, and was baptized October 18, 1643, at St. Mary's Church in Dover. He was transported to Maryland in 1665 as an indentured servant sponsored by James Warner, who had fled Virginia with the Puritans. On February 13, 1673, John witnessed the will of James Warner. However, he was in the colony well before then, as proven by his headright grant of land in 1674.[27] John Jacob married Anne Cheney, the daughter of Richard and Charity Cheney, March 1, 1674, and he received a land warrant the next day on a stream later known as Jacob's Creek.

Richard Cheyney (Cheney) immigrated to Maryland in 1658[28] with his wife Charity. She is thought to be Mary Charity Wood. Some immigration records show Charity as having immigrated in 1650, which is probably a misprint. The Cheyneys requested land from Lord Baltimore in a petition filed in 1660.[29] Richard Cheyney transported a number of settlers into the province, and in 1661 had surveyed 300 acres known as "Cheney's Rest," 400 acres known as "Cheney's Resolution," 100 acres known as "Cheney's Purchase," 100 acres known as Cheney's Hazard," and 110 acres known as "Cheneys Neck." Lord Baltimore granted these patents in 1663.

On March 1, 1674, Richard Cheney of South River deeded several parcels of land to his children including 100 acres of Cheney's Resolution to John Jacob and his wife, Anne Cheney.[30] John Jacob and Anne Cheney had nine known children. Eleanor Rosalynn Smith's ancestor Benjamin Jacob was born in Anne Arundel County in 1688. On May 1, 1711, Benjamin Jacob married Alice Westall,[31] the daughter of George Westall and Sarah Wade.

Very little is known about George Westall Sr. or Robert Wade, the father of Sarah Wade. Both seem to have arrived in the colony in the late 1650s or early 1660s. A copy of a letter from the Jacob family states "a grant of 800 acres was issued to George Westill (Westall) under date of May 2, 1659 for the transportation of 'himself and George his son and six persons more' into the Province of Maryland. The tract was on the south side of the South River and was called 'Scorton.' The proprietor of 'Scorton' apparently died intestate and nothing further is known concerning him." An 800-acre section of land called "Scorton" was surveyed for a George Wastill in 1658[32] but there appears to be no other records indicating where George emigrated from or when.

Interestingly, Scorton, George Westall's plantation, was later divided into 100 lots and became the site of London Town. The site, about eight miles southwest of Annapolis, is being excavated by archeologists as part of Anne Arundel County's "Lost Towns Project." A report on the progress of the excavation work identifies the site.[33]

Robert Wade was born in England and was transported to Maryland in 1662.[34] He was a planter in South River, Anne Arundel Co., Maryland, who died in 1694. His daughter, Sarah Wade, was born in Anne Arundel County.

George Westall's son, George Westall (II), was born in Anne Arundel County on March 1, 1690.[35] George Westall (II) and Sarah Wade were married about 1678 or 1679. Their daughter, Eleanor Rosalynn Smith's ancestor, Alice Westall, was born September 21, 1693.[36] Alice married Benjamin Jacob, the son of John Jacob and Anne Cheney. Alice's brother, George Westall (III), married Benjamin's sister, Anne Jacob.

Benjamin Jacob and Alice Westall had three known children. Our ancestor Mordecai Jacob was born May 24, 1714, in Queen Anne's Parish, Prince George's County, Maryland.[37] Mordecai married Jemima Isaac, the daughter of Richard Isaac and Sarah Pottenger, on December 7, 1745. Mordecai's sister, Sarah Jacob, married Jemima's brother, Richard Isaac (II).* Mordecai Jacob and Jemima Isaac's son and our ancestor, Benjamin Jacob, was born in 1747 in Prince George's County, Maryland. Benjamin Jacob, named for his grandfather, married Eleanor Odell, the daughter of Thomas Odell and Keziah Offutt.

On October 1, 1776, Washington County was formed and was named for Revolutionary War general George Washington, and at the same time Montgomery County was formed and named after General Richard Montgomery. Both counties were previously parts of Frederick County, which had been formed from Prince George's County in 1748. Benjamin Jacob joined Captain Jacob Sarer's Company Militia formed in the new Washington County and fought in the Revolutionary War.[38]

Benjamin Jacob and Eleanor Odell's daughter and our ancestor Martha Eleanor Jacob was born on October 8, 1780, in Prince George's County. Martha's marriage to Nathaniel Thomas Halley was the first marriage into the Halley family even though the families had lived close to each other in Prince George's County for four generations.

---

*The dates for the marriage of Mordecai Jacob and Jemima Isaac and the marriage of Sarah Jacob and Richard Isaac are taken from a lineage chart in our family records. The chart is undated but old and traces the Jacob family from John Jacob's birth in 1632 in England. For our direct lineage, the chart confirms the marriage of John Jacob and Anne Cheney and the births of their children; the marriage of Benjamin Jacob and Alice Westall (Benjamin's birth is noted as 1685, the All Hallows Church Vestry Book says 1688) and the births of their children; the marriage of Mordecai Jacob and Jemima Isaac and the births of their children; the marriage of Benjamin Jacobs and Eleanor Odell and the births of their children, including the last entries for our lineage: the birth of Martha Eleanor Jacobs on September 8, 1780, her death on March 18, 1800, and her marriage to Nathaniel Halley, for which no date is provided. Our Halley branch is not traced on the rest of the chart, which continues with the Jacobs family until the last dated entry of 1887. A notation on the chart says the record of Benjamin Jacob's birth was torn away and his birth is listed as 1746 or 1747. Unfortunately, the source records are no longer in our family's collection.

The Halley, Haley, Hailey, Hawley, Holly Family

Our ancestor John Hawley (Halley, Holly) was born in 1686 in Charles County, Maryland, and lived there his entire life until he died in September of 1755. John Hawley served in the Charles County Colonial Militia in 1746, 1747, and 1749. He married Easter (Esther) Burch on March 4, 1712, in Accokeek, Prince George's County.[39] Easter may have been the daughter of Frances Burch and there are variations of the spelling of her name, some documents referring to her as Hester. In John's will, in which his own name is spelled Holly, his wife Easter Holly is named as executrix. In her own will of September 22, 1761, she is named as Esther Halley.

Easter Holly and John Holly had three known children, who are mentioned in John Holly's will of June 10, 1755, proved January 9, 1756. Thomas Holly was given a tract of land called "Exeter" in Prince George's Co. His son, Nathaniel Holly, was given the two tracts where John lived called "Costly" and "Costly's Addition." His son, John Holly, was given a tract called "Fellowship" in Frederick County.

Our ancestor Thomas Halley was born December 17, 1713. He married Elizabeth Emerson and they had six children. Thomas died on May 17, 1769, and in his will, written on February 21, 1769, he left his plantation to his wife, Elizabeth, to use during her widowhood. In his will he named his children and gave slaves and furniture to them.[40]

Thomas Halley and Elizabeth Emerson's son and our ancestor John Hawley was born in 1739 and married Elizabeth Price. Our ancestor Nathaniel Thomas Halley was John and Elizabeth's fifteenth child. Nathaniel was born February 9, 1776,[41] and married Martha Eleanor Jacobs, the daughter of Benjamin Jacobs and Eleanor Odell, on March 19, 1800. Nathaniel and Martha moved to Georgia sometime before their daughter Martha Ellen Halley was born May 23, 1812.[42] Nathaniel was a schoolteacher and wrote several textbooks used by the state of Georgia.

The Fulford family moved to Georgia from North Carolina about the same time as the Halley family and both families had moved to Buena Vista, Georgia, a small town in Marion County. Martha Ellen Halley married James Fulford on February 4, 1838. Their first child, Mary Eleanor Fulford, was born on February 22, 1839.[43]

The Fulford and Bell Families

In contrast to Mary Eleanor Fulford's mother's ancestry of the Halley, Jacob, Isaac, Pottenger, Odell, Prather, Biggers, Brock, Ridgely, Cheney, and Westall families, very little is known about the lineage of her father James Fulford. Daniel Fulford is listed as a head of household in the 1790 census, living in Currituck County, North Carolina, with one male over 16, two males under 16, and 4 females. In the 1800 census, he is listed with one male between 16 and 25 and one female 10 thru 16, plus a male over 45 and a female 26 through 44 years old.

On December 5, 1801, William Fulford filed a petition with the Currituck County Court of North Carolina on behalf of himself and his sister for whom he was the guardian, requesting that the court appoint a commissioner and a surveyor to assess and divide the estate of his father, Daniel Fulford, who had died without leaving a will.

William's wife Mary is identified in a deed[44] in which it is recorded that William Fulford and Mary Fulford sold a parcel of land to Obadiah Capps on November 15, 1806. William and Mary then moved to Surry County and are shown as living there in the 1810 census. In the 1820 census, they are living in Battalion 3, Forks of the Yadkin, Rowan,

North Carolina. In the 1830 census, they are still in Rowan County, North Carolina. Sometime between 1830 and 1840, William died, and Mary is listed as head of household in Davie County in the 1840 census, Davie County having been formed from a part of Rowan County in 1836. William and Mary Fulford were probably James Fulford's parents although there seems to be no proof.

A family history written by Sarah Eleanor Bell, Mary Eleanor Fulford's daughter and Rosalynn Carter's grandmother, states that her grandfather James Fulford was born in December 1812 and that James Fulford's wife, Martha Halley, was born May 23, 1812. The couple were married February 4, 1838, and had nine children.

The 1850 census lists James Fulford and Martha Halley, both 37 years old, as living in Buena Vista, in Marion County, Georgia. By then, they had five children: Mary Eleanor, eleven years old; Elizabeth, seven years old; William, six years old; Martha, four years old; and James (II), two years old. James listed his state of birth as North Carolina and his occupation as mechanic. James Fulford's expertise as a mechanic was in building, maintaining, and repairing the newly invented cotton gins.

James Fulford's brother, William Fulford, enlisted as a corporal in Company H, 46th Infantry Regiment Georgia, on March 4, 1862, when the unit was formed. The 46th Regiment fought in Georgia and South Carolina. On June 16, 1862, the regiment fought in the Battle of Secessionville, defeating the Union army's attempt to capture Charleston, South Carolina. In May of 1863, after battles at Gaston and Frampton's Plantation, the unit was assigned to General Gist's Brigade and moved to Mississippi. After the Siege of Jackson, the unit joined the Army of Tennessee and fought at Chickamauga and Missionary Ridge. During or shortly after the second battle of Chickamauga in November of 1863, William was wounded or became ill and was transferred to Gilmer Hospital in Marietta, Georgia. where he died on February 26, 1864.

Our ancestor Mary Eleanor Fulford was James Fulford and Martha Halley's first child, born February 22, 1839. Mary Fulford married William Henry Bell, who was born May 31, 1843. Like the Fulford family, very little is known about the Bell family ancestry. However, the family history in our records written by their daughter and our ancestor Sarah Eleanor Bell lists her brothers and sisters and their birthdates.[45] Other family records list the parents of William Henry Bell, as Charles A. Bell who was born in Marion County in 1814 and lived there until he died in 1866. So little is known about him that his middle name is listed on documents as Abner, Adrian, and Allison. What is known is that Charles Bell married Susan Singer, the daughter of Johann Ulrich Singer and Temperance Carr.

Johann Ulrich Singer (John Singer) was born October 29, 1784, in Württemberg, Germany, and lived until August 17, 1855. He served in the Prussian army in Germany before emigrating to America. John Singer married Temperance Carr sometime around 1817 in Bibb County, Georgia. By 1833, they

A rare daguerreotype and the only known photograph of George Lynch Smith (1775–1868), a great-great-grandfather of Eleanor Rosalynn Smith.

were living in Stewart County.[46] Temperance Carr was the daughter of Robert Carr, who was born on June 30, 1760, in Randolph County, North Carolina, and Obedience, whose last name is unknown. Family legend says that Temperance Carr was an Indian but no tribe is identified.

On October 23, 1831, in Hancock County, Georgia, Robert Carr placed a legal notice in the *Georgia Journal* newspaper which said: "This is to forewarn all person from trusting my wife Obedience Carr, as I am determined not to pay any of her contracts. Signed Robert Carr."[47]

The 1850 census shows James Fulford and Martha Halley as living next door to Palestine Smith and his wife Ellen. Palestine Smith was the son of George Lynch Smith and Delanna Peddy, Eleanor Rosalynn Smith's great-great-grandparents, Rosalynn having descended from Palestine's brother Tenderson Smith. William Henry Bell's sister Willie Bell married Crittenden Jubilee Smith, son of Rosalynn Eleanor Smith's great-grandfather Tenderson Smith. Another of William Henry Bell's sisters, Laura Bell, married William Newton Smith, another of Tenderson's sons.

William Henry Bell and Mary Eleanor Fulford's daughter Sarah Eleanor Bell married William Juriston Smith and they were grandparents of Rosalynn Eleanor Smith. The Smith line can be reliably traced only to George Lynch Smith, William Juriston Smith's grandfather.

The Smiths

The Smith lineage can easily be traced back to George Lynch Smith, who arrived in Georgia shortly after 1800. However, the parents of George Lynch Smith are elusive people indeed. Our written family histories say that George Lynch Smith was the son of James Smith and Mary Lynch and his ancestry is given as the following:

James Smith and Rebecca Whitmore
George Smith (b. 1665) and Elizabeth Chesley
James Smith (b. 1701) and Teresa Bailey
James Smith II (b. 1727) and Mary Lynch (1745–1820)
George Lynch Smith (1767–1868)

The histories continue the lineage for over two hundred years after the birth of George Lynch Smith, and from his birth forward, almost every entry can be verified. Unfortunately for the ancestry of George Lynch Smith, nothing can be verified. The few published references about the lineage all say that he was the son of James Smith and Jane Ross of Spartanburg, South Carolina. Letters written to people by various family members in which they refer to cousins, aunts, and uncles are consistent with the James Smith/Jane Ross lineage, which is probably how the claim came to be made in the first place.

The Smith Family Letters

There are several existing letters written by George Lynch Smith and his son Jubilee. Among them is a letter written by George Lynch Smith in February 1859 to Caty in which he mentions the repeated cases of mortality in Tilly's family. In the letter, he names Tilly's children William, Angeline, and John as having been visited by the "Staff of Death." Caty is almost certainly James Smith and Jane Ross' daughter Catherine Smith, who married Moses Stone; and Tilly would be Catherine's sister, Matilda, who did have children named William, Angeline, and John.

Catherine Smith and Moses Stone had a daughter, Regina Minerva Stone, who married

James Wright Tracy. Not long after George Lynch Smith died, his son Jubilee wrote Regina to inform her of his father's death. The family references are excerpted:

> Americus Georgia March 18, 1867
> My Dear Cousin R.M. Tracy,
>
> I address you as cousin, from the fact that I have before me a letter in February 14 addressed to my Father George L. Smith as above. I am reduced to the painful necessity of informing you that my father G.L. Smith departed this life the third day of March 35 minutes after 8:00 o'clock A.M.... Show this letter to my aunt. I know she will rejoice to know of his happy departure.... I think it is highly probable that I shall pass through your state sometime next year. I never had the pleasure of forming the acquaintance of many of my father's relatives on his father [sic] side....
>
> [signed] Jubilee Smith

Jubilee's statement "I address you as cousin, from the fact that I have before me a letter in February 14 addressed to my Father George L. Smith as above" seems to indicate that he did not know that Regina was his cousin until he read a letter sent from her to his father, probably while sorting out his father's affairs since he is writing to her less than two weeks after George Lynch Smith died. But Jubilee was born in Georgia in 1822 and had probably never gone to South Carolina. He writes that he had "never had the pleasure of forming the acquaintance of many of my father's relatives on his father side." This statement clearly establishes kinship.

It is odd that Regina would write to George Lynch Smith and address him as cousin: "I address you as cousin, from the fact that I have before me a letter in February 14 addressed to my Father George L. Smith as above." If he was the son of James Smith and Jane Ross, George Lynch Smith would be Regina's uncle, the brother of her mother, Catherine. On the other hand, there are numerous examples from that period of terms like "uncle," "aunt" and "cousin" being used without meaning the precise relationships that we assign to them today.

The published lineage of George Lynch Smith in *Ancestors and Descendants of Smiths* conflicts with our Smith family history; and the letters I have that were written by George Lynch Smith and Jubilee strongly support the published lineage and not our family history. If the Smith family history is correct, then George Lynch Smith lived to be 100 years old. Furthermore, the letters prove that there was a close and familial relationship between George Lynch Smith and his son Jubilee and the known children and grandchildren of James Smith and Jane Ross.

The Smith Family Bibles

I also have copies of George Lynch Smith and Jubilee Smith's Bibles. Jubilee did not list a birth date for his father but he did note his passing: "George L. Smith departed this life on the 3rd day of March, 1868 in the 93rd year of his life." Jubilee's Bible entry conflicts with the letter that he wrote to Regina telling her of his father's death and which he dated 1867. There seems to be no question that George Lynch Smith died in 1868 and if he died in his 93rd year as recorded in the Jubilee Bible, then he was born in 1775. Other sources such as *The Georgia Frontier: Colonial Families to the Revolutionary War Period* place his birth date in 1779.[48]

The definitive source for establishing George Lynch Smith's date of birth would seem to be George himself and he wrote the birth dates of his family in his own Bible as follows:

George Lynch Smith was born March 15th 1779
Delanna Peddy was born September 10th 1794

Children of the above names:
Jewryston Smith was born September 14th 1813
Tenderson Smith was born August 30th 1815
Elizabeth Smith was born September 22nd 1817
Palestine Smith was born October 13th 1819
Jubilee Smith was born April 14th 1822
Rachel Smith was born May 1st 1824
Paul Smith was born September 11th 1826
Apollos Smith was born April 1st 1829
George B. Smith was born July 11th 1831
Dellany Smith was born September 3rd 1833
M.B. Smith was born July 4th 1842

George wrote a note in his Bible after the list which says, "I give you these dates of interest just so they will be in the old family Bible" [signed] G.L. Smith. George Lynch Smith writing his own birth date in his own Bible and signing the entry is very hard to refute. He was born on March 15, 1779, and died March 3, 1868, just a few days before his 89th birthday.

Having established the birth dates and that George Lynch Smith was the son of James Smith and Jane Ross, I began to look for references about his parents in order to continue tracing his ancestry. There are five references to George Lynch Smith cited in *Ancestors and Descendants of Smiths* and another five scattered in other books. One reference is listed as being in an unnamed private collection. After tracking the other nine references cited, I discovered that they all had one thing in common regarding George Lynch Smith. None of them mentioned him at all.

While tracking down those references however, I discovered another one which had not been available when other researchers were tracing George Lynch Smith and it was an excellent primary source reference indeed. The Bible of James Smith and Jane Ross was donated to the Archives of the State of North Carolina and digital images of the notations written in it can be seen on the State Library of North Carolina Digital Repository Website.

The Smith/Ross Bible is a remarkable reference. In it are meticulous records of births, marriages, and deaths in the Smith/Ross family for over two hundred years, a genealogical treasure. The entries for the births of James Smith and Jane Ross and their children are as follows:[49]

James Smith Senr. was born 15th December 1748
Jane Smith his wife was born 15th April 1752
James Smith & Jane Ross were married the 2nd August 1770
William Henry Smith was born 28th September 1771
Ross Smith was born 11th September 1773
Martha Livinia Smith was born 11th March 1776
Lettice Hancock Smith was born 1st January 1779
Scinthia Bartlet Smith born 5th March 1781
James Smith was born 24th December 1782
Susannah Smith was born 10th December 1784
Hancock Smith was born 7th March 1787
Matilda Smith was born 28th December 1790.
Mary Smith was born 28th October 1792
Ruth Smith was born 16th October 1794

Catharine Smith was born 6th May 1798

Catharine Smith married Moses Stone.
Their children:
Regina Minerva, born January 24th 182[torn page]

George Lynch Smith is not listed as a child of James Smith and Jane Ross in their Bible. He is not listed as having been married nor having died. In fact, he is not listed in the Smith/Ross Bible at all in any way, shape, or form and neither are any of his descendants. Another problem is that George Lynch Smith wrote in his Bible that he was born in March 1779. The Smith/Ross Bible records that Lettice Hancock Smith was born in January 1779. Regina had addressed him as cousin instead of uncle in her letter because he was not her uncle. George Lynch Smith was not the son of James Smith and Jane Ross.

Peter Smith of Westmoreland County, Virginia

All of the Smiths who are referred to as "cousin," "aunt" and "uncle" in the correspondence of George Lynch Smith and his son Jubilee are descendants of Peter Smith of Westmoreland County, Virginia. Peter had five sons who would carry on the Smith name: John, Peter, William, James and Thomas. The sons of Peter Smith had seventeen sons themselves who would be of the age to be George Lynch Smith's father. Some possibilities could be eliminated because they moved to different parts of the country — some to Illinois, some to Ohio and some to Indiana. Others married too late to be the father of George Lynch Smith. Eventually, even allowing for very loose interpretations of "cousin," "aunt," and "uncle," all except the descendants of William Smith seem to be eliminated as possibilities.

Peter Smith's son William was the patriarch of the families with whom George Lynch Smith and his son Jubilee corresponded. William's will, probated in Fairfax County, Virginia, on September 24, 1751, names his wife Letitia Hancock and his three sons, James, Hancock and William.[50] James was the James Smith who married Jane Ross and the meticulous and comprehensive entries in the Smith/Ross Bible seem to eliminate the possibility of his being George's father despite the published sources.

Hancock Smith was born in Virginia in the 1740s and married Jane Meaders. He fought in the Revolutionary War and was granted 200 acres of land along the Fairforest Creek a little south of Spartanburg for his service. He sold 192 acres of the land to his brother William in 1789 and the land was described as being adjacent to land owned by Peter Smith, John Smith, and others. Hancock then disappears from the records and presumably died in 1789. He does not appear in the 1790 census nor on the subsequent census records. His wife, Jane, sold the rest of her land in 1809.[51]

Hancock Smith and Jane Meaders had three sons: Elisha, John and James Smith. Elisha is very well known. He served in the Revolutionary War in the Virginia Continental Army under Lt. Col. Edward Stevens and fought against Governor Dunmore at the Battle of the Great Bridge at Norfolk and at the battles of Brandywine, Germantown, Philadelphia and Monmouth. He then reenlisted under Col. Edward Stevens and fought with George Washington at Valley Forge and reenlisted for a third time and was present when General Cornwallis surrendered at Yorktown.[52] He married Elizabeth Cannon and had three children but his marriage was after George Lynch Smith was born.

There is considerably less information about Hancock Smith's other two sons. James was born in 1770 and married a woman named Jemimah, whose last name is unknown, and John Smith was born in 1765.[53] If these dates for James and John are correct then they were too young to be the father of George Lynch Smith.

The most likely candidate to be the father of George Lynch Smith seems to be William Smith's third son, also named William. William Smith was born in Fairfax County, Virginia, in 1750, and married Catherine, whose last name is unknown. William also fought in the Revolutionary War and afterwards was granted 640 acres of land along the Fairforest Creek adjoining the land of his first cousin Peter Smith. By 1798, when he sold part of the land he inherited from his father, Hancock Smith, William had moved to Georgia. This is supported by the land transaction: "January 29, 1798 William Smith (Jackson County, GA) to Spencer Smith (Spartanburg); for £75 sold 191 acres on Fairforest Creek...."

William has three sons under sixteen years old in the 1790 census and one son over sixteen. The only one known is the oldest, William "Buck" Smith, who was born in 1771. William "Buck" Smith had a son, George Hancock Smith, who was born December 12, 1808, in Georgia. George Hancock Smith named two of his sons Tenderson and Juriston. George Lynch Smith was born in 1779 and named two of his sons Tenderson and Juriston. These are the first known occurrences in the family of the name George and the unusual names Tenderson and Juriston.

It seems very possible that George Lynch Smith was one of the three unknown sons under 16 listed by William Smith in the 1790 census. He would have been the brother of William "Buck" Smith, who named his son, George Hancock Smith, after George Lynch. George H. Smith then named his sons after George Lynch Smith's sons, who were his first cousins. There are, however, problems with this scenario, the most important being that there is not a shred of evidence supporting it beyond having eliminated other known possibilities. Furthermore, George Lynch Smith lists himself in the census as having been born in North Carolina and there is no evidence that William Smith was in North Carolina. Plus, although William Smith's wife's name is not known with certainty, when she is named, invariably with no sources and no surname, she is referred to as Catherine, not Ruth or Mary. And finally, I have contradictory though unverified information.

The Lynch Connection

Our family has lineage charts and four family histories from granddaughters of George Lynch Smith's sons Tenderson, Palestine, and Jubilee, and from a grandson of George Lynch Smith's son Molenious Benton Smith, all of which agree that George Lynch Smith's father was James Smith Sr., who was born in North Carolina and married Ruth or Mary Lynch, the daughter of Jonah Jonack Lynch. I also have an unsourced lineage from a member of the Lynch family which lists the children of Jonah Jonack Lynch as Thomas Lynch of Craven County, born about 1725; Aaron Lynch of Laurens, South Carolina, born in 1730; John Lynch Sr.; Edmond Lynch; Ruth Lynch, born in 1755; and David Lynch of Orange County, North Carolina. Ruth Lynch's husband is listed as James Smith Sr., born about 1754 in Pennsylvania. I also have a letter dated February 23, 1859, written by George Lynch Smith to Caty (Catherine Smith, daughter of James Smith and Jane Ross) recounting that he was visited on Christmas by several of his children and by "John Lynch from old Orange County who was Unkle [sic] John Lynch's grandson."

Regardless of who James Smith was, George Lynch Smith's mother was probably Ruth or Mary Lynch, the daughter of Jonah Jonack Lynch and that John Lynch "from old Orange

County" was the brother of Ruth (or Mary) Lynch and the son of Jonah Jonack Lynch. Jonah Jonack Lynch was the son of Captain Johnson Lynch and Margaret Schulf. Captain Johnson Lynch was born around 1673 and lived until 1712 and was the son of Jonah Lynch and Margaret Johnson.

Sir Nathaniel Johnson

Jonah Lynch emigrated from Gallway, in the Province of Connaught, Ireland, in 1677, sailing aboard the ship *Blessing*. On June 22, 1682, he was awarded a land grant for 780 acres on the south side of the eastern branch of the Cooper River.[54] Jonah died around 1691 and left the land to his son, Captain Johnson Lynch.

Jonah Lynch lived across the Cooper River from Sir Nathaniel Johnson's plantation. Sir Johnson had been in the British army and had been member of Parliament in London. Between 1686 and 1689 Sir Nathaniel Johnson, Knight, was governor of the Leeward Islands of Antigua, Montserrat, St. Christopher, and Treves. A staunch supporter of James II and the Church of England, he resigned his post after the ascension of William and Mary. Instead of returning to England, he moved to the colony of South Carolina. After King William III died in 1702–1703, Sir Johnson was appointed governor of Charlestowne. In 1702, he received a commission from John Lord Granville to be governor of South Carolina.

Queen Anne, suspecting correctly that Sir Nathaniel Johnson was not a supporter, placed several restrictions on him and required that he post a huge bond insuring his compliance in carrying out her instructions and implementing the laws of Parliament. Even so, his reign as governor was contentious. The first act he pushed through the assembly excluded those who were not members of the Church of England from being members of the assembly. This affected two-thirds of the population and the outraged populace forced the assembly to repeal the act. Johnson refused to sign the repeal, which led the inhabitants of Colleton County to draw up a petition imploring the Proprietors to repeal the act. John Ash, a leading dissenter, agreed to return to England to present the petition.

Governor Johnson, determined to use all of the power of his office to thwart the dissenters, banned any ship of Carolina from transporting Ash, whereupon Ash went to Virginia and sailed to London from there. The Proprietors backed Governor Johnson until Queen Anne threatened to revoke their charter.

Not to be stymied, Governor Johnson formed a court of twenty lay persons and gave them ecclesiastical jurisdiction to deprive ministers of their right to preach for what many people deemed arbitrary reasons. Johnson was accused of re-implementing King James II's Star Chamber. Amid the discord, Lord Craven gave the commission of governor of the colony to Colonel Edward Tynte and Johnson was replaced as governor in 1709.

In 1712, the South Carolina Assembly commissioned a road to be built and a ferry service to be established to provide a crossing of the Cooper River. The act proves the proximity of Nathaniel Johnson's plantation and that of Captain Johnson Lynch which he had by then inherited from his father, Jonah Lynch.[55] Sir Johnson's family and the Lynch family had known each other for years. In 1706, when Sir Johnson was governor of Charlestowne, the French and Spanish fleets attacked the city. Captain Johnson Lynch was an officer in the South Carolina militia and played an important part in defending the city against the attack. An article in the *South Carolina Historical and Genealogical Magazine*[56] gives an exciting account of the battle and Captain Johnson Lynch's part in the defense of the city under the command of Sir Johnson.

Jonah Lynch married Margaret Johnson, who is almost surely the daughter of Sir Nathaniel Johnson but not the daughter of his wife Ann Overton. You would think that the descendants of Sir Nathaniel Johnson might be somewhat reluctant to acknowledge this relationship but instead they are quite pleased to claim Margaret Johnson as Sir Nathaniel Johnson's daughter because another descendant of Jonah Lynch and Margaret Johnson signed the Declaration of Independence.

Besides our possible ancestor Captain Johnson Lynch (if the Lynch connection is accurate), Jonah Lynch and Margaret had other children: a daughter, Sarah, and another son, Colonel Thomas Lynch. Colonel Thomas Lynch married Mary Fenwick and they had a daughter named Margaret. After Mary Fenwick died in 1720, Thomas Lynch married Sabina Vanderhorst. Thomas and Sabina had seven children: a son, Thomas II, and six daughters: Mary, Sabina, Sarah, Elizabeth, and two others who died as infants. Thomas II married Elizabeth Alliston in 1745 and they had three children: Sabina, born in 1747; Ester, born in 1748; and Thomas Jr. (actually Thomas III), born in 1749. Elizabeth died in 1752 and Thomas then married Hanah Motte in March of 1775. Thomas and Hanah had a daughter, Elizabeth. Elizabeth married Major James Hamilton, and daughter Sabina married Captain William Cattell, both Revolutionary War Patriots.

Thomas Lynch was elected to the Commons House of Assembly in 1751 and served in the 1756 Stamp Act Congress in New York. His vigorous opposition to the Stamp Act brought him to the attention of the most influential leaders in the colonies. John Adams said, "We are all vastly pleased with Mr. Lynch. He is a solid, firm, judicious man." Samuel Adams described him as "a man of sense and virtue." In 1774, Thomas was elected to serve in the Continental Congress in Philadelphia and while he was there he played a major role in forming the Continental Army. In October of 1775, Thomas Lynch, along with Colonel Benjamin Harrison and Benjamin Franklin, was appointed as an advisor to General George Washington.

In February 1776, Thomas suffered a cerebral hemorrhage and was paralyzed while in Philadelphia. At the time, his son, Captain Thomas Lynch Jr., was a member of the South Carolina militia and was serving in the Provincial Congress of South Carolina. That body selected him to attend the Continental Congress in his father's place, which, incidentally, gave him and his father the distinction of being the only father-son team to serve in the Continental Congress. On August 22, 1776, Thomas Lynch Jr. became the 52nd person to sign the Declaration of Independence.

Thomas also fought in the Revolutionary War. On a march to Charleston in 1775 he became violently ill, and his health declined rapidly. Signing the Declaration of Independence was his last political act. He returned home to "Peachtree," his plantation in South Carolina, after his father died in Annapolis having suffered another stroke. In 1779, Thomas' doctors sent him to the West Indies to seek a cure for his chronic illness. Thomas and his young wife, Elizabeth Shubick, set sail on their honeymoon for St. Eustatius,* one of the Leeward Islands in the Netherlands Antilles in the Caribbean. Their ship encountered

---

*St. Eustatius, also known as Statia, has an interesting place in American history. On 16 November 1776, the brigantine *Andrew Doria*, under the command of Captain Isaiah Robinson, sailed into Oranje Harbor flying the flag of the newly independant United States. The *Andrew Doria* fired a thirteen-gun salute and Governor Johannes de Graff ordered a return salute of eleven guns to be fired, the customary salute of firing two guns less than a ship. The return of the ship's salute by St. Eustatius gave the country the distinction of being the first foreign country to officially recognize the United States of America. The governor of nearby St. Kitts immediately dispatched a ship to London to inform Parliament and the king that Holland had recognized the independent United States. The British added this offense to the list of grievances against Holland that they later used as justification to declare war on that country in 1781.

a violent storm and sank. Thomas and Elizabeth and all others on the ship were lost at sea.

Thomas and Elizabeth died leaving no heirs. His will stipulated that whoever inherited his plantation, "Peachtree," must bear the Lynch surname to continue the lineage. His sister Sabina had married John Bowman and they had a son named John Lynch Bowman. To comply with the terms of the will, John Lynch Bowman changed his name to John Bowman Lynch and inherited the plantation. John Bowman Lynch married a Miss Campbell and they had seven children, four daughters and three sons. All three sons served on the Confederate side in the Civil War. All three were killed during the war, thus ending that branch of the Lynch line.

Fortunately for us, and assuming that the Lynch connection is accurate, our Lynch ancestral line through Captain Johnson Lynch continued.

The Ancestors of the Mythical James Smith

There are four family histories of our Smith family written by the great-granddaughters and great-grandsons of George Lynch Smith. Below are a partial transcript and excerpts from a manuscript written by Lela Theresa Smith and continued by her daughters.‡

> This information was given to me by Lamartine Bostwick, Dr. Jubilee Smith's granddaughter, of Richland Ga., Stewart County.
>
> This data has been handed down in her family for several generations. Much of it was taken from many old Bible records [all of which have vanished mysteriously] that substantiate her claims....
>
> In 1652, James Smith was married to Miss Rebecca Whitmore. Their first child, George Smith, was born in 1665 after 13 long years. He was second in line in our family. He was a doctor and a dentist.
>
> He married Miss Elizabeth Chesley in 1696. He was 31 years old.
>
> Their oldest child was a girl named Amelia, their next child was a son named James. He was a minister and a school teacher born in 1701. He is third in line in our family. He was married to a Miss Teressa Daily. They had a son also named James (II) born in 1727. He was a school teacher.
>
> He married Miss Mary Lynch. He was fourth in line in our family. They had a son, George Lynch Smith born in 1767, (he is my great-grandfather). He married Miss Delannah Peddy. They were the parents of 12 children....

Other family histories recount substantially the same narrative, some spelling Rebecca Whitmore's name as Rebekka, some saying Teressa Daily was Teressa Bailey, some saying Ruth Lynch instead of Mary Lynch.

From George Lynch Smith back to the seemingly mythical James Smith who married Miss Rebecca Whitmore in 1652 nothing can be verified. There seems to be no James Smith or Rebecca Whitmore, no George Smith or Elizabeth Chesley, no James Smith who married Teressa Daily or Teresa Bailey, and no James Smith who married Mary Lynch. There is no trace of any of them.

Like the search for the family of Susan Champion, untold hours of searching for the parents of George Lynch Smith has turned up virtually nothing. I'm sure that somewhere, somebody has a family Bible listing his parents, or that there is a deed that says "because

---

*The original is now owned by Mr. Robert Hightower, who was kind enough to loan it to me.

of the natural affection I have for my son, George Lynch Smith," or maybe Theresa Smith's documentation will be found in an attic of one of our relatives. Something will either turn up or not.

And something may have. I recently came across information that in a dispute in Georgia when an estate was settled in 1863, the Lynch heirs sued the Smiths over slaves. The suit was *Thomas Lynch of Orange County v. Jubilee Smith of Stewart County*, North Carolina Court of Pleas and Quarter Sessions 1863. The information I have came from a copy of a recently acquired letter from Jubilee to John[57] complaining about Thomas Lynch suing him and asking, "How can cousins sue each other over a few slaves?"

Without even knowing whose estate it was, this is an interesting development and would seem to establish a firm connection between the Smiths and the Lynches. Unfortunately, the minutes of the Orange County, North Carolina, Court of Pleas and Quarter Sessions of 1863 are not readily available, but I will eventually track them down.

The Descendants of George Lynch Smith

George Lynch Smith and Dellana Peddy had eleven children.

Juriston Smith was born September 14, 1813. He married Miss McGuam, and they had four children. Their oldest child was Phillip Smith, who moved to Texas and reportedly lived to be 110 years old.

Elizabeth Smith was born September 22, 1817. She married Thomas McGarrah of Friendship, Georgia. Thomas and Elizabeth McGarrah were the grandparents of Robert McGarrah, the postmaster of Plains, Georgia. Eleanor Rosalynn Smith's mother was the assistant postmaster and she worked with Robert McGarrah until they both retired. Palestine Smith was born October 13, 1819. He was known as "Uncle Tine." Palestine married Ellen Belk and they had two children, Paul and Apollos, who were named for their uncles.

Jubilee Smith was born April 14, 1822. He married Mary Annie Audulf. Jubilee served as a captain in the Civil War in the 7th Regiment, Georgia Infantry. Jubilee originally enlisted in the Civil War as a surgeon but he was also a morphine addict. He was eventually removed from the surgical unit and became overseer of the Confederate arsenal in Columbus, Georgia. He posted thousands of dollars in bonds for ammunition and supplies during his service. After the war, Confederate money was worthless and Jubilee was broke. After a trip to visit his brother Molenious in Texas, he arrived back in Columbus, Georgia, with no money. He borrowed money from the Masons and traveled to Savannah and rented a room with no electricity. In the dark or by candlelight, he misjudged, and died that night of an overdose of morphine.

Rachel Smith was born May 1, 1824. She married Johnston Lawles. Paul Smith was born September 11, 1826. Paul was a doctor and he married Lucy Doster. He left town as a young man and never returned. Apollos Smith was born April 1, 1829. Family legend has it that the family received word that Apollos had been taken prisoner by Union troops in 1863 during the Civil War and was being transferred to a prisoner of war camp. He was never heard from again. His Civil War records state that he deserted. Apparently, his regiment never knew he had been captured.

George B. Smith was born July 11, 1831. He married Marshia Parham. George was a doctor and a carpenter. He lived in Benevolence, Georgia, and was the only physician for three counties. He was killed when lightning struck his house on the morning of March 29, 1790.[58] The *Terrell County* newspaper reported the ghastly tragedy:

On Wednesday morning the 29th instant, about 7 o'clock, during the prevalence of a severe thunderstorm the residence of Dr. George B. Smith near Benevolence was struck by lightning and the entire family prostrated and stunned by the shock.

To those who first recovered, an appalling spectacle presented itself.

There lay the noble head of the house with his neck broken, a lifeless corpse, while the mother and two of the little ones were grievously injured and blackened by the fluid. To add to the horrors of the scene, in an instant the entire dwelling was wrapped in flames and almost before the dead and suffering could be moved to a place of safety, the whole pile was consumed and a smoking ruin was all that remained of the pleasant home of that happy family. Books, papers, clothing, all save two feather beds, fell prey to the devouring element.

The intelligence spread like wildfire and never have we seen the entire community more startled and horror stricken by any event.

It was the privilege of the writer to know intimately and love almost with the affection of a brother, the good man and public spirited citizen who has thus been cut off in the twinkling of an eye and in the meridian of his life and usefulness.

His death will create a dark and aching void in the hearts of a large circle of devoted friends, while upon his poor family, God help them, the blow falls with crushing and overpowering effect.

We learn that Mrs. Smith has partially recovered, though severely injured and the two children will likewise probably survive.[59]

Dellany Smith was born September 3, 1833. She married Calvin Cochran.

Molenious Benton Smith was born July 4, 1842, and married Cordelia Milner. Tenderson Smith, Rosalynn Smith's great-grandfather, was born August 30, 1815, in Stewart County, Georgia. Tenderson married Frances Thomas, the daughter of John Thomas and his wife Mary, who were friends of his parents, George Lynch Smith and Delanna Peddy, when they lived in North Carolina. Two months after Frances was born, her mother left home one day and never returned. A short time later, John Thomas lost his job and then found work in Atlanta. He asked George and Delanna to keep the baby until he could move and establish himself. Unfortunately, he was killed in a construction accident soon after he moved to Atlanta. George and Delanna kept the baby and raised her instead of placing her in an orphanage and Tenderson married her on July 12, 1838.[60]

Tenderson was a farmer and lived most of his life in the Cut Off District near Dranesville in Marion County, Georgia. He and Francis Thomas had eight children: T.J. Smith, born in 1841; Teressa Smith, born in 1844; George L. Smith, born about 1847; William Newton Smith, born in 1849; Crittenden Jubilee Smith, born in 1852; Walter T. Smith, born in 1857; Wilburn Juriston Smith, born in 1858; and Lannes M. Smith, born in 1859.

A photocopy of an undated tintype photograph of Tenderson Smith (1815–1899), a great-grandfather of Eleanor Rosalynn Smith. The original of the only known photograph of Tenderson is believed lost.

Tenderson and his family lived near William Henry Bell's family. Two of Tenderson's sons married William Henry Bell's sisters. William Newton Smith married Laura Bell and Crittenden Jubilee Smith married Willie Bell. Our ancestor Wilburn Juriston Smith married Sarah Eleanor Bell, the daughter of William Henry Bell and Mary Eleanor Fulford. Wilburn Juriston Smith and Sarah Eleanor Bell are Rosalynn Smith's paternal grandparents. Tenderson Smith died on July 23, 1899, when he was 83 years old and is buried in the Champion Cemetery in Stewart County.

Wilburn Juriston Smith and Sarah Eleanor Bell had eight children. Their first child was Lela Teressa Smith, who was born August 20, 1894. Lela Teressa Smith wrote the "Smith Family History" that provides many of the clues about the ancestry of Rev. George Lynch Smith. She also recorded the birthdays of her brothers and sisters. Rosalynn Smith's father, Wilburn Edgar Smith, was born November 20, 1896. Elder Fulford Smith was born on March 5, 1899. William Tennyson Smith was born April 15, 1901. Lumas Leonidus Smith was born July 13, 1903. Oliver Crawford Smith was born in February 26, 1906. George Quitman Smith was born July 6, 1909. Sallie Will Smith was born in 1912 and died at birth.

In 1903 the Smiths moved closer to town in order for the children to attend school, and lived about 2 miles from Plains. It was at this home that Wilburn Juriston Smith died in 1918. Several years later his widow moved into Plains.

Wilburn Edgar Smith ran an auto repair shop in Plains and was seriously burned one day in an accident while welding. His burns were treated with radium, the new wonder drug. Edgar Smith died in 1940 of leukemia when he 43 years old. Frances Allethea Murray lived until 1997.

Through an amazing set of circumstances and after the astonishing journeys of their ancestors to Plains, Georgia, the son of James Earl Carter, Sr., and Lillian Gordy, James Earl Carter, Jr., married the daughter of Edgar Smith and Frances Allethea Murray, Rosalynn Eleanor Smith, on July 7, 1946.

Afterword: The Quest

Research into any family's history will always be incomplete and our family is no exception. After thousands of hours of research, there are still holes and dead ends. There are many questions left to be answered for each ancestral line.

For the Carter ancestry, the most intriguing mysteries are the identification of Kindred Carter's wife and proof that Captain Thomas Carter of Isle of Wight was the son of the William Carter who arrived in Jamestown in 1622. The origin of Adrian Gordy is still an open question. The first provable Murray was in Virginia in the mid–1700s, but the line probably extends back to David Murray, born in 1598 in Scotland. The parents of Rev. George Lynch Smith remain enigmatic.

I have not found all of our ancestors. But somewhere, someone has an old Bible that records a marriage or birth I'm still looking for, they have a will I cannot find, or they have a copy of a letter to one of our ancestors asking about a wife whose name I don't know. I haven't given up on finding any of them. After all, that's what makes it a quest. And the quest is partially fulfilled. The stories about our grandfathers and grandmothers that I've found have changed them from just names into real people.

They've become family.

Appendices

A: What's a Cousin and How Do They Get Removed?

Family relations are described by a system of degrees and removes. Degrees indicate the number of generations between the nearest common ancestors and determines first, second, third, etc. cousins. Removes indicate the number of generations between cousins after the nearest generation is established. First cousins share grandparents. Second cousins share great-grandparents but not grandparents. Third cousins share great-great-grandparents but not great-grandparents, and so on.

The child of your first cousin is not your second cousin because you do not share grandparents. He is your first cousin once removed. You and that child are considered first cousins because your own grandparents, the child's great-grandparents, are the most recent common ancestor from you yet you are separated by one additional generation. The children of that child will be your first cousins twice removed. The child of your first cousin once removed will be your child's second cousin, as they share great-grandparents but not grandparents.

If one person's grandparents are the other person's great-grandparents then they are first cousins once removed. If one person's grandparents are the other person's great-great-grandparents then they are first cousins twice removed, etc. If one person's great-grandparents are the other person's great-great-grandparents then they are second cousins once removed. If one person's great-great-grandparents are the other person's great-great-great-grandparents then they are third cousins once removed, and so on.

This is a very accurate system for describing the specific relationship between two people who share ancestors and are therefore related. Almost nobody uses it correctly.

B: Pedigree Collapse

The term "pedigree collapse" was coined by Robert Gunderson to describe the way individuals who share an ancestor cause the number of ancestors of their children to be smaller than it could be. Typically, a person would have two parents, four grandparents, eight great-grandparents, sixteen great-great-grandparents, and so on. Going back thirty generations this would amount to about a billion people, which is more people than were alive thirty generations ago. This is obviously impossible and the explanation is that people marry people who are related to them.

Below is a graphic showing the situation in which no ancestors are common. A child (c) has the expected two parents (p), four grandparents (gp1), eight great-grandparents (gp2), and sixteen great-great-grandparents (gp3) (see graphic next page).

```
gp3 gp3  gp3 gp3  gp3 gp3  gp3 gp3  gp3 gp3  gp3 gp3  gp3 gp3  gp3 gp3
  \ /      \ /      \ /      \ /      \ /      \ /      \ /      \ /
   gp2      gp2      gp2      gp2      gp2      gp2      gp2      gp2
    \        /        \        /        \        /        \        /
        gp1                gp1                gp1                gp1
         \                  /                  \                  /
                p                                       p
                 \                                     /
                 _____ child _____
```

Now suppose that the two parents are first cousins. In that case, they share one set of the child's grandparents. Instead of four sets of grandparents the child only has three, so they will have six great-grandparents instead of eight and twelve great-great-grandparents instead of sixteen. Following is a graphic representing this.

```
    gp3 gp3 gp3 gp3       gp3 gp3 gp3 gp3       gp3 gp3 gp3 gp3
      \ /     \ /           \ /     \ /           \ /     \ /
       gp2     gp2           gp2     gp2           gp2     gp2
          gp1                  gp1                   gp1
           \                  /    \                  /
            p                                         p
             \                                       /
                    _____ child _____
```

Now suppose two children marry who have a set of parents who are second cousins. In that case, instead of eight grandparents the children will only have seven. Instead of 16 great-grandparents, the children will only have 14. This is pedigree collapse. Below is a graphic representing those marrying whose parents are second cousins.

```
gp2 gp2  gp2 gp2  gp2 gp2       gp2 gp2   gp2 gp2  gp2 gp2  gp2 gp2
  \ /      \ /      \ /           \ /       \ /      \ /      \ /
   gp1      gp1      gp1   sibling  gp1       gp1      gp1      gp1
    \        /        \            /           \        /        \
     p1               p1                        p2               p2
      \               /                          \               /
       __ child1 __                               __ child2 __
```

Over a number of generations, the difference in the number of expected great-grandparents is quite large. Following is a chart showing the number of grandparents and great-grandparents to be expected if unrelated people marry as opposed to first or second cousins getting married. If the parents of a child are second cousins then the number of grandparents and great-grandparents over eight generations is decreased by 12½ percent. If the parents of a child are first cousins, then over eight generations of grandparents the number of expected grandparents for that child is reduced by 25 percent as shown in the chart.

	GPs	*2GPs*	*3GPs*	*4GPs*	*5GPs*	*6GPs*	*7GPs*	*8GPs*
Unrelated	8	16	32	64	128	256	512	1024
2nd cousin	8	14	28	56	112	224	448	896
1st cousin	6	12	24	48	96	192	384	768

The maximum amount of pedigree collapse in a single generation is 50 percent, which would occur only if siblings married each other. King Alfonso XIII of Spain, who was born in 1886, had only eight different people as his great-great-grandparents instead of the normal 16, a 50 percent collapse of his pedigree at five generations. The pedigree of Britain's Prince Charles has collapsed over 17 generations to 35 percent of the theoretical number of ancestors.

There are complex formulas to calculate the number of expected ancestors if two of your ancestors two generations ago were first cousins and two of your ancestors five generations ago were second cousins and then nine generations ago two of your ancestors were first cousins or any other combination of intermarriages between relatives. Very few people care about these formulas.

Typical American pedigree collapse, as far as I can determine, is about 21.5 percent. Your ancestors married their cousins as did mine and everybody else's.

C: The Search for Kindred Carter's Wife

One of the mysteries of the Carter lineage has been the identity of the wives of two of our Kindred Carters. Our direct ancestor Kindred Carter was born in 1750 in Bertie County, North Carolina, and died in 1805 in Columbia County, Georgia. Nothing at all is known about his wife. Kindred's uncle, also named Kindred Carter and the Kindred discussed here, was the son of Moore Carter and Jane Kindred. This Kindred was born in 1710 in Bertie County, North Carolina, and died in 1777 in Edgecombe County. From an abstract of deeds of a land transaction in which it is stated that "Kindred Carter and Mary his wife and Hardyman Pope and Sarah his wife all of Edgecombe County sell to John Hare of Bertie County, 26 May 1757, 100 acres in Northampton and Bertie County" it was known that Kindred's wife was named Mary. There has been much speculation about her identity. I have had the abstract of that deed for quite some time and I have long suspected that Kindred's wife was Mary Pope, possibly the sister of Hardyman Pope, Sr. There are numerous intertwining connections between the family of Kindred Carter of Bertie County and the Pope family.

Kindred had four daughters: Penelope, Charity, Priscilla, and Winifred. The oldest, Penelope, was born before 1740 and married Cary Whitaker. Charity Carter was born in 1740 and married Moses Knight. Charity and Moses had six children: Kindred Knight, born in 1769; James Allen Knight, born in 1770; John Carter Knight, born in 1772; Sarah Knight, born in 1774; Mary Polly Knight, born in 1776; and Pheresby Knight, born in 1778. I have seen references to Hardyman Pope's mother as Mary Polly Pope, which could connect to Charity's naming her daughter Mary Polly Knight.

Priscilla Carter married James Knight, the brother of Moses Knight, who had married her sister Charity. Winifred Carter married Rueben Taylor and they had seven children: Demsey Taylor, born in 1764; William Taylor, born in 1764; Allen Taylor, born in 1764; Elizabeth Taylor, born in 1765; Penelope Pope Taylor, born in 1767; Kinchen Taylor, born in 1782; and Mary Taylor, born in 1784. Hardyman Pope owned land next to Kindred Carter along the Swift River. When Hardyman died in 1789, Hardyman's son, Elisha, and Reuben Taylor, Kindred's son-in-law, were the executors of his will.

Kindred Carter died in 1777. In 1789, Kindred Carter Pope was born. His parents are unknown but he was not one of Kindred Carter's grandchildren, none of Kindred's daughters having married a Pope. When Kindred Carter Pope died, William Taylor, the son of Reuben Taylor and Winifred Carter and grandson of Kindred Carter, bought Kindred Carter Pope's family Bible from the estate. Having no knowledge of the Bible whatsoever beyond its being sold to William Taylor, I can only imagine that it has a complete genealogy written in it listing births, deaths, and marriages extending back generations.

In the search for Kindred Carter's wife, a lot of information has been accumulated connecting the Carters to the Pope family, all of which could be neatly tied together had Kindred married Mary Pope. It would explain how Kindred Carter and Hardyman Pope came to jointly own the land on the Swift River, why Winifred Carter and Rueben Taylor named their daughter Penelope Pope Taylor, why Reuben was the executor of Hardyman Pope's will, why Charity Carter and Moses Knight named their daughter Mary Polly Knight, and why Kindred's grandson would buy Kindred Carter Pope's Bible at the estate sale. But Kindred Carter did not marry Mary Pope.

There are deed abstracts and there are deeds. Had I lived closer to the North Carolina Archives, I would have long ago obtained a copy of the original deed that named Mary as Kindred Carter's wife, which includes much more information:

> Kindred Carter and Mary his wife and Hardyman Pope and Sarah his wife all of Edgecombe County sell to John Hare of Bertie County, 26 May 1757 for 12 pounds 13 shillings four pence current money of Va, 100 acres in Northampton and Bertie Counties on the south side of Catawiskey meadow, joining Nicholas Perry, Thomas Deans, Long Branch, land formerly belonging to Dr. Spier and land formerly belonging to Bryant O'Quin, land Walter Brown decd. purchased of Abram Oldham in 1735 and by his last will and

testament devised to his wife Mary Brown and the child she then went with which are now the wives of Kindred Carter and Hardyman Pope aforementioned. Wit: John Duke, James Wood, Barnabe Johnson. Reg. Northampton Co. May Ct. 1757 J. Edwards C. Ct.[1]

Kindred Carter married Mary Browne, the widow of Walter Browne. Hardyman Pope married Mary Browne's daughter, who had not been born when Walter Brown died.[2] Walter Browne's will confirms the bequest of his plantation to his wife Mary Browne.[3]

Although Kindred's wife is a total mystery, Walter Browne's wife is not. Walter Browne married Mary "Molly" Odum in 1731. They had two children. The eldest, Josiah Browne, was born around 1733. Walter Brown died in 1735 while Mary was with child. Mary's daughter, Sarah Browne, was born in 1736. Sarah married Hardyman Pope, proven by deeds she and Hardyman both signed as well as her legacy in Hardyman Pope's will. I suspect now that the Pope connection is through Hardyman Pope's line and that Kindred Carter Pope may be a grandchild of Hardyman Pope. Maybe, maybe not.

D: The Bethune Lineage in Scotland

The Bethune genealogy has been traced back an incredible 1400 years with reliable documentation. During that time, the family spread across Europe, but the foundation of the family empire was established in France. Around 1100 A.D. a branch of the family moved to Scotland and became highly influential in the government and the church. By 1300, Robert de Bethune had become one of the top advisors of Robert the Bruce. He negotiated the agreement between Robert the Bruce and King Edward that made Robert the Bruce king of Scotland.

Our Bethune lineage descends from the Scottish Bethunes, and the French genealogists' writings about the Scottish Bethunes differ from what the Scottish genealogists say about them over the period of 300 years between 1150 and 1450. Apparently, this argument went on for hundreds of years, with each side skewering the other in their respective academic publications.

In Paris in 1639, André Du Chesne published the definitive history of the Bethune family, *Histoire de la Maison de Bethune*. Du Chesne was, at the time, one of the most famous French historians of the era. Reporting on the bona fides of his research, he stated that the Bethunes had been connected with, and had donated so liberally to, the Catholic Church for so long that he had found in the church archives "a minute account of every important event that had occurred in the Bethune family for a *thousand years*! Every birth, marriage, and death was recorded, together with every other incident of note connected with their history. The result is that the accuracy of the narrative is unexampled; no other family can show anything like it."

Naturally, I wanted to see this book, and after quite a bit of searching, I found a copy of *A History of the Bethune Family* (translated from the French of Andre du Chesne, with Additions from Family Records and other available sources), *Together with a Sketch of the Faneuil Family, with Whom the Bethunes Have Become Connected in America,* which was published in 1884 and which gives the account of the appearance of the Bethunes in Scotland as André Du Chesne wrote of it in 1639:

HISTORY OF THE BETHUNE FAMILY
SIR JAMES BETHUNE
IS CREATED BARON OF BALFOUR, SCOTLAND.
Beginning of the Fifteenth Century.

Extract from the Funeral Oration delivered by M. Pierre Victor Cayer, Doctor of the Theological Faculty of Paris, in the Church of St. John, the last day of April, 1603, on the occasion of the death of the Lord James Bethune, Ambassador from King James of England, Scotland, and Ireland, near his Majesty, Henry IV. of France, etc. The facts related, he says, "are derived from the papers and records of the deceased."

"In the Kingdom of Scotland (1448), the question being agitated as to the marriage of the King, James II., Ambassadors Extraordinary were sent to the illustrious Duke of Gueldres and Julliers to ask in marriage, in the name of the King, the Very Illustrious Princess Marie, his daughter, who was niece to Philip, Duke of Bourgongne and of Brabant, a very powerful Prince in those times. The Ambassadors thus commissioned were the Very Hon. William, Chancellor of Scotland, the Right Rev John, Bishop of Bonquel, and Sir Nicolas d'Autriburn, a very distinguished Knight. They went to Gueldres with a great retinue, and obtained, by the favor of the Very Christian King, Charles VII. of France, the Very Illustrious Princess Marie of Gueldres and of Jullliers, and escorted her to the King, their master, to be married in Scotland, she being accompanied by the Very Rev. Bishop of Cambray and of Liege, together with the Very Illustrious Princes, the Prince of Vaire, the Prince of Bergue, and the Prince of Rauastain, and many great and valiant knights. Among them was one lord, distinguished above all the others, of the ancient race and house of Bethune of Flandres."

The person here referred to was James of Bethune, third son of John of Bethune, Lord Mareuil, and Isabeau d'Estouteville, and brother to Robert of Bethune, Chamberlain to Charles VII. The orator further states: "Having come into Scotland with this party, and being a gentleman of quality, he entered at once into the good graces of the King, who, wishing to retain him near his person, prayed him to remain in Scotland, and gave him in marriage the only daughter and heiress of the house of Balfour; this house of Balfour being one of the first in Scotland in favor and authority near the King. The title was Baron of Balfour. At that day, as in ancient times in France, it was the highest title. Since then their titles have been augmented to Counts, Marquises, and Dukes, and they have held offices and maintained their dignities, hereditary and successive, to the present day."

On the occasion of this marriage of James Bethune and the heiress of Balfour, the arms of Bethune were quartered with those of Balfour, producing the device shown in the illustration, which has since distinguished that branch of the family from all others of the same name. The crest of the original Bethune arms was a peacock's head and wings ; that of the Bethunes, Barons of Balfour, an otter's head.[1]

The Scottish genealogists disagreed. Walter Macfarlane of Arrochar was the 20th chief of the Macfarlane clan and was described in Anderson's *Diplomata Scotiæ,* published at Edinburgh in 1739, as "a most accomplished young man, Walter Macfarlane of that Ilk, Esq., Chief of the Macfarlanes, one of the most ancient of the clans, who, as he is conspicuous for the utmost urbanity, and for his acquaintance with all the more elegant, and, especially, the antiquarian departments of literature, most readily devoted much labour and industry in explaining to us the names of men and places." He is also spoken of as "the greatest genealogist I ever knew in any country, and perfectly acquainted with all the antiquities of Scotland."

Mr. Macfarlane published *Excerpts from the Genealogical Collections of Mr. Martin of Clermont: Account of the Family of Balfour Bethune as I Got It from the Present Laird of Balfour,* and in that volume Macfarlane gives a somewhat different account of the origins of the Bethunes in Scotland than Andre Du Chesne, upon whose work he comments:

> Our Historians and Genealogists all agree That The Bethuns of Scotland were not of The ancient Scottish Race, but came Originally from beyond Seas in some of The later Ages, but when or upon what Account has not been yet determined with any Certainty.
>
> Mr. Peter Cayer Author of The Funeral Panegyrick on James Arch-Bishop of Glasgow Anno 1603 tells us That amongst other considerable Gentlemen of Quality who came to Scotland Anno 1449 in The Retinue of Mary Princess of Gueldres then married to King James 2 was one Mr. Bethun for whom The King conceived a singular Fondness, and therefore to engage him to live in Scotland he married him to The Daughter and sole Heiress of The Baron of Balfour in Fife which gave Rise to The Family of Balfour Bethun and The Bethuns in Scotland.
>
> This indefinite and uncircumstantiated Account Mr. Du Chesne Author of The Great Genealogy of The House of Bethun illustrates by endeavouring to determine The Name and Person of this Mr. Bethun who had The Happiness to please The King and enjoy The Heiress. From a great many Probabilities and Conjectures he concludes That it was James (Jacotin) de Bethun Fourth Son to John Bethun Lord of Baie &c. and Isabell D'Estoutteville his Wife and younger Brother of Robert Bethun Lord of Baie &c. after his Father & Predecessor of The present Duke de Sully in France.
>
> All this fine Scheme is indeed plausible enough, but not a Word of it true or founded upon any solid Proof. We know not The least Ground Mr. Cayer could have for what he affirms. None of our ancient Historians mention any of The Name of Bethun in The Princess of Gueldres Retinue, and, as to Mr. Du Chesne's Improvements and Conjectures though Jacotin de Bethun lived at that Time, there is not The least Evidence of his ever being in Scotland. Enquerran de Monstrelet a Contemporary Historian, who speaks at Large of him and others of his Kindred, mentions no such Thing no so much as of his ever leaving The Low Countries.
>
> But, really, Mr. Cayer The Orator and Mr. Du Chesne The Genealogist, however willing they were to do Justice to The House of Balfour Bethun being at such a Distance and having no Correspondence with this Country were not sufficiently acquainted either with The Beginning or ancient History of that Family. The Bethuns were of considerable Note in Scotland many Generations before they fell in to The Estate of Balfour, and yet that happened long before The Princess of Gueldres or Jacotin de Bethun were born.[2]

Genealogy as a blood sport — couched in the academic language of gentlemen, of course.

The Bethunes

Some of the first references to the Bethunes in Scotland come from the *Genealogical Collections Concerning Families in Scotland Made by Walter MacFarlane*. MacFarlane was a distinguished Scottish genealogist who died in 1767. Of the early Bethunes he wrote the following:

> Lesly[3] and some other of our Historians tell us That The Bethuns came from France into Scotland in The Reign of Malcolm 3d., who began to reign 1057, and who died 1093. We know not now upon what Grounds they said so. However, The Thing though not absolutely certain is not at all unlikely; For we are sure That not long after this they made a good Figure in this Kingdom being Lairds of Westhall in Angus.
>
> In The Reign of King William who succeeded to The Crown A. 1165 but 72 years after The Death of King Malcolm 3d. Robert de Betun is Witness to a Charter of Rogerus de Quincy Earl of Winton to Seyerus de Seaton of an Annuity of The Mill Lands of Tranent.
>
> David De Betun and Joannes de Betun are Witnesses to a Charter by King Alexander 2d. (who began to reign A. 1214 and died A. 1249) to The Abbacy of Aberbrothick[4] de Terris in Territorio Kermuir.
>
> But a stronger Evidence of The High Station of that Family [page 2S.] in these early Times is That both Mr. Prynne and Mr. Rymer mentions Robert de Betnn present with King Edward at The Discussing of The Plea for The Crown of Scotland betwixt John Balliol and Robert Bruce. This is confirmed beyond all Doubt by some of The Seals yet preserved that are appended to King Edward's Decision A. 1292 among which is that of Robert de Betune de Scotia. It is The Arms of The Bethun Family in Artois at That Time with a File of Three Pendants in Chief as a Mark of Cadency.
>
> This Robert de Betune de Countie de Farfar and several others of that Name are mentioned by Prynne as swearing Allegiance to King Edward A.
>
> David De Betune Miles and Alexander de Betune were at The Parliament of Cambuskenneth Anno 1314 and One of their Seals is appended to The Act of Forfaulture past in that Parliament, which is The same very Coat of Arms that is upon The forementioned Seal of Robert de Betune.
>
> This Alexander continuing Loyal to The Royal Family of Bruce is particularly named by Hector Boyse as One of The Leading Men killed on that Side in The Great Battle of Duplin Anno 1332.[5]

Sir Robert Bethune, the younger son of Alexander de Bethune, married around 1360 Janet Balfour, daughter and heiress of Sir John Balfour of Balfour.[6] John Bethune, First Laird of Balfour, bought the lands of Holkettle from Duncan Earl of Fyffe sometime after 1346. He married Katherine Stewart, the daughter of Sir John Stewart of Innermay.[7] Katherine's dowry included land in the Earldom of Fyfe and is dated February 28, 1386, at Falkland. His son and heir was John Bethune, Second Laird of Balfour. He married ___ Stewart, daughter of Lord Rosaith, and his son and heir was Archibald Bethune, Third Laird of Balfour, whose son and heir was John Bethune, Forth Laird of Balfour. He married Katharine Sterling (Toshach says her name was Margaret), daughter of the Laird of Keir. Katharine was born about 1419 in Kennoway, Fife, Scotland, and died in Balfour, Fife, Scotland.

The Fourth Laird of Balfour's son and heir was John de Bethune, Fifth Laird of Balfour. He was born in 1440 in Raith, Fife, Scotland, and died 1507 in Balfour, Fife, Scotland. He married Marjory Boswall daughter of the Laird of Balmuto[8] in 1458. She was born about 1443 in Balmuto, Fife, Scotland, and died in Balfour, Fife, Scotland. They had six sons: John, David, Robert, Archibald, Andrew and James, and five daughters: Janet, Margaret, Grissel, Isobel, and Elizabeth Bethune.

John Bethune succeeded his father to become the Sixth Laird of Balfour. David became the First Laird of Creich Bethun and was the treasurer of Scotland. Robert became the first abbot of Coupar in Angus and later became abbot of Melros, Glenluss and Coupar.

James became the Chancellor of Scotland, abbot of Dumfermline, Abbot of Ardbroth, and Archbishop of Glasgow. After Archbishop Andrew Foreman died in 1524, James succeeded him and became Archbishop of St. Andrews, a position he held until his own death in 1539. James also built bridges, many of which still exist today, including the Bridge of Dairsia, the Over and Nether Bridge of Oar, the Bridge of Lochtie, the Bridge of Camron, the Bridge of Kembark, the Inner Bridge of Lewchars, the Two Bow Bridge of St. Andrews. He also completed the Guard Bridge. His coat of arms is on all of these bridges and he had it placed six times on the Guard Bridge. James built the entire foreworks of the Castle at St. Andrews.[9]

The fifth son of John Bethune, Fifth Laird of Balfour, and his wife Marjory Boswell was the ancestor of Eleanor Rosalynn Smith: Archibald Bethune of Pittochy or Capeldray, in Fife. According to the Chartulary of Glasgow, Archibald was with Cardinal Beaton at Dumfries on November 7, 1539. Archibald married Janet Duddingston about 1485.[10] She was born about 1465 in St. Ford, Fife, Scotland.

Archibald had a son named Peter who became a renowned physician in Argyllshire. His fame led to an invitation by the MacDonald and MacLeod clans for him to move to the Isle of Skye and practice his profession there. The invitation included the offer that, should he accept, he would be given as much land as he wanted, rent free, and that one of his posterity and their successors, preferably a firstborn son if they were so inclined, would be educated as a physician at no expense to that person.[11] Peter moved to Isle of Skye and married the daughter of MacDonald of Clanranald. Their first son, who became a physician, was Angus Bethune.

Angus Bethune, the third descendent from John Bethune, Fifth Laird of Balfour, had two sons, Ferquhard Senior and Ferquhard Junior. Ferquhard Junior became the physician of his generation and died in an unusual manner. He was summoned by the Earl of Sutherland to attend his wife, the countess, who was seriously ill. Upon returning home, Ferquhard and his crew stopped for the night on an uninhabited island. Their boat drifted away with all of their provisions. Twenty days later the boat drifted into Dunrobin. The earl immediately organized and dispatched a search party but by the time they were found, the doctor and his crew had starved to death. Ferquhard was found lying on a book in which he had written of their ordeal.[12]

Ferquhard Senior had a son, Angus, who became the second Dr. Angus, having studied medicine at Montpelier. He wrote a medical book entitled *Lilly of Medicine: A System of Physic*. It was said that the book contained many curious discoveries about the nature of diseases and their cures. Unfortunately, it was written for the use of the Highlanders in the Irish character and abounded with contractions. Angus' great-grandson, John Bethune, who was born around 1642, was reportedly the last person able to read it.

Angus had six sons: Ferquhard, John, Angus the Strong, Ewan, Neil, and Angus the Fair; none of whom studied medicine. Ferquhard, the eldest son, fought at the battle of Worcester on the 3rd of September 1651, along with 700 other men from the Isle of Skye. Almost all of them were either killed or taken prisoner. Ferquhard, however, escaped. He was the sixth descendent of John Bethune, Fifth Laird of Bethune, and the great-great-great-great-great-great-great-great-great-grandfather of Eleanor Rosalynn Smith.

Ferquhard's eldest son was Angus. Angus continued the family tradition and became the third Dr. Angus Bethune. John Bethune was the eldest son of the third Dr. Angus and was the eighth descendent in the male line from John Bethune, Fifth Laird of Balfour. John became minister of Braccadale in Skye and was the first minister on Isle of Skye to dispense the Sacrament of the Supper in the Protestant manner. John married Marion MacLeod of Drynoch and they had several children. Their firstborn son died while he was a student in Edinburgh. Smallpox swept through Scotland and three of Angus and Marion's four other sons contracted the disease and died. They had two sons who survived to adulthood, Ferquhard and Kenneth.

Ferquhard Bethune was the eldest son of John Bethune and moved from Isle of Skye to Kilellan where he married Isobel MacEarcharn,[13] the daughter of Colin M'Eacharn. Ferquhard was born about 1676 and Isobel about 1685. They probably had daughters but, if so, their names have been lost. They had six sons: Angus, born in 1706; Hector, born in 1708; John, Eleanor Rosalynn Smith's ancestor Colin, born in 1712; Lauchlan, born in 1714; and Duncan, born in 1716. Angus lived in Edinburgh until he died in 1766 at the age of 60. When his father, Ferquhard, died, Angus became chief of the Bethunes. Hector married Isobel MacLeod and joined the military. John married a MacLeod also and moved to America with his children. Lauchlan joined the military and never got married. Duncan became a merchant and got married very late in his life.

Ferquhard's sister married Neil MacEarcharn of Kilellan, the brother of Ferquhard's wife Isobel. When Neil died, Ferquhard inherited the Kilellan estate, which was heavily in debt to the Duchess Dowager of Argyle. Ferquhard lost a great deal of money in legal proceedings brought against him by the duchess while settling the estate's accounts. Ferquhard died in 1762, at almost one hundred years old.

Colin Bethune was the fourth son of Ferquhard Bethune and Isobel MacEarcharn and was a customs officer at Inverness.[14] Colin Bethune immigrated to South Carolina and was a great-great-great-great-great-grandfather of Eleanor Rosalynn Smith.

E: Loyal "Regulators" Association

(From Manuscript Records in the Office of the Secretary of State of North Carolina)

We the Subscribers true & Faithful subjects of our Sovereign Lord King George the third (whom may God long preserve) having for a very considerable Time past been justly alarmed at the unaccountable conduct & behaviour of a set of people, who have impudently usurped the Title of Regulators; & being now roused by the unparalleled Insolence offered by an assembled Body of them to one of his Majesty's Supr Courts of Justice begun at Hillsborough on the 22d Day of Sepr last past, & at the lawless & Brutal Violence excited against the Members of the Court in the presence of the Judge, (sedente Curia) & seeing & hearing with the heaviest Concern & most alarming apprehensions the numberless outrages committed by them in the most open & daring manner against the persons liberties & properties of many of our fellow subjects are stimulated to step forth with a manly & loyal Resolution in support of the Laws & constitution of our Country. Declaring in the Integrity of our hearts that we think it not only an authority permitted, but a duty enjoined by the Laws of God & Nation, strenuously and bravely to defend ourselves against & openly when called upon to oppose such who by these proceedings, now demonstrate to the World that they are actuated by a spirit of licentiousness sedition & Riot & that they have adopted principles & are pursuing measures dangerous to the Constitution subversive of all the ends & Designs of Good Government obstructing the Execution of wise & beneficial Laws violating the common Rights of mankind in Society & destructive to the peace & prosperity of the publick — We profess to fear God & Reverence Religion — & we mean by this our unanimous association on this awful & trying occasion to approve ourselves the declared Friends of our happy Constitution & supporters of those Glorious British Maxims & Laws whereby we are entituled to the protection of our persons & a security in the peaceable and undisturbed possession of all our boasted Rights Liberties & priviledges as freeborn English subjects — We esteem it a Duty inculcated by our Blessed Religion (the best natural institution on earth) & a Doctrine clearly established by Holy Writ that every man is by Nature a soldier aginst [sic] the Traitors of his King, & those who would disturb the peace of Society, or Violate the Laws of his Country; we further esteem it our Christion Duty to relieve the poor protect the Innocent & to redress the injured — & finally since neither the Fear of God, the sacred awe of Religion, the authority of Laws nor yet the love of Mankind are sufficient to restrain these infatuated people from the most astonishg [sic] Depredations & unheard of Acts of Barbarity & Cruelty, We feel ourselves constrained by the Dictates of self preservation a principle not imbibed by Education or inculcated by municiple obligation, but instilled in the soul & impressed upon the Human Heart at our Nativity by the God of universal Nature — to enter into this Association Wherefore We do solemnly & sincerely depose & swear on the Holy Evangelists of Almighty God that we will for the grand purposes aforementioned be true to & stand faithfully by assist & protect each other & that whenever We are called upon or required that we will immediately laying aside all other Business & Concerns repair properly accoutred for the purposes of self preservation & mutual Defence ready to enter upon any Enterprize that shall be agreed upon by a Majority of the Redressors present & continue the pursuit of such undertaking until relinquished by a consent of Majority present & that we will on every occasion in consequence of this our Engagement convene together as soon as possible & protect support & Defend each other to the utmost of our powers & abilities, so help us God.

Redressors to be our Title, & Rules for Government & Conduct of ourselves to be established occasionally by the Majority of our Body.[1]

The document was signed by several people, including John Nunn.

F: Land Grant to Ellis Marcus by the Earl of Granville

Deed executed by and between the Earl of Granville and Ellis Marcus recorded in Deed Book C, p. 229, Granville County, North Carolina.

Kingdom of Great Britain One of the Lords of his Majesty's most honourable privy Council and Knight of the most noble Order of the Garter of the one part and Ellis Marcus of Granville County in the Province of North Carolina of the other part WHEREAS his said most excellent Majesty King George the Second in and by a certain indenture bearing date the seventeenth, day of September in this the eighteenth rear of his reign and in the year of our Lord Christ one thousand seven hundred and forty four and made between his said most excellent Majesty of the one part, and the said John Earl Granville by the name and title of the right honourable John Lord Carteret of the other part did for the considerations therin mentioned give and grant release ratify and confirm unto the said Earl by the name of John Lord Carteret, and his heirs and assignees for ever a certain District Territory or parcel of land in the province of North Carolina in America and all the Sounds Creeks ports Rivers Streams and other Royalties franchises privileges and Immunities wherein the same as they are therin set out allowed and granted and confirmed to the said John Earl of Granville by the name of one eighth part of the provinces of South and North Carolina as by the said indenture duly enrolled in the high court of Chancery in Great Britain and in the Secretary's Office of the provinces of North Carolina relation being thereunto had will amongst other things more fully and at large appear. NOW THIS INDENTURE witnesseth that as well for and in consideration of the sum of three shillings promissory to the said John Earl of Granville in hand paid by the said Ellis Marcus at or before [space] and delivery of these presents the receipt whereof he the said Earl doth hereby acknowledge [space] for and in consideration of the rents covenants exceptions promises and agreements herein after mentioned reserved and contained and by and on the part and behalf of the said Ellis Marcus his heirs and assignees to be paid performed observed and kept he the said Earl Hath given granted bargained sold and confirmed and by these presents doth from himself and his heirs give grant bargain sell and confirm unto the said Ellis Marcus his heirs assignees for ever all that piece and parcel of land situated lying and being in the parish of the said county of Granville in the province of North Carolina in America beginning at black Jack oak Rob. Jonovins cornor [sic] running along his line S° 48(?) to a white oak in Gov. Johnstons line so along his line N° 76 (?) to a white oak in Rob. Jones line then along his line N 2° W55 ch. to a white oak then W 40 ch to a white oak Saplin then S° 37 ch to a white oak then E 66 ch. to the first station containing in the whole one hundred eighty and a half acres of land all which premises are more particularly described and set forth in the plan or map thereof hereunto annexed together with all woods underwoods timber lakes ponds fishings Waters Watercourses profit comodities appurtenances and hereditaments whatsoever therunto belonging or in any wise appertaining together with the privilege of hunting hawking and fowling and of waking up of all sorts of game in and upon the premises hereby granted and all mines and minerals whatsoever therin to be found, except and always reserved out of this present grant unto the Kings most excellent Majesty his heirs and successors one fourth part of all gold and silver mines to be found in or upon the premises and also except and always reserved therout unto the said John Earl of Granville his heirs and assignees one half part of the remaining three fourths of all such gold and silver mines as shall be found in or upon the said premises. TO HAVE AND TO HOLD the said piece or parcel of land and all and singular other promises hereby granted with the appurtenances, except before excepted, unto the said Ellis Marcus his heirs and assignees forever YIELDING and paying therefore yearly and every year for ever unto the said Earl his heirs and assignees the yearly rent of seven shillings p3½ which is at the rate of three shillings Sterling or four shillings prod. money for every hundred acres at or upon the two most usual feasts or days of payment in the year that is to say the feast of the Annunciation of the blessed Virgin Mary and the feast of St. Michael the Arch Angel in every year by even and equal portions and to be paid at the court house of the county of Granville aforesaid unto the said Earl or his deputy or receiver for the time being the first payment therof to be made on such of the said feast days as shall first happen after the date hereof and the said Ellis Marcus for himself his heirs and assignees forever of them doth hereby covenant promise and agree to and with the said Earl his heirs and assignees and to and with every of them by these presents in manner and form following that is to say that he the said Ellis Marcus his heirs and assignees shalt and will yearly and every year for ever well and truely pay or cause to be paid unto the said Earl his heirs or assignee or unto his or their deputy attorney or receiver for the time being on feast days and at the plates aforesaid the aforesaid yearly rent or sum of seven shillings 3 pence ½ by half yearly payments as aforesaid and further that he the said Ellis Marcus his heirs or assignees or sons or one of them shall and will within these years to be accounted from the day of the date hereof clear and, cultivate at the rate of three acres for every hundred acres of the said premises hereby granted provided always and it is hereby expressly declared and agreed by and between the said parties hereunto that if it shall happen that the said yearly rent of seven shilling 3½ or any part thereof shall at any time hereafter be behind or unpaid by the space of twenty one days next over or after any of the said feast dates appointed for payment thereof, and no sufficient distress can be found on the premises to levy such rent and arrears with the charges of distress or if the said Ellis Marcus his heirs or assignees shalt not within the space of three years after the date hereof clear and cultivate the land above granted according to the proportion of three acres for every hundred that then and in either of the said cases this present grant and all assignments thereof shall be utterly void and of no effect and it shall be lawful for the said Earl his heirs or assignees to regrant this same to any other person or persons whomsoever as if this grant or any assignment thereof had never been made IN WTTNESS whereof the parties above named have hereunto set their hands and seals this day and year first above written.

BE IT REMEMBERED that the day and year first above written the hon. Yra. Corbin and James Junes Esq. by virtue of a power of attorney and commission under the hand and seal or the above named Earl of Granville duly entered and registered in the Secretarys office of this province of North Carolina did in the name of the said Earl sign and subscribe this grant with the said Earls title and then seal and deliver the same as his the said Earls act and in present of us who in their presence have hereunto subscribed our names as Witnesses.

Wm. Churton   Wm. Johnson   GRANVILLE (L.S.)
                                by
                               James Junes
                               Yra. Corbin

At a court held for Granville County 7 June 1797
This deed was proved in due form of law by the oath of William Johnson, one of the witnesses thereto & or motion it was ordered to be registered.
Truly registered by WILL^M EATON

G: Wills

Last Will and Testament of Dr. Samuel Browne

In the name of God amen the 17th day of October 1739

I Samuel Browne in the County of Isle of Wight being at present in Bodyley Health and perfect mind and memory thanks be to God I do make and Ordain this my last will and Testament in manner and form following:

first — I give my soul to Almighty God that gave it to me and my body I commend to the Earth to be Buried at the Discretion of my Executor and as Touching what worldly goods it hath pleased God to Endow me with I give and Devise and Bequeath in manner and form following —

Item — I give unto my Son John Browne Twenty Shillings current money of Virginia.

Item — I give unto my grandson Josias Brown the Son of Walter Browne when he comes to years of Twenty and one, one Negro Boy called Dick about eight years old.

Item — I give unto my son Jesse Browne after my Decease the plantation whereon now I live and all the Lands of mine that lies in Virginia — Except the Lands that is given to Mary Drake and her son Jesse Drake I say unto my son Jesse Browne and his Issue Lawfully begotten of his Body not to be cut off by an Act of Assembly nor to go out of the Name of the Brownes — I likewise give my son Jesse Brown all my Books and Instruments and Medicens [sic] belonging to my practice and likewise I give my son Jesse Browne a Negro man called Will and a Negro woman called Bess.

Item — I give unto my daughter Mary Drake wife of John Drake a certain Tract of Land lying on the South side of the Beaver Dam Swamp containing five hundred acres land more or less I say unto my daughter Mary Drake and the Heirs lawfully begotten of her body forever — it beginning at the South prong of the Beaver Dam Swamp up the said Swamp to a marked tree on the head line so along the head line to the North prong of the said swamp and down the said swamp to the first station.

Item — I give unto my grandson Jesse Drake the son of John Drake and Mary Drake his wife three hundred acres of Land more or less on the South side of the Nottoway River across the neck to a marked poplar standing in a Branch so up the said Branch to the head of it from thence by a marked line to my head line and along the head line to his Mothers corner Tree in a Branch and down the various courses to the said Branch to Vassers corner tree in the Beaver Dam Swamp so down the said Vassers line to the first station in Nottoway River I say unto my grandson Jesse Drake and his heirs Lawfully begotten forever.

Item — I give unto my daughter Sarah Battel the wife of John Battel so much of my land that lies on the Indian Branch to be added to her deed adjacent to her plantation as will take half the Survey of the said Tract of Land being six hundred and forty acres likewise I leave the use of a Negro Boy called Dorsetshire to my daughter Sarah Battel during her life and after her decease I do give the said Negro boy called Dorsetshire to my grandson William Battel her son, likewise I leave a Negro woman called Violet to my daughter Sarah Battel during her life and after her decease to her son Jesse Battel I do give the said Negro woman called Violet.

Item — I give unto my grandson Josias Browne a negro man called Dorsetshire when he comes to the age of Twenty and one and if he dies before he comes to the above age then it is my will and desire that the above said Negro man called Dorsetshire and the aforementioned Negro Boy called Dick aged about eight years return to my Executor.

Item — I give unto my grandson Samuel Brown the son of John Brown a Negro girl called Nan.

Item — I leave the use of a Negro man called Warham unto my son John Browne during his natural life and after his decease I do give the said Negro man called Warham to my grandson Samuel Browne, his son.

Item — I give unto my granddaughter Sarah Browne the Daughter of Walter Browne a Negro girl called Cherigarllen and one feather bed and furniture when she comes to the age of Twenty and one and if she dies before she comes to the age of Twenty and one then the above said Legacies to return to my Executor.

Item — I give unto Samuel King my grandson the son of Henry King and Martha King his wife one Negro boy called London and if the said Samuel King dies before he comes to the age of Twenty and one the aforesaid Negro Boy is to return to my Executor.

Item — I give a Negro man called Hamsheire unto my grandson Samuel Nicholas Drake when he comes to the age of Twenty and one.

Item — I leave the use of a Negro Girl called Marreia unto my daughter Mary Drake the wife of John Drake during her life and after her decease I do give the said Negro girl unto Jesse Drake her son.

Item — I give unto my granddaughter Penelope Lawrence the daughter of William and Penelope Lawrence two young Negroes above Ten years and under Sixteen years old and if she dies before she comes to Twenty and one years or without Issue then the aforesaid Legacies to return to my Executor.

Item — I give unto my son Jesse Browne my plantation lying on the Indian Branch in North Carolina with one Moiety of the said Tract containing Six hundred and forty acres to him and his Heirs.

Item — I do give all the rest of my Estate both Real and Personal to my son Jesse Browne and of this my Last Will and Testament I constitute and appoint my son Jesse Browne Executor to see this my last Will and Testament fully satisfied and do hereby utterly disallow, revoke, and annul all and every other will formerely [sic] by me made or Legacies or Bequeathed by me made in anywise whatsoever before this Will or Bequeathed Ratifying and confirming this and none other to be my last Will and Testament in Witness whereof I have hereunto set my hand and fixed by Seal the day of the year above.

Samuel Browne {Seal}

Signed, Sealed pronounced and declared by the said Samuel Browne as his last Will and Testament in the presence of us. Test: Hardy Councill, Jr; John Gennill; John Dunkley; John Eley

Inventory of estate admitted to record June 22, 1741.[1]

Last Will and Testament of Francis Clinkscales, Sr.

Anderson, S.C.

I Francis Clinkscales Senr. of Anderson District being of sound and disposing mind and memory, but weak in body and calling to mind the uncertainty of life, and being desirous to dispose of all such worldly estate as it has pleased God to bless me with do make and ordain this my last will and testament, in manner following, that is to say:

First: I desire that all my estate, real and personal, be immediately sold after my decease (and my executors are authorized to make such title to my real and personal estate as I, of right, was possessed of, in my life time,) and out of the monies arising out of therefrom all my just debts and funeral expenses be paid. And after payment of my just debts and funeral expenses, I desire that my estate be divided equally among my nine children herein after named.

Secondly. Whereas I have given to my children in my life time, the sums annexed to their name; To my daughter Katharine Campbell Deceased one hundred and eighty dollars. To my daughter Priscilla Clement one hundred and twenty five dollars. To my daughter Jane B. Orr one hundred and five dollars. To my son William F. Clinkscales two hundred and sixty eight dollars. To my son John Clinkscales two hundred and sixty five dollars. To my son Levi Clinkscales two hundred and sixty five dollars. To my son Francis B. Clinkscales two hundred and sixty eight dollars. To my daughter Elizabeth Kay one hundred and thirty dollars. And to my daughter Polly Kay deceased seventy five dollars.

Thirdly: Those of my heirs who have not received an equal portion with William and Francis, in my lifetime, are to receive out of my estate, as much as, will make them equal with William and Francis before the estate be distributed among them.

Fourthly: The distributive share that is coming to Katharine Campbell deceased I do give to the lawful heirs of her body, and appoint my son William to be guardian of her heirs to act and do for them so far as pertains to her part of my estate, and to pay over money to them, after he gets it in possession, as they come of age: Should any of them die without issue, their part is to go to the surviving heirs. Also the distributive share that is coming to Polly Kay deceased I do give to the lawful heirs of her body, and appoint my son Francis B. Clinkscales guardian of her heirs to act and do for them so far as pertains to her part of my estate, and to pay over the money to them, after he gets it in possession, as they come of age. Should any of them die without issue, their part is to go to the surviving heirs.

And lastly: I do constitute and appoint my sons William F. Clinkscales and Francis B. Clinkscales, to be the executors of this my last will and testament, by me heretofore made.

In testimony whereof I have hereunto set my hand and affixed my seal the Eighteenth day of November one thousand Eight hundred and thirty one and fifty six years of the Independence of the United States of America.

Signed, sealed, published and declared, as and for the last will and testament of the above named Francis Clinkscales Senr., in presence of us

S.D. Kay
Danial Mattison
Aaron Davis

Francis Clinkscales, Sr. [2]
{seal}

Last Will and Testament of Charity Dysart

To my beloved sister-in-law Margaret Jack, widow of my brother Samuel Jack, deceased, of Clarke County, I give the proceeds from the sale of a negro woman named Jebber and her daughter Phillis, negro to be advertised and sold.

To niece Eliza D. Hodge, household furniture. To Mary Elenor Hodge, one negro girl named Diane; to Charity Grimes, my niece, household items; to Cynthia Cosby, my niece, household items, should she return home and should she never return, to her brother William H. Jack.

To George P. Nichelson a negro boy named Henry; to niece Anne Jack of Wilkes County, six tablespoons, to niece Lillian Barnett of Wilkes County _____. To nephews James H. Nichelson, John Candor Nickelson, William H. Jack, Patrick Barnett, and William Dysart Jack and beloved niece Eliza D. Hodge and my cousin Joseph William Grimes, proceeds from sale of three negroes: Mercury, Peter and Nelson, which I wish advertised and sold, proceeds equally divided between them.

To friends James Jack of Wilkes County and Thomas W. Grimes of Greene County, 287 acres of land in Washington County, plus 1,786 acres, plus 287½ acres in Greene County, six lots in the town of Gaulphinton (?), Washington County, Georgia and other tracts of land, all sold and my just debts paid with residue divided.

Appoint James H. Nickelson and Thomas Wingfield Grimes executors.
Wit.: J. G. Randle, William Muncried (Moncrief?), Daniel Coleman.

CODICIL: By laws of the state of Georgia, it is impractable by will or otherwise to emancipate a certain negro woman named Phillis and in as much as I am desirous of rewarding her for faithfulness, I do hereby appoint my friends Thomas W. Grimes and James H. Nichelson trustees on behalf of said woman, Phillis, as her trustee and guardian to exercise the right of ownership over her so far as to protect and defend her from all unlawful acts or trespasses committed on her by other persons but giving ... [the will stops here].[3]

Last Will and Testament of William Nicholson

.....unto my loving son William Nicholson the manor plantation and houses whereon I now live together with all houses and lands on western or westward side of the Holly Bush Branche excepting the new brick house which I shall hereafter direct and dispose of ... after the decease of my loving wife Alice,

.....unto my loving son Thomas (Tom) Nicholson all my land on the Eastward side of the Holly Bush Branch ... my gunn called my short gunn.

.....unto my sons George and Lemuel Nicholson all my land lying and being on the north side of the Gum Swamp Run in Princess Anne Co. to be divided in the manner following, that is to say, marking a line of trees from a place on the said land called the Cow Ponns unto another place called Little Run and that part of the land on the North side of said line, be it more or less I give unto my son Lemuel

.....and on the south side of said line, left it be more or less I give unto my son George ... the true intent and meaning of this my last will and testament is that neither of said sons George and Lemuel Nicholson shall sell or dispose of any part of said land to any out of the name Nicholson and likewise that my son William, Thomas and John Nicholson Shall have privilege to drive on and off the said land their hoggs.

.....unto my son John Nicholson a Negro named Fortune and my painted stock gun.

.....unto my grandson Joshua Nicholson, the son of my William, the first child that my Negro girl Kate brings that lives to be twelve months old.

.....unto my daughter Elizabeth my Negro girle called Kate.
.....unto my daughter Anne Butte my Negro girle, Unity.
.....unto my daughter Mary Langley a Negro boy.
.....unto my daughter Abigaill, a Negro girle.
.....unto my daughter Dinah a Negro girle.

.....unto my daughters, Elizabeth, Abigaill and Sarah after the death of my wife Alice, the new brick house for all of them to live until they are married.
.....wife Alice Nicholson ... my executrix ... my son William Nicholson my executor.

William Nicholson (seal)

Witnesses: Thos. Butte, Nath'el Tatum, George Sparrow, Peter Lowe.[4]

Last Will and Testament of Wilson Gordy

In the name of God — Amen.

I Wilson Gordy of the County of Chattahoochee and the State of Georgia, being of sound mind and disposing mind and memory and being desirous of settling my worldly affairs do make and publish this my last will and testament.

First: — I submit my soul to God who gave it and my body I desire to be buried in a decent Christian like manner according to my__ and circumstances in life.

Second: — I will and desire that my just debts be paid as soon as practicable after my death.

Third: I will and bequeath to my beloved wife Martha J. Gordy lot of land number (170) one hundred seventy and the North West one forth of lot number (140) one hundred forty, both in the sixth district of originally Muscogee now said county of Chattahoochee with all the improvements and appurtenances thereon and thereto belonging including houses of every description, Gin, Thresh, Circle Saw, Packing Screw, Sugar Mill, also, one Bureau, one Folding Leaf Table, one Gin safe, one Dozen Chairs, one Rocking Chair hair bottom, one tester bedstead, bed and mattress, one Cottage bedstead, bed and mattress, one writing desk and contents, One double barrel shot-gun, one Singer sewing machine, one cupboard, two pine tables, Dishes, knives and forks, Cooking utensils, Two large jars, Two small jars, One hand cart, One garden plow, one cow Sally and her increase, one horse and buggy, one spring clock, one patent lever double screw silver watch, three jugs, Tool chest and contents, One spinning wheel, one reel and one grind-stone, one cross-cut saw, fowl bags, swifts, fire dogs and shovel and tongs. Also, all she owned at the time of our marriage; Also one wheat saw; one syrup kettle, one corn sheller and one oat cutter.

Fourth: — I give and bequeath to my daughter Mary A. Bagley one lot of land number (150) one hundred fifty in the sixth district of originally Muscogee now Chattahoochee County, one tester bedstead and mattress, one side board, one iron safe, One wood clock, the remaining of the utensils, one pine table, the remainder of the jars and jugs, one cow Susie and her increase one tool chest No. 2 and contents, one two-horse wagon and one grindstone with solid iron crank.

Fifth: — I will and bequeath to my beloved sons James T. Gordy, Henry M. Gordy, George G. Gordy and to my Grand daughter Carrie Gordy, child of my deceased son G.P. Gordy and to the children of my deceased daughter Rebecca Webb share and share alike; That is my grandchildren taking the share to which their parents would have been entitled had said parents been living lot of land number (183) one hundred eighty three and the remaining three fourths of lot of land number one hundred and forty, after the bequest to my wife, aggregating three hundred and fifty acres more or less in Sixth district of said county.

Sixth: — I hereby nominate and appoint my dear and beloved wife Martha J. Gordy, my executrix of this my last will and testament. In testimony so hereof I have hereunto set my hand and seal this 8th day of April 1884.[5]

Wilson Gordy {seal}

Last Will and Testament of Abel Ansley

In the name of God, Amen.

I, Able Ansley, of Warren County, State of Georgia, being in a state of indisposition, but of sound mind and memory, do make, constitute, and declare this to be my Last Will and Testament, and hereby revoking and making void all others I have made heretofore.

First of all, I desire to render my soul into the hands of the Almighty God who gave it to me, and my body to be decently buried, and after my just debts is paid, it is my will that my property, both real and personal, shall be disposed of in the following manner, (to wit:)

Item 1st — I will and bequeath unto my beloved wife, Lydia Ansley, the Plantation whereon I now live with the woodland therunto belonging, together with the Plantation utensiles, stock, household and kitchen furniture, during her natural life.

Item 2nd — I will and bequeath my beloved son Jesse Ansley, the tract of land whereon he now lives, consisting of 119 acres, the aforesaid land already delivered by deed of gift, and joining Joshua Stanford and others, I deem worth $4.50 an acre. Also one mare and saddle, valued at $63, feathers and bedding, $10, one cow and yearling, $10, one ewe and two lambs, $2, one pot, $3, which is the article already delivered to him.

Last Will and Testament of Joseph Pratt

State of South Carolina Abbeville District
In the name of God Amen.

I Joseph Pratt of the State and district aforesaid being sick and weak of body but of sound and disposing memory, and knowing that it is ordained and appointed for all flesh living to die, do make and ordain this my last will and testament in manner and form following.

In the first place, I resign my soul to the hand of God that gave it and my body to be decently buried; with regard to the property of which I am possessed I will and dispose of it as follows.

1st. I will and bequeath to my dear Wife Elizabeth the plantation on which I now live during her natural life also three Negroes Dave & Harry & Putien and all the Stock on my plantation together with all the plantation Untentials [utensils] together with all the household furniture.

2nd. To my eldest daughter Emma five hundred dollars in money and a tract of land Cald the Wm. Langard tract.

3rd. to my daughter Sarah one Negro Girl named Synthy and the Dove part that is now platted on her land.

4th. To my son William one Negro boy Named Willis also two hundred Acres of land on which he Now lives and five hundred dollars in money.

5th. To my son Thomas all the land lying on the East side of little river and down sd. river to said Williams line and thence a straight line to the line of the land bought of Obadiah Fields, thence a straight line to the river & after my Wifes death a Negro called Harry.

6th. I give and bequeath to my son Joseph all that tract of land I bought of John Brownlee from sd. Thomas line to the Leonard Branch and to bind on the tract of land I gave to my daughter Emma and down McAdams line to the river also a Negro boy named Bobb.

7th. I give and bequeath to my daughter Elizabeth a Negro Girl named Winnie also a horse and saddle & a feather bed & furniture.

8th. I give and bequeath to my son John all that tract of land from Williames and Thomases Corner thence to William Youngs corner thence to Emma's line thence to the Leonard Branch down to Thomas's Corner Also a Negro boy named Elijah also a Horse and saddle & Bridle.

9th. I give and bequeath to my Daughter Nancy a Negro Girl named Jane and the first child that Patience has also a Horse and saddle a feather bed and furniture.

10th. To my niece Caroline a Negro woman named Sarah also a horse & saddle & feather bed & furniture, and at my wifes death Lyda and Dave and Patience together with all the other property /except the land/ that I gave to my Wife to be appraised and equally divided among my own children etc. Moreover I ordain and appoint my three eldest sons William, Thomas & Joseph to be Executor, this my last Will and Testament.

Given under my hand and seal this twenty seventh day of January one thousand eight hundred and twenty six.
Carod Gantt J.2.
James Pratt   Joseph Pratt L.S.
John Given

Proven by the Oathes of Cador Gantt & James Pratt and. qualified Wm. Pratt Executor 29th April 1826. & qualified Wm. Pratt Exor

Moses Taggart OAD

The part of my estate that I left my daughter Nancy seeing she has departed this life since my will was wrote I now leave it to my dear wife during her life or Widowhood and then to return to my other children equally also that part of the perishable property that I left to my son Thos. he is to receive at pleasure and settle on any part of the land he may see proper without disturbing his mother. This alteration I now make this 7th day of Apl. 1824.

          his
Test Cador Gantt   Joseph Pratt
Saml. Young   mark
John Obeven

Note: Although Joseph's will is dated January 20, 1826, his codicil, added after his daughter Nancy died and in which he states that it was added after "my will was wrote," is dated April 7, 1824.

Last Will and Testament of James Brownlee

In the name of god amen. The 20 of July 1789? I James brownlee of the state of south Carolina In ninty six district planter being very sick in body but of good and perfect memory thanks be to Almighty god for it and calling to remembrance the Uncertainty of this transitory life and that all flesh must die when it shall please god to Call them Do make and declare this my last will and testament In manner and form following first being penent and sorry for all my sins most humbly desiring forgiveness for the same I commend my soul unto Almighty god my saviour and redeemer in whom And by whos merits i trust and belive [sic] to be Saved my body I commit to the Earth to be decently buried at the discretion of my Executors hereafter Named and for the settling of my temperl state And such good chattles and ___ as is hath pleased God to be stow upon me I do order and give and dispose the same in manner and form following And first I leve to my son william one hundred acres of land to my daughter Elizabeth one hundred acres of land joining william and to my son James one hundred and sixtysix acres of land where I now live to my son william two cows and a steer the remainder of the cattel to Bee devided between bety and James I give the Negro fridy to my son James and to my son James the chist with the lock and to my son James all the plantanson tools to my son Sameull the horses and mares and he to give betty one hors the puter to be Divided between bety and James and to my son George I leve half a crown I likewise constitute make and ordain Joseph Brownlee and John Richey to be Hon Executers of this my last will and testamon and I do hereby utterly dislow revoke and all and every form of Wills and confirming this and no other to be my last will and testment in Witness wherof I have heare unto set my hand and seal this 21 of July 1789

In the presence of the witness
Joseph Brownlee
Andy Webb
Alexander Elgin   James Brownlee {seal}[6]

Last Will and Testament of George W. Carter

Georgia, Talbot County
In the name of God, Amen.

To all to whom these presents shall come, Greetings.

Know ye, that I, George W. Carter, of the state and county aforesaid, being of sound mind, but labouring under bodily afflictions which I have reason to believe will speedily terminate my earthly existence, do declare and publish this my last will and testament as follows.

I wish and desire that all the just demands against me, at the time of my decease, may be paid out of the proceeds of my estate, the estate to be disposed of in terms of the law, and that the balance of my effects or their proceeds may be equally divided between my beloved wife Winneyford and my daughter Sophronia and the child with which my wife is now pregnant, but if the child yet to be born should be dead born, or if my wife should die before my daughter Sophronia and the child yet to be born should be live born and my wife Winneyford should die and leave both the children aforenamed living, then and in that case, I desire that the estate or its proceeds as aforesaid shall belong to, and to be property of the two children as aforesaid. And I do further desire, that my beloved brother Little Berry Carter shall act, and I do hereby ordain and appoint him my executor, to carry into effect and execute in terms of the law, this my last will and testament.

In testimony as hereof, I have hereunto set my hand and affixed my seal.

Signed, dated and published, as the last will and testament of George W. Carter in his presence, and signed by us as witnesses, in the presence of the said George W. Carter and in the presence of each other, this the fourth day of March, Eighteen Hundred and forty one.

George W. Carter {seal}[7]

Joseph G. Biggs
Jubal O. Marshall
Calvin J. Branan

Last Will and Testament of Peter Gordy

Will of Peter Gordy
June 22, 1772
Worcester County, Md.

In the name of god amen the twenty second day of June in the year of our lord God one thousand seven hundred and seventy two, I Peter Gordy, of Worcester county and province of Maryland planter being in good health at present and in perfect mind and memory thanks be to God for the same therefore calling into mind the mortality of my body and knowing that it is appointed for all men once to die do make and ordain this my last will and testament.

Imprimis. I give and bequeath to my son John Gordy one Negro follow named Major to him his heirs and assigns for ever.

Item: I give and bequeath to my son Peter Gordy one hundred acres of land called Gordy's Chance lying and being in Somerset County otherwise now called Worcester county to him his heirs and assigns for ever.

Item: I give and bequeath to my son Peter Gordy all that tract of land called Addition to Gordy's Chance provided he never claim any thing or sum of money out of my Estate for what he gave Daniel Wilson on account of my part I bought of a land warrant of Peter Caliway for said land and if he does then the said land to his brother John Gordy if not I give it to Peter Gordy afore said his heirs and assigns forever.

Item: I give and bequeath to my son Peter Gordy twenty five acres of land — part of a track [sic] of land called Brandy Ridge to him and his heirs and assigns for ever.

Item: I give and bequeath to son John Gordy two tracks of Land lying and being in Worcester county — the one named Hoggard and the other named Parker's Mistake each track containing Fifty-acres as patents will more plainly appear. The aforesaid two tracts of land I give to him his heirs and assigns for ever.

Item: I give and bequeath to my son Moses Gordy one Negro girl named Patience to him his heirs and assigns forever.

Item: I give and bequeath to my Daughter Levinah, now wife to Isaac Wootton one large cupboard marked L.G. and a garnished trunk and one pair of silver sleave buttons.

Item: I give and bequeath to my son John Gordy twenty five acres of land part of a tract of land called Brandy Ridge containing fifty acres of land lying and being in Worcester county the afore-mentioned twenty five acres to be laid out for him next to his dwelling plantation the aforesaid twenty five acres I give to him his heirs and assigns for ever.

Item: I give and bequeath to my son Peter Gordy twenty five acres of land part of a tract of land called High Ridge to him and his heirs forever.

Item: I give and bequeath to my dearly beloved wife Catherine Gordy one third of my Estate after the above mentioned legacies are paid.

Item: I give and bequeath the remainder of my personal Estate to be equally divided amongst my children hereafore named (viz), Moses Gordy, Peter Gordy, John Gordy, my daughter Mary Crouch, Sarah wife to John Parker, Eunice wife to James Methvilain and Levinah wife to Isaac Wootton.

Item: I do hereby constitute and ordain my son Peter Gordy to be my only and sole executor of this my last will and testament and I do hereby utterly disanull all other wills legacies & bequests by me heretofore made ratifying and confirming this and no other to be my last will and testament in witness whereof I have hereunto set my hand and seal the day and year above written.

Signed sealed published and pronounced by the said Peter Gordy as his last will and testament in sight and presence of us (viz John Williams Sr, John Williams Junr, Mary Williams (her mark a cross) signed Peter Gordy (his mark)

July 15th 1775 then John Williams, John Williams Junr, and Mary Williams the subscribing witnesses to the foregoing will and made oath on the holy Evangalis of almighty God that they saw Peter Gordy the testator sign seal and heard him publish pronounce and declare the same to be his last will and Testament and that at the time of his so doing he was to the best of their apprehension of a sound disposing mind and memory and understanding and that they subscribed their names as witness to the said will in the presence of the testator and at his request.

Chapter Notes

Chapter 1. The Carters

1. Council of the State Virginia, *Journals of the Council and General Court of Virginia* (Richmond: Division of Purchase and Printing, 1931), 3–4.

2. Martha W. McCartney, *Virginia Immigrants and Adventurers, 1607–1635: A Biographical Dictionary* (Genealogical, 2007), 190–191.

3. Assuming William Carter was the son of John Carter, Sr.

4. John Camden Hotten, ed., *The Original Lists of Persons of Quality; Emigrants; Religious Exiles; Political Rebels; Serving Men Sold for a Term of Years; Apprentices; Children Stolen; Maidens Pressed; and Others Who Went from Great Britain to the American Plantations, 1600–1700* (London: John Camden Hotten, 1874), 121–122, http://books.google.com/books?id=J5ULA AAAIAAJ&vq.

5. Ibid.

6. "William Carter, 700 acs. James City Co., about 3 mi. from James Riv., 20 May 1636, p. 359; beg. at a reedy swampe, butting Ely. upon same, Sly. into the maine woods, & Wly. upon the rich neck otherwise upon Sunken Marsh, & Nly. upon James Riv. 50 acs. for the per. adv. of his first wife Avis Turtley, 50 acs. for the per. adv. of his second wife Ann Mathis & 50 acs. for the per. adv. of his now wife Alice Croxon & 550 acs. for trans. of 11 servts: Wm. Antherson, Andrew Robinson, Rich. Cooke, Fr. Bick, Rich. Bick, Alice Watkins, Alice Johnson, Eliza. Johnson, Henry Snow, Nich. Burrnett, Edward Bland. Note: Surrendered and Renewed by Sir John Harvey, Test: Tho. Cooke, Clr.

"William Carter, 100 acs. James City Co., about 3 mi. from James Riv., 20 May 1636, p. 359. Being a neck of land neare unto the head of the Lower Chippokes Cr., E. upon same, S. upon land of Robert Sheppard, & N. towards James Riv. Trans. of 2 servts: Mitchell Siler, Rich. Crich

"William Carter, 200 acs. James City Co., 15 Aug 1637, p. 451. Sly. upon land formerly granted to him, Ely. towards Chippoecks Cr., Wly. upon Sunken Marsh & Nly. into the bay tree.

"William Carter, 1000 acs. James City Co., 21 May 1638, p. 572. About 3 mi. from James Riv., beg. at a Reedy sw., W. into the woods, N. into the bay tree neck. Trans. of 20 pers: Avis Turtley, Ann Mathis, Alice Croxon, Wm. Atherson (or Acherson), Andrew Robinson, Richard Cooke, Fr. Bick, Richard Bick, Alice Watkins, Alice Johnson, Eliza. Johnson, Henry Snow, Nich. Barnett, Edward Bland, Math Briste, John Bell, Hercules Messenger, Tho. Streete, Wm. Higgenson, Rose Hill" (Nell Marion Nugent, *Cavaliers and Pioneers: Abstracts of Virginia Land Patents and Grants*, vol. 1 [Richmond: 1934], 42, 64, 91).

7. Ibid., 46.

8. Ibid., 171.

9. Ibid., 197–198.

10. Lyon Gardiner Tyler, ed., *Encyclopedia of Virginia Biography*, vol. 1 (New York: Lewis Historical, 1915), 243, http://books.google.com/books?id=UCgS AAAAYAAJ&dq=%22Thomas%20Godwin%20%22 %20%20virginia&pg=PA243#v=onepage&q&f=false.

11. Nell Marion Nugent, *Cavaliers and Pioneers: Abstracts of Virginia Land Patents and Grants*, vol. 1 (Richmond: 1934), 306–307.

12. Ibid., 384.

13. Ibid., 82–83.

14. Noel Currer-Briggs, *The Carters of Virginia Their English Ancestry* (Sussex: Phillimore, 1979), 21.

15. Ibid.

16. "Epaphroditus Lawson 1400 acs. Up. Norf. Co., Feb. 15, 1642, Page 822. Upon New Towne Haven River running N. W. by a bay side called Mount Lawson, adj. More Fontleroy etc ... 450 acs. by assignment from Bartholomew Hoskins...." (Nugent, *Cavaliers and Pioneers*, 135).

17. Ibid., 151.

18. Epaphroditus Lawson died in 1652, by which time he was living in Lancaster County next to Col. John Carter's plantation at Corotoman. Lancaster County, *Lancaster County, VA, Deeds, Wills and etc., Book 1, 1652–1657* (Lancaster County, Virginia, Courthouse; Archives of the State of Virginia), 33–34.

19. Nugent, *Cavaliers and Pioneers*, 132.

20. Edward Dale's will was dated Aug. 4, 1694, and proved March 11, 1695. In it, he wrote this: "Imp'mis, if it shall please God that my now wife shall happen to outlive me, I give unto her for her maintenance during her life the whole profitt of my estate whatsoever, some respect being alwaies had to her as an honest woman and gentlewoman and many years my

wife...."; Reginald M. Glencross, "Virginia Gleanings in England," *The Virginia Magazine of History and Biography* 29 (Richmond: House of the Society, 1921), 435, http://books.google.com/books?id=6tQRAAAAYAAJ&dq.

Typically, the use of the phrase "my now wife" would mean that Edward Dale had been married previously. Diana also witnessed land transactions, signing with her maiden name as late as 1655. In 2000, Charles Ward wrote an article in *American Genealogist* contesting the claim that Diana Skipwith was the mother of the Katherine Dale who was born in 1652. Ward's article was strenuously objected to by the Thomas Carter of Barford descendents because it is through Thomas of Barford's wife Katherine Dale and then through her mother's (Diana Skipwith) lineage that they claim kinship with English royalty. Fortunately, this dispute is for the Barford researchers to resolve.

21. Per Dr. Bascom Hayes.

22. Epaphroditus Lawson used the headright system aggressively even before the expansion to the north. Among others and not counting the patents he assigned to others, he claimed 200 acres in the county of Warrosquiacke (Isle of Wight), on Nansemond River, 23 Dec 1636; 200 acres in Isle of Wight County, on Nansemond River, 1 Nov 1637; 50 acres in Isle of Wight, at the mouth of Warwicksqueche river, "alias New Towne Haven," 30 Nov 1637; 250 acres on the south side of Nansemond River, 29 May 1638; 250 acres in the county of "Upper New Norfolke" (Nansemond), on "Chuckatuck River," 15 Mar 1638; 1,400 acres in Upper Norfolk, upon "New Towne haven river"; 450 acres in Upper Norfolk, on a creek "called Mount Lawson baye" and Poplar Neck Creek, 9 Jan 1643; 700 acres on Rappahannock, about 12 miles up, on the north side, 3 Sep 1649; 2,000 acres on Rappahannock, on the south side, on a creek called Lawson's Creek, 22 May 1650; 1,000 acres on Rappahannock, about 10 miles up, on the north side, 22 May 1650; 900 acres on Rappahannock, south side, and Lawson's Creek, May 1650.

23. Currer-Briggs, *The Carters of Virginia,* 86.

24. "Whereas Abraham Weeks attorney for Tho. Bannister, being arrested to this court at the suit of Major Thomas Carter for a debt of 714 lb. of tobacco and cask ... said Bannister did in consideration of the said debt assign to the said Major Carter a specialty of 880 lb. of tobacco ... pay the said 714 lbs of tobacco and cask with costs of the present suit and three years interest to the said Major Carter or his assigns within 20 days....," Lancaster County, Virginia, Courthouse Records, *Book 1—1653–1757,* 137, quoted in Noel Currer-Briggs, *The Carters of Virginia: Their English Ancestry* (Sussex: Phillimore, 1979), 82; "A judgement confessed by John Johnson to Major Thomas Carter for 500 lbs. of tobacco and cask with 2 years interest...." (Lancaster County, Virginia, Courthouse Records, Book 1:1653–1757, p. 163, quoted in Currer-Briggs, *The Carters of Virginia,* 82–83).

25. Currer-Briggs, *The Carters of Virginia,* 83.

26. Lancaster County, Virginia, Deeds and Wills Book, 1654–1661, p. 161.

27. Currer-Briggs, *The Carters of Virginia,* 84–85.

28. Ibid., 26.

29. It appears that Col. John Carter intended to be away for several years and that he was in England for about three years. He transferred some of his servants to various people and gave his power of attorney to George Marsh: "Coll. John Carter being bound for England, makes George Marsh my lawful attorney. Dated 3rd June 1656. Signed John Carter {seale}. Wit: Tho Chittwood, Jasper Baker. Recorded 5th Nov. 1656."

Beverley Fleet, *Virginia Colonial Abstracts* (Baltimore: Genealogical, Inc. 2006), 117.

30. State Papers, 1656: May (2 of 6), *A Collection of the State Papers of John Thurloe,* vol. 5: *May 1656–January 1657* (1742), 10–26, http://www.british-history.ac.uk/report.aspx?compid=55520.

31. The Captain Thomas Carter who had been captured by the Spanish "Plate" Fleet is described in the Thurloe papers as having been born in Norwich, England. Norwich was the second largest city in England and a Royalist stronghold at the time, and it was undoubtedly a major shipping port for the Vintners' Company. It is possible that our Thomas Carter could have been born there; however, it is not known where our Captain Thomas Carter was born.

32. Richard Cromwell.

33. Beverley Fleet, *Virginia Colonial Abstracts*, vol. 12 (Baltimore: Genealogical, 2006), 128, http://books.google.com/books?id=0WmgfvygR78C&lpg=PA99&ots=xWnEWaKLj6&dq=lancaster%20record%20book&pg=PP4#v=onepage&q&f=true.

34. "Page 75. 20 9br [*sic*] 1655. "Alice Carter, widow, acknowledges that Edward Pettaway married the Relict of Wm. Carter, son-in-law to Mrs. Alice Carter, and that 500 acres of land was bequeathed to the sd William Carter, Jr., by his father, William Carter, Sr., husband to Alice Carter, and that Edward Pettaway for the life of Eliza Carter, Relict of Wm. Carter, Jr., have her plantation. 145 acres, but what is leased to Thos. Culmer and Mattweh Hobson. Wit.: Nich. Perry; Rich. Blunt," in Eliza Timberlake Davis, *Surry County Records, Surry County, Virginia, 1652–1684* (Baltimore: Genealogical, 1980), 13–14.

35. "Thomas Carter, 220 acs. Nansemond Co., 4 Mar. 1658, p.259 (361). At the head of land of Edward Carter, running E. be the line of Wm. Tinse, Thomas Addiso & Richard Russell. Trans of 5 pers: Thomas Carter twice, Wm. Read, Wm. Smith" (Nell Marion Nugent, *Cavaliers and Pioneers: Abstracts of Virginia Land Patents and Grants*, Vol. 1 (Richmond, 1934), 387).

36. Secretary of state to King James I.

37. Bascom Barry Hayes, comp., "The Descendants of John Carter (ca. 1574–1630), Vintner of London, in Virginia, North Carolina, and Georgia: The First Seven Generations" (unpublished manuscript, November 2011), 41–49.

Among other transactions, Francis Moryson was

also instrumental in an unusual land deal on May 14, 1662, as recorded in the *Virginia Colonial Abstracts* by Beverley Fleet. "Francys Moryson" granted to Colo. John Carter 450 acres adjacent to the land of Thomas Chetwode. Col. Carter then assigned the land to Thomas Marshall. Thomas Marshall then assigned half of the 225 acres of the land to William Cooke and John Potter. Marshall then assigned the other 225 acres to William Hutchins. Hutchins then assigned his 225 acres to Edward King and Samuell Gooch. All this occurred on the same day. There is little proof of which land was actually owned by the Vintners' Company since it was held by individuals. This type of transaction indicates that this was the Vintners' Company land controlled by Col. John Carter. Another strong indication is that land owned at prime sites which, when the owner died, was not probated but rather was assigned to another Vintners' Company operative. There were apparently a number of sites that were made available to the Vintners' Company operatives as needed.

38. "William Cooke, John Potter, Edward King & Samuel Gough, 450 acres in Easternmost br. of Corrotoman [sic] Riv., Lancaster Co., 12 Dec 1663, p. 125. (629) Bounded upon land of Thomas Chetwood. Granted to Coll. John Carter, Esqr., 25 Sept, 1661, by him assigned to Thomas Marshall 14 May 1662, who assigned one moiety to sd. Cooke & Potter; the other half assigned to Wm. Hutchins, who assigned to sd. King & Gouch [sic]" (Nugent, *Cavaliers and Pioneers*, 436).

39. Nugent, *Cavaliers and Pioneers*, 425–28.

40. John Bennett Boddie, *Seventeenth Century Isle of Wight County, Virginia: A History of the County of Isle of Wight* (Westminster: Heritage Books, 1938), 108.

41. Ibid., 127.

42. "Col. Jno. Carter, Esqr. Councellor of the State, 4000 acs. being a neck of land on the N. side of the Rapp. Riv. bounded on the Wwd side with Cassattawoman Cr. which runneth N. & E.N.E. towards the head of Wiccocomico Riv. &c. Granted to Capt. Samll. Mathews 1 Aug 1643, by him deserted & upon petition of sd. Carter granted to him by order of the Genrll. Ct. bearing date with those presents, 12 Oct. 1665 & further due for trans 80 pers" (Nugent, *Cavaliers and Pioneers*, 536).

43. Boddie, *Seventeenth Century Isle of Wight*, 522.

44. John Burk, *The History of Virginia from Its First Settlement to the Present Day*, vol. 2 (Petersburg: Dickson & Pescud, 1805), xxxviii, http://books.google.com/books?id=ujcSAAAAYAAJ&pg=PR42&dq=%22lord+arlington%22+virginia&hl=en&ei=UVXMTNzVBMKAlAeRsf3nCA&sa=X&oi=book_result&ct=result&resnum=8&ved=0CE4Q6AEwBw#v=onepage&q=%22lord%20arlington%22%20&f=false.

45. Herbert L. Osgood, *The American Colonies in the Seventeenth Century*, vol. 3, *Imperial Control: Beginnings of the System of Royal Provinces* (New York: Macmillan, 1907), 264.

46. Ibid., 278.

47. John Bennett Boddie, *Southside Virginia Families*, vol. 2 (Baltimore: Genealogical, 1991), 43.

48. Boddie, *Seventeenth Century Isle of Wight*, 158–160.

49. Blanche Adams Chapman, *Wills and Administrations of Isle of Wight County, Virginia, 1647–1800* (Baltimore: Genealogical, 1975), 19, 21.

50. Ibid., 67.

51. Ibid., 15. This George Branch, Jr., may have been the son of Captain Francis England's son-in-law of the same name.

52. Boddie, *Southside Virginia Families*, vol. 1 (Richmond: Genealogical, 1966), 278.

53. Chapman, *Wills and Administrations of Isle of Wight County*, 113.

54. Ibid., 10.

55. Boddie, *Seventeenth Century Isle of Wight*, 166.

56. Charles W.H. Warner, "Barford Plantation and the Thomas Carters," *Northern Neck of Virginia Historical Magazine*, December 1987.

57. Dr. Joseph Lyon Miller, "Captain Thomas Carter and His Descendants," *William and Mary Quarterly Historical Magazine* 17 (Richmond: Whittey & Shepperson, 1909), 275.

58. Hayes, 29.

59. Currer-Briggs, *The Carters of Virginia*, 27.

60. Miller, "Captain Thomas Carter and his Descendants," 276–278.

61. Currer-Briggs, *The Carters of Virginia*, 29.

62. Kempson and Barford, Bedfordshire, England.

63. (Dr.) Joseph Lyon Miller, "Captain Thomas Carter and his Descendants," *William and Mary Quarterly Historical Magazine* 17 (1909), 2.

64. Dollye McAlister Elliott, "Captain Thomas Carter of 'Barford,' Lancaster County of Virginia: A Second View," *Northern Neck of Virginia Historical Magazine*, December 1987.

65. Ibid., 4216.

66. There is no proof of any of these theories. Researchers for all of the Carter lines would welcome any new documentation.

67. Warner, "Barford Plantation and the Thomas Carters," 4205–4206.

68. Ibid., 10–11.

69. Charles Warner, *Hoskins of Virginia and Related Families* (Tappahannock, VA: Charles Warner, 1971), 16.

70. McCartney, *Virginia Immigrants and Adventurers, 1607–1635*, 446.

71. Miller, "Captain Thomas Carter and his Descendants," 278.

72. Grove would be killed seven years later at Captain Francis England's house during Bacon's Rebellion.

73. John Anderson Brayton, *Colonial Families of Surry and Isle of Wight* (Memphis: J.A. Brayton, 1999), 109.

74. Ibid., 168–169.

75. Ibid., 263. There is a dispute over whether this is fifty acres or fifty-six.

76. Ibid., 642–643.

77. Isle of Wight County, Virginia, Deed Book 4, p. 301.
78. Isle of Wight County, Virginia, Deed Book 5, p, 85.
79. William Lindsay Hopkins, *Isle of Wight County, Virginia Deeds 1647–1719, Court Orders 1693–1695, and Guardian Accounts 1740–1767* (Richmond: GEN-N-DEX, 1993), 109–110.
80. Mary Best Bell, *Colonial Bertie County, North Carolina, Deed Books A–H 1720–1757* (Easley, SC: Southern Historical Press, 1963), 27.
81. Ibid., 85.
82. John Kenneth O'Quinn, Sr., comp., *O'Quinn Cousins, by the Dozens* (Spartanburg, SC: Reprint Company, 1999), 541.
83. Jacob was born around 1716; Kindred was born in 1710; our ancestor Isaac in 1717; Moor in 1718; Martha about 1720, Katherine about 1720; and Susannah in 1726.
84. Nansemond.
85. Bell, *Colonial Bertie County*, 188.
86. Margaret M. Hofmann, 1741–1759, *Abstracts of Deeds Northampton County, North Carolina Public Registry, Deed Book One and Deed Book Two* (1983).
87. Ibid.
88. Bell, *Colonial Bertie County*, 157.
89. Ibid., 94.
90. Ibid., 162.
91. Margaret M. Hofmann, *Northampton County, North Carolina, 1759–1808 Genealogical Abstracts of Wills* (Weldon, NC: Roanoke News, 1975), 15.
92. Charity Carter and Moses Knight's children were Kindred Knight, born in 1769; James Allen Knight, born in 1770; John Carter Knight, born in 1772; Sarah Knight, born in 1774; Mary Polly Knight, born in 1776; and Pheresby Knight, born in 1778.
93. Winifred Carter and Rueben Taylor's children were: Demsey Taylor, born in 1764; William Taylor, born in 1764; Allen Taylor, born in 1764; Elizabeth Taylor, born in 1765; Penelope Pope Taylor, born in 1767; Kinchen Taylor, born in 1782; and Mary Taylor, born in 1784.
94. James and his first wife had nine children: Jesse, Christian, Moore, Sarah, Elizabeth, Isaac, Parthenia, Allen, and Penelope. When his first wife died, James remarried and had another child, James Carter, Jr., Christian married Jacob Smith. Sarah Carter married Peter Hodo, who later became the first sheriff of Warren County, Georgia, and then justice of the peace. Elizabeth married twice, first to Michael Horn and second to Jonathon Burson. Parthenia Carter, named after her aunt, married John Morris. Isaac Carter married Mary Clarke and moved to Conecuh County, Alabama. Allen Carter married Sally Edmonson and James Carter, Jr., married Alsey Newsome. Jesse Carter married Phoebe Duckworth, the sister of Eleanor "Nellie" Duckworth, who married Jesse Carter's first cousin James, the son of Kindred Carter.
95. The part of Bertie County that James lived in became Hertford County in 1759.
96. Hayes, 128.
97. Benjamin Brodie Winborne, *The Colonial and State Political History of Hertford County*, no. 3 (Murfreesboro, NC: Printed for the Author by Edwards T. Brouqhton, 1906), 145.
98. Gertrude May Sloan Hay, *Roster of Soldiers from North Carolina in the American Revolution* (Durham: The North Carolina Daughters of the American Revolution [NSDAR], 1932; reprinted Baltimore: Genealogical Publishing Co., 2000), 113, 116, 118, http://books.google.com/books?id=CO-uEbXhl7IC&lpg=PR11&dq=Roster%20of%20North%20Carolina%20Soldiers%2C&pg=PA116#v=snippet&q=carter&f=false.
99. Margaret M. Hoffmann, *Northampton County, North Carolina, 1759–1808 Genealogical Abstracts of Wills, Will Bk 1* (Weldon, NC: Roanoke News), 14–15.
100. Prince George County, Virginia, Ledger B (Prince George, VA), 231.
101. William Waller Hening, *The Statutes at Large: Being a Collection of All the Laws of Virginia from the First Session of the Legislature in the Year 1619*, vol. 2 (New York: Printed for the author, by R., W., and G. Bartow, 1823), 328.
102. "May 9 1747: Isaac Carter of Society Parish to Joseph Benthall, 200 a. adj John Brown 'which was the line of Doctor Samuel Brown dec'd …' adj Moor Carter, just over the Northampton County line adj to Jacob Carter and Isaac Carter. Wit: John Brown, Samuel Brown, Enoch Lewis, Thomas Wills" (Bertie County Records, Deed Book G, 5).
103. *Carter's Executors v. Rutland:* "Negroes sent with a daughter upon her marriage, or with a son-in-law and daughter, is *prima facie* evidence of a gift; and if the property remains any length of time with them, very strong proof will be required to show that only a loan, and not a gift, was intended." The following facts were stated in this case by the parties as a *case agreed*, and submitted to a jury on the issue *non detinet*, under the direction of the court as to the law: "Facts agreed to, in the case of *Lazarus Carter*, Executor of *Isaac Carter*, v. *Shadrack Rutland* [:] *Shadrach Rutland* and *Parthena Carter*, daughter of *Isaac Carter*, of Hertford county, were married the 12th day of November, *1775*. About the middle of the year *1776*, a negro woman, *Mann*, with a young child, *Saul*, was sent by *Mr. Carter* to said *Shadrach* and *Parthena*.— *Mann's* issue since is, *Boh, Baslie, Tihhie* and *Lydia*. Some time in the year 1781, said *Shadrach* and *Parthena* were on a visit at *Mr. Carter's*, and they were directed to take a negro boy, *Peter*, home with them. Again, in the year 1782 or 1783 said *Shadrach* and *Parthena* were on a visit at *Mr. Carter's*, and they were directed to take a negro girl, *Maggy*, home with them—*Maggy's* issue is, *Homer, Penny, Violet* and *Willis*.

"Mrs. *Parthena Rutland* died in August, 178S, and *Mr. Isaac Carter* died the 8th July, 1792.

"It was also admitted on the trial, that *Isaac Carter* had bequeathed these negroes by his last will, to his grandchildren by *Parthena*, and the executor hail made the usual demand, and that the Defendant was in possession.

"*Per Curiam*— When a man sends property with his daughter upon her marriage, or to his son-in-law and daughter any short time alter the marriage, it is to he presumed *prima facie,* that the properly is given absolutely in advancement of his daughter; and when the property is permitted to remain in the possession of the son-in-law for a considerable length of time, as in this case, it will be necessary to prove very clearly, that the property was only lent by the father, and that it was expressly and notoriously understood not to he a gift at the time. The peace of families and the security of creditors, are greatly concerned in the law being thus settled.— Every transaction in human life ought to he considered under its ordinary circumstances — these will sufficiently express the intention of the parties, and generally more unequivocally than the appointed solemnities of the law. This property was given in the usual manner — that is, sent with them on their going to house-keeping, as it is called, or sent to them as soon as the parent could make the necessary arrangements in his farm or family for that purpose.

"Under this charge, there was a verdict and judgment for the Defendant" (John Haywood, Esq., *Reports of Cases Adjudged in the Superior Court of Law and Equity of the State of North Carolina from the Year 1789, to the Year 1798* (Raleigh: Jos. Gales & Son, 1832), 113–114).

104. Columbia County Superior Court, Deed Book O, 1807–1818, 404; Georgia Department of Archives and History, Drawer 91, Box 14 (Morrow, GA).

105. Talbot County, Georgia, Court of the Ordinary, Marriage Records Book A, 1828–1844, 77, Georgia Department of Archives and History, Microfilm Drawer 123, Box 30.

106. Ibid., Book B, 1844–1867.

107. Talbot County, Georgia, Court of the Ordinary, Will Book A, 1828–1856, 214, Georgia Department of Archives and History, Microfilm Drawer 123, Box 35.

108. Warren County, Georgia, Court of the Ordinary, Marriage Book 1811–1825, 256, Georgia Department of Archives and History, Microfilm Drawer 31, Box 56.

109. Keziah Carter and Robert Hinton's children were Robert Jr., born in 1828; Georgia, born in 1831; Sarah, born in 1833; Jane, born in 1835; Narcissa, born in 1837; Frances, born in 1843; and Mary, born in 1846 (1850 United States Census, 22nd District, Talbot County, Georgia).

110. Talbot County, Georgia, Court of the Ordinary, Sale Book Estates, Vol. C, 1856–1875, 411–412, Georgia Department of Archives and History, Microfilm Drawer 124, Box 19.

111. Talbot County, Georgia, Court of the Ordinary, Will Book A 1818–856, 206–208, Georgia Department of Archives and History, Microfilm Drawer 123, Box 35.

112. Warren County, Georgia, Court of the Ordinary, Marriage Records, 1824–1835, 228, Georgia Department of Archives and History, Microfilm Drawer 104, Box 13.

113. Talbot County, Georgia, Court of the Ordinary, Marriage Book A, 1828–1844, 75, Georgia Department of Archives and History, Microfilm Drawer 123, Box 30.

114. "March 16, 1860 Voucher No. 14; $285 received of Wiley Carter administrator of James Carter decd two hundred and eighty five dollars in part of distributive share of Mary Malonia Ellis and her husband, William J. Ellis in the estate of said James Carter deceased the said Mary Malonia Ellis being a daughter of Mary Archer deceased and granddaughter of James Carter deceased this 16th March, 1860" (Talbot County Court of the Ordinary, Voucher Book F, 628, Georgia Department of Archives and History, Microfilm Drawer 124, Box 11).

115. "July 8, 1869 Voucher No. 2, Jack Brown appointed agent and power of attorney for Joseph F (or H) Archer and John J. Archer of the State of Missouri who are legatees of James Carter deceased of the State of Georgia, acknowledge receipt of five hundred and thirteen and 24/100 dollars from Calvin Carter Executor under the last will and testament of Wiley Carter deceased, said Wiley Carter having been administrator of Estate of James Carter deceased who was the grandfather of said legatees mentioned in said power of attorney, Jack Brown Agt" (Sumter County, Georgia, Court of the Ordinary, Annual Returns, Volume M, 1868–1870, 160–161, Georgia Department of Archives and History, Microfilm Drawer 135, Box 35).

116. Talbot County, Georgia, Court of the Ordinary, Marriage Book A, 1828–1844, 159, Georgia Department of Archives and History, Microfilm drawer 123 Box 30.

117. Correspondence of Ken Thomas, 08 July 1978, Kenneth H. Thomas, Jr., Collection, Box 2, Jimmy Carter Library and Museum.

Chapter 2. The Morris, Cox, and Ansley Ancestors and Their Ancestors

1. James, Duke of York, would ascend to be King James II after the death of Charles II.

2. Franklin Ellis, *History of Monmouth County New Jersey* (Philadelphia: R.T. Peck, 1885).

3. William MacDonald, ed., *Select Charters and Other Documents Illustrative of American History, 1606–1775* (London: MacMillan, I899), 139.

4. Ibid. 27.

5. The Rev. Henry Miller Cox, *The Cox Family in America: A History and Genealogy of the Older Branches of the Family from the Appearance of Its First Representative in This Country in 1610* (New York: Published by the Author, 1912), 153.

6. A letter from the Court of Massachusetts Bay to the Colony of Plymouth:

"18 October 1649

"Honnored and beloved Brethren:

"We have heretofore heard diverse Anabaptists,

arisen up in your jurisdiction, and connived at; but being but few, wee well hoped that it might have pleased God, by the endeavors of yourselves and the faithful elders with you, to have reduced such erring men againe into the right way. But now, to our great griefe, wee are credibly informed that your patient bearing with such men has produced another effect, namely, the multiplying and encreasing of the same errors, and wee feare of other errors also, if timely care be not taken to supresse the same. Particularly wee understand that within a few weeks there have binne in Sea Cuncke thirteen or fourteen persons rebaptized (a swift progress in one towne; yett wee heare not of any effectuall restriction is entended thereabouts). Lett it not, wee pray you, seem presumption in us to mind you heereof, nor that wee earnestly intreate you to take care as well of the suppressing of errors, as the maintenance of the truth, God equally requiring the performance of both at the hands of Christian magistrates, but rather that you will consider our interest is concerned therein. The infection of such diseases, being so near us, one likely to spread into our jurisdiction; *tunc tua res agitur paries cum proximeus ardet.* Wee are united by confoedaracy, by faith, by neighborhood, by fellowship in our sufferings as exiles, and by other Christian bonds, and wee hope that neither Sathan nor any of his instruments shall, by thes or any other errors, disunite us of our so neere conjunction with you, but that wee shall both aequally and zealously uphold all the truths of God revealed, that wee may render a comfortable account *to Him that* hath set us in our places, and betrusted us with the keeping of both tables, of which will hoping, wee cease you further trouble, and rest,

"Your-very loving Friends and Brethren" (*Records of the Colony of Massachusetts*, vol. 3, 173–174, as quoted in John T. Christian, *A History of the Baptists*, vol. 2 [1922; reprint ed. Nashville, TN: Broadman Press, 1926], 58–59).

7. James Bowden, *The History of the Society of Friends in America*, vol. 1 (London: Charles Gilpin, 1850), 33.

8. Carol F. Karlsen. *The Devil in the Shape of a Woman: Witchcraft in Colonial New England* (London: Norton, 1987), 123.

9. Ibid.

10. Preamble of the Royal Charter of the Massachusetts Bay Colony.

11. Cox, *The Cox Family in America,* 154.

12. Ibid.

13. George Crawford Beekman, *Early Dutch Settlers of Monmouth County, New Jersey* (Higginson, 1901), 57.

14. Ibid.

15. Ibid., 58.

16. William Whitehead, ed., *Archives of the State of New Jersey*, First Series, vol. 3, 1703–1709 (Newark: Daily Advertiser Printing House, 1881), 476–481.

17. "To the Sheriff of the county of Middlesex, his under sheriff or deputy, or either of them: Whereas we are informed that Lewis Morris of Tinton, in the county of Monmouth, and province aforesaid, Gent., did in April last in Perth Amboy in the said province, seditiously assemble with others and endeavor to subvert the laws of this province and did by malicious and reproachful words, asperge the governor of said province, contrary to the peace of our Sovereign Lord the King, and the laws in such cases made and provided. These are therefore to will and require, and in His Majesty's name, strictly to charge and command you to take into your custody said Lewis Morris, and to convey him to the jail of your county, and there safely to keep, until he shall give sufficient security in the sum of three hundred pounds for his appearance at the Court of Common Rights in Perth Amboy the second Tuesday of October next, then and there to answer the premise; and in meantime to be in good behavior to His Majesty and his liege people. Hereof fail not at your peril, and for so doing this shall be your warrant. Given under our hands and seals May 11, in the eleventh year of the reign of our Sovereign Lord William the Third of England, A. D. 1699, at Perth Amboy in province aforesaid." From Whitehead, *Archives of the State of New Jersey,* vol. 3, 481–482.

18. Ibid., 482.

19. "To the Kings Most Excellent Majesty

"The Remonstrance and Humble Petition of your Majesty Loyal Subjects Inhabiting in your Majesty Province of East New-Jersey in America.

Humbly Sheweth.

"That Whereas your Majesty humble Petitioners did Remove and Settle themselves into the said Province of East New Jersey, and by Vertue of a Licence from the Honoble Coll. Richard Nicolls Governour of the said Province under his then Royal Highness the Duke of Yorke, to purchase Lands of the Native Pagans, did according to the said Licence, Purchase Lands of the said Natives at their own Proper Coasts and Charges.... Yet notwithstanding your Majesty's Loyall Subjects are Molested Disturbed, and Dispossessed of their said Lands, by the said Proprietors or their Agents, who under pretence and Colour of having bought the Government with the Soile, have distrained from, and Ejected severall Persons for and under pretence of Quitt Rent and Lords Rent.... Humbly Imploreing your Majesty will be Graciously Pleased according to your Princely Wisdom to take into Consideration Our Evill Circumstances Under the Present Proprietors, if the Right of Government is Invested in theml and that your Majesty will be Graciously Pleased to give your Royall Orders to the said Proprietors...."

20. Whitehead, ed., *Archives of the State of New Jersey,* 485.

21. Daniel J. Weeks, *Not for Filthy Lucre's Sake: Richard Saltar and the Antiproprietary Movement in East New Jersey, 1665–1707* (Cranbury, NJ: Associated University Presses, 2001), 108, http://books.google.com/books?id=FM_BrMaXR2kC&pg=PA319&dq=%22blind+tax%22+cox&hl=en&ei=0bSiTMDGPMH78AbHk8ifCg&sa=X&oi=book_result&ct=result&resnum=1&ved=0CCwQ6AEwAA#v=onepage&q=%22blind%20tax%22%20cox&f=false.

22. William A. Whitehead, ed., *Documents Relating to the Colonial History of the State of New Jersey, 1687–1703*, vol. 2 (Newark, NJ: Daily Advertiser Printing House, 1881), 363–366, http://books.google.com/books?id=WkwOAAAAIAAJ&pg.

23. http://www.iment.com/maida/familytree/morris/lewismorris.htm.

24. Colonial Dames of America, *Ancestral Records and Portraits*, chapter 1, "A Compilation from the Archives of the Colonial Dames of America" (New York: Grafton, 1910), 111.

25. Henry Fitz-Gilbert Waters, *The New England Historical and Genealogical Register* 71 (Boston: New England Historic Genealogical Society, 1917), 310, http://books.google.com/books?id=1soUAAAAYAAJ&pg.

26. Ibid.

27. The Settlers of the Beekman Patent (Online database: NewEnglandAncestors.org, New England Historic Genealogical Society, 2003). Orig. Pub. by Frank J. Doherty, Pleasant Valley, NY. Frank J. Doherty, as *The Settlers of the Beekman Patent, Dutchess County, New York: An Historical and Genealogical Study of All the 18th Century Settlers in the Patent*, six volumes, 1990–2001.

28. The Rev. John Cornell, *Genealogy of the Cornell Family: Being an Account of the Decendants of Thomas Cornell of Portsmouth, R.I.* (New York: T.A. Wright, 1902), 21–23. http://digital.library.cornell.edu/cgi/t/text/pageviewer-idx?c=ezra;cc=ezra;rgn=full%20text;idno=ezra000;didno=ezra000;node=ezra000%3A3;view=image;seq=7.

29. John Osborne Austin, *The Genealogical Dictionary of Rhode Island* (Albany: 1887).

30. Elaine Forman Crane, *Killed Strangely: The Death Of Rebecca Cornell* (Cornell University Press, 2002), http://books.google.com/books?id=RIg6y0HuKUsC&pg.

31. New Jersey Archives, Early Colonial Marriages, 1665–1799, M, Part 1: 1735–1767: 18, https://www.net1.state.nj.us/DOS/Admin/ArchivesDBPortal/ColonialMarriages.aspx.

32. Thomas Maxwell Potts and William John Potts, *Historical Collections Relating to the Potts family in Great Britain and America* (Canonsburg, PA: Published by the Compiler, 1901), 126–130, http://books.google.com/books?id=UusaAAAAYAAJ&pg.

33. Samuel Smith, *History of the Colony of Nova-Caesaria or New Jersey: Containing, an Account of Its First Settlement, Progressive Improvements, the Original and Present Constitution, and Other Events, to the Year 1721, with Some Particulars Since, and a Short View of Its Present State* (Burlington, NJ: Printed and Sold by James Parker, 1877), 108, http://books.google.com/books?id=VaUaAAAAYAAJ&pg.

34. Thomas Maxwell Potts and William John Potts. *Historical Collections Relating to the Potts family in Great Britain and America*. Canonsburg, PA: Published by the Compiler, 1901. 126–130, http://books.google.com/books?id=UusaAAAAYAAJ&pg.

35. "Thomas Potts & Mary Records solemnized their marriage at ye House of Tho: Potts (father of sd Tho.) in Burlington ye Twentieth day of June 1698 before Tho: Revell, Anthony Elton & Tho: Bibb Justices & before many witnesses."

36. "Nathaniel Records, of the Townshippe of Mansfield, in the County of Burlington within the Province of West Jersey, Yeoman, of the first part, And Thomas Potts, of the same place, Husbandman, of the other part, WITNESSETH that the said Nathaniel Records for and in consideration of a marriage allready had and Solemnized between the said Thomas Potts and Mary, the Daughter of the said Nathaniel, and as a marriage portion with her the said Mary, for their better support and supply and for the natural love and aff-ction which hee the said Nathaniel hath and beareth to the said Thomas Potts, his sonne in law, and to the said Mary, his Daughter, Hath Given, Granted...." (Potts, *Historical Collections Relating to the Potts family*, 131–135).

37. The Rev. Frank R. Symmes, *History of the Old Tennent Church*, 2nd ed. (Cranbury, NJ: G.W. Burroughs, 1904).

38. William Nelson, ed., *Archives of the State of New Jersey*, First Series, *Documents Relating to the Colonial History of the State of New Jersey*, vol. 22, *Marriage Records, 1665–1800; Edited, with an Historical Introduction on the Early Marriage Laws of New Jersey, and the Precedents on Which They Were Founded* (Paterson, NJ: 1900).

39. Ibid.

40. Colonial Records of North Carolina, vol. 8, p. 642.

41. "At a Council held in the Council Chamber at Savannah on Tuesday the 7th. February 1769. Present. His Excellency James Wright Esqr. In Council

"On reading a Petition of Joseph Maddock and Jonathan Sell two of the people called Quakers on the behalf of themselves and the rest of the Friends lately come to settle in this Province from North Carolina Setting forth (among other things) that sometime Since there was a reserve of Lands ordered to be made for Forty Families of their People it being then supposed not more than that Number would Settle in the Province but that there were already about Seventy Families come in and actually Settled and praying that a large Extent of Land might be allotted and reserved for them for a further Term they expecting a considerable Number of their Friends might yet join them. And also praying that their several Lands might be laid out; and Grant for the same passed; and a Road from their Settlement run; agreeable to the encouragement formerly given them, on the faith whereof they were come into the Province.

"It is Resolved that the Land on both Sides Germany's Creek to the Head thereof and from thence to continue the same Course 'till it intersects the Indian Line (not taken up by the People already come) be reserved for the same purpose for twelve Months next ensuing; that a Road be run from their Settlement; their Lands Surveyed in the several Tracts and proportions following and grants for the same passed and perfected to the respective persons herein after named that is to say, To [followed by a list of grants to settlers including: Thomas Ansley 200 Acres]."

42. William Nelson, ed., *Documents Relating to the Colonial History of the State of New Jersey,* vol. 21, *Marriage Records, 1665–1800* (Patterson, NJ: Press Printing, 1899), 61, http://books.google.com/books?id= YIFJAAAAYAAJ&pg. Dockwra was a very interesting man, a wealthy London merchant who in 1680 established the first private postal service in London, the Penny Post. After the Penny Post became profitable, King James II, then still the Duke of York, essentially stole it from him by having his corrupt friends bring 20 lawsuits against Dockwra. The cases went to court but a verdict was directed and William lost and settled for a pension from the Penny Post profits that was not paid for several years. After Anne became queen, he petitioned her for the redress of his grievances in a wonderful three page document which ended like this: "Your petitioner therefore prostrates himself at your Majesties feet, the throne being the refuge of the oppressed subjects and unhappy sufferers; never your Majesties incomparable goodness & intirely English heart, can let a faithful English subject be forgot, & his family languish into ruine meerly for doing good to his country; but that ye petitioner shall finde speedy redress from so admiral a Queen, whose piety and justice so conspicuous when in a private state, must, by advancing goodness, as well as Greatness, establish the throne and render it more illustrious." Queen Anne gave him a small compensation but William ended up losing several thousand pounds for setting up the Penny Post. He, however, was a wealthy man and was secretary of the Board of Proprietors of East New Jersey, New Jersey having been sold back to the Proprietors by George Carteret after Carteret received the property from King Charles II as a payoff for his support against Cromwell. At one time William Dockwra owned the town of Dunellen before it was incorporated as a borough of Piscataway, New Jersey. In 1702, he sold the town along with 2000 acres of land to his son-in-law for £400.

43. New Jersey State Archives, *Annual Report of the State Historian,* vol. 1 (1895), 533.

44. *Important Duckworth Family Dates and History,* http://www.rootsweb.ancestry.com/~mdgarret/duckworth.html.

45. Nelson, ed., *Documents ... New Jersey,* 61. http://books.google.com/books?id=PZRuAAAA MAAJ&pg.

46. Henry C. Peden, Jr., *St. John's and St. George's Parish Registers, 1696–1851* (Westminster, MD: Heritage, 1987), 59, http://books.google.com/books?id= yGzAVuYvnKgC&lpg=PP1&ots=z84Mvv_b0y&dq= St.%20John's%20and%20St.%20George's%20Parish %20Registers%201696–1851&pg=PP3#v=onepage &q=ramsey&f=false.

47. Regulator Advertisement No. 9:
"To THE GOVERNOR & COUNCIL, &c. The humble Petition of us the Subscribers sheweth that We the Inhabitants of Orange County pay larger Fees for recording Deeds than any of the adjacent Counties, and many other Fees more than the Law allows, by all that We can make out, from which a jealosie prevails that we are misused, and application has been- made to our representatives to satisfy us. But we were disregarded in the said application upon which the said discontent, growing more and more so as to threaten a disturbance of the public peace; we therefore beg that those matters may be taken under your serious consideration and interpose in our Favour, so that we may have a fair hearing in this matter, and (be) redressed where we have been wronged. Our complaints are too numerous and long to be notified in a Petition, but have sent herewith copies of the Applications, Petitions, &c, that has been made on this Occasion, with a small sketch of our misusage, and begging your protection and approbation in so just and equitable an undertaking and an opportunity to be heard, We conclude, your humble Petitioners...." (William Edward Fitch (M.D.), *Some Neglected History of North Carolina, Being an Account of the Revolution of the Regulators and of the Battle of Alamance, the First Battle of the American Revolution* (New York: Published by the Author, 1914), 136–7).

48. "Read a Petition of Jeremiah Duckworth setting forth that he had been some time in the province had a Wife and Six Children but never had any Land granted him and being now desirous of Obtaining Land for Cultivation Therefore praying for three hundred Acres of Land on the little Kioka about four Miles above the Mouth thereof. RESOLVED That on Condition &c the prayer of the said Petition is granted" (*Colonial Records of the State of Georgia: Proceedings and Minutes of the Governor and Council from August 6, 1771, February 13, 1782* (Atlanta: Franklin-Turner, 1907), 170.

49. Warren County Court of the Ordinary, Marriage Book 1833–1848, p. 107, Georgia Department of Archives and History, Microfilm Drawer 104, Box 14.

50. Ibid., 13.

51. Wiley Carter Beckwith was born in 1841, Sarah Beckwith was born in 1843, Amanda Jane Beckwith was born 10 February 1844, James Turner Beckwith was born 10 April 1846, Martha Lorenda Beckwith was born 10 September 1847, and Antoinette Beckwith was born 10 November 1853 (Jimmy Carter, *Family of Wiley Carter, 1798–1998* (Atlanta: Darby, 1998),14).

52. Sarah Ann, or Sallie, Carter was born in 1850. Sarah probably died as an infant. Carter family records say that another daughter, also named Sarah Ann Carter or Sallie Carter, was born in 1851. Lula G. Carter was born in 1857, William C. Carter was born in 1866, David Alonzo Carter was born in 1855, Jesse Neil Carter was born in 1852, John Vincent Carter was born in 1848 (Carter, *Family of Wiley Carter,* 106).

53. Warren County Court of the Ordinary, Marriage Book 1833–1848, p. 539, Georgia Department of Archives and History, Microfilm Drawer 104, Box 14.

54. Warren County Court of the Ordinary, Marriage Book 1848–1873, p. 20, Georgia Department of Archives and History, Microfilm Drawer 104, Box 14.

55. Ibid., 95.

56. James Wiley Abbot, born in 1850; John Calvin Abbot, born in 1853; John Quincy Abbot, born in 1853; Sterling Quincy Abbot, born in 1855; Stirling Gibson Abbot, born in 1855; Alice Amanda Caroline Abbot, born in 1859; and William Wright Abbot, born in 1861.

57. Warren County Court of the Ordinary, Marriage Book 1848–1873, p. 44, Georgia Department of Archives and History, Microfilm Drawer 104, Box 14.

58. Warren County Court of the Ordinary, Marriage Book 1833–1848, p. 353, Georgia Department of Archives and History, Microfilm Drawer 104, Box 14.

59. Calvin Hart; John Hart was born in 1854, Olin Hart was born in 1867, Emmett Russell Hart was born in 1869, and Minnie Hart was born September 9, 1872 (Carter, *Family of Wiley Carter*, 58).

60. Jonithon Louis Mize, George Mize, Willie Mize, Daisy Mize, Joe Mize, Frank Mize, Jr., and Ella Mize (Carter, *Family of Wiley Carter*, 63).

61. John was born in 1865, John Calvin was born in 1866, Margaret was born in 1869, Elizabeth was born in 1868, Maggie was born in 1870, Maud was born in 1875, Caywood was born in 1877, Harvey was born in 1880, Martha Blanch was born December 29, 1874, Albert Thomas was born in 1883, Claudia was born in 1887, James Henry Ray was born in 1889, and Wiley David Carter was born in 1890 (Carter, *Family of Wiley Carter*, 46).

62. Camilla Rumph, born about 1856; James Oscar Rumph, born about 1859; Charlie Clifford Rumph, born about 1866; Jesse Myrtle Rumph, born about 1869; and Ralph Hartwell Rumph, birth date unknown (Carter, *Family of Wiley Carter*, 51).

63. Ann Carter was born December 16, 1869, Fort Carter was born around 1871, Charles David Carter was born August 2, 1872, Samuel Thomas Carter was born November 11, 1876, Sallie Murray Carter was born June 14 1879 and Jesse Floyd Carter was born April 2, 1883. After Nancy died, Jesse married Susan Ann Augusta Jones October 1, 1899. Jesse Taliaferro Carter and Susan had two children. Bobbie Carter was born in 1900. William Jackson Carter was born in 1901 in Richland, Georgia (Carter, *Family of Wiley Carter*, 24).

64. W. Jake Hardin, *The Wiley Carter Story* (Avera, GA: 1977).

65. Warren County Government Online, *Sheriffs of Warren County*, http://www.warrencountyga.org/Departments/SheriffsOffice/SheriffsOfWarrenCounty.aspx.

66. Harden, *The Wiley Carter Story*, 3.

67. Warren County Court of the Ordinary, Marriage Book 1848–1873, Georgia Department of Archives and History, Microfilm Drawer 104, Box 14, 3.

68. "Compiled Service Records of Confederate Soldiers Who Served in Organizations from the State of Georgia" (electronic record), M266, "Carded Records Showing Military Service of Soldiers Who Fought in Confederate Organizations, compiled 1903–1927, documenting the period 1861–1865," Record Group 109, National Archives and Records Administration (hereinafter referred to as NARA), www.footnote.com/image/29870936, www.footnote.com/image/29871011, www.footnote.com/image/29871107.

69. Ibid., www.footnote.com/image/29871045.

70. Ibid., www.footnote.com/image/29870975.

71. Ibid., www.footnote.com/image/29871191, www.footnote.com/image/29871227, www.footnote.com/image/29871230.

72. Ibid., www.footnote.com/image/29870992, www.footnote.com/image/29871087, www.footnote.com/image/29871217, www.footnote.com/image/29870986, www.footnote.com/image/29871081, www.footnote.com/image/29871212.

Chapter 3. Ancestors of Mary Ann Diligent Seals

1. Virginia Lee Hutcheson Davis, *Tidewater Virginia Families* (Baltimore: Genealogical, 1989), 267.

2. In the colonies under English common law, women could inherit land and widows had a common law right known as dower rights, which gave her a one-third interest in all lands owned by her husband during their marriage. During the couple's marriage the woman became a "feme covert," essentially suspending her legal existence during the marriage. However, before land could be sold by the husband, the wife had to also renounce any claim to title. This protection was included in her dower rights, and land deeds from the period usually have a separate addendum attached in the form of a release of the dower rights. Women whose husband died intestate received at least one-third of the property her husband owned while they were married. Even if the husband died and left a will, if the wife was not satisfied with her bequest she still had the option of claiming one-third of the property.

3. Davis, *Tidewater Virginia Families*, 268.

4. Edwin H. Terrell, *Further Genealogical Notes of the Tyrrell-Terrell Family of Virginia and Its English and Norman-French Progenitors* (San Antonia: 1901), 39, http://books.google.com/books?id=AVETAAAAYAAJ&dq=Genealogical%20Notes%20On%20The%20Tyrrell%20And%20Terrell%20Family%20Of%20Virginia&pg=PA39#v=onepage&q&f=false.

5. Ibid., 270.

6. Ibid.

7. Ibid., 271–272.

8. Anne Terrell married David Lewis and they had a daughter, Hannah. Hannah Lewis married James Hickman and they had a daughter, Susannah. Susannah Hickman married James Browning and they had a daughter, Anne. Anne Browning married Robert Overall and they had a son, George Washington Overall. George Washington Overall married Louisiana Duvall and they had a daughter, Susan. Susan Overall married Christopher Columbus Clark and they had a daughter, Gabriella. Gabriella Clark married Harry

Armour and they had a daughter, Ruth. Ruth Armour married Ralph Waldo Emerson Dunham and they had a son, Stanley. Stanley Dunham married Madelyn Lee Payne and they had a daughter, Stanley Ann. Stanley Ann Dunham married Barak Hussein Obama, Sr., and they were the parents of President Obama, who is Jimmy Carter's seventh cousin.

9. Goochland County adjoins Hanover. Thomas Jefferson was born there before it was divided.

10. Gary Boyd Roberts, *Ancestors of American Presidents*, Preliminary Edition (Boston: New England Historic Genealogical Society, 1990).

11. Emma Dicken, comp., *Our Burnley Ancestors and Allied Families* (New York: Hobson Book Press, 1946), 75.

12. Ibid., 79.

13. Sarah Donelson Hubert, *Genealogy of Part of the Barksdale Family of America* (Atlanta: Franklin, 1895), 25, http://contentdm.lib.byu.edu/cdm4/document.php?CISOROOT=/FH9&CISOPTR=90957&REC=3.

14. Dicken, *Our Burnley Ancestors and Allied Families*, 93–95.

15. Dicken, *Our Burnley Ancestors and Allied Families*, 87.

16. Ibid., 94–96.

17. Captain John A. Barksdale, *Barksdale Family History and Genealogy* (Richmond: William Byrd, 1940), 44.

18. Ibid., 50.

19. Yates Publishing, *U.S. and International Marriage Records, 1560–1900* (online database), Provo, UT, USA: Generations Network, 2004, ancestry.com.

20. Will of James Muse, Sr., 1758, in Dorothy Ford Wulfeck, *Marriages of Some Virginia Residents, 1607–1800*, vol. 5.

21. Duane Meyer, *The Highland Scots of North Carolina, 1732–1776* (Chapel Hill: University of North Carolina Press, 1957, 1966) 156–160, http://books.google.com/books?id=-5_7YVUyI1AC&pg=PA159&dq.

22. Robert Digges Wimberly Connor, *Cornelius Harnett: An Essay in North Carolina History* (Raleigh: Edwards and Broughton, 1909), 114–121, http://books.google.com/books?id=ZsIEAAAAIAAJ&dq.

23. Wilkes County, Georgia, Deed Books A-VV (1784–1806), 68, 93, 143.

24. Gary Boyd Roberts, *Ancestors of American Presidents*, 2009 ed. (Boston: New England Historic Genealogical Society, 2009), 167.

25. Allen Johnson, *Union and Democracy* (Boston, New York, Chicago: Houghton Mifflin, 1915), 168, www.gutenberg.org/files/22461/22461-h/22461-h.htm.

26. Article I, Section 10, Clause 1.

27. Roberts, *Ancestors of American Presidents*, 2009 ed.

28. Marriage license, in Warren County Ordinary Court, Marriage Book A, 1794–1814, 16, Georgia Department of Archives and History (Morrow, GA), Microfilm Drawer 104, Box 13.

29. Warren County Ordinary Court, Marriage Book, 1848–1873, 43, Georgia Department of Archives and History (Morrow, GA), Microfilm Drawer 104, Box 14.

30. *Weekly Sumter Republican* (Americus, GA), November 21, 1873.

31. Ibid., November 28, 1873.

32. Ibid., December 5, 1873.

Chapter 4. Ancestors of Captain James Pratt

1. South Carolina State Archives, *Pratt, William, Account Audited (file no. 6106) of Claims Growing out of the American Revolution*, http://www.archivesindex.sc.gov/onlinearchives/RecordDetail.aspx?RecordId=125236.

2. Gary Boyd Roberts, *Ancestors of American Presidents*, 2009 ed. (Boston: New England Historic Genealogical Society, 2009).

3. Colyer Meriwether, *Publications of the Southern History Association*, vol. 2 (Southern History Association, 1898), 156, http://books.google.com/books?id=VtQRAAAAYAAJ&pg.

4. South Carolina Department of Archives and History, *Kay, James, Plat for 258 Acres on Branch of Hogskin and Corner Creek, Abbeville County, Ninety Six District, Surveyed by Benjamin Arnold*, http://www.archivesindex.sc.gov/onlinearchives/RecordDetail.aspx?RecordId=200474.

5. Roberts, *Ancestors of American Presidents*, 166–167.

6. "Compiled Service Records of Confederate Soldiers Who Served in Organizations from the State of South Carolina" (electronic record), M267, "Carded Records Showing Military Service of Soldiers Who Fought in Confederate Organizations, compiled 1903–1927, documenting the period 1861–1865," Record Group 109, National Archives and Records Administration, http://www.footnote.com/image/77085790.

7. Ibid., Chapter 6, File No. 702, 14, http://www.footnote.com/image/77085961, #77085877.

8. Ibid., *Inspection Report P*, No. 53, inclosure [sic] 4, http://www.footnote.com/image/77085990.

9. Ibid., Chapter 6, File No. 186, 546, http://www.footnote.com/image/77085995.

Chapter 5. Ancestors of Sophronia Cowan

1. Augustus Hunt Shearer, ed., *Ireland by Patrick Weston Joyce and Scotland*, vol. 12 (Philadelphia: John D. Morris, 1906), 166, http://books.google.com/books?id=y9XLBpnw8nwC&pg=PA166&lpg=PA166&dq#v=onepage&q&f=false.

2. Charles A. Hannah, *The Scotch-Irish in America*, vol. 2 (New York and London: G.P. Putnam's Sons;

Knickerbocher Press, 1902), 172–176. http://books.google.com/books?id=KHeAAAAAIAAJ&dq.

3. Ruth Dudley Edwards and Bridgette Hourican, *An Atlas of Irish History*, 3rd ed. (New York: Routledge, 2005), 137.

4. Robert Witherspoon, *Witherspoon Genealogies*, quoted in Charles A. Hannah, *The Scotch-Irish in America*, vol. 2 (New York and London: G.P. Putnam's Sons; Knickerbocher Press, 1902), 26–28, http://books.google.com/books?id=KHeAAAAAIAAJ&dq.

5. http://web.wctel.net/~kfleming/bt.html.

6. Roberts, *Ancestors of American Presidents*.

7. Elise Greenup Jourdan, *Early Families of Southern Maryland*, vol. 6 (Heritage, 2007), 118.

8. Howard Malcolm Jenkins and George Overcash Seilhamer, *Memorial History of the City of Philadelphia from Its First Settlement to the Year 1895* (New York: New York History Company, 1895), 217, http://books.google.com/books?id=-lwUAAAAYAAJ.

9. *Muster Rolls and Other Records of Service of Maryland Troops in the American Revolution, 1775–1783* (Published by Authority of the State, Under the Direction of the Maryland Historical Society, 1900), 377.

10. Revolutionary War pension application for Edward Miles, S11069, in "Revolutionary War Pension and Bounty-Land Warrant" (electronic record), M804, "Case Files of Pension and Bounty-Land Warrant Applications Based on Revolutionary War Service, compiled ca. 1800–ca. 1912, documenting the period ca. 1775–ca. 1900," Record Group 15, National Archives and Records Administration, http://www.fold3.com/image/24786180.

11. James Calvin Hemphill, *Men of Mark in South Carolina: A Collection of Biographies of Leading Men of the State*, vol. 3 (Washington, DC: Men of Mark, 1906), 83, http://books.google.com/books?id=0SsEAAAAYAAJ.

12. South Carolina Department of Archives and History, S108093: South Carolina Will Transcripts (Microcopy No 9), *Clinkscales, Francis, of Anderson District, Will Transcript*, Mss Will: vol. 1, 74, Estate Packet: Pkg. No. 140, http://www.archivesindex.sc.gov/onlinearchives/ViewImage.aspx?imageNumber=S108093000400605000a.jpg&recordId=308909.

13. Janie Revill, comp., *A Compilation of the Original Lists of Protestant Immigrants to South Carolina* (Baltimore: Genealogical, 1968), 5–7, 104–106.

14. The image was found on a Website with an irreproducible address in an unknown language which resembled (but was not) Thai. "Belfast News Letter, October 6, 1767" was written in the margin.

15. Yates Snowden, ed. *History of South Carolina*, vol. 5 (Chicago and New York: Lewis, 1950), 272.

16. U.S. and International Marriage Records, 1560–1900, Ancestry.com.

17. George and Sarah Brownlee's oldest child, John A. Brownlee, was born about 1779 and stayed in the Abbeville area his entire life with his wife, Jane Agnew. George Brownlee (II) was born in 1782. He married Anna Richey and moved to Texas. Martha Matilda Brownlee was born in 1787 and married John Stuart Richey, Anna Richey's brother. They moved to Mississippi. Elizabeth Brownlee was also born in 1787, Jane Brownlee in 1790, our ancestor Eleanor Brownlee in 1791, Sarah Brownlee in 1795 and Isabella Brownlee in 1798.

18. J.W. Richards, *The Baker and Gibson Families and Allied Lines* (Colorado Springs: 2001), 42.

19. Revill, *A Compilation of the Original List of Protestant Immigrants to South Carolina, 1763–1773*.

20. Nell Seawright Reeves, *The Saga of the Seawrights* (Greenwood, SC: Bagpipe Press, 1987) 42–43.

21. Revolutionary War pension application of John Miller, S1702, transcribed by Will Graves, http://www.southerncampaign.org/pen/s1702.pdf.

22. Ibid.

23. One of the men killed in the Cloud's Creek Massacre was one of my wife's many-generations-past great-grandfathers.

24. At that time Ninety-Six was a huge district covering the western part of South Carolina. On January 1, 1800 the Ninety-Six District was abolished and replaced by Abbeville, Edgefield, Greenville, Laurens and Newbury districts.

25. Last Will and Testament of John Cowan, 1874.

26. Jimmy Carter, *An Hour Before Daylight* (New York: Simon and Schuster, 2001), 237.

27. *Americus (GA) Times Recorder,* "Fatal Affair at Arlington," September 4, 1903, pp. 4–5.

28. *Americus (GA) Times Recorder,* "Death Results From Injuries," September 5, 1903, Section 4, p. 3.

Chapter 6. Ancestors of James Jackson Gordy

1. Robert Ellington Torbert, *The Gordys of Georgia and Relatives,* part 6, "Peter Gordy III" (Robert Ellington Torbert, 1994), 4–7.

2. Ibid.

3. N.K. Rogers, *The History of Chattahoochee County: Scotts in America* (Columbus: Columbus Office Supply, 1933).

4. Fred J. Cook, "Allan McLane, Unknown Hero of the Revolution," *American Heritage* 7, no. 6 (October 1956).

5. "Compiled Service Records of Soldiers Who Served in the American Army During the Revolutionary War" (electronic record), M881, "Compiled Service Records of Soldiers Who Served in the American Army During the Revolutionary War, compiled 1894–ca. 1912, documenting the period 1775–1784," Record Group 93, National Archives and Records Administration; http://www.footnote.com/image/#11816493.

6. Cook, "Allan McLane."

7. Ibid.

8. "Captain Allen McLane's Partisan Company of Foot, in the Service of the United States, taken for the Months of March, April, May, and June, 1779."

Captain, Allen McLane, commissioned January 13. 1777
First Lieutenant, A. M. Dunn, commissioned January 13, 1777.
Second Lieutenant, William Jones, commissioned January 13, 1777. Killed at Wyoming, April 17, 1779.
First Sergeant, John Edenfield.
Second Sergeant, John Hegan.
Third Sergeant, George Rowan.
Fourth Sergeant, Robert Farrell.
First Corporal, Matthew Cusick.
Second Corporal, John Vandegrift.
Drummer, Philip Wheylon.
Fifer, Eliazer Crane.
Privates. James Burk, John Rowles, Lidford Berry, William Stratton, Edward Hines, Robert Soloway, Thomas Finn, Perry Scott, Thomas Wells, Charles McMunigill, Thomas Parker, James Longo, Barret Alley, Henry Harneyman, Francis Bilstone, Moses McLane, Ezekiel Clark, Patrick Dagney, Lazarus Carmedy, John Butcher" (John Thomas Scharf, *History of Delaware, 1609–1888*, vol. 1, *General History* (Philadelphia: L.J. Richards, 1888), 269).

9. Alexander Garden, *Anecdotes of the Revolutionary War in America, with Sketches of Character of Persons the Most Distinguished, in the Southern States for Civil and Military Service* (Charleston: A.E. Miller, 1822), 392–393.

10. Baldwin Ordinary Court, Marriage Book A, 1806–1842, p. 55, Georgia Department of Archives and History, Microfilm Drawer 122, Box 60.

11. That part of Muscogee County would later become Chattahoochee County, in 1833.

12. Torbert, *The Gordys of Georgia* (1994), 14, 25–26.

13. 1850 U.S. Census.

14. "Compiled Service Records of Confederate Soldiers Who Served in Organizations from the State of Louisiana" (electronic record), M320, "Carded Records Showing Military Service of Soldiers Who Fought in Confederate Organizations, compiled 1903–1927, documenting the period 1861–1865," Record Group 109, National Archives and Records Administration, http://www.footnote.com/image/66094342, http://www.footnote.com/image/66094344, http://www.footnote.com/image/66094349, http://www.footnote.com/image/66094350, http://www.footnote.com/image/66094352.

15. N.K. Rogers, *History of Chattahoochee County, Georgia* (Columbus, GA: Columbus Office Supply, 1933).

16. 1850 U.S. Census.

17. "Compiled Service Records of Confederate Soldiers Who Served in Organizations from the State of Georgia" (electronic record), M226, "Carded Records Showing Military Service of Soldiers Who Fought in Confederate Organizations, Compiled 1903–1927, Documenting the Period 1861–1865," Record Group 109, National Archives and Records Administration, http://www.footnote.com/image/77085790, http://www.footnote.com/image/30752624, http://www.footnote.com/image/30752626, http://www.footnote.com/image/30752627.

18. Kristen Wyatt, "Confederate Uniform is Rescued," Associated Press, *Deseret News* (Salt Lake City, UT), April 20, 2002.

19. 1850 U.S. Census.

20. "Compiled Service Records of Confederate Soldiers Who Served in Organizations from the State of Georgia" (electronic record), M226, "Carded Records Showing Military Service of Soldiers Who Fought in Confederate Organizations, Compiled 1903–1927, Documenting the Period 1861–1865," Record Group 109, National Archives and Records Administration, http://www.footnote.com/image/58559930, http://www.footnote.com/image/58559938, http://www.footnote.com/image/58559951, http://www.footnote.com/image/58559957, http://www.footnote.com/image/58559965, http://www.footnote.com/image/58560001, http://www.footnote.com/image/58560022, http://www.footnote.com/image/58560027, http://www.footnote.com/image/58560051, http://www.footnote.com/image/58560098.

21. 1850 U.S. Census.

22. Also known as the Battle of Sharpsburg, particularly in the South.

23. Chattahoochee County Confederate Pensions and Records, "H.M. Gordy," Georgia Department of Archives and History, Microfilm Drawer 271, Box 70.

24. "Compiled Service Records of Confederate Soldiers Who Served in Organizations from the State of Georgia" (electronic record), M226, "Carded Records Showing Military Service of Soldiers Who Fought in Confederate Organizations, Compiled 1903–1927, Documenting the Period 1861–1865," Record Group 109, National Archives and Records Administration, http://www.footnote.com/image/20|35766312, http://www.footnote.com/image/20|35766321, http://www.footnote.com/image/20|35766342, http://www.footnote.com/image/20|35766375.

25. Rogers, *History of Chattahoochee County*.

26. Ibid.

27. Chattahoochee Ordinary Court, Marriage Book A, 1854–1907, p. 256, Georgia Department of Archives and History Microfilm Drawer 144, Box 68.

28. 1850 U.S. Census.

29. William Robert Scaife, *Joe Brown's Pets: The Georgia Militia, 1861–1865* (Macon, GA: Mercer University Press, 2004), 280.

30. Chattahoochee Ordinary Court, Marriage Book A, *1854–1907*, 4, Georgia Department of Archives and History, Microfilm Drawer 144, Box 68.

31. Union County was formed from Anson County and Mecklenburg County in 1842. Most of the early records for the Helms family are from Anson County.

32. Mrs. E.E. Moffitt, *The North Carolina Booklet: Great Events in North Carolina History*, vol. 12 (Raleigh: North Carolina Daughters of the American Revolution, 1912), 6–8.

33. Ibid., 11.

34. Robert L. Jolley, *Descendants, Relatives, and Ancestors of Ida Lucille Moore* (Winnepeg: Robert L. Jol-

ley, 2007), 232, http://contentdm.lib.byu.edu/cdm4/document.php?CISOROOT=%2FFH37&CISOPTR=77045&REC=8&CISOBO.

35. Ibid., 241.

36. Anson County, North Carolina, Will Book 2 (Wadesboro, NC), 124.

37. Thomas Presley was the son of Andreas Preslar, a German Palatine refuge who immigrated to New York in 1720, and his wife Antje Wells. Thomas and Antje later moved to Cecil County, Maryland, where Thomas was born. Andrew Presley, Jr., the brother of Thomas Presley, was born in 1732 and had five sons: Charles, John, Andrew III, Peter, and Joseph. John Presley was born in Rowan County in 1748 and fought in the Revolutionary War. He filed for and received a Revolutionary War pension after he moved to Monroe County, Tennessee. John Presley was the father of Dunnan (Dunning) Presley, Sr., born in Lancaster, South Carolina, in 1780. He married for the second time to Catherine and their son Dunnan Presley, Jr., was born July 1, 1827, in Monroe County, Tennessee. Dunnan Jr. enlisted at Knoxville as a private in Captain Jonathan C. Vaughn's Company C of the 5th Regiment of Tennessee Volunteers and served in the War with Mexico. When the war was over, he received a land grant for his service. After Dunnan's first wife died, he married Martha Jane Wesson on August 15, 1861.

Dunnan and Martha Jane's first child was Rosella Elizabeth Presley, born in February of 1862 in Fulton, Mississippi. Rosella never married but had nine illegitimate children, all of whom she gave the last name of Presley. Jessie McDowell Presley was born April 9, 1896, and lived until 1973. Jessie married Minnie Mae Hood on July 20, 1913, and their firstborn child, Vernon Elvis Presley, was born April 10, 1916, in Fulton, Mississippi.

Vernon Presley married Gladys Love Smith in Pontotoc County, Mississippi, on June 17, 1933. They moved to Tupelo, Mississippi, and their firstborn child, Elvis Aaron Presley, was born there on January 8, 1935. Elvis Aaron Presley was the sixth cousin once removed of President Jimmy Carter.

38. Jolley, *Descendants, Relatives, and Ancestors of Ida Lucille Moore,* 252–262.

39. Gerald C. Helms, comp., *Tilman, George and Jonathan Helms, Brothers, 1720–1881: History and Genealogy of the Helms Family* (NC: Published by the author and Jo Ann Stevenson, 1984), 12.

Chapter 7. Ancestors of Mary Ida Nicholson

1. John Blinn and William H. Egle (M.D.), eds., *Pennsylvania Second Series Archives,* vol. 9 (Harrisburg: Lane S. Hart, 1880), 11, http://books.google.com/books?id=PnMFAAAAQAAJ&pg=PA11&dq.

2. J.L. Ziegler, *Authentic History of Donegal Presbyterian Church, Located in East Donegal Township, Lancaster Co., Pa.* (F. McManus, Jr., 1902), 125, http://www.archive.org/stream/authentichistory00zieg/authentichistory00zieg_djvu.txt.

3. Brent H. Holcomb, *Mecklenburg Co. North County, Deed Abstracts,* Book 3 (Greenville, SC: Southern Historical Press, 1981), 225.

4. Ibid., Book 4, pp. 600–602.

5. C.L. Hunter, *Sketches of Western North Carolina Historical and Biographical, Illustrating Principally the Revolutionary Period of Mecklenburg, Rowan, Lincoln and Adjoining Counties Accompanied with Miscellaneous Information, Much of It Never Before Published* (Raleigh: Raleigh News Steam Job, 1887), 61–64.

6. Ibid.

7. Ibid., 667–69.

8. Colonial Dames of America, *Ancestral Records and Portraits: A Compilation from the Archives of Chapter I,* vol. 1 (New York: Grafton, 1910), 127, http://books.google.com/books?id=hYl2AAAAMAAJ&pg.

9. Samuel A'Court Ashe, *Biographical History of North Carolina from Colonial Times to the Present,* vol. 4 (Greensboro, NC: Charles L. Van Noppen, 1906), 221, http://books.google.com/books?id=EdKLfhkJIWEC&vq.

10. Ibid., 72–80.

11. Service source: North Carolina Revolutionary War Army Accounts, Vol. # 1, 66, Folio 4, Roll #72.1.

12. Brent H. Holcomb, *Mecklenburg Co. North County, Deed Abstracts,* Book 10 (Greenville, SC: Southern Historical Press, 1981), 9.

13. *Jan 1786: Wilkes County Georgia Deeds,* 586.

14. *Minutes of Mecklenburg Co NC, Court of Common Pleas and Quarter Sessions,* 1790 April Session, Book 2, 93.

15. Hunter, *Sketches of Western North Carolina,* http://infomotions.com/etexts/gutenberg/dirs/1/2/9/5/12953/12953.htm.

16. Mrs. Howard H. McCall, comp., *Roster of Revolutionary Soldiers in Georgia,* vol. 1 (Baltimore: Genealogical, 1968), 78.

17. "Greene County, State Of Georgia, Know all men by these present that I, Sterling Grimes of said state and county for consideration hereinafter expressed, have this day bargained and delivered unto William G. Grimes in the Town of Greensborough Lot #5, consideration of $532. Wit: John C. Nickelson, Nicholas Lewis JIC [Justice of the Inferior Court], Recorded April 1882" (*Green County, Georgia, Land Records, Books FF, GG, HH, 1816–1818,* vol. 3 [n.p.: Bory: 2006], 212).

18. "Notice. The subscribers inform their friends and the public in general, that they have opened a House of Entertainment, in the town of Greensborough, in the house lately occupied by Mr. William G. Grimes — where their house, bar, and stables will at all times be supplied with the best the country can afford. (signed) Samuel J. Nicholson, John C. Nicholson" (Fred R. Hartz and Emilie K. Hartz, *Genealogical Abstracts from the Georgia Journal (Milledgeville) Newspaper, 1809–1840,* vol. 1, 1809–1818, October 26, 1814 issue, 326).

19. "KNOW ALL MEN BY THESE PRESENTS, that we John C Nicholson, Thomas W Grimes, Joseph W Grimes, & William G Grimes are held and firmly bound unto the honorable, the Justices of the Inferior Court, sitting for Ordinary purposes, for the county of Greene and state of Georgia, in the just and full sum of Sixteen thousand Dollars, which payment will and truly to be made, we and each of us, do bind ourselves, our heirs, executors, administrators and assigns, firmly by these presents, sealed with our seals and dated this ninth day of August 1826.

"The condition of this obligation is such, that if the above bound John C Nicholson administrator of the goods, chattels and credits of Joseph Nicholson, deceased, do make a true and perfect inventory of all and singular the goods, chattels, and credits of the said deceased, which have, or shall came to the hands, possession or knowledge of the said John C Nicholson or into the hands or possession of any other person, or persons, for him and the same so made, do exhibit to the Court of Ordinary when thereunto required; and such goods, chattels and credits, do, well and truly administer according to law, and do made a just and true account of his actings and doings therein, when required by the Court aforesaid; and all the rest of the goods, chattels, and credits, which shall be found remaining upon the account of the said administration, the same being first allowed by the said Court, shall deliver and pay to such persons respectively as are entitled to the same by law, and if it shall hereafter appear, that any last will and testament was made by the said deceased, and the executors obtain a certificate of the probate thereof, and the said John C Nicholson do in such case, if required, render and deliver up said letters of administration, then this obligation to be void, else to remain in force, power and virtue.

"Signed, sealed, and delivered in the presence of
John C Nicholson (seal)
Thos. W Grimes (seal)
Joseph W Grimes (seal)
William G Grimes (seal)
Attest: Ebenezer Torrence Clerk"

20. "Between the usual hours of sale, will be sold on the 1st Tuesday in February next, in the town of Greensborough, Greene County, the following property, to wit: ... All the undivided interest of George P. Nicholson in 187 acres of land ... levied on to satisfy fi fas in favor of George Heard ... and other fi fas vs. said Nicholson. All the undivided interest of John C. Nicholson in 187 acres of land ... levied on to satisfy a fi fa in favor of George Heard, adm'r., etc., and other fi fas vs. said Nicholson. (signed) William Greer, Sheriff" (Hartz and Hartz, *Genealogical Abstracts from the Georgia Journal (Milledgeville) Newspaper, 1824–1828*, vol. 3, January 2, 1827 issue, 598).

21. Or the brother's son, also named Sterling Grimes.

22. Colonial and State Records of North Carolina, Vol. 22, *Payroll for David Hart's Company of the Orange County Militia* (1771), 418–419, http://docsouth.unc.edu/csr/index.html/document/csr22-0147.

23. Howard H. McCall, *Roster of Revolutionary Soldiers in Georgia* (Baltimore: Genealogical, 1996), 7, http://books.google.com/books?id=VuXEmBJOP7gC&dq=%22john+nunn%22+revolutionary&source=gbs_navlinks_s.

24. Paul K. Graham, *1805 Georgia Land Lottery Fortunate Drawers and Grantees* (Decatur, GA: Genealogy, 2004), 227.

25. Rogers, *History of Chattahoochee County*, 362–363.

26. "Compiled Service Records of Confederate Soldiers Who Served in Organizations from the State of Georgia" (electronic record), M226, "Carded Records Showing Military Service of Soldiers Who Fought in Confederate Organizations, Compiled 1903–1927, Documenting the Period 1861–1865," Record Group 109, National Archives and Records Administration, http://www.footnote.com/image/42164478, http://www.footnote.com/image/42164479, http://www.footnote.com/image/42164480.

27. Ibid., http://www.footnote.com/image/4837 1862.

28. Ibid., http://www.footnote.com/image/4216 4482 through http://www.footnote.com/image/4216 4507.

29. Ibid., http://www.footnote.com/image/4216 4492.

30. N.K. Rogers, *The History of Chattahoochee County Georgia* (Columbus, GA: Columbus Office Supply, 1933), 373.

31. Joseph W. Dawson, *Record of the Dawson Family from 1743 to 1900*, Kenneth H. Thomas, Jr., Collection, Box 2, Jimmy Carter Library and Museum. The family history was written by Joseph Dawson in 1875 and updated by Walter Ernest Dawson August 26, 1900.

32. South Carolina Department of Archives and History, *Dawson, Jonathan, Account Audited (Aud #1831, Roll #32) of Claims Growing Out of the American Revolution*, Series: S108092, Reel: 0032, Frame: 00324, http://www.archivesindex.sc.gov/onlinearchives/RecordDetail.aspx?RecordId=119498.

33. "Revolutionary War Pension and Bounty-Land Warrant Application Files" (electronic record), M804, "Case Files of Pension and Bounty-Land Warrant Applications Based on Revolutionary War Service, compiled ca. 1800–ca. 1912, documenting the period ca. 1775–ca. 1900," Record Group 15, Pension Number: S17920, National Archives and Records Administration, http://www.footnote.com/image/15221692, http://www.footnote.com/image/15221729, http://www.footnote.com/image/15221733.

34. Charles Fleming McIntosh, *Brief Abstracts of Norfolk County, Virginia, Wills, 1710–1753* (Heritage Books, 1922), 118.

35. Edgefield County Historical Society, comp., *Genealogy of Nicholson and Allied Families* (Edgefield Advertiser, 1944), 16–17.

36. South Carolina Department of Archives and History, Nicholson, Wright, Account Audited (File No. 5514) of Claims Growing Out of the American

Revolution, Series: S108092, Reel: 0111, Frame: 00451, http://www.archivesindex.sc.gov/onlinearchives/RecordDetail.aspx?RecordId= 124567.

37. South Carolina Department of Archives and History, Nicholson, Wright, of Edgefield County, Will Transcript (Mss Will: Book A, Page 244; Estate Packet: Box 43, Pkg. 1784), http://www.archivesindex.sc.gov/onlinearchives/ViewImage.aspx?imageNumber=S108093000800434000a.jpg&recordId=3494.

38. Carol Wells, *Edgefield County, South Carolina: Deed Books 19, 20, 21, and 22* (Westminster, MD: Heritage Books, 2007), 76, http://books.google.com/books?id=GYCpZqXaW48C&pg=PA98&lpg=PA98&dq.

39. 1850 U.S. Census, District 86, Upson County, Georgia, Roll M432-85, Page 288A, Image: 14.

40. Hunting for Bears, comp., *Georgia Marriages, 1699–1944* (online database), Provo, UT, Ancestry.com, 2004. http://search.ancestry.com/cgi-bin/sse.dll?db=gamarriages_ga&h=50818&ti=0&indiv=try&gss=pt&ssrc=pt_t11567819_p-439839327_g32768.

41. L.P. Gaines, rev. by Mary Kathryn Gaines Cooley Korstian, *History of the Gaines Family: One Line from 1620 to the Present Time, 1918* (Rome, GA: Brazelton-Wallis, 1973), 11.

42. Gaines, *History of the Gaines Family*, 17; Janice L. Abercrombie and Richard Slatten, *Virginia Revolutionary "Publick" Claims*, vol. 2 (Athens: Iberian, 1992), 226; *NSDAR Lineage Book*, vol. 157, 1920 (Washington, DC: 1937), 187.

43. Gaines, *History of the Gaines Family*, 18.

44. Travis Jackson Hagler, *Bonner, Brown, Boswell Family History: Southeastern Alabama Era* (Huntsville, AL: T.J. Hagler, 1995), 89.

45. Personal Carter family records. Certified marriage certificate from the Ordinary and ex-officio clerk of the Court of Ordinary, Baldwin County, Georgia.

46. South Carolina Department of Archives and History, Marcus, Daniel, Account Audited (File no. 4769 B 1/2) of Claims Growing Out of the American Revolution, Series: S108092, Reel: 0093, Frame: 00291, http://www.archivesindex.sc.gov/onlinearchives/RecordDetail.aspx?RecordId=123310.

47. South Carolina Department of Archives and History, Marcus, Ellis Of Edgefield County, Will Typescript (Mss Will: Book A, pages 7–8; Estate Packet: Box 42, Pkg. 1757), Series: S108093, Reel: 0008, Frame: 00032, http://www.archivesindex.sc.gov/onlinearchives/Thumbnails.aspx?recordId=297470

48. 1850 U.S. Census, *Slave Schedules*, Roll M432.

49. Morgan D. Jones, *Brown Genealogy* (privately printed, 1965).

50. Ibid.

51. 1850 U.S. Census.

52. Ibid., *Slave Schedules*.

53. "Compiled Service Records of Confederate Soldiers Who Served in Organizations from the State of Georgia" (electronic record), M266, "Carded Records Showing Military Service of Soldiers Who Fought in Confederate Organizations, Compiled 1903–1927, Documenting the Period 1861–1865," Record Group 109, National Archives and Records Administration, http://www.footnote.com/image/29879552, http://www.footnote.com/image/29879589, http://www.footnote.com/image/29879594, http://www.footnote.com/image/29879596, http://www.footnote.com/image/29879615, http://www.footnote.com/image/29879606.

54. Mary Elizabeth Dawson and Nathaniel Nunn Nicholson's son.

55. "Compiled Service Records of Confederate Soldiers Who Served in Organizations from the State of Georgia" (electronic record), M266, "Carded Records Showing Military Service of Soldiers Who Fought in Confederate Organizations, Compiled 1903–1927, Documenting the Period 1861–1865," Record Group 109, National Archives and Records Administration, http://www.footnote.com/image/43375686, http://www.footnote.com/image/43375778, http://www.footnote.com/image/43375788, http://www.footnote.com/image/43375801.

56. Jean F. Wheeler, *Malachi Dawson Family History*, Collection of Kenneth Thomas, Box 2, Carter Library and Museum.

Chapter 8. Ancestors of John William Murray

1. Alton Murray, *Kindred Murrays: A Story of the Murrays Who Migrated from the Cape Fear River in North Carolina to the Province of Georgia in 1769 and Their Kindred* (St. Marys, GA: Alton Murray, 1981).

2. Ibid., 15.

3. I can't tell them apart from the deeds.

4. Onslow County, North Carolina, Deed Book B (Jacksonville, NC), 21.

5. Murray, *Kindred Murrays*, 16.

6. Personal Carter family records. This will is in Onslow County Will Book A, 95–96, December 8, 1808, in the Onslow County Courthouse in Jacksonville, NC.

7. Bobby G. Albritton, *Albrittons of the Second Millennium*, rev. ed. (Alpharetta, GA: Balbritt, 2003), 26, http://contentdm.lib.byu.edu/cdm4/document.php?CISOROOT=/FH36&CISOPTR=77356&REC=1.

8. Ibid., 28–29.

9. Pitt County, North Carolina, Deed Book F (Greenville, NC), 75–77.

10. Personal Carter family records. This deed is recorded in Laurens County Deed Book F, 1818–1821, 222. The official records are in the Laurens County, Georgia, courthouse in Dublin, Georgia.

11. Ibid., Deed Book 1, 1836–1831, 18–19.

12. Ibid., 94.

13. Zae Hargett Gwynn, *Abstracts of the Records of Onslow County, North Carolina, 1734–1850*, vol. 2, North Carolina, Onslow County Court, 1141, http://books.google.com/books?id=W3AlAAAAMAAJ&q.

14. Ibid., 1000.

15. Blanche Adams Chapman, *Wills and Administrations of Isle of Wight County, Virginia, 1647–1800* (Baltimore: Genealogical, 1975), 35–36.

16. Yates Publishing, *U.S. and International Marriage Records, 1560–1900* (online database), Provo, UT, ancestry.com.

17. William Champion and Mary Fort also had at least two daughters: Mary Martha Champion was born in 1777 and Elizabeth was born in 1782.

18. This deed is recorded in Laurens County Deed Book H, 1823–1826, on pages 29–30.

19. Unpublished family history written by Alethea Lawhon held in the personal Carter family records.

20. Alexander McQueen Quattlebaum, Linda Grabeman and Stephen Hoffius, eds., *Clergymen and Chiefs: A Genealogy of the MacQueen and MacFarlane Families* (Charleston: South Carolina Historical Society, 1990), 34, http://books.google.com/books?id=T-6oCucIvsMC&dq.

21. David Dobson, *Directory of Scots in the Carolinas, 1680–1830* (Baltimore: Genealogical, 1986), 322.

22. Robert Archibald Logan, "Highlanders from Skye in North Carolina and Nova Scotia: 1771–1818," *Scottish Genealogist* 12, no. 4 (February 1966), 92–107.

23. Laughlin Bethune, the son of Colin and brother of our ancestor Martin Bethune, was born in Isle of Skye, Scotland. He was for several years a state senator of North Carolina. From 1831 to 1833 he was a representative from North Carolina to the twenty-second and twenty-third congresses. Laughlin died in 1856 in Fayetteville, NC.

24. Robert Digges, Wimberly Conner, William Kenneth Boyd, and Joseph Grégoire de Roulhac Hamilton, *History of North Carolina*, vol. 6, North Carolina Biography (Chicago and New York: Lewis, 1919), http://www.archive.org/stream/historyofnorthca06conn/historyofnorthca06conn_djvu.txt.

25. Eugene M. Wiseman, *The Wiseman Family and Allied Lines*, vol. 1 (Franklin, NC: Genealogy, 1991), 254, http://books.google.com/books?id=FdlfAAAAMAAJ&q.

26. Unpublished family history written by Alethea Lawhon.

27. Personal Carter family records.

28. Ibid.

29. Personal Carter family records; unpublished family history written by Alethea Lawhon.

30. Lucian Knight, *Georgia's Roster of the Revolution, Containing a List of the States Defenders, Officers and Men, Soldiers and Sailors, Partisans and Regulars, Whether Enlisted from Georgia or Settled in Georgia After the Close of Hostilities: Compiled Under Authority of the Legislature from Various Sources, Including Official Documents, Both State and Federal, Certificates of Service, Land Grants, Pension Rolls, and Other Records* (Atlanta: Index, 1920), 107–108.

31. "Compiled Service Records of Confederate Soldiers Who Served in Organizations from the State of Georgia" (electronic record), M266, "Carded Records Showing Military Service of Soldiers Who Fought in Confederate Organizations, Compiled 1903–1927, Documenting the Period 1861–1865," Record Group 109, National Archives and Records Administration, http://www.footnote.com/image/#35560992.

32. Willie Zuela was born in 1861, married John Godwin and lived until 1953. Margaret Elizabeth was born in 1866. She married Thomas Anderson and lived until 1949. Drue Parker Murray was born in 1869 and lived until 1944. Drue married Maude Jennings. Susan Alethea was born August 18, 1874 and lived until 1959. Susan married Ichabod Lafayette Balcom. Alma Murray was born in 1879 and lived until 1937. He married Florris Estelle Stevens. Anna Josephine Murray was born in 1883 and married William Thomas Mackey. She lived until 1980. Nathan Fulwood Murray was born in 1887 and lived until 1964. Nathan married Kathleen McGarrah (Beth Murray Walters, *Murray Lineage* [privately printed, 1983], 7).

Chapter 9. The Ancestors of Rosa Nettie Wise

1. One of my wife's ancestors, Rene de St. Julian, had his land confiscated and was given a week to dispose of the rest of his property. He fled France and eventually made his way to South Carolina.

2. A corruption of "Deutsch."

3. E.B. Hallman, "Early Settlers in the Carolina Dutch Fork, 1744–1760" (master's thesis, Wofford College, n.d.).

4. http://dutchforkchapter.org/html/bickley_hans.htm.

5. South Carolina Council Journal, vol. 21, p. 48.

6. Frederick Calhoun Wyse, Jr., rev. by Sybil and Wallace Harmon, *History of The Wise and Wyse Families of South Carolina* (Wolfe City, TX: Herington, 1992), 27.

7. This family and their journey are described in an out-of-print book by Jack V. Lybrand entitled *From Kleiningersheim to Dutch Fork: Lybrand Descendants of Johann Heinrich Leibbrand* (Columbia, SC: Jack V. Lybrand, 1992), which I have not been able to find.

8. South Carolina Council Journal, vol. 21, part 1, p. 340.

9. B.H. Holcomb, *Petitions for Land from the South Carolina Council Journals*, vol. 2, 1752–1753 (Columbia, SC: SCMAR, 1997), 210.

10. *(Columbia) South Carolina Gazette*, December 1752.

11. Gottlieb Mittelberger, *Gottlieb Mittelberger's Journey to Pennsylvania in the Year 1750 and Return to Germany in the Year 1754*, trans. Carl Theo. Eben (Philadelphia: John Jos. McVey), 1898, http://books.google.com/books?id=4KYlAAAAMAAJ&dq.

12. Gottlieb Mittelberger was passenger number 486 on the ship *Osgood*, William Wilkie Captain, by way of Cowes.

13. *Family of Johann Heinrich Lybrand and Catharina Weiss*, Palmetto Genealogy Association, http://www.palmettoroots.org/Family_Lybrand.html.

14. Elizabeth Lybrand was born about 1797. Sarah Sally Lybrand was born January 21, 1799, and married Daniel Smith. Mary Lybrand was born about 1802 and married Frederick Gable. Rebecca Lybrand was born about 1805. Catherine was born in 1807. Levi was born January 1, 1812, and Christina was born about 1814.
Descendants of Hans (Leibbrand, Lybrand) Leuprandt, http://www.leibbrandt.com/leibbrandt_Archive/William_Maxfield_Harris/Hans_Leuprandt.htm.

15. "The Southern Claims Commission" (electronic record), M1407, "Southern Claims Commission," Roll 046, National Archives and Records Administration, http://www.footnote.com/image/668120, http://www.footnote.com/image/668120.

16. "Where as Barnet Lybrand, late of Lexington District, died seized of a considerable Real Estate leaving a widow to whom by his L.W.&T. devised said Real Estate during her natural life, and the sd. Widow having recently departed this life leaving six daughters to wit, Elizabeth intermarried with John Coogle, Sally intermarried with Daniel Smith, Mary intermarried with Frederick Gable, Rebecca Lybrand, Catharine Addy, widow, formerly Catharine Lybrand, and Christena Lybrand ... heirs sell for $391, 229 acres to Frederick Gable adj. John S. Swygert, John Drehr, the heirs of Valentine Gable, and others" (deed of sale for 229 acres in the estate records of Barnet Lybrand).

17. John Thomas Coogle was born May 24, 1817. James Bernard Coogle was born November 15, 1820. Caroline Coogle was born sometime around 1825 and married William J. Taylor. Peter Coogle was born about 1828, *Macon County (GA) Citizen* Obituary, May 27, 1891.

18. Sally Kleckley born in 1814 and Daniel Kleckley born in 1817.

19. *Marriage and Death Abstracts from the Journal of Rev. Godfrey Dreher*, http://www.palmettoroots.org/DreherJournal.html.

20. Dan O. Harvill, *History of Mt. Zion Lutheran Church, 1938–1958*. http://files.uswarchives.net/ga/macon/churches/mtzion.txt.

21. "Compiled Service Records of Confederate Soldiers Who Served in Organizations from the State of Georgia" (electronic record), M266, "Carded Records Showing Military Service of Soldiers Who Fought in Confederate Organizations, Compiled 1903–1927, Documenting the Period 1861–1865," Record Group 109, National Archives and Records Administration, http://www.footnote.com/image/32|37403221, http://www.footnote.com/image/32|37403280.

22. Ibid., http://www.footnote.com/image/32|37403383.

23. Ibid., http://www.footnote.com/image/32|35761004, http://www.footnote.com/image/32|35761026, http://www.footnote.com/image/32|35761074, http://www.footnote.com/image/32|35761098, http://www.footnote.com/image/32|35761109.

24. Ibid., http://www.footnote.com/image/32|35761171, http://www.footnote.com/image/32|35761327, http://www.footnote.com/image/32|35761332, http://www.footnote.com/image/32|35761346.

25. Carl W. Nichols and Ann Corum, *Palmetto Connections: The Kölle Family Of Blaubeuren Germany*, http://www.palmettoroots.org/Family_Kelly.html.

26. Elizabeth Wise was born January 28, 1800. Elizabeth married John Derrick and after he died she married Jacob Caughman. Nancy Wise was born March 19, 1803, and married John McNeary. Their only son, Levi, married Elizabeth Etheridge. John McNeary, Levi and Elizabeth migrated to Botsford around 1869 after Nancy died. John and Levi served on the first Church Council. They later moved back to South Carolina.
Christina Wise was born January 20, 1805. She married Captain Frederick Kinard, the son of her father's second wife, Catherine Elizabeth Chapman. Catherine Chapman had previously been married to Frederick Andrew Kinard, who died in 1811; their son, Captain Frederick Kinard, was born in Newbury, South Carolina, in 1800. Catherine's first husband, Frederick Andrew Kinard, was the son of another Palatine immigrant, Martin Kinard, an upstanding citizen of Dutch Forks and a member of the Bethlehem Church there. Martin joined Colonel Philemon Waters' regiment at the beginning of the Revolutionary War and served with Col. Waters during the entire war (George Leland Summer, *Newberry County, South Carolina: Historical and Genealogical Annals* (Baltimore: Genealogical Inc. 1950), 246).
Sarah Wise was born December 28, 1806, and married John Singley. Mary Margaret Wise was born December 13, 1817, and married Michael Shealy. Jemima Wise was born November 24, 1815, and married George Addy and moved to Botsford. Her daughter Amanda Elizabeth Wise would later marry Guilford Etheridge, and her brother David would marry Guilford's sister.
George Wise was born May 14, 1801. Joseph was born in 1805. David Wise, our ancestor, was born April 30, 1809 and married Rosannah Elizabeth Etheridge. Jesse Wise was born January 6, 1811, and married Martha Etheridge. After Martha died, Jesse married her sister, Jane (or Jency) Etheridge. Jane and her three married daughters moved to Botsford. Jeremiah Wise was born January 27, 1813. He married Letitia Jennings. Joel Wise was born either June 27 or June 28, 1820. Joel married Melissa Schumpert, and after she died he married Mary Jane Moore. Joel and Mary Jane also moved to Botsford. Levi Wise was born in 1822 and died very young. George Wise married Mary Roberts on October 15, 1819. According to old family records, George married Mary Shealy around 1829. It seems that both wives lived until 1885. The story seems to have been lost in time (Frederick Calhoun Wyse, Jr., rev. by Sybil and Wallace Harmon, *History of the Wise and Wyse Families of South Carolina* (Wolfe City, TX: Herington, 1992), 53–55, 82–84).

27. *Confederate Archives*, Chapter 10, File Number 33, 118.

28. Ibid., File Number 10, 226.

29. Wyse, *History of The Wise and Wyse Families of South Carolina*, 111.

30. "Compiled Service Records of Confederate Soldiers Who Served in Organizations from the State of South Carolina" (electronic record), M267, "Carded Records Showing Military Service of Soldiers Who Fought in Confederate Organizations, Compiled 1903–1927, Documenting the Period 1861–1865," Record Group 109, National Archives and Records Administration, http://www.footnote.com/image/32|71189974, http://www.footnote.com/image/32|71189990, http://www.footnote.com/image/32|71189993, http://www.footnote.com/image/32|71189995, http://www.footnote.com/image/32|71189997, http://www.footnote.com/image/32|71190000, http://www.footnote.com/image/32|71190004, http://www.footnote.com/image/32|71190008, http://www.footnote.com/image/32|71190012.

31. Ibid., http://www.footnote.com/image/32|75863525, http://www.footnote.com/image/32|75863542.

32. Ibid., http://www.footnote.com/image/32|75558848, #32|75558904.

33. Ibid., http://www.footnote.com/image/32|75558677, http://www.footnote.com/image/32|75558737, http://www.footnote.com/image/32|75558750, http://www.footnote.com/image/32|75558766.

34. *Confederate Archives*, Chapter 10, File 33, 123.

Chapter 10. Ancestors of Wilburn Edgar Smith

1. *Colonial Churches in the Original Colony of Virginia*, 2nd ed. (Richmond: Southern Churchman, 1908), 144.

2. Oswald Tilgman, *History of Talbot County, Maryland, 1661–1861*, vol. 1 (Baltimore: Williams and Wilkins, 1915), 134, http://books.google.com/books?id=nGYlAAAAMAAJ&dq.

3. Daniel R. Randall, *A Puritan Colony in Maryland*, ed. Herbert B. Adams, Johns Hopkins University Studies in Historical and Political Science, Fourth Series (Baltimore: Johns Hopkins University, 1886), 25.

4. Hotten, *The Original Lists of Persons of Quality*, 246 (Hotten says 20 years old).

5. Now Newport News, Virginia.

6. Sharon J. Doliante, *Maryland and Virginia Colonials: Genealogies of Some Colonial families* (Baltimore: Genealogical, 1991), 651, http://books.google.com/books?id=1KvkiaQks-kC&pg.

7. Charles Francis Stein, *A History of Calvert County, Maryland*, 2nd ed. (Baltimore: Calvert County Historical Society, 1961), 237, http://books.google.com/books?cd=3&id=MWozAAAAIAAJ&dq.

8. "John Bigger aged 24 yeares or thereabouts sworne 14 January 1658 Sayth that formerly he used to trade much in horses, in buying & selling them for many yeares together, & being desyred by MTM ffenwick to looke in her Roand, horses mouth doth declare th' the sd Roand horse is five yeares old, next foaling time, according to this Depon's best skill in the age of horses, & further sayth not. Sworne before me Hugh Stanley John Bigger" (Maryland State Archives, Benard Christian Steiner, ed., *Proceedings of the Provincial Court of Maryland, 1658–1662*, vol. 41 (Baltimore: Lord Baltimore, 1922), 219).

9. William Hand Browne, ed., *Archives of Maryland, Proceedings of the Council of Maryland, 1693–1697*, vol. 20 (Baltimore: Maryland Historical Society, 1900), 108, 541–542.

10. F. Edward Wright, *Anne Arundel County Church Records of the 17th and 18th Centuries* (Lewes, DE: Colonial Roots, 2004), 5.

11. Joshua Dorsey Warfield, *The Founders of Anne Arundel and Howard Counties, Maryland: A Genealogical and Biographical Review from Wills, Deeds and Church records* (Baltimore: Kohn & Polloch, 1905), 75–79, http://books.google.com/books?id=vgINAAAAYAAJ&dq.

12. Ibid., 77.

13. These records are mentioned on page x of the preface to the *Proceedings of the Council of Maryland, 1698–1731*, vol. 25: "In the night of Oct. 17, 1704, the State house was burned and many of the records destroyed. This calamity was followed the next year by a fire which destroyed the court house, to which the records had been removed, and several other buildings. These fires were believed to be the work of conspirators who wished to destroy the evidence of their indebtedness. Their ringleader, Richard Clarke, was tried for this and other offences, found guilty and executed." Many people subsequently restored these lost records by reregistering their transactions.

14. "Nicholas Ridgely, son of Henry (who was the son of Colonel Henry and Sarah, his wife), and Catherine, his wife (who was the daughter of Colonel Nicholas Greenberry and Ann, his wife), all of Anne Arundel County, in the Province of Maryland), the said Nicholas was born the 12th day of February, A. D., 1694, and was married to Sarah Worthington (the daughter of Captain John and Sarah, his wife, of Anne Arundel County, aforesaid), the 26th day of December, 1711" (Warfield, *The Founders of Anne Arundel and Howard Counties*). It was Colonel Nicholas Greenberry, the father of Henry's wife Catherine, who restored the Ridgely-Warner land transaction records lost in 1704.

15. "I give to my wife Mary, my home, plantation, 'Cotton'; 'Mary's Delight' and 'Larkin's Folly,' which I bought of Thomas Larkin, to an unborn child.... If 'Mary's Delight' is not possessed by an heir, it is to be divided between John Brewer, Joseph Brewer, Thomas Odall and Henry Odall, sons of Thomas Odall (elsewhere written Odell). I give to my daughter, Sarah Odall, wife of Thomas, a negroe girl; to all my grandchildren, £10; to my god-daughter, Martha Duvall, £51, and a cow and calf" (Warfield, *The Founders Of Anne Arundel And Howard Counties*, 78).

16. There is a strong likelihood that James Murray

was the father of Jonathon Murray although there is no proof. If James was Jonathon's father, then 220 years later and having moved through three states, James Murray's descendant, Rosalynn Carter's father, would marry Thomas Odell's descendant, Rosalynn's mother.

17. *Proceedings of the Council of Maryland, 1681–85/6*, 261.

18. "June the 19, 1714. Then came Mareen Duvall and Ninian Beal and John Wall being the within three witnesses to the will and did make oath before the Holy Evangelists and Almighty God, that they were present at the time and place and did see the within Edward Brock which is now deceased sign, seal and acknowledge the with written to be his last will and testament and at the same time he was in his perfect senses to the best of their knowledge. Sworn before me Benjamin Berry, Dept Comisory Prince George's County Maryland: these are to certify the whereas Mr. Edward Brock last of Prince George's County deceased hast thought fit to nominate and appoint William Offutt, executor of his last will and testament and the said William Offutt for divers reasons do by these presents renounce and relinquish and make void and null the said executorship and pray that the same be granted unto William Nichols and his Wife being the next kindred as witness my hand and seal this 19 day of June 1714.
William Offutt (seal)
Signed in the presence of us
Joseph 'X' Storry
Phil Gotting, Junior.
Commisy General — to the Honorable Wm. Bladen Esqr. George's County
before me Benj. Berry Dept. Comns, Pr, June the 19th 1714 the within acknowledged" (Will of Edward Brock, Sr.).

19. Hester Dorsey Richardson, *Side-lights on Maryland History: With Sketches Of Early Maryland Families* (Baltimore: Williams and Wilkins, 1913), 9, http://books.google.com/books?id=l_oMAAAAYAAJ&pg.

20. Prince George's County, Maryland, Land Records, Liber C (Upper Marlboro, MD), folio 20 and 22.

21. Prince George's County, Maryland, Land Records, 1717–1726 (Upper Marlboro, MD), folio 692.

22. Zada Wade Beadles, *The Wades: The History of a Family, Dealing with the Kith and Kin of Zachary and Mary Hatton Wade, Their Descendants and Related Lines, Male and Female, in Maryland, Virginia, Tennessee, South Carolina, North Carolina, and Other States* (Cairo, IL: Published by the author, 1963), 54, http://books.google.com/books?id=7QlaAAAAMAAJ&q.

23. Doliante, *Maryland and Virginia Colonials*, 559.

24. Henry C. Peden, *Colonial Maryland Soldiers and Sailors, 1634–1734* (Westminster, MD: Heritage, 2008), 194, http://books.google.com/books?id=wSye_RpvnnwC&dq.

25. George Norbury Mackenzie, *Colonial Families of the United States of America in Which Is Given the History, Genealogy and Armorial Bearings of Colonial Families Who Settled in the American Colonies from the Time of the Settlement of Jamestown, 13th May, 1607, to the Battle of Lexington, 19th April, 1775*, vol. 6 (Baltimore: Seaforth, 1917), 279–280, http://books.google.com/books?id=J1tlAAAAMAAJ&pg.

26. *Ancestral Records and Portraits*, vol. 1, *A Compilation from the Archives of Chapter 1, the Colonial Dames of America* (New York: Grafton, 1910), 87, http://books.google.com/books?id=hYl2AAAAMAAJ&dq.

27. "2nd December 1674. Came John Jacob of Ann Arundell County and proved hid Right to fifty acres of Land for his time of Service performed in this province to James Warner nine years since. Warrant then granted the Said John Jacob for fifty acres of Land Due to him for his time of Service performed in this province. Cert. retur the 2nd of March next" (Liber #18, f. 128, Hall of Records, Annapolis, Maryland, quoted in Sharon J. Doliante, *Maryland and Virginia Colonials: Genealogies of Some Colonial Families* (Baltimore: Genealogical, 1991), 382, http://books.google.com/books?id=1KvkiaQks-kC&pg=PA391&dq).

28. Gus Skordas, *The Early Settlers of Maryland: An Index to Names of Immigrants Compiled from Records of Land Patents, 1633–1680, in the Hall of Records, Annapolis, Maryland* (Baltimore: Genealogical, 1968), 88, http://books.google.com/books?id=RSCnJFLE-90C&dq.

29. "January 23 1659/60, CECILIUS [Lord Baltimore] absolute Lord and proprietary of the provinces of Maryland and Avalon Lord Baron of Baltimore &c To All persons to whom these presents shall come Greeting in our Lord God Everlasting Know yee that we for and in consideration that Richard Cheney hath transported himself and Charity his wife into this our province here to inhabit and upon such conditions and terms as are expressed in our conditions of plantation of our said province of Maryland, under our great Seal at armes bearing date London the Second day of July in the year of our Lord God 1649, and remaining upon record in our s^d province of Maryland, with such alteration as in them is made by our declaration bearing date the Six and twentieth day of August Anno. 1651 likewise remaining upon record in our said province of Maryland Do hereby grant unto the said Richard Cheyney a parcell of Land called Cheney Hill lying on the West side of Chesapeak Bay, on the South side of a River in the said Bay called South River and on the South side of a Creek in the said River called the fflat Creek Beginning at a markd oak standing upon a hill near the Creek side...." (Patents, Liber 4, f. 262, Hall of Records, Annapolis, quoted in Doliante, *Maryland and Virginia Colonials*, 106, http://books.google.com/books?id=1KvkiaQks-kC&pg=PA391&dq).

30. "Now know ye that I the sd Richard Cheney for & in consideration of the Natural Love & fatherly affection I have & do beare unto my beloved Son in Law John Jacob & to my Daughter Anne the now wife

of the said John of South River in Ann Arundell County afd. Planter ... and with the consent of of [sic] [blank] my wife I have Given & Granted ... unto said Jacob and Anne his wife a parte and parcell of the afd 400 a. of land...." (Anne Arundel County Land Records, Liber I H #1, ff. 47–9, quoted in, Doliante, *Maryland and Virginia Colonials,* 107).

31. F. Edward Wright, *Anne Arundel County Church Records of the 17th and 18th Centuries,* Westminster, Maryland: Family Line, 1994), 25.

32. Hester Dorsey Richardson, *Side-lights on Maryland History: With Sketches of Early Maryland Families* (Baltimore: Williams and Wilkins, 1913), 356, http://books.google.com/books?id=6vkMAAAAYAAJ&pg.

33. "Soils prime for tobacco planting and a close proximity to water brought colonists to the land now known as London Town in Edgewater, Maryland. Plantations were scattered along the shore, allowing for boats to dock and exchange tobacco for goods brought from England. The land known as 'Scorton' was granted to George Westall from Lord Baltimore in 1658, which was then sold to William Burgess, Sr., in 1673" (Lisa E. Plumley and Erin N. Cullen, "A London Town Burial: A Study in Past and Present Customs," *Maryland Archeology* 40, no. 2, 9–18 (September 2004): 9, http://losttowns.com/publications/articles/londontownburial.pdf).

34. Elise Greenup Jourdan, *Early Families of Southern Maryland,* vol. 4 (Westminster, MD: Heritage, 2007), 236, http://books.google.com/books?id=u9JMSeAgLfcC&pg.

35. Wright, *Anne Arundel County Church Records of the 17th and 18th Centuries,* 2.

36. Jourdan, *Early Families of Southern Maryland,* 238, http://books.google.com/books?id=u9JMSeAgLfcC&pg.

37. Elise Greenup Jourdan, comp., *Colonial Settlers of Prince George's County Maryland* (Westminster, MD: Heritage, 2009), 181.

38. "Compiled Service Records of Soldiers Who Served in the American Army During the Revolutionary War" (electronic record), M881, "Compiled Service Records of Soldiers Who Served in the American Army During the Revolutionary War, Compiled 1894–ca. 1912, Documenting the Period 1775–1784," Record Group 93, National Archives and Records Administration. http://www.footnote.com/image/17156093.

39. Janina M. Winegard Hawley, comp., *The Ancestors and Descendants of William Carl Hawley* (2008), 1.

40. "— to son John Hally, my Negro boy Frank and a feather bed and furniture.

— to son Samuel Hally, my Negro boy Harry and a feather bed and furniture.

— to son James Burch Hally, Negro boy Will and a feather bed and furniture.

— to dau. Bathsheba Hally, Negro boy Leonard, a feather bed and furniture and a mare called the white footed mare.

— to dau. Elizabeth Hally, my Negro named Jane and a feather bed and furniture.

— I have not mentioned my loving dau. Sarah Gordon from any disrespect or less affection, but owing only to my having heretofore given her on and since her marriage a part of my estate that is equal at least to what will be the part of my other children" (Jourdan, comp., *Prince George's County, Md., Will Book No. 1 (1698–1770),* 617–8).

41. Elinor J. Britton Hartstone, *Family Connections: Some Southern Ancestors and Allied Lines* (Family, 1991), 118.

42. Family history written by Sarah Eleanor Bell, granddaughter of Martha Ellen Halley.

43. Ibid.

44. Currituck County Land Record, Book 9 (Currituck, NC), 307.

45. Annie Elizabeth Bell, born 12 October 1866; Martha Edna Bell, born 1 March 1868; James Oscar Bell, born 28 January 1870; Mary Susan Bell, born 27 November 1872; Charles Edgar Bell, born 25 September 1873; Sarah Eleanor Bell, born 27 June 1875; William Benjamin Bell, born 8 August 1877; George Thomas Bell, born 16 June 1879; Laura Bell, born 10 August 1881; James Nathaniel Bell, born 5 September 1883.

46. Getha Gina Bell, *The Bells in U.S.A. and Allied Families, 1650–1977* (Ann Arbor, MI: Edwards Brothers, 1977), 358.

47. *(Milledgeville) Georgia Journal,* October 23, 1831, 369.

48. Jeannette Holland Austin, *The Georgia Frontier: Colonial Families to the Revolutionary War Period* (Baltimore: Genealogical, 2005), 47, http://books.google.com/books?id=0Ojje2nFwisC&source=gbs_navlinks_s.

49. North Carolina State Archives, NC Family Records Collection, James and Jane Ross Smith Family Bible Records 1748–1949, http://digitalstatelibnc.cdmhost.com/cdm4/document.php?CISOROOT=/p15012coll1&CISOPTR=6194&REC=1.

50. Abstracts of Wills and Inventories, Fairfax County, Virginia, 1742–1801, 9, http://search.ancestry.com/Browse/bookview.aspx?dbid=49017&iid=FLHG_AbstWilInvFairfaxCntyVA-0013&desc=William+Smith+from+1751-1751.

51. Wilmer Lane Smith, *Peter Smith of Westmoreland County, Virginia (Died 1741), and Some Descendants* (Chelsea, MI: 1996), 33–34.

52. Ibid.

53. Ibid., 44.

54. I have copies of land grants for Jonah Lynch from William Earl of Craven in 1682: Captain Johnson Lynch from Governor Robert Gifford, 27 July 1711; and to Thomas Lynch from King George II in 1732.

55. "7th of June 1712 — An Act for the Appointing a Ferry Over the Eastern Branch of the T of Cooper River, and for the Making of Causways, Landings and Bridges, for the Better Conveniency of Said Ferry.

"For the more easy conjunction of the forces of this Colony, in times of war and danger, and for the conveniency of business and commerce,

I. *Be it enacted,* by his Excellency, the Palatine, and the rest of the true and absolute Lords and Proprietors of this Province, by and with the advice and consent of the rest of the members of the General Assembly, now met at Charlestown for the south-west part of this Province, and by the authority of the same, That with all convenient speed, after the ratification of this Act, there be laid out, made and kept clear, one common highway, in the nearest and most convenient place, from the broad path that leads from the plantation commonly called Clowter's plantation, to the Honorable Sir Nathaniel Johnson's plantation, called Silk Hope; the said path or highway to lead through Captain Johnson Lynch his swamp, lying on the eastern branch of the T of Cooper river, over to the landing of Anthony Bonneau, that plantation being the most convenient for crossing the said river, in the road to the ferry on the western branch of the said T of Cooper river; and that the said high road be laid out by the advice and direction of the commissioners hereafter named, or any three of them" (David J. Mccord, ed., *The Statutes at Large of South Carolina: Acts Relating to Roads, Bridges and Ferries*, vol. 9 (Columbia: State of South Carolina, 1841), 20).

56. *South Carolina Historical and Genealogical Magazine* 40, no. 75.

57. Last name unknown.

58. Harold Havelock Kynett, D.G. Brinton, Samuel Worcester Butler, eds., *Medical and Surgical Reporter* 22 (January–June 1870) (Philadelphia: 1870), 400, http://books.google.com/books?id=GjqgAAAAMAAJ&pg.

59. *Terrell County (GA) Newspaper*, "Awful Calamity," April 7, 1870. It's strange to find stuff like this.

60. Stewart County Ordinary Court Marriage Book, Georgia Department of Archives and History, Microfilm Drawer 37, Box 37.

Appendix C: The Search for Kindred Carter's Wife

1. Margaret M. Hoffmann, *1741–1759 Abstracts of Deeds Northampton County, North Carolina Public Registry, Deed Book One and Deed Book Two*, (Weldon, NC: Roanoke News Co., 1983).

2. After I found this, I thought that I had uncovered an important piece of new information only to find later that Dr. Barry Hayes had discovered it at least 20 years earlier.

3. Browne, Walter, Bertie County, October 17, 1735, February Court, 1735, Son: Josiah Browne ("dwelling plantation"); Cousin: Jesse Drake; Wife: Mary Browne ("plantation on the South side of Cattawaske marsh"); Executrix: Mary Browne; Witnesses: Jesse Browne, John Battle, John Browne; Clerk of the Court: John Wynn; Remarks: The date of probate is evidently incorrect, as the will is dated eight months later. Probably this date was 1736, as the will was recorded March 2, 1736 (John Bryan Grimes, *Abstract of North Carolina Wills Compiled from Original and Recorded Wills in the Office of the Secretary of State* (Raleigh: E.M. Uzzel, 1910), 52).

Appendix D: The Bethune Lineage in Scotland

1. Mrs. John A. Weisse, *A History of the Bethune Family*, "Translated from the French of Andre du Chesne, with Additions from Family Records and Other Available Sources, Together with a Sketch of the Faneuil Family, with Whom the Bethunes Have Become Connected in America" (New York: Trow's, 1884), 11–12, http://www.archive.org/stream/historyofbethune1884weis/historyofbethune1884weis_djvu.txt.

2. James Toshach Clark, ed,. *Genealogical Collections Concerning Families in Scotland made by Walter MacFarlane, 1750–1751*, vol. 1 (Edinburgh: University Press for the Scottish History Society, 1900), 18–19, http://books.google.com/books?id=Gv0cAAAAMAAJ&pg=PA1&dq.

3. Bishop John Lesly, Scottish historian and philosopher (September 29, 1527–May 31, 1596).

4. Aberbrothock, now Arbroath, is the largest town in the council area of Angus in Scotland. It is on the North Sea coast, around 16 miles ENE of Dundee and 45 miles SSW of Aberdeen.

5. *Publications of the Scottish History Society* 33 (Edinburgh: Printed at the University Press by T. and A. Constable for the Scottish History Society, 1900), 20.

6. Walter Wood, *The East Nuek of Fife: Its History and Antiquities, Geology, Botany, and Natural History in General* (Edinburgh: Oliver & Boyd, 1862), 261.

7. Toshach, *Genealogical Collections Concerning Families in Scotland*, 5.

8. Ibid.

9. Ibid., 6.

10. Wood, *The East Nuek of Fife*, 261.

11. Lieut. Col John MacInnes, *The Brave Sons of Skye* (Edinburgh: Eyre and Spottiswoode, 1899), 165; http://books.google.com/books?id=IRo9AAAAYAAJ&dq.

12. Thomas Whyte, *An Historical and Genealogical Account of the Bethunes of the Island of Sky* (reprint) (London: A. Chilver for Alfred A. Bethune-Baker, 1893), 9.

13. Ibid., 34.

14. Ibid., 35.

Appendix E: Loyal "Regulators" Association

1. William A. Saunders, ed., Colonial and State Records of North Carolina, *Association by Edmund Fanning et al. Concerning the Actions of the Regulators Fanning, Edmund, 1739–1818; Nash, Francis, 1720–1777; Martin, Alexander, 1740–1807; Et Al.* (1770, vol.

8), 273–275, http://webcache.googleusercontent.com/search?q=cache:http://docsouth.unc.edu/csr/index.html/document/csr08-0164

Appendix G: Wills

1. The will of Dr. Samuel Browne of Isle of Wight Co, Virginia, dated October 17, 1739, and proved June 23, 1740, was transcribed by Sally Moore Koestler.

2. South Carolina Department of Archives and History, S108093: South Carolina Will Transcripts (Microcopy No 9), Clinkscales, Francis of Anderson District, Will Transcript, Mss Will: Vol. 1, Page 74; Estate Packet: Pkg. No. 140, http://www.archivesindex.sc.gov/onlinearchives/ViewImage.aspx?imageNumber=S108093000400605000a.jpg&recordId=308909.

3. Freda Reid Turner, comp., *Green County, Georgia, Wills, 1786–1877*, vol. 1 (Fernandina: Wolfe), 140–141.

4. Charles Fleming McIntosh, *Brief Abstracts of Norfolk County, Virginia, Wills, 1710–1753* (Heritage Books, 1922), 118.

5. Chattahoochee County Ordinary Court, Will Book A, 1854–1935, pp. 97–99, Georgia Department of Archives and History, Microfilm Drawer 144, Box 70.

6. South Carolina Department of Archives and History, S108093: Brownlee, James, of Ninety Six District, Will Typescript (Mss Will: Estate Record Book 1, Page 218; Estate Packet: Box 105, Pkg 2676, http://Www.Archivesindex.Sc.Gov/Onlinearchives/Viewimage.Aspx?Imagenumber=S108093000400605000a.jpg&recordId=308909.

7. Talbot County Court of the Ordinary, Will Book A, 1828–56, p. 97. Microfilm Drawer 123, Box 35.

BIBLIOGRAPHY

Abercrombie, Janice L., and Richard Slatten. *Virginia Revolutionary "Publick" Claims*. Vol. 2. Athens, GA: Iberian Pub. Co., 1992.

Abstracts of Deeds, Edgecombe Precinct, Edgecombe County, North Carolina, 1732–1758. Weldon: Roanoke News, 1976.

Abstracts of Wills and Inventories, Fairfax County, Virginia, 1742–1801. http://search.ancestry.com/Browse/bookview.aspx?dbid=49017&iid=FLHG_AbstWillnvFairfaxCntyVA-0013&desc=William+Smith+from+1751–1751.

Albritton, Bobby G. *Albrittons of the Second Millennium*. Rev. ed. Alpharetta, GA: Balbritt, 2003. http://contentdm.lib.byu.edu/cdm4/document.php?CISOROOT=/FH36&CISOPTR=77356&REC=1.

Anne Arundel County, Maryland. Land Records, Liber I H #1, ff.

Anson County, North Carolina. Will Book 2.

Ashe, Samuel A'Court. *Biographical History of North Carolina from Colonial Times to the Present*. Vol. 4. Greensboro, NC: Charles L.Van Noppen, 1906. http://books.google.com/books?id=EdKLfhkJIWEC&vq.

Austin, Jeannette Holland. *The Georgia Frontier: Colonial Families to the Revolutionary War Period*. Baltimore: Genealogical, 2005. http://books.google.com/books?id=0Ojje2nFwisC&source=gbs_navlinks_s.

Austin, John Osborne. *The Genealogical Dictionary of Rhode Island*. Albany, NY: 1887.

"Awful Calamity." *Terrell County (GA) Newspaper*, April 7, 1870.

Baldwin Ordinary Court. Marriage Book A, 1806–1842.

Barksdale, Captain John A. *Barksdale Family History and Genealogy*. Richmond: William Byrd Press, 1940.

Beadles, Zada Wade. *The Wades: The History of a Family, Dealing with the Kith and Kin of Zachary and Mary Hatton Wade, Their Descendants and Related Lines, Male and Female, in Maryland, Virginia, Tennessee, South Carolina, North Carolina, and Other States*. Cairo, IL: Published by the Author, 1963. http://books.google.com/books?id=7QlaAAAAMAAJ&q.

Beekman, George Crawford. *Early Dutch Settlers of Monmouth County, New Jersey*. Higginson, 1901.

Bell, Getha Gina. *The Bells in U.S.A. and Allied Families, 1650–1977*.

Bell, Mary Best. *Colonial Bertie County, North Carolina, Deed Books A-H 1720–1757*. Easley, SC: Southern Historical Press, 1963.

Bertie County, North Carolina, Records, Deed Book G.

Blinn, John, and William H. Egle (M.D.), eds. *Pennsylvania Second Series Archives*. Vol. 9. Harrisburg, PA: Lane S. Hart, 1880. http://books.google.com/books?id=PnMFAAAAQAAJ&pg=PA11&dq.

Boddie, John Bennett. *Seventeenth Century Isle of Wight County, Virginia: A History of the County of Isle of Wight*. Westminster: Heritage Books, 1938.

___. *Southside Virginia Families*. Vol. 1. Richmond: Genealogical, 1966.

___. *Southside Virginia Families*. Vol. 2 Baltimore: Genealogical, 1991.

Brayton, John Anderson. *Colonial Families of Surry and Isle of Wight*. Memphis: J.A. Brayton, 1999.

Browne, William Hand, ed. *Proceedings of the Council of Maryland, 1693–1697*. Vol. 20. Baltimore: Maryland Historical Society, 1900.

Burk, John. *The History of Virginia: From Its First Settlement to the Present Day*. Vol. 2. Petersburg: Dickson & Pescud, 1805. http://books.google.com/books?id=ujcSAAAAYAAJ&pg=PR42&dq=%22lord+arlington%22+virginia&hl=en&ei=UVXMTNzVBMKAlAeRsf3nCA&sa=X&oi=book_result&ct=result&resnum=8&ved=0CE4Q6AEwBw#v=onepage&q=%22lord%20arlington%22%20&f=false.

Carter, Jimmy. *Family of Wiley Carter 1798- 1998*. Atlanta: Darby, 1998.

___. *An Hour Before Daylight*. New York: Simon and Schuster, 2001.

Chapman, Blanche Adams. *Wills and Administrations of *Isle of Wight County, Virginia, 1647–1800*. Baltimore: Genealogical, 1975.

Chattahoochee County (GA). Confederate Pensions and Records. "H.M. Gordy." Georgia Department of Archives and History (Morrow, GA), Microfilm Drawer 271, Box 70.

Chattahoochee County (GA) Ordinary Court. Marriage Book A, 1854–1907.

Chattahoochee County (GA) Ordinary Court. Will Book A, 1854–1935. Georgia Department of Archives and History (Murray, GA), Microfilm Drawer 144, Box 70.

Christian, John T. *A History of the Baptists*. Vol. 2. 1922. Reprint Nashville, TN: Broadman Press, 1926.

Clark, James Toshach, ed. *Genealogical Collections Concerning Families in Scotland*. "Made by Walter MacFarlane, 1750–1751." Vol. 1. Edinburgh: University Press for the Scottish History Society, 1900. http://books.google.com/books?id=Gv0cAAAAMAAJ&pg=PA1&dq.

Clark, Walter, ed. The State Records of North Carolina. Vol. 22 Miscellaneous, *Payroll for David Hart's Company of the Orange County Militia, 1771*. (Goldsboro, NC: Nash Brothers Book and Job Printers, 1907). http://ia700407.us.archive.org/23/items/staterecordsofno221nort/staterecordsofno221nort.pdf.

Colonial Churches in the Original Colony of Virginia. 2nd ed. Richmond: Southern Churchmen Company, 1908.

Colonial Dames of America. *Ancestral Records and Portraits*. Vol. 1. Chapter 1, "A Compilation from the Archives of the Colonial Dames of America." New York: Grafton, 1910. http://books.google.com/books?id=hYl2AAAAMAAJ&dq.

Colonial Records of the State of Georgia: Proceedings and Minutes of the Governor and Council from August 6, 1771, February 13, 1782. Atlanta: Franklin-Turner, 1907.

Columbia County (GA) Superior Court. Deed Book O, 1807–1818. Georgia Department of Archives and History (Morrow, GA), Drawer 91, Box 14.

"Compiled Service Records of Confederate Soldiers Who Served in Organizations from the State of Georgia." Electronic Record. M266. "Carded Records Showing Military Service of Soldiers Who Fought in Confederate Organizations, Compiled 1903–1927, Documenting the Period 1861–1865." Record Group 109, National Archives and Records Administration.

"Compiled Service Records of Confederate Soldiers Who Served in Organizations from the State of Louisiana." Electronic Record. M320. "Carded Records Showing Military Service of Soldiers Who Fought in Confederate Organizations, Compiled 1903–1927, Documenting the Period 1861–1865." Record Group 109, National Archives and Records Administration.

"Compiled Service Records of Confederate Soldiers Who Served in Organizations from the State of South Carolina." Electronic Record. M267. "Carded Records Showing Military Service of Soldiers Who Fought in Confederate Organizations, Compiled 1903–1927, Documenting the Period 1861–1865." Record Group 109, National Archives and Records Administration.

"Compiled Service Records of Soldiers Who Served in the American Army During the Revolutionary War." Electronic Record. M881. "Compiled Service Records of Soldiers Who Served in the American Army During the Revolutionary War, Compiled 1894–ca. 1912, Documenting the Period 1775–1784." Record Group 93, National Archives and Records Administration.

Connor, Robert Digges Wimberly. *Cornelius Harnett: An Essay in North Carolina History*. Raleigh: Edwards and Broughton, 1909. http://books.google.com/books?id=ZslEAAAAIAAJ&dq.

Cook, Fred J. "Allan McLane: Unknown Hero of the Revolution." *American Heritage* 7, no. 6 (October 1956).

Cornell, Rev. John. *Genealogy of the Cornell Family: Being an Account of the Decendants of Thomas Cornell of Portsmouth, R.I.* New York: T.A. Wright, 1902. http://digital.library.cornell.edu/cgi/t/text/pageviewer-idx?c=ezra;cc=ezra;rgn=full%20text;idno=ezra000;didno=ezra000;node=ezra000%3A3;view=image;seq=7.

Council of the State Virginia. *Journals of the Council of the State of Virginia*. Richmond: Division of Purchase and Printing, 1931.

Cox, Rev. Henry Miller. *The Cox Family in America: A History and Genealogy of the Older Branches of the Family from the Appearance of Its First Representative in This Country in 1610*. New York: Published by the Author, 1912.

Crane, Elaine Forman. *Killed Strangely: The Death of Rebecca Cornell*. Ithaca, NY: Cornell University Press, 2002. http://books.google.com/books?id=RIg6y0HuKUsC&pg.

Currer-Briggs, Noel. *The Carters of Virginia: Their English Ancestry*. Sussex, England: Phillimore, 1979.

Davis, Eliza Timberlake. *Surry County Records, Surry County, Virginia, 1652–1684*. Baltimore: Genealogical, 1980.

Davis, Virginia Lee Hutcheson. *Tidewater Virginia Families*. (Baltimore, MD: Genealogical Publishing, 1989.

Dawson, Joseph W. *Record of the Dawson Family from 1743 to 1900*. Kenneth H. Thomas, Jr., Collection, Box 2, Carter Presidential Library, Atlanta, Georgia. Note: The family history was written by Joseph Dawson in 1875 and updated by Walter Ernest Dawson 26 August 1900.

"Death Results from Injuries." *Americus (GA) Times Recorder*, September 5, 1903. Section 4.

Dicken, Emma, comp. *Our Burnley Ancestors and Allied Families*. New York: Hobson Book Press, 1946.

Dobson, David. *Directory of Scots in the Carolinas, 1680–1830*. Baltimore: Genealogical, 1986.

Documents Relating to the Colonial History of the State of New Jersey. Vol. 21, *Marriage Records, 1665–1800*. Patterson, NJ.: Press Printing, 1900. http://books.google.com/books?id=PZRuAAAAMAAJ&pg.

Doherty, Frank J. *The Settlers of the Beekman Patent, Dutchess County, New York: An Historical and Genealogical Study of All the 18th Century Settlers in the Patent*. 6 vols. Pleasant Valley, NY: Frank J. Doherty, 1990–2001. Accessed through online database: NewEnglandAncestors.org. New England Historic Genealogical Society, 2003.

Doliante, Sharon J. *Maryland and Virginia Colonials: Genealogies of Some Colonial Families*. Baltimore: Genealogical, 1991. http://books.google.com/books?id=1KvkiaQks-kC&pg.

Edgefield County Historical Society, comp. *Genealogy of Nicholson and Allied Families*. Edgefield Advertiser, 1944.

Edwards, Ruth Dudley, and Bridgette Hourican. *An Atlas of Irish History*. 3rd ed. New York: Routledge, 2005.

Elliott, Dollye McAlister. "Captain Thomas Carter of 'Barford,' Lancaster County, of Virginia: A Second View." *Northern Neck of Virginia Historical Magazine*, December 1987.

Ellis, Franklin. *History of Monmouth County, New Jersey*. Philadelphia: R.T. Peck, 1885.

"Fatal Affair at Arlington." *Americus (GA) Times Recorder*, September 4, 1903. Section 4.

Fitch, William Edward (M.D.). *Some Neglected History of North Carolina: Being an Account of the Revolution of the Regulators and of the Battle of Alamance, the First Battle of the American Revolution*. New York: Published by the Author, 1914.

Fleet, Beverley. *Virginia Colonial Abstracts*. Vol. 12. Baltimore: Genealogical, 2006. http://books.google.com/books?id=0WmgfvygR78C&lpg=PA99&ots=xWnEWaKLj6&dq=lancaster%20record%20book&pg=PP4#v=onepage&q&f=true.

Gaines, L.P. *History of the Gaines Family: One Line from 1620 to the Present Time, 1918*. Revised by Mary Kathryn Gaines Cooley Korstian. Rome, GA: Brazelton-Wallis, 1973.

Garden, Alexander. *Anecdotes of the Revolutionary War in America, with Sketches of Character of Persons the Most Distinguished, in the Southern States for Civil and Military Service*. Charleston: A.E. Miller, 1822.

Glencross, Reginald M. "Virginia Gleanings in England." *Virginia Magazine of History and Biography* 29. Richmond: House of the Society, 1921. http://books.google.com/books?id=6tQRAAAAYAAJ&dq.

Green County, Georgia. Land Records. Books FF, GG, and HH, 1816–1818. Vol. 3. N.p.: Bory, 2006.

Grimes, John Bryan. *Abstract of North Carolina Wills Compiled from Original and Recorded Wills in the Office of the Secretary of State*. Raleigh: E.M. Uzzel, 1910.

Gwynn, Zae Hargett. *Abstracts of the Records of Onslow County, North Carolina, 1734–1850*. Vol. 2. Onslow County, NC: Onslow County Court. http://books.google.com/books?id=W3AlAAAAMAAJ&q.

Hagler, Travis Jackson. *Bonner, Brown, Boswell Family History: Southeastern Alabama Era*. Huntsville, AL: T.J. Hagler, 1995.

Hallman, E.B. "Early Settlers in the Carolina Dutch Fork, 1744–1760." Master's thesis, Wofford College, 1944.

Hannah, Charles A. *The Scotch-Irish in America*. Vol. 2. New York and London: G.P. Putnam's Sons; Knickerbocker, 1902. http://books.google.com/books?id=KHeAAAAAIAAJ&dq.

Hardin, W. Jake. *The Wiley Carter Story*. Avera, GA: 1977.

Hartstone, Elinor J. Britton. *Family Connections: Some Southern Ancestors and Allied Lines*. Family Publications, 1991.

Hartz, Fred R., and Emilie K. Hartz. *Genealogical Abstracts from the (Milledgeville) Georgia Journal Newspaper, 1809–1840*. Vol. 1., *1809–1818, October 26, 1814*. Vidalia, GA: Gwendolyn Press, 1990.

Harvill, Dan O. *History of Mt. Zion Lutheran Church, 1938–1958*. http://files.usgwarchives.net/ga/macon/churches/mtzion.txt.

Hawley, Janina M. Winegard, comp. *The Ancestors and Descendants of William Carl Hawley*. Privately printed, 2008. https://dcms.lds.org/view/action/ieViewer.do?from_proxy=true&dps_pid=IE61810&dps_dvs=1329589183745-562&dps_pid=IE61810&change_lng=en.

Hay, Gertrude May Sloan. *Roster of Soldiers from North Carolina in the American Revolution*. Baltimore: Daughters of the American Revolution of North Carolina, 2000. http://books.google.com/books?id=CO-uEbXhl7IC&lpg=PR11&dq=Roster%20of%20North%20Carolina%20Soldiers%2C&pg=PA116#v=snippet&q=carter&f=false.

Hayes, Bascom Barry, comp. "The Descendants of John Carter (ca. 1574–1630), Vintner of London, in Virginia, North Carolina, and Georgia: The First Seven Generations." Unpublished, November 2010.

Helms, Gerald C., comp. *Tilman, George, and Jonathan Helms, Brothers, 1720–1881: History and Genealogy of the Helms Family*. NC: Published by the author and Jo Ann Stevenson, 1984.

Hemphill, James Calvin. *Men of Mark in South Carolina: A Collection of Biographies of Leading Men of the State*. Vol. 3. Washington, DC: Men of

Mark , 1906. http://books.google.com/books?id=0SsEAAAAYAAJ.

Henning, William Waller. *The Statutes at Large: Being a Collection of All the Laws of Virginia from the First Session of the Legislature in the Year 1619.* Vol. 2. New York: R & W. & G. Bartow, 1823.

History of North Carolina. Vol. 7. North Carolina Biography. Chicago and New York: Lewis, 1919. http://www.archive.org/stream/historyofnorthca06conn/historyofnorthca06conn_djvu.txt.

Hoffmann, Margaret M. *Northampton County, North Carolina, 1759–1808, Genealogical Abstracts of Wills, Will Bk 1.* Weldon, North Carolina: Roanoke News, 1975.

___. *1741–1759, Abstracts of Deeds, Northampton County, North Carolina Public Registry, Deed Book One and Deed Book Two.* Weldon, NC: Roanoke News Co., 1983.

Holcomb, B.H. *Petitions for Land from the South Carolina Council Journals.* Vol. 3, 1752–1753. Columbia, SC: SCMAR, 1997.

Holcomb, Brent H. *Mecklenburg Co. North County, Deed Abstracts, Book 3.* Baltimore, MD: Genealogical Publishing Company, 2009.

___. *Mecklenburg Co. North County, Deed Abstracts, Book 10.* Greenville: Southern Historical Press, 1981.

Hopkins, William Lindsay. *Isle of Wight County, Virginia Deeds, 1647–1719, Court Orders, 1693–1695, and Guardian Accounts, 1740–1767.* Richmond: GEN-N-DEX, 1993.

Hotten, John Camden, ed. *The Original Lists of Persons of Quality; Emigrants; Religious Exiles; Political Rebels; Serving Men Sold for a Term of Years; Apprentices; Children Stolen; Maidens Pressed; and Others who went from Great Britain to the American Plantations, 1600–1700.* London: John Camden Hotten, 1874. http://books.google.com/books?id=J5ULAAAAIAAJ&vq.

Hubert, Sarah Donelson. *Genealogy of Part of the Barksdale Family of America.* Atlanta: Franklin, 1895. http://contentdm.lib.byu.edu/cdm4/document.php?CISOROOT=/FH9&CISOPTR=90957&REC=3.

Hunter, C.L. *Sketches of Western North Carolina Historical and Biographical, Illustrating Principally the Revolutionary Period of Mecklenburg, Rowan, Lincoln and Adjoining Counties, Accompanied with Miscellaneous Information, Much of It Never Before Published.* Raleigh: Raleigh News Steam Job Print, 1887.

Hunting for Bears, comp. *Georgia Marriages, 1699–1944.* Provo, UT: Ancestry.com, 2004. http://search.ancestry.com/cgi-bin/sse.dll?db=gamarriages_ga&h=50818&ti=0&indiv=try&gss=pt&ssrc=pt_t11567819_p-439839327_g32768.

Isle of Wight County, Virginia, Deed Books 4 and 5.

Jenkins, Howard Malcolm, and George Overcash Seilhamer. *Memorial History of the City of Philadelphia from Its First Settlement to the Year 1895.* New York History, 1895. http://books.google.com/books?id=-lwUAAAAYAAJ.

Jolley, Robert L. *Descendants, Relatives, and Ancestors of Ida Lucille Moore.* Winnepeg: Robert L. Jolley, 2007. http://contentdm.lib.byu.edu/cdm4/document.php?CISOROOT=%2FFH37&CISOPTR=77045&REC=8&CISOBO.

Jones, Morgan D. *Brown Genealogy.* Privately printed, 1965.

Jourdan, Elise Greenup, comp. *Colonial Settlers of Prince George's County Maryland.* Westminster, MD: Heritage Books, 2009.

Jourdan, Elise Greenup. *Early Families of Southern Maryland.* Vol. 4. Westminster, MD: Heritage Books, 2007. http://books.google.com/books?id=u9JMSeAgLfcC&pg.

___. *Early Families of Southern Maryland.* Vol. 6. Heritage Books, 2007.

Karlsen, Carol F. *The Devil in the Shape of a Woman: Witchcraft in Colonial New England.* London: Norton, 1987.

Knight, Lucian. *Georgia's Roster of the Revolution: Containing a List of the States Defenders, Officers and Men, Soldiers and Sailors, Partisans and Regulars, Whether Enlisted from Georgia or Settled in Georgia After the Close of Hostilities: Compiled Under Authority of the Legislature from Various Sources, Including Official Documents, Both State and Federal, Certificates of Service, Land Grants, Pension Rolls, and Other Records.* Atlanta: Index, 1920.

Kynett, Harold Havelock, D.G. Brinton, and Samuel Worcester Butler, eds. *Medical and Surgical Reporter* 22 (January–June 1870). Philadelphia: 1870. http://books.google.com/books?id=GjqgAAAAMAAJ&pg.

Lancaster County, Virginia, Courthouse Records, Book 1: 1653–1757. As quoted in Currer-Briggs, *The Carters of Virginia.*

Lancaster County, Virginia. Deeds and Wills Book, 1654–1661.

Land Records of Prince George's County, Maryland, 1717–1726. Folio 692.

Laurens County, Georgia, Deed Books F and I.

Logan, Robert Archibald. "Highlanders from Skye, in North Carolina and Nova Scotia, 1771–1818." *Scottish Genealogist* 12, no. 4 (February 1966).

MacDonald, William, ed. *Select Charters and Other Documents Illustrative of American History, 1606–1775.* London: MacMillan, 1899.

MacInnes, (Lieut. Col.) John. *The Brave Sons of Skye.* Edinburgh: Eyre and Spottiswoode, 1899. http://books.google.com/books?id=IRo9AAAAYAAJ&dq.

Mackenzie, George Norbury. *Colonial Families of the*

United States of America in Which Is Given the History, Genealogy and Armorial Bearings of Colonial Families Who Settled in the American Colonies from the Time of the Settlement of Jamestown, 13th May, 1607, to the Battle of Lexington, 19th April, 1775. Vol. 6. Baltimore: Seaforth, 1917. http://books.google.com/books?id=J1tlAAAAMAAJ&pg.

Marriage and Death Abstracts from the Journal of Rev. Godfrey Dreher. http://www.palmettoroots.org/DreherJournal.html.

McCall, Howard H., comp. *Roster of Revolutionary Soldiers in Georgia.* Baltimore: Genealogical Com, 1996. http://books.google.com/books?id=VuXEmBJOP7gC&dq=%22john+nunn%22+revolutionary&source=gbs_navlinks_s.

McCall, Mrs. Howard H., comp. *Roster of Revolutionary Soldiers in Georgia.* Vol. 1. Baltimore: Genealogical, 1968.

McCartney, Martha W. *Virginia Immigrants and Adventurers, 1607–1635: A Biographical Dictionary.* Baltimore: Genealogical, 2007.

McCord, David J., ed. *The Statutes at Large of South Carolina: Acts Relating to Roads, Bridges and Ferries.* Vol. 9. Columbia: State of South Carolina, 1841.

McIntosh, Charles Fleming. *Brief Abstracts of Norfolk County, Virginia, Wills, 1710–1753.* Heritage Books, 1922.

Meriwether, Colyer. *Publications of the Southern History Association.* Vol. 2. Southern History Association, 1898. http://books.google.com/books?id=VtQRAAAAYAAJ&pg.

Meyer, Duane. *The Highland Scots of North Carolina, 1732–1776.* Chapel Hill: University of North Carolina Press, 1957, 1966. http://books.google.com/books?id=-5_7YVUyI1AC&pg=PA159&dq.

Miller, (Dr.) Joseph Lyon. "Captain Thomas Carter and His Descendants." *William and Mary Quarterly Historical Magazine* 17. Richmond: Whittey & Shepperson, 1909.

Minutes of Mecklenburg County, North Carolina, Court of Common Pleas and Quarter Sessions, 1790 April Session, Book 2.

Mittelberger, Gottlieb. *Gottlieb Mittelberger's Journey to Pennsylvania in the Year 1750 and Return to Germany in the Year 1754.* Translated by Carl Theo. Eben. Philadelphia: John Jos. McVey, 1898. http://books.google.com/books?id=4KYlAAAAMAAJ&dq.

Moffitt, Mrs. E.E. *The North Carolina Booklet: Great Events in North Carolina History.* Vol. 12. Raleigh: North Carolina Daughters of the American Revolution, 1912.

Murray, Alton. *Kindred Murrays: A Story of the Murrays Who Migrated from the Cape Fear River in North Carolina to the Province of Georgia in 1769 and Their Kindred.* St. Marys, GA: Alton J. Murray, 1981.

Muster Rolls and Other Records of Service of Maryland Troops in the American Revolution, 1775–1783. Published by Authority of the State, Under the Direction of the Maryland Historical Society, 1900.

Nelson, William, ed. *Archives of the State of New Jersey: Documents Relating to the Colonial History of the State of New Jersey.* First Series. Vol. 22, *Marriage Records, 1665–1800, Edited, with an Historical Introduction on the Early Marriage Laws of New Jersey, and the Precedents on Which They Were Founded.* Paterson, NJ: 1900.

___. *Documents Relating to the Colonial History of the State of New Jersey.* Vol. 21. Patterson, NJ: Press Printing, 1899.

New Jersey Archives. Early Colonial Marriages, 1665–1799. M, Part 1: 1735–1767. https://www.net1.state.nj.us/DOS/Admin/ArchivesDBPortal/ColonialMarriages.aspx.

New Jersey State Archives. *Annual Report of the State Historian.* Vol. 1. 1895.

Nichols, Carl W., and Ann Corum. *Palmetto Connections: The Kölle Family of Blaubeuren Germany.* http://www.palmettoroots.org/Family_Kelly.html.

North Carolina State Archives, North Carolina Family Records Collection. *James and June Ross Smith Family Bible Records, 1748–1949.* http://digitalstatelibnc.cdmhost.com/cdm4/document.php?CISOROOT=/p15012coll1&CISOPTR=6194&REC=1.

Nugent, Nell Marion. *Cavaliers and Pioneers: Abstracts of Virginia Land Patents and Grants, 1623–1666.* Vol. 6. Baltimore: Genealogical, 1963.

___. *Cavaliers and Pioneers: Abstracts of Virginia Land Patents and Grants.* Vol. 1. Richmond, 1934.

Onslow County, North Carolina, Deed Books A (December 8, 1808) and B.

O'Quinn, John Kenneth, Sr., comp. *O'Quinn Cousins, by the Dozens.* Spartanburg: Reprint Company, 1999.

Osgood, Herbert L. *The American Colonies in the Seventeenth Century.* Vol. 3, *Imperial Control: Beginnings of the System of Royal Provinces.* New York: Macmillan, 1907.

Palmetto Genealogy Association. *Family of Johann Heinrich Lybrand and Catharina Weiss.* http://www.palmettoroots.org/Family_Lybrand.html.

Peden, Henry C. *Colonial Maryland Soldiers and Sailors: 1634–1734.* Westminster, MD: Heritage Books, 2008. http://books.google.com/books?id=wSye_RpvnnwC&dq.

Peden, Henry C., Jr. *St. John's and St. George's Parish Registers, 1696–1851.* Westminster, MD: Heritage Books, 1987. http://books.google.com/books?id=yGzAVuYvnKgC&lpg=PP1&ots=z84Mvv_b0y&dq=St.%20John's%20and%20St.%20George's%20Parish%20Registers%201696-1851&pg=PP3#v=onepage&q=ramsey&f=false.

Plumley, Lisa E., and Erin N. Cullen. "A London Town Burial: A Study in Past and Present Customs." *Maryland Archeology* 40, no. 2 (September 2004), 9–18. http://losttowns.com/publications/articles/londontownburial.pdf.

Potts, Thomas Maxwell, and William John Potts. *Historical Collections Relating to the Potts Family in Great Britain and America.* Canonsburg, PA: Published by the Compiler, 1901. http://books.google.com/books?id=UusaAAAAYAAJ&pg.

Prince George County, Virginia. Ledger B.

Prince George's County, Maryland. Land Records. Liber C, folio 20 and 22.

Prince George's County, Maryland. Will Book No. 1: 1698–1770.

Publications of the Scottish History Society. Vol. 33. Edinburgh: University Press by T. and A. Constable for the Scottish History Society, 1900.

Quattlebaum, Alexander McQueen, Linda Grabeman and Stephen Hoffius, eds. *Clergymen and Chiefs: A Genealogy of the MacQueen and MacFarlane Families.* Charleston: South Carolina Historical Society, 1990. http://books.google.com/books?id=T-6oCucIvsMC&dq.

Randall, Daniel R. *A Puritan Colony in Maryland.* Edited by Herbert B. Adams. Johns Hopkins University Studies in Historical and Political Science, Fourth Series. Baltimore: Johns Hopkins University, 1886.

Reeves, Nell Seawright. *The Saga of the Seawrights.* Greenwood, SC: Bagpipe, 1987.

Revill, Janie, comp. *A Compilation of the Original List of Protestant Immigrants to South Carolina, 1763–1773.* Baltimore: Clearfield, 1939. Reprt. Genealogical, 1996.

"Revolutionary War Pension and Bounty-Land Warrant Application Files." Electronic Record. M804. "Case Files of Pension and Bounty-Land Warrant Applications Based on Revolutionary War Service, Compiled ca. 1800–ca. 1912, Documenting the Period ca. 1775–ca. 1900." Record Group 15, National Archives and Records Administration.

Richards, J.W. *The Baker and Gibson Families and Allied Lines.* Colorado Springs: 2001.

Richardson, Hester Dorsey. *Side-lights on Maryland History: With Sketches of Early Maryland Families.* Baltimore: Williams and Wilkins, 1913. http://books.google.com/books?id=6vkMAAAAYAAJ&pg.

Roberts, Gary Boyd. *Ancestors of American Presidents.* Boston: New England Historic Genealogical Society, 1990, 2009.

Rogers, N.K. *History of Chattahoochee County, Georgia.* Columbus, GA: Columbus Office Supply, 1933.

Saunders, William L., ed. The Colonial and State Records of North Carolina. Vol. VIII, 1769 to 1771, *Concerning the Actions of the Regulators* (Raleigh, NC: Joseph Daniels, 1890). http://webcache.googleusercontent.com/search?q=cache:http://docsouth.unc.edu/csr/index.html/document/csr08-0164.

Scaife, William Robert. *Joe Brown's Pets: The Georgia Militia, 1861–1865.* Macon, GA: Mercer University Press, 2004.

Scharf, John Thomas. *History of Delaware: 1609–1888: General History.* Vol. 1. Philadelphia: L.J. Richards, 1888.

Shearer, Augustus Hunt, ed. *Ireland by Patrick Weston Joyce and Scotland.* Vol. 12. Philadelphia: John D. Morris, 1906. http://books.google.com/books?id=y9XLBpnw8nwC&pg=PA166&lpg=PA166&dq#v=onepage&q&f=false.

Skordas, Gus. *The Early Settlers of Maryland: An Index to Names of Immigrants Compiled from Records of Land Patents, 1633–1680, in the Hall of Records, Annapolis, Maryland.* Baltimore: Genealogical, 1968. http://books.google.com/books?id=RSCnJFLE-90C&dq.

Smith, Samuel. *History of the Colony of Nova-Caesaria, or New Jersey: Containing, an Account of Its First Settlement, Progressive Improvements, the Original and Present Constitution, and Other Events, to the Year 1721, With Some Particulars Since, and a Short View of Its Present State.* Burlington, NJ: James Parker, 1877. http://books.google.com/books?id=VaUaAAAAYAAJ&pg.

Smith, Wilmer Lane. *Peter Smith of Westmoreland County, Virginia (Died 1741), and Some Descendants.* Chelsea, MI: 1996.

Snowden, Yates, ed. *History of South Carolina.* Vol. 5. Chicago and New York: Lewis, 1950.

South Carolina Council Journal, Vol. 21.

South Carolina Gazette (Columbia), December 4, 1752.

South Carolina Historical and Genealogical Magazine 40. Baltimore: Williams & Wilkins, 1939.

"The Southern Claims Commission." Electronic Record. M1407. "Southern Claims Commission." Roll 046, National Archives and Records Administration.

Stein, Charles Francis. *A History of Calvert County, Maryland.* 2nd ed. Baltimore: Calvert County Historical Society, 1961. http://books.google.com/books?cd=3&id=MWozAAAAIAAJ&dq.

Steiner, Bernard Christian, ed. *Maryland State Archives.* Vol. 41, *Proceedings of the Provincial Court of Maryland, 1658–1662.* Baltimore: Lord Baltimore Press, 1922.

Summer, George Leland. *Newberry County, South Carolina: Historical and Genealogical Annals.* Baltimore: Genealogical, 1950.

Sumter County Court of the Ordinary. Annual Returns, Vol. M, 1868–1870, Georgia Department of Archives and History (Morrow, GA), Microfilm Drawer 135, Box 35.

Symmes, Rev. Frank R. *History of the Old Tennent Church.* 2nd ed. Cranbury, NJ: George W. Burroughs, Printer, 1904.

Talbot County (GA) Court of the Ordinary. Marriage Records, Book A, 1828–1844. Georgia Department of Archives and History (Morrow, GA), Microfilm Drawer 123, Box 30.

___. Marriage Records, Book B, 1844–1867, Georgia Department of Archives and History (Morrow, GA), Microfilm Drawer 123, Box 30.

___. Sale Book Estates, Vol. C 1856–1875, pp. 411–412, Georgia Department of Archives and History (Morrow, GA), Microfilm Drawer 124, Box 19.

___. Voucher Book F, p. 628. Georgia Department of Archives and History (Morrow, GA), Microfilm Drawer 124, Box 11.

___. Will Book A, 1828–1856, p. 214. Georgia Department of Archives and History (Morrow, GA), Microfilm Drawer 123, Box 35.

Terrell, Edwin H. *Further Genealogical Notes of the Tyrrell-Terrell Family of Virginia and Its English and Norman-French Progenitors.* San Antonia: 1901. http://books.google.com/books?id=AVET AAAAYAAJ&dq=Genealogical%20Notes%20On %20The%20Tyrrell%20And%20Terrell%20 Family%20Of%20VirGinia&pg=PA39#v=one page&q&f=false.

Thurloe, John. State Papers, 1656: May (2 of 6). *A Collection of the State Papers of John Thurloe.* Vol. 5, *May 1656–January 1657* (1742). http://www.british-history.ac.uk/report.aspx?compid=55520.

Tilgman, Oswald. *History of Talbot County, Maryland, 1661–1861.* Vol. 1. Baltimore: Williams and Wilkins, 1915. http://books.google.com/books? id=nGYlAAAAMAAJ&dq.

Timberlake, Davis, Eliza. *Surry County Records, Surry County, Virginia, 1652–1684.* Baltimore: Genealogical, 1980.

Torbert, Robert Ellington. *The Gordy's of Georgia.* 1994.

Turner, Freda Reid, comp. *Green County, Georgia Wills 1786—1877.* Vol. 1. Fernandina, FL: Wolfe Pub., 1998

Tyler, Lyon Gardiner, ed. *Encyclopedia of Virginia Biography.* Vol 1. New York: Lewis, 1915. http:// books.google.com/books?id=UCgSAAAAYAAJ& dq=%22Thomas%20Godwin%20%22%20%20 virginia&pg=PA243#v=onepage&q&f=false.

Virginia Colonial Abstracts. Baltimore: Genealogical, 2006.

Walters, Beth Murray. *Murray Lineage.* Privately printed, 1983.

Warfield, Joshua Dorsey. *The Founders of Anne Arundel and Howard Counties, Maryland: A Genealogical and Biographical Review from Wills, Deeds and Church Records.* Baltimore: Kohn & Polloch, 1905. http://books.google.com/books? id=vgINAAAAYAAJ&dq.

Warner, Charles. *Hoskins of Virginia and Related Families.* Tappahannock, VA: Charles Warner, 1971.

Warner, Charles W.H. "Barford Plantation and the Thomas Carters." *Northern Neck of Virginia Historical Magazine,* December 1987.

Warren County, Georgia, Court of the Ordinary. Marriage Book, Vol. 1, 1848–1873. Georgia Department of Archives and History (Murray, GA), Microfilm Drawer 104, Box 14.

___. Marriage Book, 1811–1825. Georgia Department of Archives and History (Murray, GA), Microfilm Drawer 31, Box 56.

___. Marriage Records, 1824–1835. Georgia Department of Archives and History (Murray, GA), Microfilm Drawer 104, Box 13.

Waters, Henry Fitz-Gilbert. *The New England Historical and Genealogical Register.* Vol. 71. Boston: New England Historic Genealogical Society, 1917.

Weeks, Daniel J. *Not for Filthy Lucre's Sake: Richard Saltar and the Antiproprietary Movement in East New Jersey, 1665–1707.* http://books.google.com/ books?id=FM_BrMaXR2kC&pg=PA319&dq=%2 2blind+tax%22+cox&hl=en&ei=0bSiT MDGPMH78AbHk8ifCg&sa=X&oi=book_re sult&ct=result&resnum=1&ved=0CCwQ6AEwA A#v=onepage&q=%22blind%20tax%22%20cox &f=false.

Weisse, Mrs. John A. *A History of the Bethune Family.* "Translated from the French of Andre du Chesne, with Additions from Family Records and Other Available Sources, Together with a Sketch of the Faneuil Family, with Whom the Bethunes Have Become Connected in America." New York: Trow's, 1884. http://www.archive.org/stream/his toryofbethune1884weis/historyofbethune1884wcis _djvu.txt.

Wells, Carol. *Edgefield County, South Carolina: Deed Books 19, 20, 21, and 22.* Westminster, MD: Heritage Books, 2007. http://books.google.com/ books?id=GYCpZqXaW48C&pg=PA98&lpg=PA 98&dq.

Wheeler, Jean F. *Malachi Dawson Family History.* Collection of Kenneth Thomas, Box 2. Carter Presidential Library, Atlanta, Georgia.

Whitehead, William A., ed. *Archives of the State of New Jersey,* First Series. Vol. 3. 1703–1709. Newark: Daily Advertiser Printing House, 1881.

___. *Documents Relating to the Colonial History of the State of New Jersey.* Vol. 2, *1687–1703.* Newark, NJ: Daily Advertiser Printing, 1881. http://books. google.com/books?id=WkwOAAAAIAAJ&pg.

Whyte, Thomas. *An Historical and Genealogical Account of the Bethunes of the Island of Sky.* Edinburgh: Neill and Company 1778. Reprt., London: A. Chilver for Alfred A. Bethune-Baker, 1893.

Wilkes County. Georgia. Deed Books A—VV, 1784–1806.

Williams, Ruth Smith, and Margarette Glenn Griffin. *Abstracts of the Wills of Edgecombe County, North Carolina, 1733–1856*. Rocky Mount, NC: Joseph W. Watson, 1980.

Winborne, Benjamin Brodie. *The Colonial and State Political History of Hertford County.* "Issue 3." Murfreesboro. NC: Edwards T. Broughton, 1906.

Wiseman, Eugene M. *The Wiseman Family and Allied Lines*. Vol. 1. Franklin, NC : Genealogy, 1991. http://books.google.com/books?id=Fdlf AAAAMAAJ&q.

Witherspoon, Robert. *Witherspoon Genealogies*. Quoted in Charles A. Hannah, *The Scotch-Irish in America* (vol. 2). New York and London: G.P. Putnam's Sons, Knickerbocker, 1902. http://books.google.com/books?id=KHeAAAAAIA AJ&dq.

Wood, Walter. *The East Nuek of Fife: Its History and Antiquities, Geology, Botany, and Natural History in General*. Edinburgh: Oliver & Boyd, 1862.

Wright, F. Edward. *Anne Arundel County Church Records of the 17th and 18th Centuries*, Westminster. MD: Family Line Publications.

___. *Maryland Calendar of Wills, 1774–1777*. Vol. 16. Westerminster, MD: Family Line publications, 1994.

Wulfick, Dorothy Ford. *Marriages of Some Virginia Residents*. Boston: New England Historic Genealogical Society, 2009.

Wyatt, Kristen. "Confederate Uniform Is Rescued." Associated Press. In *Deseret News* [Salt Lake City, UT], April 20, 2002.

Wyse, Frederick Calhoun, Jr. *History of the Wise and Wyse Families of South Carolina*. Revised by Sybil and Wallace Harmon. Wolfe City, TX: Herington, 1992.

Ziegler, J.L. *Authentic History of Donegal Presbyterian Church, Located in East Donegal Township, Lancaster Co., Pa.* F. McManus, Jr., 1902. http://www.archive.org/stream/authentichistory00zieg/authentichistory00zieg_djvu.txt.

INDEX

Abbeville 70, 71, 72, 78, 79, 80, 81, 82, 178
Abbot, Cato 59
Albemarle County 7, 113
Albrighton, Francis 36
Albritton, George 36, 116
Albritton, James 36, 115, 116
Albritton, Martha 36, 113, 115, 116
Albritton, Matthew 36, 116
Albritton, Ralph 36, 115
Albritton, Thomas 36, 115
Alexander, Mary 100
Almy, Christopher 54
Almy, Elizabeth 54
Almy, William 52
Annapolis 144, 149, 158
Ansley, Abel 58, 177
Ansley, Ann 43, 58, 60, 70
Ansley, James 58
Ansley, Joseph 58
Ansley, Mary 55, 58
Ansley, Rebecca 55, 58
Ansley, Thomas 55, 56, 57, 58
Ansley, William 55, 58
Appomattox 8, 38, 44, 61, 73, 102, 123, 126
Arnold, Benedict 62
Athel 145

Bacon, Nathaniel 21, 22, 39
Bailey, Teresa 152, 159
Baliol 120
Barcroft, Charles 13
Barksdale, Collier 65, 66
Barksdale, Lucy 66
Barksdale, William 44, 62, 65
Barlowe, Audrey 52, 53
Barnett, Jane 100
Battle, John 19, 36, 37
Bay Tree Neck 11, 12
Beale, Ninian 147, 148
Beall, Mary 147, 148
Beaton, Martin 121
Beckwith, Hansel 59

Belfast 74, 75, 76, 77, 79, 80
Belk, Ellen 160
Bell, Charles A. 151
Bell, Laura 152, 162
Bell, Sarah Eleanor 140, 151, 152, 162
Bell, William Henry 151, 152, 162
Bell, Willie 152, 162
Bennett, Edward 140, 141
Bennett, Richard 141, 142
Benthall, Joseph 35, 36, 39
Bertie County 7, 34, 35, 36, 37, 39, 40, 166, 167
Bertie Precinct 7
Bethune, Alexander de 170
Bethune, Angus 171
Bethune, Archibald 170
Bethune, Colin 119, 120, 121, 171
Bethune, Ferquhard 171
Bethune, John 170, 171
Bethune, Laughlin 120
Bethune, Martin 121, 122
Bethune, Sarah 113, 119, 122
Bickley, Anna Barbara 130, 136
Bigger, Elizabeth 143
Bigger, James 143
Bigger, John 140, 143
Billender Oliver 78
Bishop, Greer 117
Blackbeard 114
Bladen County 66
Bland, Edward 11, 18, 182
Blessing (ship) 157
Boage, Captain John 143
Boonesborough 76, 77, 79, 80, 82
Boswell, Marjory 170
Bounty Act 80
Brandywine 139, 155
Brewer, Sarah Ridgely 144
Brig Lord Dungannon 79
Brightwell, Samuel 103
Bristoe Campaign 61, 73, 137
Broadmouth Creek 72
Brocas, William 13, 15
Brown, Brady Mitchell 107, 108

Brown, Hollinger 106, 107, 108, 109
Brown, John 35, 63, 79, 106, 107, 174, 178
Brown, Mary Marcus 103, 106, 107, 109
Brown, Millie 107
Brown, Walter 36, 167, 168, 174, 175
Browne, Dr. Samuel 34, 35, 36, 37, 174
Browne, Sarah 19, 36, 37, 38, 39, 168, 175
Brownlee, George 77, 79, 82
Brownlee, James 74, 79, 180
Brownlee, John 79, 178
Bryn, James 35
Bucher, Ann 78
Bucher, Hans Martin 78
Buck Yard Branch 121
Burgoyne, Battle of 64
Burnley, Elizabeth 66, 68, 69
Burnley, Henry 64, 66, 68, 69
Burnley, Israel 64
Burrington, Governor George 114

Caldwell, Sarah 79
Campbell County 64
Candor, Jennet 95, 96
Candour, Joseph 96
Candour, Mary 96
Candour, Rose 96
Cape Fear River 67, 103, 121, 122
Carpenter, Mary 72, 78, 79
Carr, Obedience 152
Carr, Robert 44, 152
Carr, Temperance 151, 152
Carrell, John 24
Carroll County 68
Carter, Amanda 58
Carter, Ann 42, 59, 70
Carter, Calvin 43, 70, 84, 85
Carter, Calvin G. 59
Carter, Caroline 59
Carter, Charity 36, 38, 39, 167

Carter, Eliza Ann 70
Carter, Epsey 42, 58
Carter, Ethel 84
Carter, Euphrasia 59
Carter, Felix 42
Carter, George W. 42
Carter, Georgia Ann 42
Carter, Henry 40, 41
Carter, Isaac 19, 34, 35, 36, 37, 38, 39
Carter, Jacob 35
Carter, James 13, 34, 37, 39, 40, 41, 42, 43, 58
Carter, James D. 42, 43
Carter, James Earl 3, 36, 84, 85, 95, 101, 162
Carter, James Earl, Jr. 36, 95
Carter, Jane 35, 59
Carter, Jeanette 84
Carter, Jeremiah Calvin 70, 84
Carter, Jesse 38, 58, 106
Carter, Jesse L. 42
Carter, Jesse Taliaferro 59, 60
Carter, John 9, 10, 12, 13, 14, 15, 16, 17, 18, 19, 20, 24, 25, 26, 27, 29, 30, 31, 114, 167, 182
Carter, Joseph 35
Carter, Julia A. 59, 70
Carter, Katherine 35, 36
Carter, Keziah 42
Carter, Kindred 35, 36, 39, 40, 58, 106, 163, 166, 167, 168
Carter, Lazarus 38
Carter, Littleberry 42
Carter, Louisiana Virginia 59
Carter, Lula 84
Carter, Magdalen 117
Carter, Marina 43
Carter, Martha 34, 35, 36, 40, 41, 42, 43
Carter, Mary 43
Carter, Mirabeaugh 42
Carter, Moore 17, 19, 33, 34, 35, 36, 37, 39, 166
Carter, Parthenia 39
Carter, Priscilla 36, 167
Carter, Susannah 35, 36
Carter, Thomas 2, 3, 5, 9, 10, 12, 13, 14, 15, 16, 17, 18, 19, 20, 23, 24, 25, 26, 27, 28, 29, 30, 31, 32, 33, 34, 37, 118, 163
Carter, Walker 44, 59, 60, 61, 62, 70, 84
Carter, Wiley 1, 43, 58, 59, 60, 61, 70
Carter, William 3, 9, 10, 11, 12, 13, 14, 15, 16, 17, 18, 19, 20, 24, 25, 26, 27, 30, 31, 33, 34, 84, 85, 163, 182
Carter, William Alton 84
Carter, William Archibald 70, 84, 85

Carter, Winifred 36, 167
Carteret, Sir George 45, 114
Cary, Thomas 114
Caswell, Colonel Richard 67
Cedar Run 123, 135
Champion, Benjamin 118
Champion, Edward 117, 118
Champion, Edward, Jr. 117
Champion, Elias Fort 117, 118
Champion, Hart 118
Champion, John 70, 118
Champion, Micajah Fort 118
Champion, Orlando 117
Champion, Priscilla 117, 118
Champion, Rhoda 70
Champion, Susan 36, 113, 116, 117, 118, 123, 159
Champion, Susannah 118
Champion, William 118
Chancellorsville, Battle of 61, 73, 91, 102, 125, 137
Charlemagne 52, 127
Charles II 7, 14, 16, 17, 20, 23, 27, 44, 45, 48, 55, 74, 75, 97, 114, 142, 144
Charles Town 67, 76, 80, 129, 130, 131, 135, 136
Chattahoochee Beauregards 90, 102
Cheney, Anne 148, 149
Cheneys Resolution 148
Chesley, Elizabeth 152, 159
Chestnut Hill, Battle of 64
Chetwood, Thomas 18
Cheyney, Charity 140
Chiles, Agatha 63
Chiles, Henry 63
Chowan River 7
Church of England 63, 75, 97, 114, 141, 157
Civil War 3, 8, 45, 48, 60, 62, 63, 66, 70, 82, 89, 90, 91, 102, 109, 123, 134, 135, 136, 137, 159, 160
Clapham, William 12
Clark, Agnes 138
Clinkscales, Adam 77, 78
Clinkscales, Andrew 74, 78
Clinkscales, Francis 72, 78, 79, 175, 176
Clinkscales, Francis B. 72, 79, 82, 175
Clinkscales, Levi 175
Clinkscales, William 78
Cochran, Calvin 161
Cold Harbor, Battle of 73, 91, 102, 125, 137
Cole, Lydia Wadsworth 108
Cole, Nancy 108
Columbia County 39, 40, 41, 42, 68, 166
Conquest, Richard 141

Coogle, David 135
Coogle, John 134, 135
Coogle, John Thomas 134, 135
Coogle, Peter 134
Cooke, Elinor 13, 20, 23, 25, 32
Cooke, William 13, 16, 17, 18, 24, 27, 32, 33
County Attrim 74
County Down 44, 74, 82
Cowan, Andrew 74, 77
Cowan, Isaac 82, 83
Cowan, John 79, 82, 83
Cowan, Sophronia 72, 73, 74, 75, 77, 79, 82, 83, 84
Cox, Rebecca 55, 56, 58
Cox, Thomas 44, 46, 47, 49, 50, 54, 55
Craven County 66, 71, 156
Cripps, George 24
Cromwell 7, 9, 14, 16, 17, 18, 44, 45, 48, 67, 74, 147
Croxon, Alice 182
Culloden Moor 119
Cumberland County 66, 104, 117, 120, 121, 122
Cunningham, Col. William 71, 80, 81, 82
Currituck 7, 115, 150
Currituck County 115, 150
Cutawhiskie River 34, 35

Dale, Edward 13, 27, 30, 31
Dale, Katharine 28, 31
Davis, Mary 59
Davis, Phoebe 64
Davis, Rachel 41
Dawson, Brady 110
Dawson, Davis 110
Dawson, Elizabeth 95, 102, 103, 109, 111
Dawson, Hollinger B. 110
Dawson, Jonathan 95, 103, 105, 106, 109
Dawson, Malachi 103, 106
Dawson, Repsy 106
Dawson, William 104, 105
Deep Bottom, Battle of 125, 137
Deep River 66
Dickinson, John 34, 35
Dickson, Mary Eleanor 74, 80, 82
Dockwra, William 57
Donald, Brigadier General 67
Dove, Nancy 138
Dreher 130, 134
Drennan, Mary 71
Drew, Edward 11
Du Chesme Andre 168, 169
Duckworth, Jeremiah 42, 57, 58, 101
Duckworth, John 57

Duckworth, Joseph 5, 57, 58
Duckworth, Nellie 43
Duckworth, Phoebe 58
Duckworth, William 57, 58
Duddingston, Janet 171
Due West 82
Durand, William 141
Duvall, Maureen 145
Dysart, Charity 100, 176
Dysart, Dr. Cornelius 99

Eden, Charles 114
Eden, Governor 114
Edgecombe County 7, 36, 40, 106, 117, 118, 122, 138, 166, 167
Edwards, Elizabeth 113
Elgin, Grace 72
Elizabeth Cittie 143
Eltonhead, Jane 18
Emerson, Elizabeth 150
England 6, 8, 23, 143, 168
England, Francis 13, 23, 24
English Civil War 45, 48, 67
Enniskillen, Ireland 96
Etheridge, Aaron 138
Etheridge, Caleb 138
Etheridge, Caleb, Sr. 138
Etheridge, Guilford 73, 137
Etheridge, Joseph 137
Etheridge, Robert 138
Etheridge, Rosannah 127, 137, 139
Etheridge, Thomas 138
Etheridge, Tyre 137
Etheridge, William 138
Everhard, Sir Richard 114

Falling Water, Battle of 73, 137
Fifth Virginia Continental 64
Flake, Robert 13
Flake, Robert, Sr. 13
Floyd House and Ocmulgee Hospital 110, 135
Ford, Jericho 137
Ford, John J.W. 59
Fort, Mary 118
Frazer, Janet 119
Fulford, Daniel 150
Fulford, James 150, 151
Fulford, Mary 150, 151
Fulford, Mary Eleanor 150, 151, 152
Fulford, William 150, 151

Gaines, Captain Daniel 106
Gaines, Mildred 106, 107
Gaines, Richard 107
Gaines, Richard, Jr. 107
Georgia Ann 42
Germantown, Battle of 139
Gettysburg, Battle of 73, 91, 102, 111, 125, 137

Gift of God (ship) 140
Glasgow, Scotland 44, 74, 77
Godwin, Thomas 11
Gordy, Bessie Lillian 85, 95, 101, 111
Gottlieb, Mittelberger 132
Granville, Lord John 114, 157
Gray, Eli 43
Greene, General Nathanial 139
Greene County 68, 100, 176
Greenville Presbyterian Church 79, 83
Grimes, John 100
Grimes, Sterling 100, 101
Grimes, Thomas Wingfield 100, 101, 176
Grimes, William G. 100
Grimsley, Owen 108
Grove, William 23, 32, 33

Halifax County 69, 106, 117, 118, 138
Halifax Resolves 67
Halley, Martha 151, 152
Halley, Nathaniel 149
Halley, Nathaniel Thomas 149, 150
Halley, Thomas 149, 150
Hamilton, Andrew 50, 51, 147
Hamiter, Jacob 134
Hamiter, Thomas 130
Hanover County 62, 63, 64
Harnett County 121
Harris, Eliza 69, 70
Harris, Nathan 70
Harrison, Benjamin 64, 158
Harrison, Reverend Thomas 141
Hart, Barnabas 59
Hart, Isaac 59
Hart, Mary Virginia 59
Harvey, Sir John 14, 18, 182
Henry, Patrick 62, 68
Hertford County 7, 37, 38, 40
Hinton, Robert 42, 43
Hogskin Creek 71
Hollinger, Mildred 107
Hopewell 140
Hoskins, Bartholomew 10, 12, 29
House of Stuart 9, 16, 119, 142
Howard, Elizabeth 140, 144
Huguenots 75, 128
Hull, John 65
Hunt, George J. 108
Hyde, Edward 52, 114

Ireland 5, 8, 32, 44, 47, 57, 70, 74, 75, 76, 79, 80, 82, 86, 87, 95, 96, 97, 103, 105, 113, 129, 143, 157, 168
Isaac, Jemima 147, 148, 149
Isaac, Joseph 146, 147
Isaac, Richard 146

Isack, Richard 140
Isle of Skye 119, 120, 121, 171
Isle of Wight 3, 5, 12, 13, 17, 18, 20, 23, 24, 25, 26, 32, 33, 34, 37, 115, 117, 118, 122, 140, 163, 174

Jack, Lillis McAdoo 97, 99, 100
Jack, Patrick 97, 98, 99, 100
Jackson, Stonewall 8, 91, 123
Jackson Hospital 73, 90, 135, 137
Jacob, Anne 149
Jacob, Benjamin 147, 148, 149, 150
Jacob, John 135, 136, 148, 149
Jacob, Mordecai 147, 148, 149
Jacob, Sarah 149
Jacobite 96, 119
Jacobs, Martha Eleanor 149, 150
Jefferson, Thomas 64
Jenkins, Charity 114, 115
Jennings, John 138
Jennings, Lucy 138
Jennings, William 19, 138
John, Martha 102
Johnson, Margaret 157, 158
Johnson, Sir Nathaniel 157, 158
Jones, John 34, 36
Jordan, Rachel 63
Joyce, Flake 13
Joyce, Jane 146

Kay, James 44, 72, 79
Kay, Mary 72
Kay, Robert 72
Kelly, Anna Mary 136, 137
Kelly, John George 136
Kelly, Rachel 122, 123
Kelly, William 123
Kindred, Jane 17, 19, 34, 35, 36, 37, 39, 166
Kindred, John 17, 19, 33
Kleckley, Jacob 134, 135
Kleckley, Joel Thomas 135
Kleckley, Johannes 130, 133, 134
Kleckley, John 135
Knight, James Allen 167
Knight, John Carter 167
Knight, Kindred 167
Knight, William 36
Kolle, Johann Jacob 131, 133

Lancaster Battalion 98
Lanier, Elizabeth 36, 115
Laurens County 116, 117, 118
Lawhon, Alethea 113, 119, 121, 122, 123
Lawhon, Noel 113, 122
Lawrence, Robert 19
Lawson, Epaphroditus 12, 14, 18, 24, 25

Lawson, Rowland 14, 25, 26
Leibbrand, Johann Heinrich 131, 133
Lindsay, Robert 6, 71
Lindsay Cemetery 83, 84
Little Falling River 64
Little River 72, 92
Littleton, Edward 43
Lloyd, Edward 142
Louis XIV 5, 8, 45, 127, 128, 129
Loyalist 66, 67
Luther, Martin 7, 102, 110, 127, 128
Lybrand, Barnet 134
Lybrand, Christopher 133, 134
Lybrand, Elizabeth 134, 135
Lybrand, Johann Christian 133
Lynch, John, Sr. 156
Lynch, Aaron 156
Lynch, Edmond 156
Lynch, Jonah Jonack 156, 157
Lynch, Mary 152, 156, 157, 159
Lynch, Thomas 156, 158, 160

MacDonald, Flora 119, 120
MacFarlane, Walter 170
Mackay, Mary 143
Madison County 68
Magruder, Gen. John B. 110
Marcus, Daniel 107
Marcus, Ellis 107, 172, 173
Marcus, Mary 103, 106, 107, 109
Marcus, Sarah Cassandra 106, 107, 109
Margaret, Mary 92, 136
Marie Providence (ship) 143
Marsh, Thomas 141, 142
Maryland 5, 21
Mathis, Ann 182
McAdoo, Lillis 97, 99, 100
McCarthy, Justin 96
McClellan, Gen. George B. 111
McCullough, Elizabeth 82
McGarrah, Elizabeth 160
McGarrah, Robert 160
McGarrah, Thomas 160
McKay, Jane 140
McLeod, Colonel 67
Meaders, Jane 155
Mecklenburg County 96, 97, 99
Menefie, George 10
Middleton, Martin 35
Miller, George 81
Miller, John 81
Miller, Dr. Joseph Lyon 25
Milner, Cordelia 161
Mine Run, Battle of 61, 73, 125, 137
Mize, Francis M. 59
Monmouth, Battle of 139

Montgomery, General Richard 149
Moore, George 13, 19, 24, 32, 33, 34, 117, 118
Moore, Colonel James 67
Moore, John 13
Moore, Katherine 13
Moore, Magdalen 13, 19, 24, 32, 33, 34, 118
Moore, Sir Nathaniel 114
Moore, Richard 147
Moore, Ruth 147
Moore, Thomas 13, 22, 24, 117, 118
Moore County 120
Morris, Jacob 55
Morris, Job 54, 55, 58
Morris, Lewis 48, 49, 50, 51, 52, 54, 56
Morris, Lydia 58
Morris, Richard 54
Morris, Robert 22
Moryson, Francis 13, 18, 20
Mosley, William 65
Munday, William 19
Munger, John 12, 13, 24
Murray, Ann Elizabeth 118
Murray, Charity 115
Murray, David 5, 112, 163
Murray, Drury 36, 113, 115, 116, 117, 118, 119, 123
Murray, Francis Allethea 36, 112, 162
Murray, James 8, 112, 113, 114, 115, 145
Murray, John William 36, 112, 126
Murray, John William Fulwood 36, 113, 118, 119, 123, 125, 126, 129
Murray, Jonathan 114
Murray, Nathan 36, 113, 115, 116, 123
Murray, Susannah 117
Murrays Addition 145
Muscogee County 43, 68, 87, 89, 100, 101
Muse, James, Sr. 66
Muse, John 66
Muse, Sophia Pope 66
Muse, Thomas 66
Muse, William Seale 66, 68

Nansemond County 10, 14, 18, 24, 113, 141
Neal, Sarah 41
New Kent County 62, 64
Newbury County 79
Nichols, Rachel 130, 133
Nicholson, Cuthbert 95, 96, 99
Nicholson, Daniel Melson 103

Nicholson, George 96, 99, 105, 106
Nicholson, Ira Brady 103
Nicholson, James John 102
Nicholson, John 95, 99, 100, 101, 102, 105, 106, 176
Nicholson, John Candor 95, 99, 100, 101
Nicholson, Joseph 99, 100
Nicholson, Lemuel 105, 106, 176
Nicholson, Mamie I. Vera 103
Nicholson, Martin Luther 102, 110
Nicholson, Nathaniel Nunn 94, 95, 100, 101, 102, 103, 109, 111
Nicholson, Rebecca Lucinda 103
Nicholson, Repsema 105
Nicholson, Sallie Estelle 103
Nicholson, William 105, 176, 177
Nicholson, William Jefferson 102
Nicholson, Wright 106
North Anna, Battle of 73, 91, 102, 137
Northampton County 7, 35, 37, 39
Norwood, Captain John 71, 80, 81

Odell, Eleanor 147, 149, 150
Odell, Henry 143, 145, 147
Odell, Thomas 143, 144, 145, 147, 149
Odum, Mary 168
Offutt, Keziah 145, 146, 147, 149
Offutt, Mary 146
Offutt, William 145, 146
Oliver, Cromwell 9, 14, 16, 44
Ong, Esther 57
Onslow County 113, 114, 115, 116, 117
O'Quinn, Patience 35
Orange County 56, 71, 92, 156, 157, 160
Oxford, Elizabeth 62, 63

Pace, John 106
Palatine 5, 78, 127, 129, 130, 132, 135, 137
Parham, Marshia 160
Parker, Alethea Josephine 36, 123
Parker, John Prescott 122
Parker, Rebecca 143
Parker, William John 113, 119, 122, 123
Pasquotank, County 7, 105
Peddy, Delanna 152, 153, 161
Perquimas County 7
Pettaway, Edward 17
Pettaway, Robert 11

Piland, Richard 13, 24
Plymouth 53, 78
Polecat Creek 63
Polecat Swamp 62, 63
Pope, Hardyman 166, 167, 168
Pope, Humphrey 66
Pope, Sofia 66
Pope Leo X 127, 128
Port Tobacco 77
Porter, Mary 54
Potecasi Creek 34, 35
Pottenger, John 147, 148
Potts, Rebecca 54, 55
Potts, Thomas 54, 55
Powell, John 143
Powell, Judith 62
Powell, Mary 143
Prather, Jonathan 140, 143, 145
Pratt, Griffin 71
Pratt, James 70, 71, 72, 73, 74, 79, 82, 83, 84, 178
Pratt, John 71, 72
Pratt, Joseph 71, 83, 178
Pratt, Nina 70, 74, 79, 82, 84, 85
Pratt, William 71
Price, Elizabeth 150

Quintyne, Margaret 142

Ramsey, Christiana 42, 58
Ramsey, John 58
Randolph, Henry 44, 62
Records, Mary 54, 55
Revolutionary War 6, 8, 37, 38, 62, 64, 65, 66, 67, 68, 69, 71, 78, 79, 80, 82, 87, 88, 92, 93, 98, 99, 101, 103, 105, 106, 107, 123, 136, 139, 149, 153, 155, 156, 158
Rhodes, Elizabeth 130, 133
Richerson, Lieut. Col. Holt 107
Ridgely, Colonel Henry 140, 144, 145
Ross, Jane 152, 153, 154, 155, 156
Rouse, Francis 103, 105
Rozier, Alexander 41
Rozier, Anderson 40, 41
Rozier, Robert 40, 41
Rumph, John H. 59
Russel, Catherine 113, 116
Rutland, Shadrack 38, 39

Safety (ship) 10, 24, 29, 67, 98
St. Barnabas Episcopal Church 145
St. Paul's Parish 62, 63
Sampson, James 13
Savage, Dorothy 72
Schulf, Margaret 157
Schumpert, Melissa 137

Scorton 148, 149
Seale, Charles 66
Seals, Mary Ann Diligent 62, 70, 84
Seals, Spencer 68, 69
Seals, William 60, 68
Seals, William Archibald 69, 70
Seawright, Andrew 5, 44, 74, 77, 80, 81, 82
Seawright, James 74, 77, 81, 82
Seawright, Jane 82
Sharpe, Elizabeth 140
Sharpsburg, Battle of 91, 137
Shepard, Captain Richard 143
Sherwood, William 19, 33
Siege of Petersburg 73, 91, 102, 135, 137
Sigler, Anna Catharina 131, 133, 136
Singer, Jacob 151
Singer, Johann Ulrich 151
Singer, Susan 151
Smith, Apollos 154, 160
Smith, Catharine 155
Smith, Crittenden Jubilee 152, 161, 162
Smith, Eleanor Rosalynn 3, 7, 36, 112, 115, 121, 122, 126, 133, 134, 139, 140, 142, 143, 145, 146, 148, 149, 152, 160, 170, 171
Smith, Elizabeth 154, 160
Smith, George B. 154, 160, 161
Smith, George Lynch 3, 140, 152, 153, 154, 155, 156, 159, 160, 161, 162, 163
Smith, Hancock 154, 155, 156
Smith, Jewryston 154
Smith, Jubilee 152, 153, 154, 159, 160, 162
Smith, Lettice Hancock 154, 155
Smith, Martha Livinia 154
Smith, Mary 154
Smith, Matilda 154
Smith, Molenious Benton 156, 161
Smith, Palestine 152, 154, 160
Smith, Paul 154, 160
Smith, Peter 155, 156
Smith, Rachel 154, 160
Smith, Ross 154
Smith, Ruth 154
Smith, Scinthia Bartlet 154
Smith, Susannah 154
Smith, Tenderson 152, 154, 161, 162
Smith, Wilburn Edgar 36, 139, 140, 162
Smith, William Henry 154
Smith, William Newton 152, 161, 162
Snead, Peter 108

Snow Rowan 130, 131, 134, 135
Spivey, Nancy Jane 59
Spotswood, Alexander 114
Spotsylvania 73, 91, 102, 125, 137
Stampe, Thomas 19
Steele Creek Presbyterian Church 99
Stone, Moses 152, 155
Strother, Dorothy 72
Strother, Elizabeth 72
Strother, Robert 72
Strother, William 72
Stuart, Charles 119
Suffolk 64
Sunken Marsh 12, 182
Surry County 11, 12, 13, 32, 118, 150
Switzerland 8, 78, 127

Taliaferro County 68
Taylor, Reuben 167
Taylor, President Zachary 72
Teach, Edward 114
Telfair, Governor 68
Terrell, Anne 63
Terrell, David 63
Terrell, Hannah 64
Terrell, Major Henry 64
Terrell, Joel 63, 64
Terrell, John 63
Terrell, Captain Peter 64
Terrell, William 62, 63
Tetzel, Johan 127
Thomas, Frances 161
Thomas, John 94, 134, 135, 161
Thurloe, John 16
Tooke, James 14, 17, 18
Truelock, Ann 143
Turtley, Avis 182
Tyrrell Precinct 7

Urquhart, Barbara 121
Usry, Carroll 59

Valley Forge 8, 64, 87, 88, 155
Vinson, Charity 38, 39
Virginia Company 9, 11, 14, 140, 143

Wade, Richard 140
Wardner, James 144
Warner, Sarah 145
Warren County 39, 42, 58, 59, 60, 65, 68, 69, 70, 101, 122, 177
Warroscoyack 140
Washington, Augustine 72
Washington, George 62, 72, 87, 92, 149, 155, 158
Washington County 68, 122, 123, 149, 176

Waters, Susannah 63
Webb, Jean 79
Weiss, Catherina 131, 133
Weiss, Johann Georg 131, 135, 136
Westall, Alice 148, 149
Westall, George 140, 148, 149
Whitemarsh 87
Whitmore, Rebecca 152, 159
Wilderness, Battle of 61, 91, 102, 125, 135, 137
Wilkes County 37, 64, 65, 68, 99, 100, 101, 176
Wilkinson County 101, 116, 118

William, King 50, 75, 146, 157, 170
Williams, Elizabeth 118
Williamsburg 62, 64, 90, 102
Wilson, Margaret 100
Wingfield, Elizabeth 100
Wise, David 137, 139
Wise, George Calhoun 127, 135, 137, 139
Wise, James 136
Wise, John 3, 136, 137
Wise, John A. 136
Wise, Lemuel 136
Wise, Michael 136

Wise, Patrick 136
Wise, Rosa Nettie 5, 36, 112, 126, 127, 139
Wise, Tyre 137
Witherspoon, Robert 76
Wood, Mary Charity 148
Woodward, Katharine 19
Worth County 42, 118
Wright, Mary 47

Yazoo Land Fraud 67, 68
Yeardley, Governor 143
Yeardley, Sir George 10
Yorktown 8, 64, 78, 102, 155

www.ingramcontent.com/pod-product-compliance
Ingram Content Group UK Ltd.
Pitfield, Milton Keynes, MK11 3LW, UK
UKHW050528150426
5217IPUK00026B/1853